Edited by Jörg Schröder,
Maurizio Carta,
Maddalena Ferretti,
Barbara Lino

DYNAMICS OF PERIPHERY

ATLAS FOR EMERGING CREATIVE AND RESILIENT HABITATS

jovis

DYNAMICS OF PERIPHERY

Atlas for Emerging Creative and Resilient Habitats

DYNAMICS OF PERIPHERY

Jörg Schröder, Maurizio Carta, Maddalena Ferretti, Barbara Lino

How can dynamic factors and dynamic phenomena outside of metropolitan cores be displayed for debates about territorial futures? *Dynamics of Periphery* showcases emerging creative and resilient habitat futures to develop concepts for metropolitan, urban, and rural networks—with a perspective not on urban margins, but on new places of community. The atlas displays integrative process-design, pro-active context-building, and conceptual narratives as accelerators of change and new concepts in urbanism. These new concepts combine bottom-up and participatory approaches, the use of territorial capital, and the qualities of liveable spaces to create processual and strategic innovations across scales and disciplines. Starting from architecture, urban design, and territorial planning, the book aims to explore interfaces between design and research that contribute towards dynamic roles of peripheries as accelerators of change towards sustainable territorial futures.

Dynamics of Periphery is an issue being discussed internationally as a topic that is important for economically and socially critical situations. Both in Europe and as part of a global debate, integrative and balanced development of metropolitan peripheries and of areas outside of new metropolitan regions is being stressed in research, planning practice, and politics. In addition to offering a wide range of current research concepts and approaches, the atlas aims to point towards future research into integrative urbanism and territorial development with a multi-disciplinary and multi-actor focus. It builds on the shared experiences of many contributors in the national Italian research project *Re-Cycle* (2012–16, funded by MIUR), which was based on the exhibition *Re-Cycle* at MAXXI in Rome 2011, and it connects with a large range of national and European research projects realized by several contributors including *Responsive City*, *Augmented City*, *SmartLand*, *Agri-Cultures/Agro-Cities*, *Rurbance*, *Regiobranding*, *Alpine Building Culture*, etc.

The atlas offers twenty-five contributions taken from projects in both research and practice and from emerging research approaches in Germany, Italy, Spain, Brazil, Colombia, Uruguay, and Indonesia. A transversal structure of three voices across all contributions addresses important topics of current academic debate on dynamic territorial transformation:

Voices—Dynamics of Transformation (for an introduction, see p. 95):
In-transition Processes
Place: Managing the Change
Narrative: Stories from the Periphery

The exploration of the themes and topographies of *Dynamics of Periphery* is guided by a group of three chapters that offer complementary approaches to the topic:

Approaches—*Dynamics of Periphery*:

Habitat Vision (p. 109)

Reserves of Resilience (p. 175)

Territorial Creativity (p. 233)

The book puts forward a Habitat Vision of rural and urban polarities as a contribution to mono-directional debates that in fact mainly call for social and economic stabilisation, with a primary focus on infrastructural support for shrinking areas. Land-flight in the south of Europe is being enforced de facto by high unemployment of young people and is also related to a search for perspectives for urban centres. Finding perspectives for peripheries is also a highly relevant contemporary issue in Germany. Migration movements and refugees further call for new linkages between the city and the countryside. Resettling, recycling, and reconnecting of peripheries are new phenomena. The relevance of an action-oriented, space- and place-centred contribution towards political and cultural debates in Europe might gain fresh input from looking at *Dynamics of Periphery* for future places of work, living, and culture.

Peripheries are precious Reserves of Resilience for reactivating the urban metabolism in post-metropolis systems that, more and more, resemble archipelagos and matrices of places rather than satellite systems. Even if declining suburbs and peripheral regions still contain active cells (active communities, landscapes, agriculture, and manufacturing) that are capable of restarting jammed mechanisms of evolution, it will be necessary in the future to pass from the dangerous, constant state of a metropolis in unsustainable expansion to a state of dynamic neighbourhoods that are in progress towards resilience. Policies, projects, and actions can reactivate the possibilities and energy of peripheries to enhance the dynamism of a new development model.

The idea of Territorial Creativity that can serve as a basis for innovative arts, entrepreneurship, and communities, and which aims at development rather than merely the valorisation of heritage, is in fact one of the most discussed themes in cultural and economic policies in Europe. A territorial focus in this debate is one main objective of *Dynamics of Periphery*.

The introductory section of the atlas relates these three approaches to larger frameworks of research, its academic context, and further perspectives (p. 9–75). A report from a preparatory international workshop in Favara, Italy (p. 76–93) additionally evaluates transdisciplinary methods and actual topics of emerging research by design.

The atlas *Dynamics of Periphery* is funded through the programme Hochschuldialog Südeuropa of the DAAD, which is financed by the German Ministry of Foreign Affairs. The organising university partners from the Department of Architecture of the University of Palermo and from the Chair for Regional Building and Urban Planning of Leibniz Universität Hannover wish to thank all the contributors for their collaboration in the atlas project of *Dynamics of Periphery*.

DYNAMICS OF PERIPHERY

INTRODUCTION

Open Habitat

Jörg Schröder

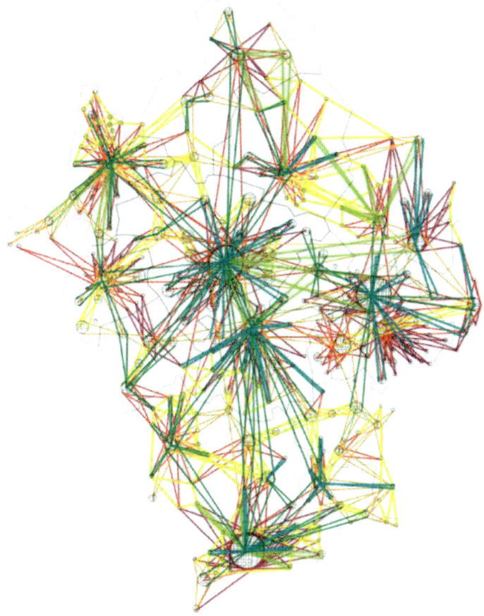

Figure 1. Creative Clusters Vision, metropolitan region Hannover Braunschweig, Göttingen, Wolfsburg. Graphic: Jan Philipp Drude, Raphaela Djalili, Lisa Iglseder, Valentin Zellmer, LUH Regionales Bauen und Siedlungsplanung 2017

At least since the economic crisis of 2008, from which Europe appears to be recovering only now, ten years later, our notion of innovation has been enriched by a spatial focus. This focus has entailed merging, superimposing, and hybridising innovations in technology and digitalisation with the founding of social and cultural communities, and with—as is the aim of *Dynamics of Periphery* to show—new qualities in lived space and in territories. Parallel to the increased consciousness of spatial change, these new qualities evolved in different velocities with new connotations: slow, which also assumes advantages for supporting resilience; fast, opening up to a targeted use of timeframes and temporality. Dynamic factors, dynamic constellations, and dynamic processes nevertheless remain bound to and shed light on cultural, social, and economic frameworks in which spatial transformation is constructed and influences visions of life. In urbanism (used as term for a projective approach) over the last ten years, most voices kept to a mind-set and to concepts that took the city as a starting point—even if the very idea of city has, since globalisation in the nineteen-nineties, finally become blurred, along with that the assumption of modernism that dynamics are only bound to clustering and to centres of ever larger size. Parallel to a multiplicity of spatial phenomena, structures, and multi-actor constellations, the notion of dynamic positioning in space has also been exponentially extended (the flat world of digitalisation and mobility) and, at the same time, limited, as it has become re-centred for many people and in many aspects. On the one hand, this is the hypothesis of a (mostly silent) process of powerful centralisation, and on the other, a search to actively—in a larger extension—link to new modes of shaping nodes and networks between space and society that *Dynamics of Periphery* aims to address. This background is also the reason we have constructed this book as an atlas: to discover new territories of spatial change. It displays integrative process-design, pro-active context-building, and conceptual narratives as

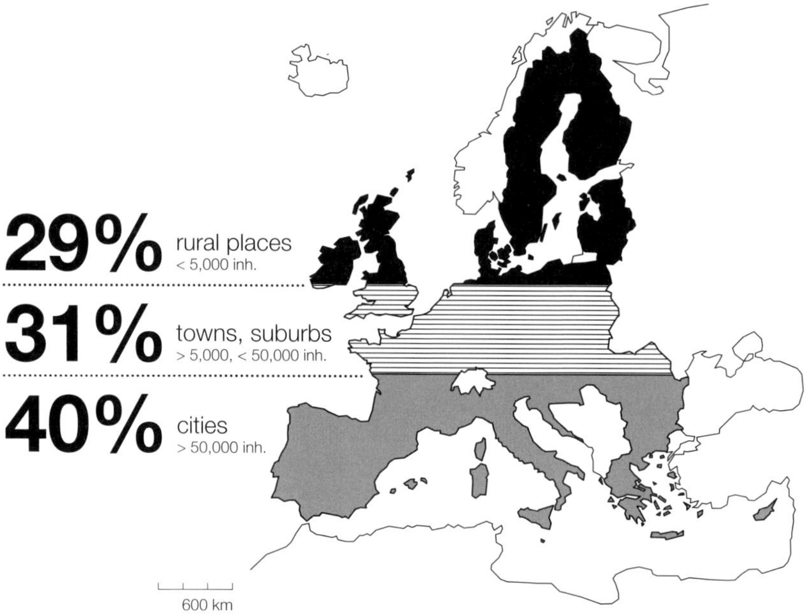

Figure 2. EU-28 population according to settlement typologisation, projected by graphic share (precision: municipal level, LAU2). Data: Dijkstra, Poelman 2014. Graphic: Jörg Schröder

accelerators of change and new concepts in urbanism. These new concepts combine bottom-up and participatory approaches, the use of territorial capital, and the qualities of liveable spaces into processual and strategic innovations that cross scales and disciplines. Starting from architecture, urban design, and territorial planning, this book aims at interfaces between design and research towards lived space and territories. In extending the view of urbanism (and architecture) into new explorations and unknown lands of territorial constellations, the atlas aims to link with important initiatives currently underway: the Italian Pavilion in the Biennale 2018 will focus on "Archipelago Italia," and on architecture as catalyst for territorial innovation beyond metropolis; the Biennale Rotterdam 2018–20, "Architecture, Climate Change, and Society," will focus on a shared and comprehensive narrative for spatial qualities; the European Year of Cultural Heritage 2018 is promoting sharing heritage in an enlarged sense as integrative process for spaces and society; and the conference "Creative Heritage: International Platform for Regenerative Cities, Resilience and Territorial Innovation" in October 2017 elaborated a "Hannover Creative Heritage Agenda".[1]

Discovering Places beyond Metropolis

In this context, *Dynamics of Peripheries* wants to be understood as a provocation, questioning long-running beliefs of urbanism disciplines, and of the public and political mainstream. "Periphery" is understood by many in the sense of "urban periphery" (a term used since industrialisation and the disruptive expansion of cities), or in a more general sense as "not being central". We propose to reconnect with the origin of the word, *peri-phero*, which in ancient Greek means "to carry around, to move around", digging into relations and dynamics of constellations of living spaces. And, finally, in order to refresh a theme and a debate for politics, we refer to the idea of polis = city. The rediscovery of places beyond the metropolis—and of connecting to the metropolis in a new way, and of being connected to transformations of the metropolis itself—as guiding themes can be based on a great variety of cultural, social, and economic innovations of recent years: a new awareness for regional dimensions in terms of food provision (e.g. *Foodscapes* project in the *Food Revolution 5.0* exhibition; Fig. 4–5);[3] a new awareness of resources, energy, heritage, culture (*Landraum*: Schröder, Weigert 2010); of *Re-Cycle* as an architectural and urbanistic movement (Ricci, Schröder 2016); of the renaissance of Europe as a secure and sustainable tourism and leisure destination (e.g., *Baltic Coast* project; Fig. 6); of new mobile lifestyles, migration and resettlement movements, and pioneering place-making in European peripheries (Schröder 2017); and, not least of all, digital-material transformation that leads to new role and new importance of material space (*Territories: Rural-Urban Strategies*; Schröder, Carta, Ferretti, Lino 2017).

In fact, metropolisation, much more than diffuse "urbanisation" or the "urban age", can be seen to represent the peaks and nodes of the flows of the "information age". Digitalisation—apart from making new lifestyles possible by shrinking, enlarging, or virtualising materials space—has effectively deepened spatial and material divides and caused new marginalisation. This is especially true for European spaces, which is provoking ongoing transformations in Europe's highly structured and articulated settlements. The relative distribution of the living spaces of Europeans in 2014 shows this variety of settlement: 40% of Europeans live in cities (of more than 50,000 inhabitants), 31% live in towns and suburbs (of between 5,000 and 50,000 inhabitants), and 29% live in smaller settlements (of less than 5,000 inhabitants), as can be seen in Fig. 2 as the size of these shares on a map of the continent. Yet beyond the deep polarities of urban/rural—and the blurring of their meaning in different scales—these data still do not communicate the character or even types of these living places and especially of their contexts. Nevertheless , the lenses through which we think and act politically work differently with different centralities and different networks in ways that highlight the roles of large cities, of medium and small cities (with different definitions), and towns, quarters, villages, hamlets, and other forms of settlement.

Peripheries Are for Real

This challenge becomes even clearer with the mapping of the metropolitan regions in Germany in 2017 (Fig. 3), which originated in global economic positioning and are underway to becoming platforms of territorial governance of all sectorial policies and of development programmes beyond the increased cultural and economic (and population) concentration in the metropolitan cores that is provoking major disruptions in real estate markets. Eleven metropolitan regions cover 50%t of the area, with a total of 63% of the population (fifty-two million inhabitants). These regions exist in the forms of associations of territorial bodies of different sizes, and in most cases also with economic

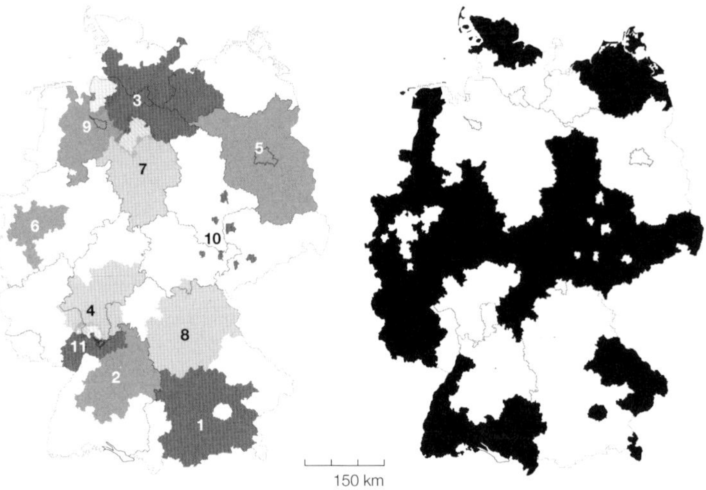

63% of people
50% of surface
in eleven metro-regions
52 mio. inh., 179,000 km²

37% of people
50% of surface
outside metro-regions
30.5 mio. inh., 177,000 km²

Figure 3. Eleven metropolitan regions in Germany in 2017, NUTS3 composition: 63% of population, 50% of surface, 289 inh/km². Non-metropolitan region areas in Germany in 2017, NUTS-3 composition: 37% of population, 50% of surface, 172 inh/km². Data source: Statistisches Bundesamt, 2017. Graphic: Jörg Schröder

1 München (5.7 mio.)
2 Stuttgart (5.2 mio)
3 Hamburg (5 mio.)
4 Rhein-Main (5.6 mio.)
5 Berlin/Brandenburg (6 mio.)
6 Rhein-Ruhr (10 mio.)
7 Hannover Braunschweig Göttingen Wolfsburg (3.8 mio.)
8 Nürnberg (3.5 mio.)
9 Bremen/Oldenburg (2.7 mio.)
10 Mitteldeutschland (2.4 mio.)
11 Rhein-Neckar (2.3 mio.)

and civil society organisations as partners; in Germany, no new institutional bodies for metropolitan cities have been created as in France or Italy in recent years. A part from the challenge of increased pressure in most of the metropolitan cores, at the same time the large associations (that extend in order to in reach the goal to include at least five million inhabitants, and because of having a dynamic of their own that is both an attractive network and attracts networks) increasingly face debates about how to steer very different territorial realities in their configuration—or, to simply to call them by their old names, very different urban and rural parts. In fact, urban-rural cooperation, new concepts of polycentricism in a wider range, transversal strategies that comprehend /balance/ combine phenomena of (often discontinuous) shrinkage and growth in different parts, and alliances for subspaces have become recurrent topics in metropolitan regions (see Schröder, Carta, Ferretti, Lino 2017). One example that shows this is the recent study *RegioDesign* for cultural and creative industries as a new force of cohesion and a motor to activate territorial capital in the metropolitan region of Hannover Braunschweig Göttingen Wolfsburg (Fig. 1).[2] At the same time, to speak about global or European major metropolises, not all eleven metropolitan cores qualify for that designation, and some metropolitan regions are even organised in polycentric constellations. Hence, the metropolitan regions display growing differences among themselves not only in economic fields, but also in spatial challenges and chances.

The Other Half of Germany

The other interesting question that the map of Fig. 3 puts forward is the areas outside of these eleven metropolitan regions: these have been significantly moved out of public, political, and specifically media-related awareness, debates, and communication, even if they cover the other half of the 50% of area and 37% of the population of Germany (30.5 million inhabitants). Obviously not all these areas "outside of metropolis" are "remote" in geographic or economic sense, even if some are, and various urban forms and new forms of regional associations can be observed, for example, the international alliance around Lake Constance that connects activities of development cooperation with the economic positioning of a growth area outside of metropolis (Schröder, Hartmann 2016). The areas "outside" include cities that can be defined as small (50,000–100,000 inhabitants) and medium-sized (100,000–250,000 inhabitants) in European terminology, and a rich range of smaller settlement realities.

Peripheries Are Everywhere

The new realities and ongoing trends in centralisation and marginalisation—especially in the larger territorial scales—mirror similar fragmentations in smaller scales. Still, concepts of urbanism that lean, for example, towards the ideas of Soja (2011) are still working along the line of the diffusion of "the city" into the region and sticking to perspectives of the 1990s. This is the case even when growing inequalities can be seen to call for reflections on spatial structures on a metropolitan scale (Secchi 2013) that can be extended beyond. Here the provocation of *Dynamics of Periphery* is to combine observation and reasoning about new peripheries in all parts of territories, and to look for new connections that perhaps begin directly from the variety of these parts. Critical observers such as Guilluy already subsumed many different notions of periphery into a wide-ranging cultural and political debate about a major social division, in his books *Fractures françaises* (2010) and *La France périphérique* (2015). Issues of separation, fragmentation, specialisation, polarisation, periurban, and neo-rural are merged in a critical assessment of a France "threatened by social and cultural separatism" and by a "profound crisis of living together", but which is not being perceived because of "intellectual and media-related blindness". And—just to add one more factor—because of an urbanism discipline that is increasingly trapped in good practices and process evaluation, without structural, critical, or creative force. Still, the growing interest in "territory" as cultural creation and as development chance has been manifest already since the crisis of 2008 (Barca 2009; Roncayolo 2016), and is beginning to spread.

By subsuming many notions of periphery and asking about the role and impact of this trend in lived space, urbanism needs to face the task of refreshing approaches in the discipline, its concepts, and its practices . In fact, already in the constellations of urban expansion and urban diffusion, spatial strategies for larger scales that combine metropolitan cores with urban peripheries have regularly encountered limitations in the autonomy of municipalities, in many economic and social factors, and in superimposed large infrastructures (transport, energy, etc.); and these strategies have not been effectively combined with protection movements for nature and heritage—both today increasingly important themes. Already the notorious Milan Intermunicipal Plan of 1963 co-ordinated by Giancarlo De Carlo was effectively never realised. More than fifty years later, we continue to face all of these questions in a similar manner, and the need for spatial strategies is ever more urgent. Hence, spatial fragmentation as key issue since the globalisation of the 1990s gave impetus to a wide and varied debate in urbanism about new concepts and strategies in large-scale urban-metropolitan development.

Fragmentation as a key issue can be observed equally in and outside of the metropolitan cores: in voids (Solà-Morales 2001), in new borders, and in loosed connections. In fact, zoning—though declared to be a tool of a remote modernist past—is constantly having even more impact, erecting new borders not only in building typologies or urban morphology, but also very much in a territorial scale of spatial segregation and des-integration in the mosaics of superimposed urban, rural, and natural patches: voids, borders, and loosed connection can be found in metropolitan centres, in transformed suburban fringes, in medium-sized cities, in all forms of differently sized and shaped settlements in the territory. This spatial fragmentation corresponds very intimately to increasing social segregation (Secchi 2013). For an urbanism pushing to work on the the roles and meanings of space as positive agent in rapid changes of society, climate change, and technology, this can be seen as major chance for actualisation: new tools are needed for recognising spatial phenomena, for concepts and strategies in transdisciplinary and multi-actor constellations to activate and shape living spaces, and for drawing new lines of connection in space, projects, communities, and collaboration.

Sharing Narratives of Cooperation—Enhancing Transformative Visioning

Narratives as a projective tool in urbanism (Salmon 2007, Matthey 2014) imply a critique of description, scripts, and indicators, especially if they are derived from non-spatial backgrounds and do not consider spatial criteria . The critique of an immanent "descriptive urbanism" (already formulated by Secchi 1992), together with the call to construct new stories and to push towards new narratives as part of urbanistic activities, may reconnect us to more visionary urban concepts of the 1960s and 1970s. However, the critique of pre-categorised description and ex-ante evaluation strongly pertains to the gap between ever more sectorial and at the same time more comprehensive sets of objectives in spatial development (Resilience Agendas, UN Sustainable Development Goals, EU Urban Agenda, etc.); it also touches on spatial strategies desired to be developed for a long period of time and at the same time to be immediately very effective. Innovative, non-established stories are difficult to merge to fixed indicator sets and process scripts. The chance to exit stable imbalances towards activating potential energies of peripheries, and to become dynamic factors for new development models with larger spatial networks and new instances of cooperation, reveal the multiscalar and multiperspective capacity of narratives. Their design is confronted with these implicit questions, as has become clear in recent important analytical and conceptual research, e.g., on spatial strategies for the Ruhr area (Polívka, Reicher, Zöpel 2017), for the *Territorial Mosaic City* in Catalonia (Llop 2017), on a new analytical basis for *Postmetropolitan Territories* in Italy (Balducci, Fedeli, Curci 2017), or on projects as knowledge producer (Viganò 2016). The construction of narratives is crucial for strengthening bottom-up and social innovation projects (Murray, Caulier-Grice, Mulgan 2010) in their desired role beyond fixed compounds and limited social groups. Construction of shared narratives for city and territory is also part of—and may become even more important for—newly gathering communities that are materially, digitally, and virtually assembled in the circular economy (Webster 2015), the *Regenerative City*, the *Augmented City* (Carta 2017) and the *Responsive City* (Gausa 2015)—passing from becoming "smart" (Goldsmith, Crawford 2014) in data technologies towards more interactive, more material, and more emotional qualities of space. All these concepts are very much linked to the idea of moving from the observation/evaluation of abstract spatial transformation towards invention strategies for complex spatial change and dynamics.

Concepts of space as an aggregator of inclusion and as a newly attractive material reality call for refreshed abilities in urbanism to work on and with territorial creativity— abilities linked to activities and agents—and for expertise in constructing new interaction of space and society. This is very much opposed to the old concept of "using territorial capital" as passive asset to be put into action. Thus, "shared territorial visions" (as formulated in *Rurbance*; Schröder 2015) or "explorative scenarios" (in *Regiobranding*; Schröder, Ferretti 2018) can become accelerators rather than outputs of integrative and interactive processes of spatial change in different scales. This new demand in abilities in urbanism is not limited to co-designing processes in strong relation to space and communities. It also calls for new forms and new roles of designing visions, for exploring capacities and potentials in a projective sense, and for co-constructing free spaces as "socially interactive machines (that are) highly adaptable to the shifting conditions of their time and place," as Cedric Price postulated with *The Fun Palace* and *The Potteries Thinkbelt* (Matthews 2006). Territorial creativity can be seen as major driver for innovative arts, entrepreneurship, and communities that also aims at developing more than mere valorisation of heritage, and it is a widely discussed themes in cultural and economic policies in Europe.

Open Habitat

How can dynamic factors and dynamic phenomena outside of metropolitan cores be displayed for debates about territorial futures? New approaches, tools, and strategies in architecture, urban design, and territorial planning are called to promote spatial qualities, capacities, and dynamisms, and to respond to an actual demand for the quality of lived space in ongoing cultural and political

Figure 4. Food-towers on the Elbe river, Regio-spot food centre, Swimming restaurants. Design project *Foodscapes—New architectures of food for the metropolis Hamburg*. Rica Arnold, Carlotta Nilius, Sina Raupert, Kristin Welc, Lena Lauermann, Aleksandra Eggers. LUH Regionales Bauen und Siedlungsplanung 2017

debates. On a conceptual level, the move from staying fixed to oppositions towards the consideration of dynamic factors and polarities and towards crossing the limits of systems implies extending the notion of peripheries from sectorial indicators towards more complex spatial relationality and the inclusion of externalities. Thus, the rediscovery of "peripheral" phenomena and situations and their transformation in relation to multiple contexts may influence and charge structural dimensions (in space, programming, and meaning) as well as refresh creativity and communities.

Habitat—living spaces in city and territory with an open perspective and as open devices—in this sense refers to debates of the 1950s. The *Doorn Manifesto* of Team Ten from 1954, as drawn by Alison and Peter Smithson (Chung 2005), indicated with its "valley section" a framework larger than the city, thus exploring manifold activities of association interlinked in this vision and connected to natural factors. The video *La città degli uomini* (The human city) by Giancarlo De Carlo at the X Triennale of Milan (Zucci 1992) in the same year is exemplary of a shared debate in Europe—and worldwide—for a new attention to the cultural and social dimensions in interaction towards which architectural and urban design was desired to evolve. And already in 1950, Lina Bo Bardi in São Paulo began to co-direct and design the magazine *Habitat* (Terenzi 2007) with the aim to create a cultural context for innovative performative arts, design, architecture, and urbanism in a modern society, and for its cultural and social involvement as engaged in a discovery of the vernacular and the natural in the rich diversities of Brazil. And as an idea that is quite near to the idea of modernist redesign of all living and cultural expressions (in Europe at the same time, Max Bill in Germany and Ernesto Nathan Rogers in Italy promoted the motto "from the spoon to the city" as a field of modernist *Gestaltung* or performative shaping), today the openness and passion in this movement support the call for creative, synthetic, experimental approaches in shaping human living surroundings. The universality and locality intended with the Anthropocene Age of human implication in geological change strongly calls for a re-reasoning of human living space—and this will have to go

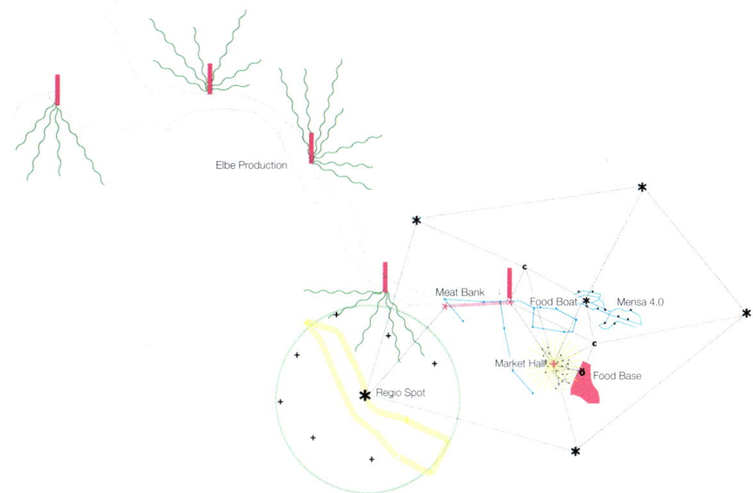

Figure 5. Foodscape Map. *New architectures of food for the metropolis Hamburg*. Jörg Schröder, LUH Regionales Bauen und Siedlungsplanung 2017

beyond the ecological meaning of habitat as niche. This is discussed in ecology itself—in relation to changes and complex systems—and also to a great degree in urbanism, against the overall and increasing trend of fragmentation.

The "Open City" as opposed to the "Closed City" is an idea proposed by Richard Sennett (2013) as a place where citizens actively try to "found new communities" based on "agreeing in differences" and where urbanism also supports "experiments in urban forms and space."[4] Sennett states critically that in urban design and urban development "we have more resources to use than in the past, but resources we don't use very creatively". He sees the reason for this paradox in the "over-determination both of the city's forms and its social functions". With a definition of attributes of closed systems—fixed shape, equilibrium, and integration—Sennett points out that as one main characteristic of the "Open City", over time "an open system can be non-linear, and within that frame range from path-dependency to the patterns of chance", in interaction between spatial creation and social behaviour that together form "agency" in the city. This reasoning can be transferred to a wider understanding of habitat as living space in and beyond the metropolis. Especially in the further spatial definition of boundaries and walls as characteristic for the "Closed City", and—in opposition—porosity and borders as characteristics of the "Open City", Sennett states that porosity and borders "create liminal space; that is, space at the limits of control, limits which permit the appearance of things, acts, and persons unforeseen, yet focused and sited". In the reasoning of "Open Habitat" for living space, one may well argue that the liminal space today can be found everywhere and that fragmentation thus becomes a major site and chance for desired change.

The experiments in urban design studio work of the following three projects aim at exploring the concepts of path-dependency, patterns of chance, and liminal space—at stressing knowledge production through performative analysis and projective design, programming and visioning.

Liminal Spaces—Co-Habitat

Venice Lagoon: Urban Design for a Productive Archipelago (Fig. 13–18)[5]

Venice and its lagoon are a unique territory, characterised by hybrid cultural and natural spatial forms, flows, and networks. Beyond the islands of Venice this focus includes sixty-eight islands in the lagoon, many of which are no longer used and inhabited. The aim of the design and research project *Venice Lagoon* is to develop creative readings of the lagoon space in an architectural perspective, starting from spatial potentials and moving towards drawing innovative patterns and processes of spatial change, and which are connected with new economic and social perspectives. Architecture and urban design projects for spatial catalysts are revealed as explorative tool and a strong strategic contribution to address borders between water and land, fresh water and salt water, city and country—as well as towards borders of protection zones and planning zones, regulation, and sectorial policies and disciplines. Crossing borders and offering linkages and permeability are shown to be creative fields of innovation that lead towards enhancing capacities of space. The lagoon as newly founded cultural hybrid sphere can systemise aspects of building and settlements and of natural forces: renewable resources; water; agriculture; fishery; white, green and blue economies; crafts and industries; arts and R&D. Also in reference to debates about Venice's future as city, the potential and demand of stronger ties across the lagoon emerge to further point towards the harbour, the mainland, and the regional scale. Architecture's possible incentive perspective for the lagoon with experimental spatial interventions aims at setting and strengthening cultural and economic impulses. By weaving territorial networks in a call to cross borders and scales, *Venice Lagoon* explores a *co-habitat* vision of a newly productive Archipelago.

The methodology developed in the *Venice Lagoon* laboratory is directed at understanding and learning from the lagoon as a territorial system of interconnected layers in a diachronic and spatial perspective. The investigation into promising points, lines, fields, and networks includes digging into the past of land/water design and dynamics in order to understand social, cultural, and economic issues from a spatial perspective; it also includes understanding the spatial dependencies and fields of changes in its potentials and limitations. The sharpening of concepts and tools of qualitative research in a spatial-architectural perspective offers concepts of space not as a separated "physical problem" for abstract superimpositions, but as a hybrid construction of figurative, material, functional, and meaningful flows leading to hybrid concepts of configuration. The work on the lagoon in the reading phase of the laboratory is connected to explorations into actual urban perspectives of the city of Venice, with an interpretation of Venice—not only as specific entity but as symbol for today's urban questions—in flows, segregations, heritage, and global dimensions.

New Lagoon Network: Hybrid Linkages across City and Territory: In this sense, a discovery of capillary living and activities in the lagoon describes spatially permanent, semi-permanent, and temporary settlement developments by looking at their links with natural forces and resources and the embedded knowledge of how to sustainably use and develop them, and thus to also use the knowledge of how to feed innovation into new set-ups of rural-urban linkages. Spatial potentials identified in a design approach in the *Lost Islands* project as first part of the lagoon laboratory are being elaborated in mind/space mapping research and evaluated in the context of territorial networks. The artistic ingredients and paradigms in the research process thus lead to an actualised multifarious vision of the islands' role in a lagoon network model. Emerging projects of tourism as global exchange, rooted in places of good life and creativity as attractors, are shown to directly influence this research.

Islands as Catalysts of Change: In the next steps of the design process, a reflective yet audacious range of proposals deliberately questions limitations and offers points of interventions for the lagoon. The "freezing" introduced in the paradigmatic plan of 1962 for Venice by Giuseppe Samonà subsequently also had a strong influence on the islands' planning frameworks to accelerate social and economic changes towards separation: the islands became manifold peripheries. With the added "freezing" to achieve ecological protection and the debates about the ecological future of the lagoon, the positive effects of protection are now being questioned in ways that allow for the evolution of future possibilities. The call for "development" and creative use of heritage—and not only for "valorisation"—in the guiding strategies for the UNESCO site of Venice and its lagoon (established in 1987) can be related to public debates in concrete cases of privatisation of islands, complex public ownership setups, exclusive economic use, and public space and natural values, as has happened over the last years in the cases of Poveglia or the Lagoon North park. In the architectural perspective of *Venice Lagoon*, this background is mirrored in a multi-relational configuration of programmes. The impulse of architectural and urban design thus inherently offers to facilitate inclusiveness and involvement, and also strongly points towards economic perspectives in a renewed understanding of territorial productivity.

Path Dependency—Co-Programming
A New Architecture for the Baltic Sea Coast—Mecklenburg-Vorpommern (Fig. 6–12)[6]

With 1700 kilometres of coastline, Mecklenburg-Vorpommern was the national *Wunderland* of tourism in 2016, and a further rise in tourism happened in 2017, not least of all because of international insecurities and risks. Focused on the Baltic Sea coast, this master design studio aims at two connected questions: How can a possibly short-term "Baltic hype" be transformed into strategic impulses for urban and regional development? How does this transformation of the coast change architectural practices and paradigms in leisure and tourism, and what impulses towards and interferences with other sectors do these transformations generate? The *Baltic Coast* project addresses urbanistic strategies and architectural concepts that react to changes and influence the shaping of trends themselves. The methodological steps are oriented towards a design-based knowledge production, starting with an exploration of spatial and socio-economic context, in field surveys, mapping, and interviews, that is connected to conducting urban and architectural design research on territorial, local, and object scales and is combined with presentations, debates, posters, and models. The possibly short-term effect of capitalising on security may be extended to a strengthening of the location in the longer run, especially considering an increased awareness for

Prerow
Seebad Prora
Rügen
Stralsund
Poel
Rostock
Greifswald
Usedom
Boltenhagen
Wismar
Lübeck
border
Germany/
Poland
Stettin

6

8

9

10

Figure 6. *A New Architecture for the Baltic Coast*, 350 km in Germany, Mecklenburg-Vorpommern. Graphic: LUH Regionales Bauen und Siedlungsplanung, 2017
Figure 7. Vertical analysis. Graphic: Nils Hiddessen, Max Pape
Figure 8. Platform Stettiner Haff. Graphic: Juliane A. Doniek, Patrick Rahe
Figure 9, 10. New mobility Stettiner Haff. Graphic: Lesley-Anne Fischer, Sören Tanke
Figure 11. Darss-Rügen network. Graphic: Guangji Zhu, Yidan Zhang
Figure 12. Stettinger Haff network. Graphic: Juliane A. Doniek, Patrick Rahe

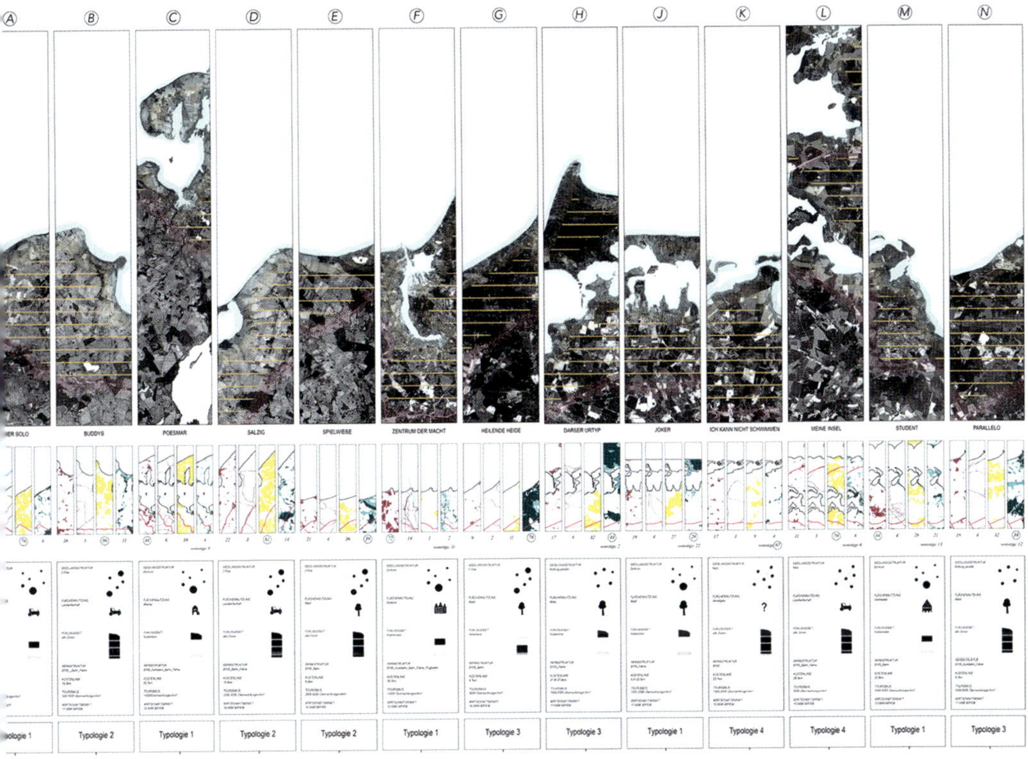

7

11

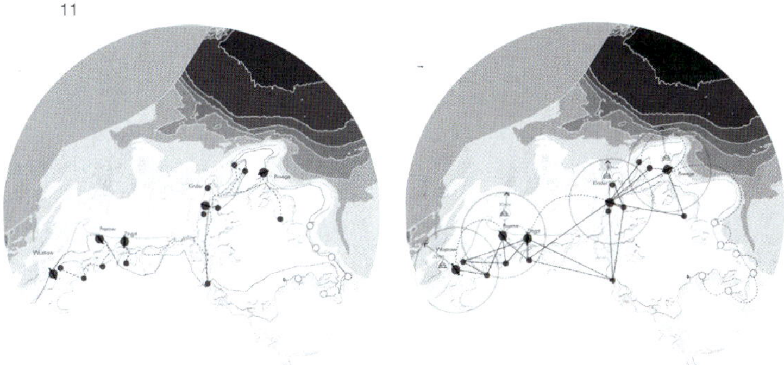

12

Figure 13. Lagoon islands. Photos: Maddalena Ferretti
Figure 14. Venice Lagoon, between land and sea. Image: Google Earth 2016
Figure 15. *Venice Lagoon—Productive Archipelage*: eight zooms in 500 km².
Graphic: LUH Regionales Bauen und Siedlungsplanung, 2016
Figure 16. Pellestrina cultural industries. Graphic: Yihan Zhou, Ruo Shen
Figure 17. Pavilions Lagoon Park North, Torcello. Graphic: Constantin Tibor Bruns
Figure 18. Venice connected. Graphic: Moritz Engel, Lisa Flöter

13

14

16

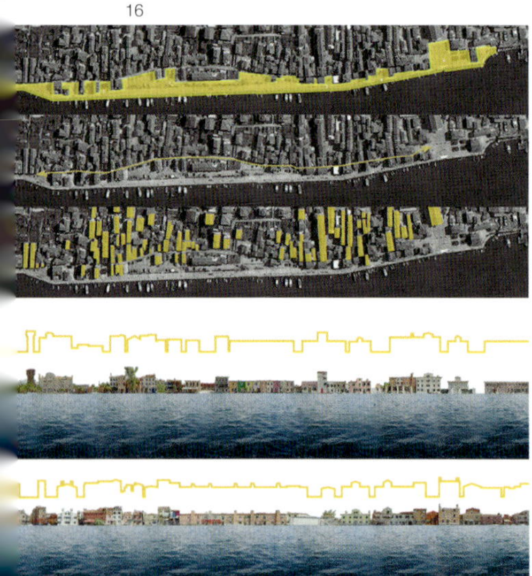

17

15

Torcello
Mazzorbo
Campalto
Certosa
Sacca San Biagio
Santo Spirito
Poveglia
Pellestrina

18

19

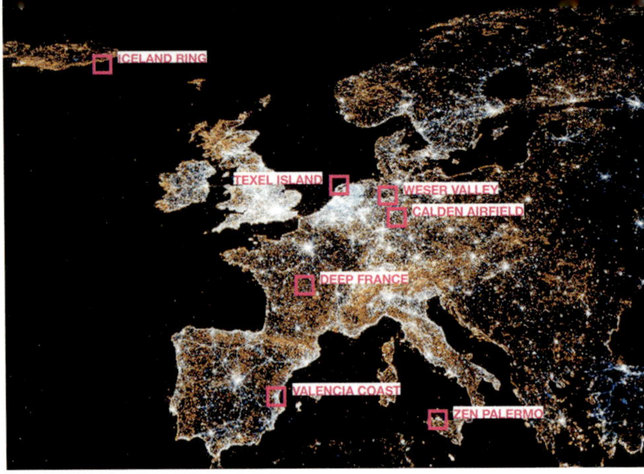

20

Figure 19. *Dynamics of Periphery*, Case studies. Graphic: LUH Regionales Bauen und Siedlungsplanung, 2018

Figure 20. Northern Iceland. Photo: Laura Baden. La Perche, France. Photo: Pierre Martin. Zen Palermo, Italy. Photo: Matti Hänsch. El Cabanyal, Valencia, Spain. Photo: Felix Rutenbeck

21

22

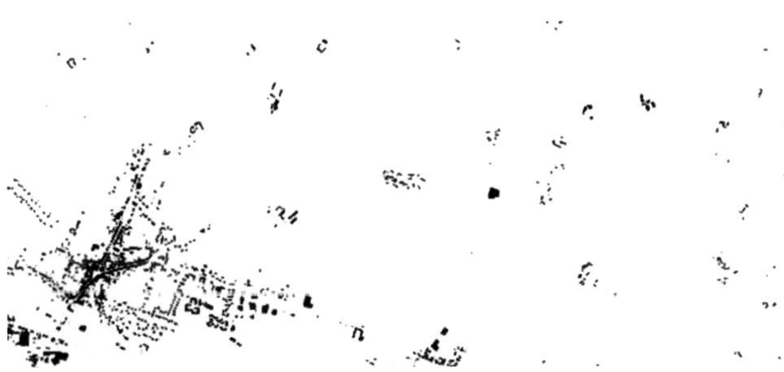

23

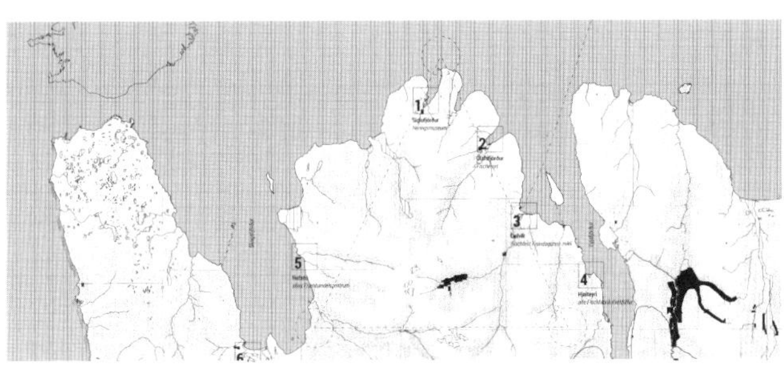

24

25

Figure 21. Texel Science Platform, Netherlands. Graphic: Julia Hermanns
Figure 22. en Palermo, Italy. Graphic: Matti Hänsch
Figure 23. La Perche, France. Graphic: Pierre Martin
Figure 24. Northern Iceland Ringroad. Graphic: Laura Baden
Figure 25. Texel water system, Netherlands. Graphic: Julia Hermanns
Dynamics of Periphery, Case studies,
LUH Regionales Bauen und Siedlungsplanung, 2018

regional values, for the origin of products, and for spatial, social, ecological, and economic sustainability. Therefore, the quality of touristic offerings and of the overall living quality of the context are seen as major values and future goals for development. Tourism can thus become a catalyst for regional development. Hence, in this research, both the role of architecture for larger contexts and urban design and planning for places on the coast in dimensions beyond tourism are seen as crucial. The relations of activities and space between coastline and hinterland, and between small places, towns, and cities along the coast are of specific interest to tie together and explore new regional networks and patterns or activities and spatial qualities. This discussion of relevance and of novel aspects lead to a specific methodological setup of the *Baltic Coast* project. The project connects scales of territorial context, settlement and landscape context, and architectural context and construction processes in spatial analysis and conceptual design work. The production of knowledge in the process of design together with the methodological and scientific enhancement of design processes form the core idea of the *Baltic Coast* project. In exploring spatial processed in interrelation with the touristic sector and with other sectors, and with social, cultural, and ecological aspects, the project aims to conceptually formulate new knowledge about spatial possibilities and possible push-factors in the form of transferable models. By analysing and evolving spatial models, the project connects together and discusses a series of places along the 1700 kilometres of this coastline in order to enhance knowledge of common and individually different potentials, of interfaces, and of interdependencies of territorial and urban development, architecture, and mobility with leisure and tourism.

Chance Mutations—Co-creative Scenarios

Dynamics of Periphery, Thesis Projects (Fig. 19–25)[7]

A series of thesis projects develop a focus on very different constellations of settlement, landscape, and infrastructure in different contexts across Europe: the island of Texel in the Netherlands (Science Platform); the Zen quarter in Palermo, Italy (Quarter Upgrading); the region of La Perche in France (New Crafts and Resources); Iceland's ring road (Tourism); the El Cabanyal quarter in Valencia/Spain (Quarter Upgrading); the airport town Calden/Germany (Town Upgrading); and the Weser Valley in Germany (New Agriculture and Living). These projects are developed in the scales of connected urban design, architectural planning, and territorial planning in order to grasp dynamics in spatial, cultural, and social possibilities and to discover possible dimensions of spatial futures—not (only) as local articulations of global trends but as evolution of spatial capacities. New centralities, new networks, and multi-layered connections to (reshaped) networks in space, functions, and meanings are called upon to imply pro-active design and place-making in architectural, cultural, and community-related senses, while also exploring possible governing processes as narratives as tools of interpretation and strategic action. In every of the case studies, the chance mutations generated in this form of laboratory have been connected to fieldwork on site and to interviews and research into spatial and stakeholder constellations; and it is the aim of these projects to contribute to chance mutations through university research and to engage with the very places of change towards *Open Habitat*.

1 Symposium funded by Volkswagen Foundation. The "Hannover Creative Heritage Agenda" is available online at: www.staedtebau.uni-hannover.de/schroeder. Accessed: 20 December 2017.

2 "RegioDesign", Seminar project M.Sc. architecture and urbanism, LUH Regionales Bauen und Siedlungsplanung, 2017. Academic direction: Prof. Jörg Schröder, Arch. Emanuele Sommariva PhD. Publication: Schröder J., Sommariva E. eds. (2017) RegioDesign: *Mapping and Visioning in the Metropolitan Region Hannover Braunschweig Göttingen Wolfsburg*. Hannover, Regionales Bauen und Siedlungsplanung.

3 "Foodscapes", Design studio project M.Sc. architecture and urbanism, LUH Regionales Bauen und Siedlungsplanung, 2017. Academic direction: Prof. Jörg Schröder, Arch. Maddalena Ferretti PhD, Dipl.-Ing. Sarah Hartmann. Publication: Schröder J., Hartmann S. eds. (2017) *Foodscapes: From the Spoon to the City. Architectures of Food for the Metropolis Hamburg*. Hannover, Regionales Bauen und Siedlungsplanung.

4 Lecture in 2013; Sennet's new book on this topic, Building and Dwelling: Ethics for the City, has been announced for 2018.

5 "Venice Lagoon", Design studio project M.Sc. architecture and urbanism, LUH Regionales Bauen und Siedlungsplanung, 2016. Academic direction: Prof. Jörg Schröder, Arch. Maddalena Ferretti PhD, Dipl.-Ing. Sarah Hartmann. Publication: Schröder J., Ferretti M. eds. (2016) *Venice Lagoon: Urban Design for a Productive Archipelago*. Hannover, Regionales Bauen und Siedlungsplanung.

6 "Baltic Coast", Design studio project M.Sc. architecture and urbanism, LUH Regionales Bauen und Siedlungsplanung, 2017. Academic direction: Prof. Jörg Schröder, Arch. Maddalena Ferretti PhD, Dipl.-Ing. Sarah Hartmann, Arch. Emanuele Sommariva PhD. Publication: Schröder J., Ferretti M. eds. (2017) *Baltic Coast: A New Architecture for the Baltic Coast, Mecklenburg-Vorpommern*. Hannover, Regionales Bauen und Siedlungsplanung.

7 "Dynamics of Periphery: Case Studies in Europe", Thesis projects, LUH Regionales Bauen und Siedlungsplanung, 2017. Supervisors: Prof. Jörg Schröder, Arch. Maddalena Ferretti PhD, Dipl.-Ing. Sarah Hartmann, Arch. Emanuele Sommariva PhD.

Balducci A., Fedeli V., Curci F. eds. (2017) *Post-Metropolitan Territories: Looking for a New Urbanity*. Oxford, Taylor & Francis.

Barca F. (2009) *An Agenda for a Reformed Cohesion Policy: A Place-Based Approach to Meeting European Union Challenges and Expectations*. Available on line at: http://ec.europa.eu/regional_policy/archive/policy/future/pdf/report_barca_v0306.pdf. Accessed: 20 December 2017.

Caminada G. (2005) "Neun Thesen für die Stärkung der Peripherie". In: Schlorhaufer B. (2005) *Cul zuffel e l'aura dado. Gion A. Caminada*. Luzern, Quart. pp. 133–136.

Carta M. (2017) *Augmented City. A Paradigm Shift*. Trento-Barcelona, ListLab.

Chung C. ed. (2005) *The Charged Void: Urbanism*. Peter and Alison Smithson. New York, Monacelli Press.

Dijkstra, Poelman (2014) *A Harmonised Definition of Cities and Rural Areas*. DG Regio Working Paper 1/2014. Brussels, European Commission.

Goldsmith S., Crawford S. (2014) *The Responsive City: Engaging Communities Through Data-Smart Governance*. San Francisco, Jossey-Bass.

Guilluy C. (2015) *La France périphérique*. Paris, Flammarion.

Guilluy C. (2010) *Fractures françaises*. Paris, Bourin éditeur.

Llop Torné C. ed. (2017) *Ciudades, territorios metropolitanos y regiones urbanas eficientes. Estrategias y propuestas de proyecto para la regeneración de la Ciudad_Mosaico_Territorial*. Barcelona, Universitat Politècnica de Catalunya.

Mathews S. (2006) *From Agit-prop to Free Space: The Architecture of Cedric Price*. London, Black Dog Publishing.

Matthey L. (2014) *Building up stories: Sur l'action urbanistique à l'heure de la société du spectacle intégré*. Geneva, A-Type.

Murray R., Caulier-Grice J., Mulgan G. (2010) *The Open Book of Social Innovation*. London, Nesta and Young Foundation.

Polívka J, Reicher C., Zöpel C. eds. (2017) *Raumstrategien Ruhr 2035+: Konzepte zur Entwicklung der Agglomeration Ruhr*. Dortmund. Verlag Kettler.

Ricci M., Schröder J. eds. (2016) *Towards a Pro-active Manifesto: PRIN ReCycle Series, New Life Cycles for Architectures and Infrastructures of City and Landscape*. Roma, Aracne.

Roncayolo M. ed. (2016) *Territoires*. Paris, Editions Rue d'Ulm.

Salmon C. (2007) *Storytelling: La machine à fabriquer des histoires et à formater les esprits*. Paris, La Découverte.

Schröder J., Weigert K. eds. (2010) *Landraum*. Berlin, Jovis.

Schröder J. (2015) "Integrated Territorial Visions". In: Regione Lombardia ed. (2015) *RURBANCE Rural-Urban Governance. For a Balanced Development of Rural and Urban Areas*. Final Publication ERDF Alpine Space project. Milano, Directorate General for Environment, Energy and Sustainable Development of Lombardy Region. pp. 20–37.

Schröder J. (2017) "Towards an Architecture of Territories". In: Schröder J., Carta M., Ferretti M., Lino B. eds. (2017) *Territories—Rural-Urban Strategies*. Berlin, Jovis. pp. 14–35.

Schröder J., Carta M., Ferretti M., Lino B. eds. (2017) *Territories—Rural-Urban Strategies*. Berlin, Jovis.

Schröder J., Ferretti M. (2018) *Scenarios and Patterns for Regiobranding*. Berlin, Jovis.

Secchi B. (1992) "Urbanistica descrittiva. Descriptive City Planning". In: *Casabella* 588, 1992. pp. 22–23, 61–62.

Secchi B. (2013) *La città dei ricchi e la città dei poveri*. Bari, Laterza.

Sennett R. (2018) *Building and Dwelling: Ethics for the City*. New York. Farrar, Straus and Giroux.

Sennett R. (2013) *The Open City*. Lecture at GSD Harvard 19.9.2013. Available online at: www.richardsennett.com/document-download.axd?documentresourceid=2. Accessed: 20 December 2017.

Soja E. (2011) "From Metropolitan to Regional Urbanization". In: Banerjee T., Loukaitou-Sideris A. eds. (2011) *Companion to Urban Design*. London, Routledge. p. 552–561.

Solà-Morales I. (2002) *Territorios*. Barcelona, Gustavo Gili.

Terenzi Stuchi F. (2007) *Revista Habitat: um olhar moderno sobre os anos 50 em São Paulo*. São Paulo, FAUUSP.

Viganò P. (2016) *Territories of Urbanism. The Project as Knowledge Producer*. Lausanne, EPFL Press.

Webster K. (2015) *The Circular Economy: A Wealth of Flows*. Cowes, Ellen MacArthur Foundation.

Polipheries: Heterotopic Cities and Plural Communities of a Different Present in Southern Europe

Maurizio Carta

Figure 1. Palermo, Ecomuseo del mare. Photo: author

Reboot Ethics and Politics of Cities

In Europe, cities have always been theatres that put utopian thinking on the stage. The European city is a "mediation between mediations", to quote Henri Lefebvre, one of the most lucid philosophers of the city, since the city is a permanent interface for several types of relationships: relationships between individuals, structured and unstructured relationships, and relationships with and between social, institutional, and normative organisations. And in an increasingly urban world where most of the world's population lives in cities, with levels close to 80% in Europe, cities are the living organisms that breath the breath of change, especially the change in the relationships, visions, and responsibilities needed to reactivate the future we want. However, contemporary cities are also the places where inequalities and marginalities are emerging with ever greater virulence, triggering real epidemics that arise from the peripheral areas that are the most lacking in quality and equity, extending to the entire urban organism, and mining the cooperative status that is the basis of the birth of the city. The answer can not be a generic anti-urban sentiment, but it should be a more aware and responsible claim for the respect of the "right to the city", which is not only a guarantee of essential services, but a right to work, participation, safety, reception, cohesion, welfare. It is a right to the future. And the most powerful antidote for the anti-city epidemic is to reaffirm the city of inherently urban rights: access to city resources and the opportunity to experience an urban life that is alternative to the logic and uneven processes of industrialisation and of capital accumulation, the to quality of relational life, and to the opportunity to increase our wellbeing in non-egoistic ways. "The right to the city," Henri Lefebvre wrote in 1967, "manifests itself as a superior form of rights: right to freedom, to individualisation in socialisation, to habitat and to inhabit. The right to the oeuvre, to participation and appropriation (clearly distinct from the right to property), are implied in the right to the city" (Lefebvre 1967). That right is therefore eminently political and acts in the very heart of urban democracy; it sinks its roots in the polis, the mother of politics as responsibility and art of guiding collective life. Hence it is the right to build "the human city" every day—as invoked in 1960 by Adriano Olivetti, Italian entrepreneur, urbanist, and utopist—that breaks the devices for control and homologation of the daily life of our metropolises, and gives times and spaces of urban living back to more and more plural and nomadic, fluid, and cosmopolitan citizens, thus reconfiguring social, political, and economic relations starting from an enlargement of the decision-making agora. Adriano Olivetti believed in the idea of community as the only way to overcome the division between production and culture. The idea was, in fact, to create a community of "shareholders" who share vision and responsibility: public authorities, universities, entrepreneurs, workers' representatives, civil society. It is his human city, an unrealised but clearly defined dream in his homonymous book, that traces a clear map of iof this community and still proves useful today for discussing urban democracy.[1]

In a Europe that wants to rediscover its cultural roots before resuming financial reforms, in a Europe that wants to begin again with ethics and urban politics instead of erecting walls or closing doors, the militant teachings of Giorgio La Pira, the most beloved mayor of Florence, again become relevant. La Pira lived his life as a daily example of the idea that he asserted in 1955: "the right to the cities of present generations is the rise to use—but not to destroy or ruin—a visible and built heritage, a heritage that is real and ideal, delivered to the present by past generations and destined to be passed down to future generations having been enhanced and improved. Use, improve, and pass down our common home! Cities are not things that belong to us alone and are available to us at will: they are the things that belong to other people and to the next generations, whose rights and turn should be violated by nobody" (La Pira 1955). Therefore, discussing about the human city means reflecting on the new state-form of cities that become metropolises, connecting to global networks, fighting for human rights, coming to be "world rulers"—as Benjamin Barber lucidly writes in a book that he 2013 dedicated to mayors (Barber 2013). Thus the metropolis becomes an atelier—as defined by David Harvey in the book on rebel cities (Harvey 2012)—in which the relationship between financial, manufacturing, and cultural capital can find new balance points. And for this reason, today the city—and especially its peripheries—is also the place of resistance, social movements, and active citizens contesting the regime of accumulation that uses finance to circumvent the blocking points of the production flow, claiming a new political leading role, being not only the sensors of criticality but also the actuators of change, new "urban mechanics" according to Nigel Jacob's fruitful intuition.[2]

In a new vision of the future of peripheries, a vision that at first concerns politics and then urban planning, the metropolis must overcome its purely functional vision (as attractor, aggregator, engine, portal, platform, etc.) to become a "community of communities", an intelligent interface between space and society that enables and encourages virtuous bottom-up behaviours, giving visibility to individual and collective advantages, to quote Giancarlo De Carlo, the visionary and militant Italian urbanist. A metropolis not only as a conceived (institutional) space but as a perceived space (made up of sensations and identities) and above all as a lived space, inhabited by multiple rooted or migrant communities, and animated by a civic pluralism that today is made up of activists, "makers", urban farmers, digital artisans, creative people, smart citizens, co-workers, prosumers, etc.—protagonists of the contemporary city but above all new protagonists of politics as commitment to the common good. Contemporary metropolises—post-metropolises with respect to the traditional sense—are increasingly inclined to provide collective responses to new and diverse questions: demanding not only homes, work, and services, but assistance, safety, integration, beauty, quality of life, happiness, innovation, participation, and democracy. And in the human city the answer to these questions is coming less and less solely from institutional and formal subjects, such as mayors or administrators, technicians or service providers, institutions or businesses, to become a collective response that sees proactive engagement of new citizens in the human city. This new political humanism, which draws democracy from the ground up toward a civic protagonism but also from the top toward a politics of proximity, is the most up-to-date legacy of a political idea that has found some prominent exponents in the Europe of origins (Robert Schuman in France, Konrad Adenauer in Germany, Aldo Moro, Giorgio La Pira, and Giuseppe Dossetti in Italy), all of whom theorised and realised a concrete relationship between ethics and politics, responsibility and practice, which finds its field of action in the city. It is still in Giorgio La Pira's words that we find a precious map to guide us: cities are "like living books of human history and human civilisation: destined for the spiritual and material formation of next generations. They are like neverending reserves of those essential human goods—from high goods, religious, and cultural, to basic goods, technical, and economic—of which all generations are in unavoidable

Figure 2. Messina, Toti Ringo. Photo: author
Figure 3. Ex-Fadda, San Vito Normanni. Photo: author

need." And it is precisely for this so vital and permanent relationship between cities and man that the city is the most appropriate instrument "to overcome all possible crises to which human history and human civilisation are subjected over the centuries" (La Pira 1955). In the face of the search for a more political and social post-urbanity, and to contain the anti-city epidemic resulting from the conflict between centres and peripheries, we must have the courage to implement a renewed ethic of political responsibility and a more sensitive urbanism, to be more creative in the use of natural and cultural resources, more sustainable in economy, more open in governance, more intelligent in transportation, and more resilient in life cycles.

It is in Southern Europe that the new urban humanism was able to show its first complete forms, proposing itself as a laboratory of a different possible future for the Mediterranean European regions in search of reboot. A laboratory for remedying the abandoned historic centres and the great peripheries of the twentieth-century urban model, which has greatly limited their development by relegating them to the spatial and conceptual margins of urban planning action. Today, now that the exhilaration of unlimited debt growth and voracious soil consumption has ceased, peripheries find themselves able to be the protagonists of a city model fuelled by resilience, recycling, and culture, but above all by reactivation of their vital human capital, and they are offering themselves as a precious laboratory, not of a consolatory mending, but of a powerful, disruptive urban and human regeneration.

Peripheries is also the keyword for understanding the pontificate of Pope Francis: going forth, going out, taking root in those places that are the real heart of cities, this is his magisterium. Pope Francis's teaching is a true "theology of city" that begins again from peripheries to rebuild the city. A city that is rebuilt from a stronger alliance between politics and urbanism, but above all which returns to be a favourable environment for human communities. Today, it is in the peripheries that the challenge of refugees and the integration of immigrants is at play, but integration is not carried out by institutions. Communities are those that connect and integrate, but the neighbourhood communities have crumbled. That is why we have to bring back to life a great civil passion for peripheries, to reinhabit them, to reactivate their spatial and cultural communities as a fabric to regenerate space, but above all society. From urban criticalities, bearers of marginality, and generators of conflict, contemporary peripheries can evolve—for those who know how to look at them with new eyes and govern them with wise hands—into significant components of urban metamorphosis. Considered as aggregations of stigma and concentration of prejudices, peripheries see the flourishing of new—and ever younger—activists who claim to renegotiate the localisation of social, cultural, or sport facilities, to demand new collective transportation systems, or to propose peri-urban landscaping patterns as new infrastructure for sustainable mobility. Associations of citizens who experience a true subsidiarity by managing community services and requalifying places and spaces to contain neighbourhood labs, increasingly new factories for the return of urban manufacture.

Figure 4. Milano, Ringhiera. Photo: author

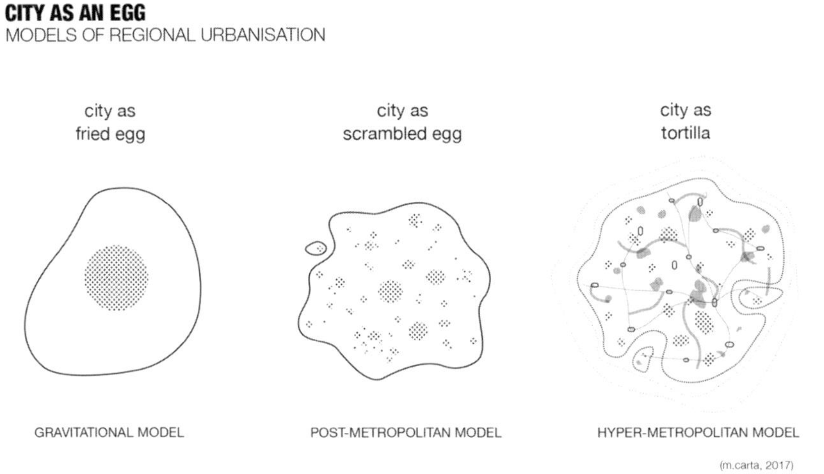

Figure 5. City as an egg. Sketch: author

It is clear that the human city cannot be reduced to its urban or social components, or even less to its economic one. But it requires the political synthesis of all of these, and above all it requires requires a renewed political humanism, that is, human participation in political responsibility. It therefore needs a paradigm shift and a true system innovation. It is not just the invocation of good politics to defeat bad populism, but the discussion of a new development model led by a new alliance between society, culture, and politics. To get out of the political crisis that has followed economic and social crises, an ethical push is needed in order to bring out our civic virtues by overcoming the vices and errors that have stifled them over the years. A new vision that modifies all the behaviours is needed, one that becomes a project, but it is disruptive to dangerous conformism and even more so to dangerous racism. Not being content with small maintenance and partial repairs of urban development mechanisms, but pursueing a radical innovation, true renewal of the city, even starting from its peripheries.

New Post-Metropolitan Patterns in Italy

To redefine the dynamics of peripheries proactively, I think it is time to rethink the gravitational metropolitan model towards more fluid and reticular forms, capable of including instead of separating, of enabling rather than regulating. The need has already been expressed by postmetropolitan theorists since the beginning of the century; among them the most innovative has been Edward W. Soja with his revolutionary post-metropolis studios, which in 2000 already signalled the emergence of new multiscalar models that redefined space and governance of urban settlement (Soja 2000). And most recently, in 2012 Enrico Moretti, a young economist at Berkeley and an economic advisor to Obama, had redesigned the new geography of jobs resulting from the change of productions and professions on both sides of the Atlantic, breaking down the myth of local work systems (Moretti 2012). The fact that triumphal technology was redefining the relationship between people and work by remodelling the daily life was known to Erik Brynjolfsson and Andrew McAfee, who 2014 at MIT announced the advent of the "second machine age" (Brynjolfsson, McAfee 2014). Likewise, the circular society and the collective intelligence that impose new paradigms on production, relational, and urban systems have been very well described, including even an effective infographic poster by Aldo Bonomi, Roberto Masiero, and Federico Della Puppa in their book dedicated to the circular society and to the consequences of a new non-linear interaction between economy, space, and society (Bonomi, Della Puppa, Masiero 2016).Urbanisation and urbanism have also been subject to rethinking and redefinition of knowledge, to interpretative parameters, and to paradigms and tools for imagining and designing more liveable, creative, and sustainable cities able to embrace post-metropolitan metamorphosis that is underway.

Using the famous metaphor by Cedric Price that in 1982 represented the metropolitan relations through different ways of cooking eggs, we moved from the gravitational model represented by the fried egg with a yellow and dense yolk (the tasty metropolis of all functions) and an albumen that surrounds and protects the yolk as a surrounding mantle (the belt towns, a bit bland without the yolk), to the "scrambled eggs" that represent the post-metropolitan model in which yolk and albumen blend, hierarchies are mixed, and the result is an alternation of softness and substance, of primary and secondary urban centres where the functions are distributed across the metropolitan territory. Today we have to make another leap in Price's metaphor, because today our polycentric urban systems are more like "tortillas", that is aggregations that are not composed only of yolk and albumen, the traditional components of the city now mixed in a non-hierarchical system, but that are the result of the incorporation of new ingredients of different consistency, sapidity, shapes, and colours that enrich the flavour and diversify the result. There are now many "tortilla-cities" in Europe that mix new ingredients, that put urban values together with rural resources, that add to the local ingredients the flavour of some cosmopolitan endowments resulting from global relationships and multiculturalism; some of these "tortilla-cities" mix the ingredients found in the territory by experimenting with new combinations, for example between agricultural production and digital innovation, others enrich through the cultural and social contributions of migrants hybridising manufactures and lifestyles. In the tortilla-cities the rurality-urbanity relationship does not disappear, the countryside is not cancelled by being swallowed up by the city, but the relationship between artifice and nature, between densities and porosity, is intensified, intersecting with other values and relationships. In the "tortilla-city" peripheries take on new consistency and function, contributing to the sapidity and flavour of the dish. It is time to put them in the menu, it is time that these new urban articulations, fluid and poly-material joints, which are already present in many centre and south-European experiences, enter into Italy's developmental agenda. Because only through new spatial models of regional urbanisation could we offer to peripheries the opportunity to put to good use the dynamism they are expressing. To turn reaction into action, conflict into co-operation. By comparing fruitful experiences, especially French ones, the Italian metropolitan cities need to be rethought—and redefined in identifications and perimeters—to act above all as new and more powerful drivers around which to reorganise both the peri- and sub-metropolitan contexts and the inner areas, in a renewed polycentric and reticular organisation of Italy. The vision of metropolitan cities as a gravitational functional system, that is, as a system of autonomous urban communities that exchange flows (material and immaterial) with a large territorial context, acting as an interchange node of a network of municipalities, has to be overcome. We can no longer limit ourselves to extending the effects of urban aggregation and integration beyond the municipal dimension to engage the broad cultural, social, and economic systems that characterise their multiple identities and contribute to the reinforcement of metropolitan relations, since they have often reached their efficiency threshold and begun a process of system decline.

Before we leave for the post-metropolis dirge, content to celebrate the death of an inefficient and congested model, it is imperative to accept the challenge of finding a new paradigm that supports the new kind of settlement, that supports cultural relationships that are productive and more fluid, open, and changing. We need a new generation of metropolitan cities more capable of seizing the opportunities of development metamorphosis and more able to reactivate territorial metabolism, especially in lagging regions. We need to develop new non-gravitational paradigms that are capable of recognising and guiding the new hyper-metropolitan relationships of which local territories—urban and rural territories in renewed combinations—let us catch a glimpse.

The aggregator, centripetal, and dual metropolitan model (between metropolitan cities and inner areas), has to be replaced with a model that I would define "hyper-metropolitan" because it is made up of settlement systems capable of interpreting the various forms of urban agglomeration. An advanced model, not post-something but decisively something else, based on a strategic—and therefore selective—approach that articulates the territory into different settlement and production configurations: strategic platforms, metropolitan super-organisms, joint territories, territorial archipelagos. An Italy made up of hyper-metropolis—systems of systems as said before—with distinct identities, magnitudes, specialisations and territorial relationships that can guide the vision, the project, and the norm of future metropolitan strategic plans and of urban agendas more clearly, so that they are not the tired reproposal of traditional practices and the ritual use of well-established but already blunt instruments. Returning to the egg metaphor, there are two types of tortilla-city. The one that we could call "gourmet"—compact and with a well-defined form and mix of different ingredients—creates the "super-organism", a new and recognisable system of regional urbanisation which is proposed as an intermediate, authoritative, and well-defined competence level between the region and the local authorities. For all intents and purposes a new level of territorial governance comparable to many of the most established European metropolitan realities. In the super-organism, peripheries assume well-defined roles, functions, and hierarchies by allocating service or pivotal functions of new metropolitan relationships. But we also have the "rustic" tortilla-city, more unformed and with different ingredient aggregations, which do not have a well-defined geometry and extension but mutate into the dish. These give life to the territorial archipelago, a more flexible and variable governance system that draws competences and authority from the ability to aggregate local authorities around a well-defined goal and project. More similar to French

Figure 6. San Berillo. Photo: author

"pôles métropolitaines" or German rur-urban systems. In the archipelago model peripheries retain their identity as porous and rarefied settlements, offering different living places that are capable of intercepting the growing demand for differentiated lifestyles over the hyper-urban (Schröder, Carta, Ferretti, Lino 2017). In the selective model we want to pursue, we must therefore recognise the value of both super-organisms and archipelagos. First of all, since international competition requires it, we must activate the added value of some "metropolitan super-organisms" that are multi-urban systems composed of cohesive and specialised communities, not merely connected with unidirectional gravitational relationships. Communities in which all components have a clear and defined role and—as the components of a perfect mechanism—act in unison by competing in a differential and incremental way to the pursuit of the organism's development. The metropolitan super-organism is therefore not the sum of the parts, but a new polycentric urban system characterised by the reticular specialisation of functions, which enhances both nodes and networks within a new super-urban relationship. The metropolitan super-organism is not the convenient aggregation of its components, but it is a new multi-city of innovation, creativity, and differentiated opportunities that privileges the recovery of what already exists and reduces the waste of resources, making them an opportunity to diversify functions. It is a metropolitan city that is sensitive to the landscape and that aims to requalify underused areas as enhancement of diversified centralities capable of reactivating social regeneration and economic vitality. As previously mentioned, in Italy, there are not only metropolitan super-organisms, but we have to recognise the existence—or rather we have to facilitate the development—of "territorial archipelagos" as settlement systems. These are systems that draw from their own local stories, that cross the palimpsest of time and their apparent marginalisation, are that are now able to offer themselves as alternatives to metropolitan aggregation and congestion. They are polycentric and reticular settlement systems that overcome the antinomy between aggregation and dispersion, characterised by more circular life cycles, that are capable of acting as hubs for the connection to the necessary global networks (e.g. through thematic networks) of small rural and urban areas, which are otherwise excluded from direct connection to larger networks.

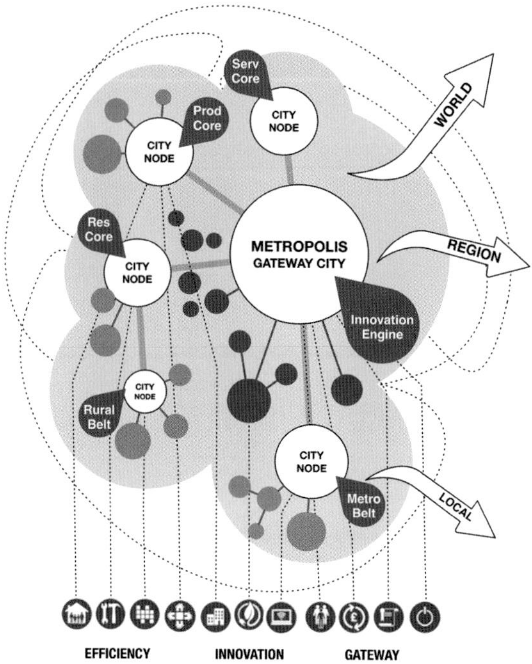

Figure 7. Metropolitan super-organism: innovative cooperative relation. Graphic: author

The territorial archipelago is a system of rural/urban settlements linked by traditional productive patterns and landscape infrastructure whose connective system is often composed of green and blue ecological networks. We can imagine it as a system of small urban cells thickened by green interfaces—agricultural or natural—with different functions: agricultural/productive park, river corridor, areas of renaturalisation, sports activities, etc. Therefore, the park-archipelago becomes the connective tissue of the urban islands and their scenario of resilience. Territorial archipelagos are the sites of local care, circular metabolism based on the communities' knowledge, they are the places of collective—earlier then technological—intelligence. These are places that return to be "pasture and nurturer of society", as Plato puts it, places that can accommodate communities in transition searching less erosive life cycles. Places that pulsate in different rhythm. The territorial archipelago does not act as a single system like the previous super-organism, but uses the energy of its reticular relationships to share identities, roles and hierarchies. For years in Europe, several rur-urban polycentric systems (such as Lower Saxony along the Elbe in Germany, Andalusia and Murcia in Spain, Provence and Languedoc-Roussillon in France, the network of green towns of Murgia and Madonie, and the historic centres of Val di Noto in Italy) have been experimenting rural-urban development strategies through the local rootedness of mobility infrastructure and digital infrastructure, the interconnection between green networks, cultural armour and slow life cycles, and the diffusion of technological skills and innovation within the local government. This local self-management capability empowers minor local actors to reap the competitive benefits offered by reticular systems in the new challenge for a polycentric Europe.

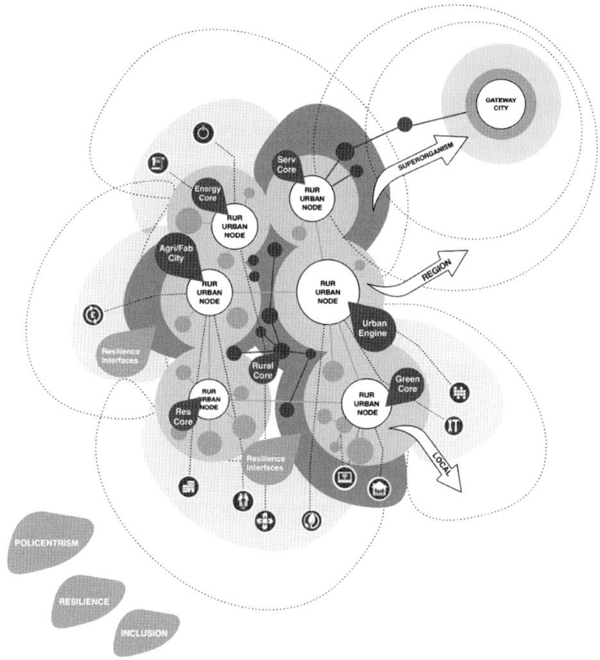

Figure 8. Territorial archipelago:
Rur-urban connective interfaces. Graphic: author

<u>Peripheries of a different present</u>

In his short but powerful movie "La forma della città" of 1974, Pier Paolo Pasolini—a sublime Italian poet, intellectual, writer and director—wonders while looking at the peripheral large buildings of Orte (near Rome). "What is it that gives me so much trouble?...What offends me in them? It's because I'm a void, an upset of form and style...And how many times have you seen me suffer, fidget, swear because of this image, this absolute purity of the shape of the city was ruined by something modern, by some foreign body that it was not any part of this form of the city." Pasolini gives voice and image, with his own body, to the criticism of the modern periphery as a foreign body, separated from that extraordinary relationship of form and norm, between space and society, as an element that disfigures the city that falls within the walls of his history, relegating the peripheries, which it had itself generated, more and more to the domain of stigma, aesthetic ugliness, and social wickedness. Nowadays, were Pasolini to return to the Italian suburbs, he would love them; he would also find them places teeming with life, dense relationships, and new forms of contemporary cities. Alongside the ugly and vulgar palaces that have ruined them, new communities appear, animating them for a new urbanity. The revolution of the future in Italy can start from suburbs, because today the places located in the margins of the centres of the unsustainable development, want to be resilient, socially innovative, and creative. These places must be protagonists of a different development and not only an object to be rethought. Faced with the pursuit of post-urbanism that characterises the times in which we are living—in order to contain the anti-city

Figure 9. Favara Sette cortili. Photo: author

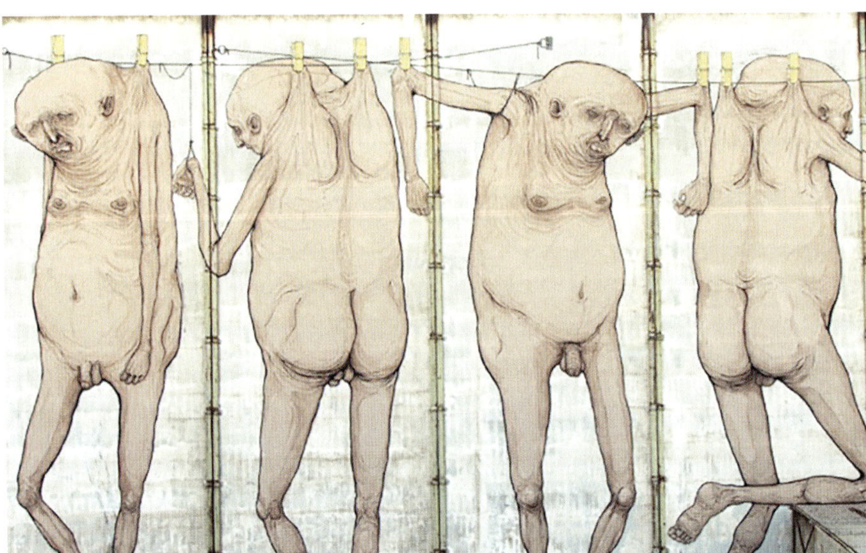

Figure 10. Messina, NemOS. Photo: author

as result of the conflict between centres and suburbs, and which is produced by the unsustainable soil consumption that is eroding our plant and cultural palimpsests—we must have the courage to fully enter into the Neoanthropocene of which we already see the first manifestations in a rediscovered ecological collective consciousness. In the circular and creative society, facing the challenges of climate change and sharing opportunities, cities can once again be the most powerful platforms of social innovation. They become what I define as Augmented Cities, vibrant systems of places and communities, data and information, actions and reactions. They are transformed into a new metabolism created by a new interaction between people and the environment, between centres and margins (Carta 2017).

And it is in Southern Europe that the urban Neoanthropocene might be able to show its first forms, to enhance the abandoned historic centres and large suburbs—children of the twentieth-century urban model—which has greatly restricted development by relegating them to spatial and conceptual margins of the urban planning. Today, after the absinthe-effect of unlimited debt-growth and vigorous land-consumption has worn off, external and internal peripheries have become the protagonists of a city model fostered by the interaction of resilience, recycling, and human capital reactivation, and which are offered as a precious laboratory—not as a comforting repair but of a powerful, disruptive regeneration, urban and human together. These are the places where Georg Simmel invokes "rootedness" and from which can revive a city's architecture (Simmel 1903). As Lars Lerup writes "after-the-city is just another city" (Lerup 2001).

Studying the Parisian banlieues, Henri Lefebvre wrote negagtively as early of 1967 that "with 'suburbanisation' a process is set into motion which decentres the city. Isolated from the city, the proletariat will end its sense of oeuvre. Isolated from places of production, available from a sector of habitation for scattered firms, the proletariat will allow its creative capacity to diminish in its conscience" (Lefebvre 1996). Nowadays, the revival of an urban consciousness in the periphery, the formation of a community consciousness is bound up with security issues and the struggle against terrorism, which must find the solutions in peripheries, since it is here that problems have been produced and that have created fertile soil for rebellion and conflict. In Italy, the *Atlas of Metropolitan Suburbs* edited by the General Directorate of Art and Contemporary Architecture and Urban Peripheries of the MiBACT with the scientific direction of Paolo Cottino is a precious guide—not yet finished but already significant—for interpreting how the peripheries are changing from "dysfunctional places" to creative and innovative communities and places. The survey has taken as field of analysis nine metropolitan cities—taking a census of, and interpreting and representing, the mix of activities and services as a factor of urban quality and the problem of rarefaction of diversity in metropolitan territories—by proposing a metropolitan geography of the typologies of functional peripheries, to reactivate their regenerative factors of space, but above all social connections, which are often facilitated by culture and creativity. Located along a clear dorsal that crosses Italy, the experiences of resilience and creativity in the periphery are multiplying, creating an atlas of places, people, models, and prototypes that are generated both by the North and the South, by metropolises and inner areas, such as a collaborative writing of a new code of development for the cities of the future:

starting with the pioneering experiences of Farm Cultural Park in Sicily or where social innovation meets design at the Ringhiera Theater in Milan that does not want to lose its roots while while it also allows the construction of skyscrapers; from the urban Ecomuseum "Mare Memoria Viva" of Palermo which rediscovers its liquid dimension to the "Urban Cultural Sea of Milan" where water is the collaborative creativity that satisfies the desire for change; or the new creative metaphors of Parma's WOPA, and the productive recycling of Ex Fadda at San Vito dei Normanni, just to mention a few exciting experiences of initiatives that are parts of the creative city. Just look at the 429 urban and human innovation projects that participated in the 2017 "Call of Culturability" promoted by the Unipolis Foundation to design a threedimensional map of Italy that rejects the stigma of the suburbs and, from margins, launches powerful signals of a future made of regeneration of quarries as cultural epicentres, of a dream school in Gramsci's home, of new artistic languages accessible to everyone, of music and politics in the memory of Fabrizio De Andrè, and of developing ignored spaces through cinematic storytelling, just to mention the five winning projects. We could continue an unlimited list which is updated every month that a new urban regeneration initiative is born to show that peripheries are vital areas of new urbanism.

The Second Half of the Chessboard: from Practices to Protocols

The number of peripheral regeneration practices doubles with dizzying rhythm, with a nearly logarithmic progression, risking an end like that of the Emperor Gupta, submerged by rice grains. I am referring to one of the most efficient metaphors for the problems of managing exponential growth, which reminds us that we must learn to manage the "second half of the chessboard". The futurologist Ray Kurzweil, in his essay from the year 1999, tells us a story to better understand the power of exponential progression (Kurzweil 1999). In the fourth century BC, the inventor of the game of chess went to Pataliputra to show his creation to Emperor Gupta, who was so impressed by that nice and hard game that he invited the inventor to decide for himself the compensation he should recieve. The inventor praised the generosity of the emperor, and then he asked for just a little bit of rice to feed his family. The man suggested using the chessboard to decide the amount of rice to be allocated. "Emperor," he said, "put a single grain of rice on the first box of the table, two on the second, four on the third, and so on, so that each square has twice as much of the previous one." The emperor, impressed by the apparent modesty of the inventor, agreed. But the Emperor, wise and brave leader, did not know the power of logarithms: sixty-three doublings give us an incredibly large number, even if we begin only with one. If his request were to be fully honored, the inventor would end up with over eighteen trillion grains of rice, an amount of rice greater than produced throughout the history of the planet. Of course, the emperor failed to honour the request. Kurzweil's great intuition is that even though the numbers may become excessive in the first half of the chessboard, we are still in the real world. On the second half of the chessboard, when the numbers run into trillions, quadrillions, quintillions, we lose the notion of quantity. This story allows us to clarify that the many and growing practices in the peripheries of social innovation, urban and human regeneration are happily—or dangerously—close to the second half of the chessboard. These practices claims to replace a purely recognitive and celebratory approach with a more effective, responsible, delicate

Figure 11. Castelbuono, Piazza Castello. Photo: Roberto Panucci

Figure 12. Castelbuono, Piazza Castello. Photo: Stefano Masselli

Figure 13. Mazzara, Cava, and wall painting by MOMO. Photo: author

management approach. Approaching the second half of the chessboard asks us to begin to govern the new life of the Italian peripheries, incorporating experiences, experiments, informal actions within the new creative and responsible urbanism we want.

Peripheries nowadays are no longer heresies resistant to the modernist paradigm of the competitive city, but a great resource of resilience, a place where we can find settlement, community, landscape identity values from which cities can resume after having been marked by an imperfect modernity that has so insolently crossed us. Cities move from the margins to re-energise social, territorial, and cultural capitals and to definitively save us from the dramatic drug addiction of a "subprime" urbanism that has anaesthetised our ability to imagine, plan, and take root. The commitment to deal with the issue of peripheries' regeneration—spatial, social, or economic—finds a new impetus not only for their physical recovery, for their environmental improvement or mobility accessibility, but instead for acting on their more total regenerative ability of social, spatial, economic and productive tissues within new visions of cities in metamorphosis: schools as devices of legality and libraries as places of knowledge, visions that lovingly recapture fragments of agricultural landscapes, that recycle neglected areas and buildings. In Italy, large peripheral neighbourhoods from the nineteen-fifties and nineteen-sixties, abandoned historic centres, or middle cities' neighbourhoods centrifuged by the urban dispersion and rural micro-urban patterns of internal areas, must be rethought; avoiding cold reconnections tissues or inhabitants desertification, and refusing an extremely invasive and erosive surgical approach that is characterised by consuming vast material and immaterial resources, and above all by undefined outcomes with the risk of rejection (Di Biagi 2008). It is no longer the time of cosmetic overthrow, aesthetic grafting, purely volumetric demolition and reconstruction, and the urban radiotherapy caused by the bombardment of resources through peripheral transformations or forced engagement of centrality services or large shopping malls is also no longer adequate. What is more effective—continuing this healthcare metaphor—is a "stem" urbanism that introduces some urban quality cells extracted from the same identity tissue: multifunctional agriculture, schools as collective services and citizenship, libraries as new spaces of knowledge and aggregating associative spaces, co-working, digital manufacturing and creative ateliers, but also smart and efficient buildings and sustainable mobility. And, let's not forget, the most powerful stem cells that can regenerate the wounded tissue of the suburbs: women and men living in peripheries, the good Anthropocene.

Polipheries: New Generation of Cities

Reimagining suburbs means not just looking at them with new eyes and designing them with renewed tools, but also redefining them epistemologically, starting from our vocabulary. We should speak of them no longer as "surrounding places" of the central city where all values are concentrated, as areas without identity, but as new centres. I propose here, with all the disruptive and heretical charge of the term, to call suburbs "polipheries" as a combination of the two words *pòli* (multiple) and *phérein* (to bring), plural sites capable of generating the new polycentric city. But polipheries also designate the combination of *pólis* (city) and *phérein*, intense places able to generate new forms of creative, intelligent, and equal cities. The polipheries are therefore the epiphanies of a new generation of Neoanthropocene cities and no longer the imperfect version of the city of the twentieth century. When polipheries are viewed with new eyes and mapped in new ways, they become precious reserves of identity and futurity; they become respositories of heritage and creativity that are essential for their planning and design as living organisms. The cells that resisted changes in wild urbanisation—fragments of agricultural landscapes, parts of infrastructure, functional reconversions transforming landscapes and abandoned areas—today allow the city to be more resilient, less resistant to innovation and less adaptive. These reserves are used to activate ecological and social resilience processes that can successfully address more interactive problems, engage the plurality of actors and different social archipelagos in decision-making, and implement governance-capable forms of balancing competition between central cities and their settlement belts in an ecosystem relationship. Polipheries are resilience cells capable of reactivating a more creative, intelligent, and ecological "hyper-metabolism" in marginal areas that have been excluded from the rhetoric of turbo-development: transitional suburbs, industrial restructuring districts, port areas, and recycled rail infrastructure.

First of all, we need a new urban and territorial policy to strengthen the quality, connectivity, and competitiveness of cultural ecosystems through the adoption of strategies to enhance the potential of the territory (history, resources, connections, and identities) and to promote its integration by overlaying them with dimensions to increase both their mass and amplitude, and thus their power. What should not be overlooked is the importance of interventions for the expansion and strengthening of human capital and the level of skills and professionalism available through training and research and through facilitating interaction between actors within the ecosystem and between inter-ecosystems, even through the emergence of brokers (agencies, mixed companies, pacts). In the urban transition that we must cross over, we must also change the social and economic importance of the many cultural resources (culture and creativity are the basis of almost all urban regeneration practices) present or reactivated in the suburbs, linking new cultural policies with human development policies. It is therefore necessary that the cultural capital, made up of capital assets but more and more of social assets (as demonstrated by the numerous practices I mentioned), be structurally integrated into the regeneration and development portfolio, that it distributes in an extended and fair manner a dividend that it is capable of engendering and competing in dispersing the effects of this renewed cultural dimension of development in the everyday life of communities.

If we believe in peripheries as a new centre of an urban archipelago that remodels spaces and economies, we must create and distribute a real "creative and cultural dividend" of conservation and valorisation policies of landscape, building recovery and development, stimulating entrepreneur- ship, and security assurance. The cultural dividend of the regeneration of the suburbs is therefore a new currency of exchange in the transition economy, and an equity instrument capable of entering the market of interest negotiation, redefining priorities and developmental paths, acting on the domain of collective interests and common goods. A territory can realise the cultural dividend by definitely focusing on an initial investment, both in terms of funding and human resources, and on the enhancement of material heritage. But then innovation is needed, both in solving known vulnerabilities, but also in identifying in a timely manner the variables that can limit the propagation of the positive effects of intervention to other sectors of the chain (quality and safety of living, mobility, production, environmental protection). And above all, we need a new partnership with the private sector and with civil society, to activate the widest range of interventions with adequate returns on investment for new policies, projects, and cultural and social infrastructure, interconnected in real ecosystems, in plural and generative terms: as "polipherical".

Finally, the European peripheries are crying out to us: no more masterplan! Their complexity and fragility, their desire for redemption, and the social activism of their communities require us to abandon a conformational and regulatory design that pretends to foresee their development trajectory and to crystallise their design with no flexibility for change based on conditions of context. And, with even greater strength, peripheries do not accept a top-down approach. Instead, new strategic approaches are needed, engaged and negotiated with a precise timeline, which is incremental compared to a necessary first phase, more colonising, to bring life cycles back into the suburbs and to a second stage more focused on consolidation and predeployment to a development based on a new urban environment capable of supporting its costs, financial and social.

In conclusion, we need adaptive approaches that model the evolving needs of reborn communities and of a space that is remodelled to accommodate them. In short, the polipheries of a different present claim the use of "cityforming" (Carta 2017), a protocol that generates the necessary urban atmosphere that is capable of developing a new urban and human metabolism.

Figure 14. Favara SOU. Photo: author

Notes/Bibliography

1 The "Human City" is the book-manifesto gathering together Adriano Olivetti's speeches and interventions from the nineteen-fifties, which was published in 1960, when his death was imminent, as a theoretical seal to cap his unitary vision of enterprise, community, politics, and urbanism. See: Olivetti A. (2001) *Città dell'uomo*. Torino: Edizioni di Comunità. On the concept of communities as bricks to build the great building of an integrated democracy that starts from the hundreds of small homelands to reconstructs the state by focusing on scientific, social, and aesthetic values, see: Olivetti A. (2013) ***Il cammino della Comunità***. Roma: Edizioni di Comunità, especially the beautiful introduction by Salvatore Settis. To deepen the relevance of Olivetti's thinking and the modernity of his community concept, see the beautiful book by Aldo Bonomi, Marco Revelli and Alberto Magnaghi (2015) *Il vento di Adriano. La comunità concreta di Olivetti tra non più e non ancora*. Roma: DeriveApprodi.

2 Nigel Jacob is the cofounder of the Mayor's Office of New Urban Mechanics, a civic innovation incubator and R&D Lab within Boston's City Hall. Nigel's work is about making urban life better via innovative, people-oriented applications of technology and design.

Barber B.R. (2013) *If Mayors Ruled the World. Dysfunctional Nations, Rising Cities*. New Haven, Yale University Press.

Bonomi A., Della Puppa F., Masiero R. (2016) *La società circolare. Fordismo, capitalismo molecolare, sharing economy*. Roma, DeriveApprodi.

Brynjolfsson E., McAfee A (2014) *The Second Machine Age: Work, Progress, and Prosperity in a Time of Brilliant Technologies*. Boston, W W Norton & Co.

Carta M. (2017) *Augmented City. A Paradigm Shift*. Trento-Barcelona, ListLab.

Di Biagi P. (2008) *Città pubbliche. Linee guida per la riqualificazione urbana*. Milano, Giorgio Mondadori.

Harvey D. (2012) *Rebel Cities: From the Right to the City to the Urban Revolution*. New York, New Left Books.

Lerup L. (2001) *After the City. Cambridge* MA, MIT Press.

Kurzweil R. (1999) *The Age or Spiritual Machines*. New York, Penguin.

La Pira G. (1955) "Per la salvezza delle città di tutto il mondo", speech held at the meeting of the mayors of world capitals, Firenze, 2 October 1955.

Lefebvre H. (1967) "Le droit à la ville". L'Homme et la société, Volume 6, n. 1.

Lefebvre H. (1996) *Writings on cities*. Oxford, Blackwell Publishers.

Moretti E. (2012) *The New Geography of Jobs*. Boston, Mariner Books.

Schröder J., Carta M., Ferretti M., Lino B. (2016) *Territories. Rural-urban Strategies*. Berlin, Jovis.

Simmel G. (1903) *Die Großstädte und das Geistesleben*. Dresden, Petermann.

Soja E. W. (2000) *Postmetropolis: Critical Studies of Cities and Regions*. New York, Wiley.

New Lifecycles for the Peripheries

Mosè Ricci

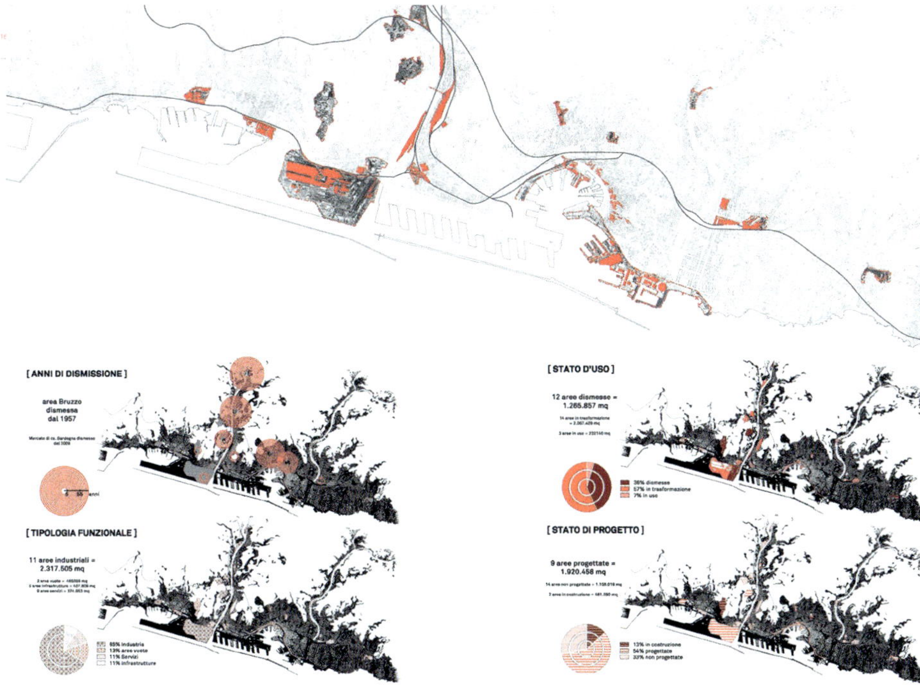

Figure 1. Recycle Footprint Genova: state of transformation and reuse potentials of abandoned areas. Graphic: L. Nazzari and B. Pignatti (2014)

Periphery does not exist. Or at least it does not exist in the way we always thought about it until today. The marginal parts, the *spread* tissue, the non-centre no longer exist and no longer only exist around (from the etymology of the word *periphero* = to bring around) the compact city. These parts are inside, they constitute its black holes. To invert the image, one could actually say that the majority of the connective tissues of the contemporary city is what we once called the peripheral tissue. Central and compact nucleuses flow in the infinite peripheries of the European city, as we have learned to recognise it and described it over the last decades. We cannot even say that those tissues of the infinite city are unresolved, they they simply lack significant public spaces, monuments, or anything that would make them more similar and homologous to the compact and historical city. All attempts of homologation of this type of urban spaces have failed. Because they have another logic. They are differently experienced and their places of aggregation and monuments are different, and not always easy to interpret through design. However, if we abandon the topological references (in-out-around), and if by peripheries we mean the spaces of social difficulty and housing abandonment (which often coincide), then our cities are constellations of these spaces. As is often the case in American metropolises or in the Swiss, Greek, and Italian mountains, the old centres are the most peripheral areas in terms of territorial development, at least as it was intended in the last century. And just as often in the middle of the global crisis and in the full digital divide of shared information, these "peripheries" are the most capable of resilience and those that are worth social investment. The building boom of the last twenty years has left several cadavers on the territory. In Italy between 1999 and 2012 (CRESME data 2012), about 300 million cubic meters of new buildings were built. On these, the percentage of abuse is irrelevant, less than 5%. In a game where everybody believed they were earning money—the owners who secured their savings, the building companies that undertook the construction, the administrations that survived with the burden of urbanisation, the politics that was continually rewarded with the rhythm of the construction cycle—a bloody and unprecedented invasion of Italian landscapes was perpetrated. The outcomes are evident for everybody. Since the collapse of the real estate market in 2007, the territories affected by the economic and environmental crisis suffer from disasters of abandonment and disposal, often also of the most recent buildings. In Italy, there are at least six million empty homes on more than ten million "blocked" properties. Twenty million square meters of dismantled or about-to-be-dismantled railway areas. At least five thousand kilometres of railway lines not in use. Twenty thousand kilometres of abandoned roads, of which two thousand six hundred are unused.

It is also not possible to exactly calcuate the number of businesses and abandoned industrial buildings. The new infrastructure, the cornerstones of government-based development, often remain unused and become a burden to the development. The cost of their senselessness is paid by everyone. Gioia Tauro, Tiburtina Station, Bre-Be-Mi, the Expo are just the most obvious examples of a policy that always wastes twice as much for building new fetishes of past modernity and let the largest historical, cultural, and touristic heritage in the world perish without any strategic investment for its valorisation. The situation does not differ in other European countries. In Spain, for example, between Madrid and Toledo a new city for 300,000 inhabitants has been completely built—up to garbage baskets and street lamps—and remains completely empty and unsold.

And even in the richest countries in northern Europe, the problem is well known. The Dutch Pavilion at the 2010 Venice Biennale presented an empty hall with the threat of suspended models hanging from the ceiling representing all the empty Ramstadt buildings weighing above the visitor's head. At the 2012 Biennale, the Dutch Pavilion was called "Reset" and the German one "Reduce, Reuse, Recycle". In 2014, it was Portugal that dramatically raised the same theme, and in 2014 the Korean Pavilion staged "The Fair Game", which designated tactics of reuse and urban recycling suggesting a new form of the city just by extending, modifying, and parasitising the existing one. The crisis that today seems to curb the urban dispersion processes is nothing but the detonator of a deeper change that is altering the geography of our desires, our lifestyles, and our expectations for the future.

In the economic and environmental juncture that we all know, we are experiencing the revolution of shared information technologies. It is a subtle revolution that we sometimes barely recognise,

Figure 2. The Italian *Recycle* Footprint, elaboration from Soil consumption database 2012, Confiscated/unsold properties 2013, Real Estate Growth from 2001–2011. Source: Recycle Italy Atlas database (PRIN 2012–2016). Graphic: E. Sommariva (2016)

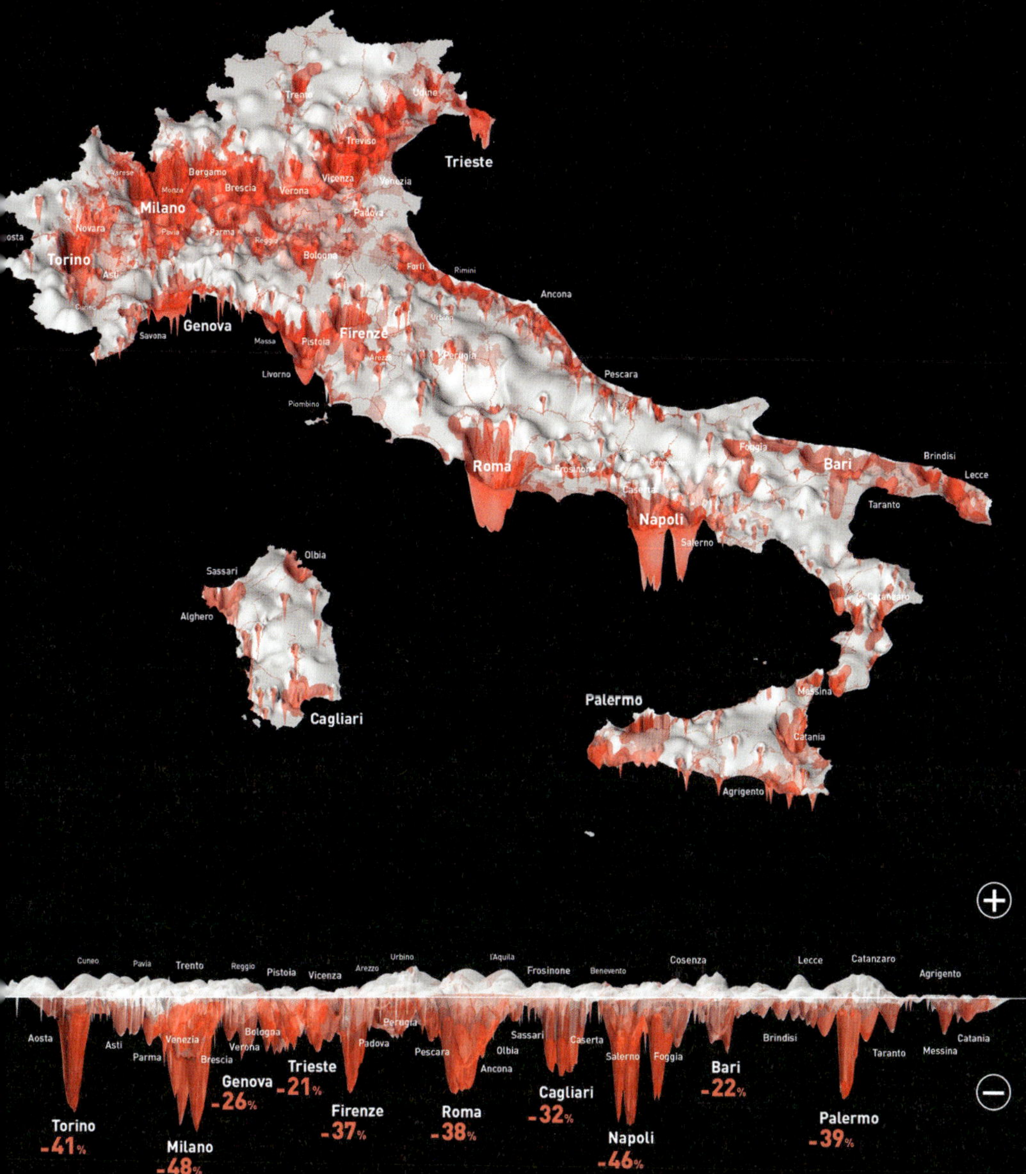

Trento
Udine
Treviso
Trieste
Varese
Bergamo
Monza
Brescia
Verona
Vicenza
Venezia
Milano
Padova
Novara
Pavia
Parma
Reggio
Torino
Bologna
Asti
Forlì
Rimini
Ancona
Genova
Savona
Massa
Pistoia
Firenze
Arezzo
Perugia
Livorno
Pescara
Piombino
Foggia
Bari
Brindisi
Lecce
Roma
Taranto
Caserta
Napoli
Salerno
Olbia
Sassari
Alghero
Catanzaro
Messina
Palermo
Cagliari
Catania
Agrigento
Cuneo
Pavia
Trento
Reggio
Pistoia
Vicenza
Arezzo
Urbino
L'Aquila
Frosinone
Benevento
Cosenza
Lecce
Catanzaro
Agrigento
Aosta
Asti
Parma
Venezia
Brescia
Verona
Bologna
Perugia
Padova
Sassari
Pescara
Olbia
Ancona
Caserta
Salerno
Foggia
Brindisi
Taranto
Messina
Catania
Genova -26%
Trieste -21%
Torino -41%
Milano -48%
Firenze -37%
Roma -38%
Cagliari -32%
Napoli -46%
Bari -22%
Palermo -39%

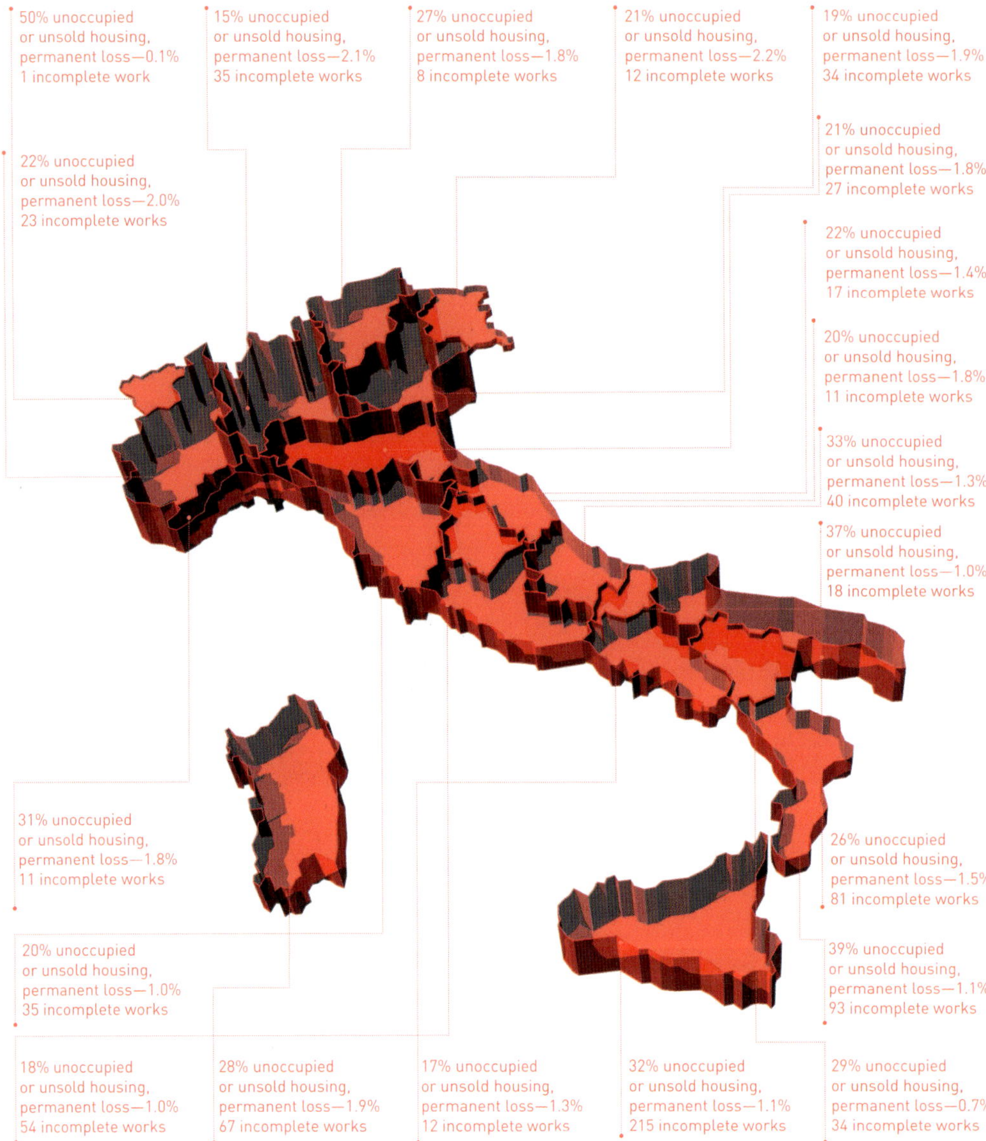

Figure 3. The Italy of Opportunities, elaboration from ISTAT population 2011–2014, unfinished works Codacons 2014, Housing market scenario 2012–2015
Source: Recycle Italy Atlas database (PRIN 2012-2016). Graphic: J. Sordi, C. Rizzi (2016)

as change occurs in our lives and our behaviours in subsidiary and molecular form. Day by day we look at the world from new perspectives, and we do the same things we did before in a different way. We learn to use ever-more powerful, artificially minded, instantaneous tools. We occupy more and more spacious virtual spaces. To manage our lives and to spend our time, we have less and less need of dedicated physical places. There is a thin wire that inseparably binds recycling and smart systems. Perhaps the real causes for the abandonment of living spaces that have so deeply affected Western cities and landscapes are computers, smart phones, tablets, interactive televisions, and new apps—and all sophisticated devices and distortion and time-cancelling technologies, such as those for sharing information, decisions, and actions.

You can meet, establish a relationship, or give a talk via Skype or other social media without physically being present where this takes place. Now everything happens in the video, but soon our presence will be virtually expressed by holograms that can also simulate physical appearance, emotion, and meaning. Today, it is best to buy consumer goods, clothing, books, or furniture on the net, as on Amazon, and we will need less and less retail space in the city. Anyone can become a part time taxi driver and sell his journeys on Uber or share the car with Car to Go or even political choices at the click of Avaaz.

In a few years with a 3D printer we will be able to produce construction components and whole buildings. At home, you can make spare parts of any object in common use, and in a basically equipped laboratory you can also make blenders and washing machines. While new figures of digital artisans are emerging, the appliances factories in Friuli and Veneto have already closed. One buys train tickets online, and there is much less need of train stations, in the traditional way they were designed. For example, the building of the Tiburtina Station in Rome, recently built, proved to be unneeded even before it was opened, and now there are official guards posted to encourage people to use the station. Each of us can find thousands of similar examples that show how you always need less functional spaces to live and work because many of the uses that used to occupy solid spaces in the city have been transferred or moved to the virtual spaces of the internet.

If all of this is about to happen or already happens, it is clear that many essential paradigms of the modern ages, and not only those of the close relationship between function and form of architecture or town, will be emptied of meaning. Ultimately the revolution in information technologies for sharing will displace the certainties of the modern project, suddenly making all theories and practices related to it appear out-of-date. The zoning, the functional organisation of urban contexts or that of the architectural spaces, the model's theories, the best practices—all of these seem to be manifestations of a logic that belongs to another era, theoretical and behavioural models conceived to handle a three-dimensional solid space that is now no longer the only possible design space.

This is the point. The simultaneous action of three key factors— the economic crisis, the environmental crisis, and the revolution in sharing information technologies—is so deeply changing our lifestyles and the way in which we imagine and we want the solid forms of our future that all our design knowledge suddenly seems inadequate both as an interpretative tool for the current condition and as a device capable of generating new environmental, social, economic performativity and new beauty. Turning to the positive effects of the digital revolution, one might say that what is happening to the most evolved societies through the effect of shared information is the possibility of being able to to live much more in physical space than in the past and not necessarily have to conform to specific pre-established destinies. Simply, we have a huge amount of built-in volume that is no longer needed or that we still do not know how to use. The same is already happening for infrastructure and open spaces. This is not surprising. In the history of architecture and of the city, great technological changes have also greatly changed ways and forms of living and consequently the ways and forms of design. One of the main theoretical questions of modernity was that of the best possible spatial synthesis between the function and shape of architecture and the organisation of the city in homogeneous functional areas. Today, with the revolution in information technology, we have the opposite problem. That is, to give meaning, narrative, and uses—albeit temporarily—to spaces that have already been given forms. And to transform them into attractive, ecologically performing, habitable places. The dissipation of modernity requires new paradigms like new perspectives on the future—or on the present—and a new idea for the design of physical spaces. This is an important challenge for architectural culture: to value existing structures and resources through conceptual devices working on a shift of sense and on new habitats' life cycles. This is a challenge that considers the context as an occasion for design, the landscape as a piece of infrastructure that produces ecological value, and the future of the city as a collective and non-authoritative project.

In this framework recycling becomes the main physical and conceptual space of the architect's action. The design practice of recycling is necessarily contextual and adaptive. It can't be implemented with stereotyped techniques or with traditional tools. Any architectural, urban, or landscaping material is different from another. Each place and each case can have different projects. There is no point in talking about "guide projects" or "good practices". One could rather refer to different adaptive and local tactics that always respond to intervention strategies geared to building new sense and new ecologies. The very idea of recycling provides a vision. As "detectives of space", architects are interested in the possibility of revitalising existing structures, of finding new meanings for them, of creating new conveniences and new beauty by the recycling of built spaces that so rapidly are abandoning their usage and meaning. Recycling means putting back into circulation, re-using waste materials which have lost value and/or meaning. Recycling protects the environment and is economically convenient. It is a practice that allows one to limit the presence of waste, to reduce disposal costs and to contain those of new production. *Recycle* means creating new value, in new way. To begin a new cycle, another life. In this lies the propulsive content of recycling. *Recycle* is an ecological action that intervenes into meaning, pushing the existing structures into the future by transforming waste into prominent figures. Too often *recycle* rhetoric speaks about the ethics of the process. As architects, we do not recycle because it is a good and just action. We study how to recycle, since to recycle is to design.

Figure 4. *Recycle* Footprint Genova: numbers of the abandoned heritage and infrastructure. Graphic: L. Nazzari and B. Pignatti (2014)

Figure 5. *Tivoli the Other Rome: The Strategic Master Plan for Aniene Riverpark*, proposed for Roma 2025 Metro-Region, exhibited at the MAXXI Foundation in Rome (2015). Photo: author

Bibliography

Gausa M. (2016) "Decalogues for a New Informational Era". In: Ricci M., Schröder J. eds. (2016) *Towards a Pro-Active Manifesto.* Roma, Aracne editrice. pp. 46–55.

Ricci M., Schröder J. eds. (2014) *Productive Grounds, Transalpine Trajectories. Re-cycle Italy Series*, nr. 11. Roma, Aracne editrice.

Ricci M. (2014) "The Recycle Paradigm. Learning from Detroit". In: Younès C., D'Arienzo R. eds. (2014) *Recycler l'Urbain. Pour une écologie des milieux habités.* Metis Presses, Collection: vuesDensemble Essais, pp. 241–260.

Ricci M. (2014) *Rigenerazione per lo sviluppo.* In: *RIVISTA*, nr. 10. pp. 12–13.

Ricci M., Schröder J. eds. (2016) *Towards a Pro-Active Manifesto. Re-cycle Italy Series*, nr. 16. Roma, Aracne editrice.

Ricci M. (2013) "Recycle footprint_Impronta da riciclo". In: Marini S., Santangelo V. eds. (2013) *Nuovi cicli di vita per architetture e infrastrutture della città e del paesaggio, Re-cycle Italy Series*, nr. 1. Roma, Aracne editrice. pp. 40–45.

Ricci M. (2016), *DETROIT_ITALIA Manifesto proattivo per il riciclo della architettura, dei paesaggi e delle città.* n. 36–37.

Latouche S. (2007) *La scommessa della decrescita.* Milano, Feltrinelli.

—(2007) *Come sopravvivere allo sviluppo.* Torino, Bollati Boringhieri.

Jacobs J. (1992) The Death and the Life of Great American Cities. London, Vintage.

CRESME (2010) *Il Mercato delle Costruzioni 2011, XVIII Rapporto Congiunturale e Previsionale CRESME 2010–2015 l'avvio del VII ciclo edilizio.* Organizzazione e direzione di Lorenzo Bellicini e Francesco Toso. Rome.

WWF Italia (2010) *2009 l'anno del cemento. Processi e stime immobiliari da CRESME/SI.* Roma.

Consiglio Nazionale dei Geologi (2010) *Terra e sviluppo. Decalogo della terra 2010. Rapporto sullo stato del territorio italiano.* Con la consulenza scientifica del centro di ricerca CRESME. Roma.

SUPERELEVATA FOOT[PRINTS]

Genoa, 21|09|2014

For one day the area of the Ancient Harbour and the seaside promenade were finally connected, creating one five-kilometre-long path open to the public and closed to vehicle traffic.

Superelevata Foot[prints] has opened the area of Genova Shipyards in Calata Gadda to citizens, with art performances and events to raise awareness of strategic areas in the Old Port that are still being neglected. Photos: Mosè Ricci

UPERELEVATA FOOT[PRINTS]
ecycle, Reuse, Urban Happy Mood

Urban happiness can be found in the discovery of new emotions as well as in the sense of security that familiar and liveable places provide. But we believe it also has to do with the feeling of being part of the process of contributing to the creation of a better place to live in.

Periphery–Peripherals, 1980–2015: From the Postmodern Era to the Information Age

Manuel Gausa Navarro

Figure 1. Manolo Lagullo: *Diagonal Sur*, Barcelona,1989. Source: COAG

1980s–1990s.
Another Form, Another Place: The Periphery as "Alternative Landscape"

The revisionist response to the crisis of modernity (historicism, "turning back", reconstruction and evocation, mannerist eclecticism, etc.) marked most of the postmodern urban cultures of the late twentieth century. Confidence in formal architectural language and design were the main strengths of models that were more attentive to the lyrical and punctual approach than to possible holistic conceptions of the city.

In the face of the diverse figurative expressions—emphatically "stylistic" or gently "calligraphic"—of this retroactive vision which saw in the evocation of a referential centre (ideally civic, cohesive, and harmonious) its main reference (but which also, in the face of the dream, sought to recover "lost paradises"), the critical reaction favoured during a good part of the nineteen-eighties by certain theoretical positions would be to return to the basis of modern production—more contemporary (abstract, objective, technical)—as accepted in all its "dry and hard radicalism". In this context it is possible to interpret the interest manifested by the research produced in this period as focused around a "new" expressive landscape: the landscape of the periphery (the "suburb", the "crown" of the "broken" city, its crust more or less cracked) as "alternative scenario" (Mateo 1987).

Faced with the decadent harmony of a recreated history and with the impossible sentimentality of the traditional city, the periphery became, in effect, an alternative "new place" (present in a systemic and almost interchangeable way in most large cities) revealing a new epic scale open to the possibility of entering into the city's own latent potentials (Steiner 1993).

The attention to the periphery would then appear, for much of the 1980s and 1990s, as the "impossible" dream of a "possible"—if "interrupted"—lost modernity: the quasi-poetic scenario of a failed city that is nevertheless also susceptible of being potentially reinterpretable, that contrasts the rigorous, austere, and abstract intensity of the modern city to the evocative model of the historical city. The urban schematism, its productive mechanics, and generally the poor constructive quality that had been in most cases the main characteristics of the "modern city" in post-war Europe (thus converting its architectural translation into a symbol of fragmentation, dislocation, imposition, as epic as it was autistic, as "self-sufficient" as it was indifferent to the environment) did not prevent the interpretation of the peripheral space as big spaces of possibilities, of "expectant scenarios" rather than "significant spaces" (Wenders, Kollhoff 1988).

A space more strict than ceremonious; more severe than solemn; more purist than pure:
The subtle border line between the "periphery" of the nineteen-eighties as an alternative "cult landscape"—a space of latencies but also of values—and the "suburb" of the nineteen-sixties as a political scene of social denunciation—deficient, conflicting, belligerent, socially "resistant"—traced an ambiguous scenario of contradictions and intersections at the same time. However, inside of this scene, one would find prevailing and continuing to underly these notions the very idea of the periphery as a "limit" (or perimeter).

This notion of peripheral perimeter would, however, be the one which at the end of the nineteen-nineties mutated and changed to give way to a more diffuse, fractalised, and ambiguous scenario in its expressions and manifestations.

In this sense, if the dichotomy between a "centre frozen by history" and an "expectant periphery" had for some time constituted a revitalizing leitmotiv of urbanism at the end of twentieth century, it had also limited the debate to a sort of aesthetic confrontation between two figurative landscapes: that of the morphological continuity of the historical city and that of the objective freedom of modern growth; this reduced the perception—and the approach—of space to a problem of forms: old or new forms, old or new scenarios—inner fabrics or perimeter boundaries—located, in any case, in the familiar context of what had traditionally been conceived as "city". Thus, it is a recognizable and virtually coherent and continuous enclosure (or object), a scenario whose old geometries have already begun to fray.

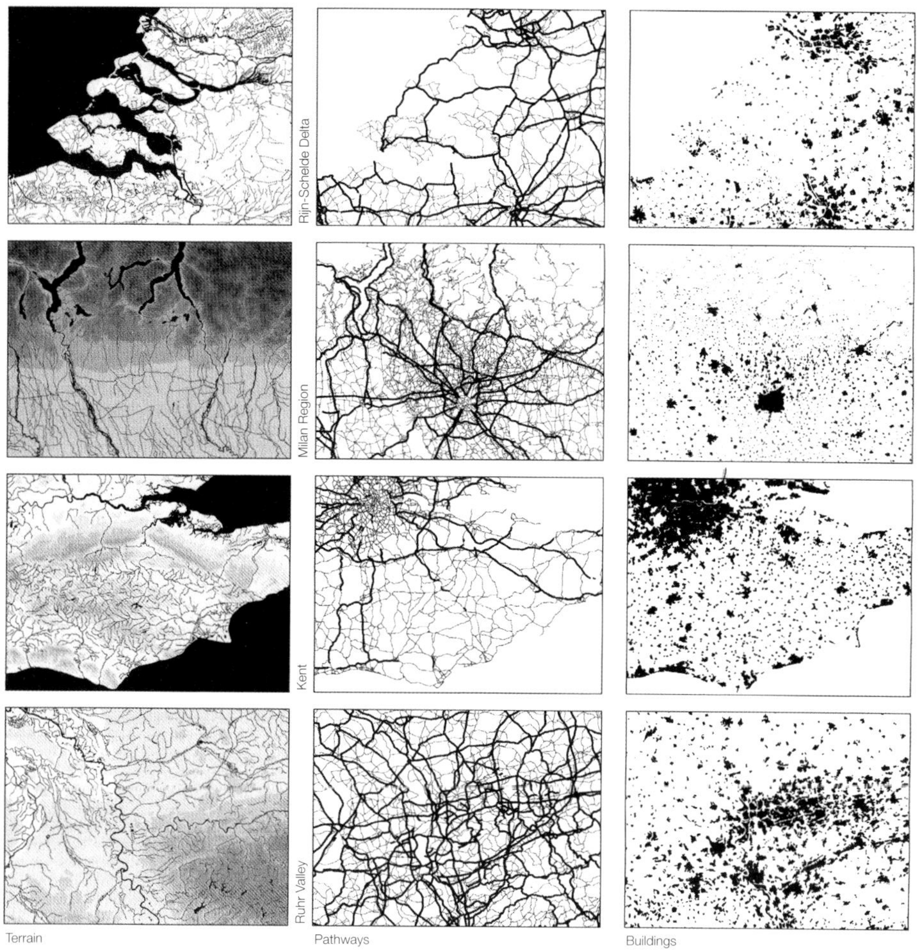

Figure 2. Processes of interconnection among infrastructural networks and urban spattering in different European regions: the Rijn-Schelde Delta, the Milan Region, Kent and the Ruhr Valley. Based on MUST S/A Lab. Images: De Verkenning Van de Hoeksche Waard

Figure 3. Sprawl Cities, Urbanalisation processes. Photo: Francesc Muñoz, 2010

1990s–2000s.
In the "Urban-Territorial" Space: Dispersions, Decohesions, Dis-densities.
The Periphery as "Multi-Place"

At the end of the twentieth century, it was evident that the geographical limits of what had been understood as a city had, almost suddenly, given way to the new scales of a new urban- territorial space in constant vibration and reconfiguration. In this context, what had been understood as the periphery could no longer be conceived as a "location" (a precise place or landscape: the boundary of the city, its border), but rather as a "condition" in the womb of a process (that of the dissolution of the urban in the territory), in which consolidated realities and scattered, often contradictory realities would coexist, alluding to a new entropic and definitively unfinished definition of the "new city".

The widespread increase of new phenomena of transformation associated with the impact of mobility and distant communication in the territorial occupation itself, the appearance of new "territorialities in network", the refocusing of the city in its outskirts, demographic or real estate explosions (with no necessary connection between them), the emergence of hypertrophied "world-cities" and specialised ghettos (produced at all levels, spatial and social), and, in a nutshell, the emergence of urban "forms" and "targets" of irregular development were effectively provoking local and global transformations that hardly seemed to have been anticipated, addressed, or foreseen by an urban science enclosed in the linear imposition-composition of those traditional models that were often limited to themselves. The field of the periphery now pointed to that "eccentric" space, with no limit (coherent or apparent). An n-borderland called to express its condition as multinter (multilayered and inter-networks, multi-level and inter-territories) becomes vast and vague, more and more ambiguous in its expressions or manifestations (Neutelings 1992).

The more or less defined old boundaries (and the old enclosures) of the old city "perimeter"—still with "flanks" and "rear"—had almost "succumbed" to the many demands of a new type of "geo-strategic-territorial" arrangement, just as the old genuinely compositional factors had done in the face of the evidence of an increasingly polyhedral, elusive, and vital reality.

In the incipient networked nature of the new multiple structures of urban-territorial exchange and development, a new kind of more elastic condition—a fractal and irregular topology—could be noted: the old expansive forms of "metropolitan" accumulation, with large referential centres and "aureolar" peripheries, would gradually give way to less hierarchical, polycentric, polyhedral, and poly-cooperative groups; discontinuous and related, "concerted" or "arranged", and not always univocal but articulated differentials; destined to combine "centres" and "edges" at the same time (large nuclei as attractors and new intermediate nuclei, connection meshes and surfaces of relation, boundary landscapes, and in-between landscapes) in a new type of network structures—more complex, elastic, and flexible—between "in(ter)dependent identities" rather than between "subordinate entities": structures defined beyond the traditional "metropolitan areas" or the eternal dichotomies "urban/rural", "centre/periphery" (Batty 1997, Harvey 1985).

In the case of European and especially Mediterranean realities this geo-urban condition would be even more explicit in highlighting the value of a varied geography, usually rich in populations and directly related to living and exchange spaces. The current dynamics of global development, multiplied by the information revolution itself, have given rise to the conditions of a new type of flexible and open (polyhedral and polyphonic) order in the territory: an order that would give special prominence to the interactive nature of the processes and phenomena associated with them, and whose most obvious manifestation would be an organism (the city) constantly reinformed (redefined and transformed) by continuous operations of action and reaction, adjustment and readjustment, between material and immaterial realities ("layers" of "information" and networks of articulation) in constant evolutionary combination.

These dynamics construct a new global framework, more complex and plural, for a new projective interpretation of the territory: that of a pluri-city (poli-polis) agreed to a multiple network of infrastructure and intra-structure, landscapes and in-between-landscapes, density nodes and exchange cores, with relational and differential vocation, integrated and balanced at the same time, in a poly-territory that would no longer be manifested as a "single place" (associated with a centrifugal or radial movement around a large centre) but as a multiple set of dynamic scenarios of relationship and interaction (see some variations in Gausa 2010). A structure of variable geometry that today expresses, conclusively, its definitely dynamic condition and requires a new integrated and relational interpretation; with the capacity to articulate new visions, new schemes, and, therefore, new connections between old and new polycentric structures implicit in this new complex system of independent and interdependent "sets" at a time, where strata and layers intersect and overlap (Ascher 1995).

Strategic Issues—and Criteria

From these considerations various questions can then arise regarding the "multiple", strategic, and relational meaning and impact of the current conjunction city-territory, centre/centres-periphery/peripheries and their own network articulation:

How should the geo-urban scale of the city be approached?

- From what guiding criteria could this new geo-urban dimension of the city be approached "in", "with", and "towards" the territory, and how would this dimension be oriented in a new assemblage of structures "in set" and "in net", capable of conjugating municipal realities and intermunicipal relations, networks of articulation and pockets of cohesion, development matrices and landscapes as links, in new integrated models?
- What role should the main attracting centres and the various intermediate nuclei play in these polymorphic models, and how could an effective articulation between mobility, growth, nature, and landscape be defined in and between them?

Figure 4. Barcelona Land-Grid. Topographical Model. Graphic: Actar Arquitectura, 1998–2000

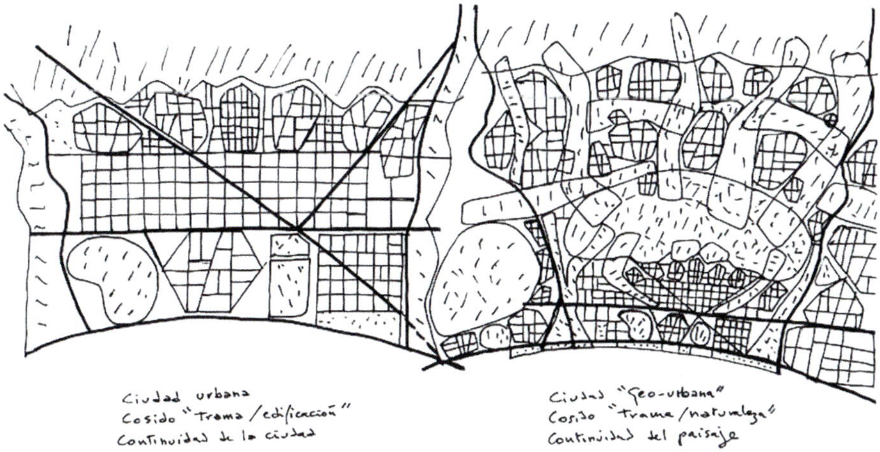

Figure 5. Urban City, Geo-Urban City. Continuity City/City, Connectivity City/Landscape. Graphic: author

Figure 6. Barcelona Land-Grid. Topographical Model. Graphic: Actar Arquitectura, 1998–2000

How should the new mobility scenarios be defined?

- With what inter-scalar criteria should infrastructure be considered and how should a new integrated definition of the transport and energy systems themselves—as "compressor" agents (and "tensors") in the territory—be addressed?

What new active role should the landscape play?

- What new functional condition should be taken by the great natural spaces, understood not only as landscape reserves but as active scenarios?
- What new programmatic and resilient role could be given to the landscape as urban and territorial "infrastructure", related to the great environmental topics (water, energy, land use, matter, and recycling, etc.)?
- What kind of new poly-functional approach could be foreseen for the traditional primary agricultural spaces, transforming today's spaces into new playful mixed scenarios for combining primary and tertiary activities: agriculture, tourism, research, green economy?
- What should be the new social space: public and/or collective?

How should our own life surroundings and relationships be?

- How could a new type of more stimulating habitats be generated?
- How, beyond the old extensional or polygonal models, should cities be developed to translate a new environmental sensitivity associated with a new conception of habitat into a possible relational landscape?

From which models should our urban scenarios be developed and/or redefined?

- In what way should the old core cores and density spots be reinformed (recycled, recalibrated, renewed) to ensure necessary processes of qualitative reactivation?
- With what kind of innovative actions should the recycling of existing fabrics be promoted, be they "historic neighbourhoods" (mature stages or consolidated fabrics that are more or less obsolete) or "modern peripheries" (residential complexes, industrial estates or tourism scenarios that are often deficient in their performance and/or in their necessary programmatic and functional re-evaluation processes)?

What new type of urban metabolism—and urban models—would have to be formulated?

- With what criteria should these parameters be combined—redefinition, recycling, re- naturalization and/or restructuring—with new innovative and inductive repertoires (multifunctional, mixed, hybrid) to ensure genuine qualitative actions, diversity, and variety at the same time, in a territory potentially able to reconcile culture, life, production, leisure, and knowledge, from an adequate integrated enhancement of its own infrastructure?

What should be the interplay between contemporary architecture, society, and culture in the new information society?

- From what new creative and technological, spatial, and environmental ambition should the new challenges of an emerging society and its translation be addressed in new collective and interactive scenarios: conceived for activity, enjoyment, and knowledge, but also as possibly interactive or reactive—that is, responsive—and more sustainable interface or mediation spaces between individuals, their environment, and new information technologies?

Today it is a matter of rethinking the possible propositive quality implicit in the dynamic potential of this new "geo-urban" scenario, of displacement, mobility, and exchange—but also of landscape and inter-landscapes, of the connectivity and the (inter) relationship—connecting to a new understanding of the idea of place or context: as a field of forces "articulated", in network, as well as with a new projectional and conceptual tool, emerging today, associated to the new information technologies; thus recovering a certain optimistic— ambitious—epic of the "glocal" involved in the profound changes of scale and structures characteristic of the new metropolitan forms; favouring a positive and at the same time critical action, attentive to those conflicts, tensions, and deficits generated by the phenomenon that is approached. These tensions and deficits—social and spatial and environmental—appeal to new approaches, resilient and integrated at the same time, of our life scenarios and relationships (Gausa *et.al.* 2003).

2000s–2015
Expanded Realities: The Periphery as "Disconnection"

The first decades of the twenty-first century are opening up to the exponential development of new technologies that have multiplied the potentials of interaction between spaces, contexts, media, and users, thus opening up a new stage of increasingly ubiquitous, augmented, and embedded capabilities in a new material-virtual dimension called to define one's own "expanded" condition of contemporary reality.

The launch of new, more personalised interfaces—from the emergence in the nineteen-nineties of the first personal computers to the multiplication of new portable devices, from the idea of intercities to the idea of a global network, from multi-layer interaction (Windows, GIS, Scan) to multi-environment interaction (apps, sensors, IA)—translates the progressive perfection of the operational programmes and operative systems as a corollary of these processes, destined to extend the possibilities of interaction among means and between means and users, favoured by the consolidation and increase of applications for mobile and open programmes (Open Source) and Real-Time readings.

The research developed at this third stage tends to deepen the exploration of these new capacities associated with the accelerated progression of the encounter (and crossing) between reality and virtuality, materiality and digitality (integrated digitisation), associated with the augmented interactions

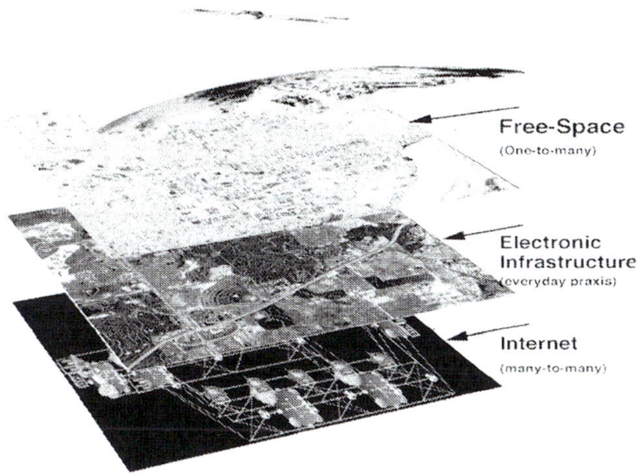

Figure 7. Stephen Perella, *Haptic Horizon*, 1998

Figure 8. Data Maps Energy 01, Barcelona Torre Baró. A new reactivated peri-urbanity, interactive model, IAAC Global Summer School 2014. Graphic: IAAC

between materiality (reactive) and environment (reactivated), but also between the environment (actuated) and involved agents (actuators): agents and materials (Agents & Matters) raise new focuses of attention, from interest to the hyper-collectivity of new urban co-production processes (co-participatory, co-decision-making) and its implicit empathic quality (new communities and new collective behaviours, Commons & Behaviours), as paradigms directly associated with a new interchange system.

The exploration of a new co-participatory definition (empathic or eco-empathic) for the inhabited surroundings, but also of a new endo-sensitive definition of/for an environmentally responsive materiality (ubiquitous, embedded) related with the environment (nano-technologies, bio-technologies, etc.) today marks many of the experiments of this new era.

Information understood as input-output (shared, cooperative) or as indicator-actuator (supra- environmental) leads, effectively, to new formulations inclined towards deepening new active and interactive responses that are not only relational but decidedly synergistic (empathic) with a medium and with a reality. They are, as it has been pointed out, not only distributed but ubiquitous, augmented in their own capacities of hyper-connectivity and sensing; an expansive, systemic, responsive, and "collective/connective" condition, associated with an endo-technological definition, as an increased relational capacity in and between systems (Gausa 2013).

Parallel to this type of advanced environments, the inertias associated with other, less positive global situations are related to the conflicts and threats linked to climate change and their devastating effects on less developed populations (environmental risks, housing devaluation, pollution and contamination, ghettoification, rising poverty, etc.).

The informational capacity of the de-localised productive exchange has increased the plural complexity (rich, varied, diverse) of scenarios and relationships, but it has also contributed to increasing the entropic effects on land-use and the progressive inequality between realities and communities—leading therefore to the emergence of a new type of periphery, no longer only physical but also socio-economic (and cultural?) (Rifkin 2014).

The coexistence of hyper-connected and hypo-connected societies thus expresses a new reality to be managed and balanced with a new type of governance that is more sensitive to a new type of holistic, equitable, and empathic logic (empathicities) (Guallart 2012).

The old urban notion of "periphery" (*peri-pheros*, the city displaced around itself) seems to give way to a new concept, the "para-feria" (*para-pheros*, the city displaced by the margin and on its margins) in which the urban would pass from being a single place to become a "place of places": real and virtual, diverse, irregular, differential, and (potentially and qualitatively) (re)orientable and/or interlaceable.

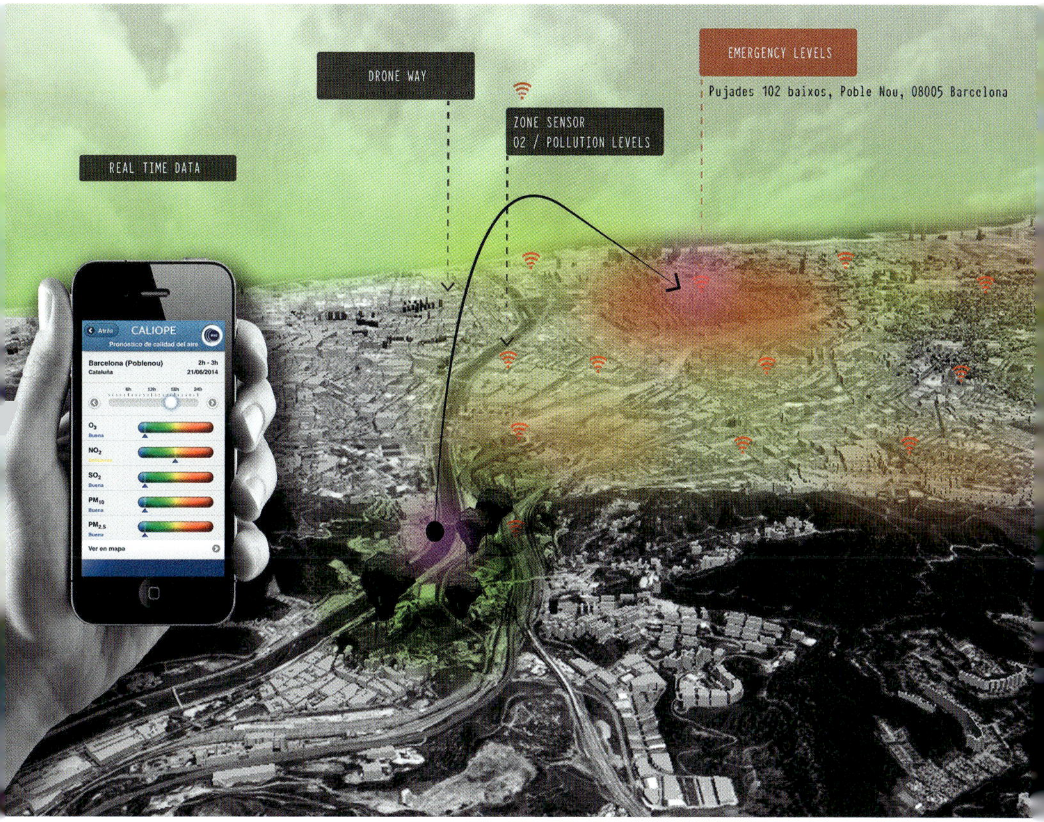

Figure 9. IAAC MAA01- A new hyper-connected multicity: Master in Advanced Architecture, Introductory Studios, Markopoulou-Diez-Rubio-Bravo-Ros, course 2012–2013. Graphic: IAAC

Bibliography

Ascher F. (1995) *Métapoles ou l'Avenir des villes*. Paris, ed. Odile Jacob.

Batty M. (1997) "The Fractal City". In: *Architectural Design*. Nr. 9/10, vol. 67, 1997. pp. 74–83.

Gausa M., Guallart V., Muller W. (2003) *HiperCatalunya, Territories of Research.* Barcelona, ed. Actar, Generalitat de Catalunya.

Gausa M. (2010) *Open-Espacio-Tiempo-Información*. Barcelona, ed. Actar.

Gausa M. (2013) "City Sense. Territorialising Information". In: Capelli L. ed. (2013) *City Sense. Shaping our Environment with Real-Time Data*. Barcelona, ed. Actar-IAAC. pp. 6–13.

Guallart V. (2012) *La ciudad autosuficiente.* Barcelona, ed. RBA.

Harvey D. (1985) *The Urbanisation of Capital*. Baltimore, Johns Hopkins University Press.

Mateo J. (1987) "No existe el centro. The centre does not exist". In: *Quaderns d'Arquitectura i Urbanisme*. Colegio de Arquitectos de Cataluña. Nr. 175, 1987. pp. 2–3.

Neutelings W. (1992) *Patchwork City.* Rotterdam, 010 Publishers.

Rifkin J. (2014) *The Zero Marginal Cost Society: The Internet of Things, the Collaborative Commons, and the Eclipse of Capitalism.* London, Palgrave Macmillan.

Steiner D. (1993) "Vielleicht eine Biographie der Peripherie". In: *Daidalos*. Nr. 50, 1993. p. 86.

Wenders W., Kollhoff H. (1988) "La ciudad = The city. Conversación entre Wim Wenders y Hans Kollhoff. A Conversation between Wim Wenders and Hans Kollhoff". In: *Quaderns d'Arquitectura i Urbanisme*. Colegio de Arquitectos de Cataluña. Nr. 177, 1988. pp. 44–79.

Favara Futures: Research Workshop

Barbara Lino, Sarah Hartmann, Jessica Smeralda Oliva,
Maurizio Carta, Jörg Schröder

Figure 1: Favara urban regeneration. Photo: Maurizio Carta

Favara Futures: Research Workshop

Urban regeneration and impulses for local development in new constellations of peripheries and centres are the focus of the research workshop "Dynamics of Periphery". What are research, practice, design, and planning contributions to successful initiatives and models in small cities? How are they linked with innovative models of urban design, architecture, *re-cycle* and artistic creativity? How can sustainable use of territorial capital, concepts of social innovation, and governance improvements enhance creative dynamics of specific assets and spatial characteristics?

In a research project between the University of Palermo and Leibniz Universität Hannover, "Dynamics of Periphery" were discussed in a workshop in Palermo. These conceptual approaches were combined with a research workshop in Favara with master's students from both universities; in collaboration with the municipality of Favara and with FARM Cultural Park Favara. These workshops were funded with the University Dialogue Programme Southern Europe of the DAAD. The transversal research between architecture, urban design, arts, local and regional development highlights the need and the potential of new ways of integrating "Dynamics of Periphery" into debates and policies about the futures of habitat in Europe.

With the research workshop in Favara, further possible and promising areas of regeneration are addressed in the contributions by the master's students from Palermo and Hannover, in international working groups, and in discussion with the local experts and stakeholders. The range of the ideas for themes, approaches, and branding are drawn from buildings to open spaces and nature, from urban spaces to infrastructure, from steps and "cityforming" processes to visioning. As a creative and innovative collection of different contributions, the students´ works were presented in Favara to gain new perspectives for further discussions.

The research workshop "Dynamics of Periphery" focused on areas of access that link the consolidated city with periphery, urban planning with landscape design, the architectural with the planning scale. The methodological approach is based on the Cityforming Protocol developed by Maurizio Carta. This method is divided into three phases (colonisation, consolidation, and development) and makes it possible to think about future scenarios of the territory. The workshop focused on urban regeneration, and it unveiled new design solutions for the inner city and its peripheries in reference to the creative and innovative milieu, which is seen as a local resource for designing and restoring cities based on culture, communication, cooperation, energy, and sustainability.

The educational objective of the workshop was to trigger students' imagination and their ability to interpret contemporary city identifying structures, hierarchies, and relationships in order to produce innovative proposals. The international workshop aimed to design future scenarios of evolving territories, especially the regeneration of urban areas characterised by marginalization and decline, abandoned buildings and infrastructure, functional underuse, or weak reactivation cycles. For this task the Cityforming Protocol will be used. This method permits the adoption of a temporalised and

Figure 2. Favara, Vallone Cicchillo. Photo: Jessica Smeralda Oliva

adaptive guiding programme, which is able to compose a comprehensive vision due to a gradual implementation. This method is capable of temporary actions and, at the same time, generates long-lasting forces for new futures. Based on the first step, the process of territorial regeneration, values are produced which trigger subsequent investments and generate creative power for new housing and production as well as for commercial and cultural functions. An urban design project will be developed for the selected focus area of the valley, with urban tactics to understand the functions assigned to the area and especially the necessary transformations of the public space: the interaction between buildings and their surroundings, the accessibility and mobility that is coherent with the new function, and the capability to activate the next phase of the "consolidation". This is, therefore, to deepen the first phase of Cityforming, the step of colonisation that involves all the components of the colony: space and people; infrastructure and landscape; social and economic components; those of the built environment and those of the open spaces. In this way, each group of students will develop an independent proposal (in some cases they may also propose alternative solutions) by redesigning the areas and connections between the historic centre and the periphery. The workshop follows the idea of constructing a systemic and metabolic approach

Figure 3. Favara, view from the castle over Favara. Photo: Annalisa Contato

to identify the necessary integration between functions and in particular complementary actions between each colony, creating the new image of the city of Favara by applying the Cityforming Protocol. The international workshop was developed in two phases and took place in Palermo (two days) and in Favara (three days). The structure of the workshop was divided into three phases that directed the students toward the final presentation. The first phase concerned the use of techniques and paradigms that participants used to elaborate new visions for the area; the second phase was structured in two different parts focused on case study analysis and scenario sketches; finally, the third part was dedicated to the presentation of the work:

Phase 1 - Methodological approach and case study description
Phase 2 - SWOT analysis, conceptual elaborations, site visit, and scenario sketches
Phase 3 - Presentation

The Focus Area of the Project

The focus area of the project is the city of Favara, located at the southern boarder of Sicily. The city is characterised by its peripheral location distant from the sea and by a considerable urban extension, as well as by many empty buildings in the centre. In the context of the urban regeneration process that is ongoing in the city of Favara, the area called "Vallone Cicchillo" has been selected as an area of intervention for the workshop. The site is characterised by being an example of a rural-urban in-between, dense, but with open space and opportunities at the same time. The project questions can be grouped into three main themes:

1. the margins (historic centre/periphery, built-up/green areas)
2. accessibility, crossing, and connections
3. agricultural landscape within the city

The area called "Vallone Cicchillo" is a natural wedge-shaped cultivated valley within the city of Favara, a green spot along the north-south axis, located at the southern edge of the built-up area. On the west side of the valley, there is the historic centre of the city, while on the east side the urban fabric has expanded following the path of the abandoned railway line, unused since 1958. Part of the former railway infrastructure, *ponte tre archi* (three arches bridge) crosses the valley and has been restored as a connection element to link those two parts of the city. In recent years the area has been the object of two projects. One is "Ortus", an intervention of consolidation and requalification of urban farms started in 2003 and funded by the Italian Ministry of Infrastructures and Transportation and the Regional Department for Public Works and led by the city of Favara in collaboration with the University of Palermo. The other intervention is "H.O.R.T.U.S." (Harmoniser les Opérations de Restauration Territorial du paysage Urbain Soutenable), an EU project aimed at the sustainable development and environmental regeneration of peripheral areas of Mediterranean cities, through interventions on green areas and landscape.

Therefore, the area raises some relevant questions, representative of marginal and in-between contexts and emblematic of peripheries and their dynamics. These questions are mainly related to three themes: margins, connections, and agricultural landscape within the city. The margins are the space where the historic centre and the periphery, the built-up and the green areas meet, physically and metaphorically, and call for designing new relationships. Accessibility, crossing and connections demand not only that the relationship between the two parts of the city be reshaped, but also that we rethink the use of this area as a device for reestablishing connection through new mobility paths, and also through new functions, thereby making the area more attractive. The theme of agricultural landscape within a city opens the reflection on multifunctional landscape and human-nature interdependence and helps us think about new sustainable life-styles for a better future.

Figure 4. FARM Favara Cultural Park. Photo: Annalisa Contato

FARM Cultural Park in Favara

An interesting reference project for the re-design and re-structuring of the valley is the ongoing experiment of the FARM Cultural Park in Favara, a creative social catalyst with an international reputation. Favara is a small town just eight kilometres from Agrigento's Unesco Archaeological and Landscape Park "Valley of the Temples". Seven years ago it was not to be found on any tourist map. Today FARM acts powerfully in the current debate about how to make small communities resilient to global changes and economic crisis, and how to identify unused resources to make them an empowering instrument of sustainable growth and social innovation. The project was born in 2010 from the desire, passion, and ability of its key figures, Andrea Bartoli (a "cultural agitator", as he calls himself) and his wife Florinda, who recycled an abandoned area, turning it into an international cultural centre devoted to contemporary art, architecture, design, and social innovation. The creative district, called "Sette Cortili" (seven courtyards), includes a breakthrough contemporary art museum, a residence for artists from around the world, an innovation-oriented co-working space, a space dedicated to a School of Architecture for Children, a leisure garden—called "riad" as tribute to the Moroccan tradition—with a hotel suite for art travellers, a bookshop, a concept store, and several ethnic food spaces that mix Sicilian and African culinary traditions. The exteriors of the buildings are used as canvases for huge paintings and sculptures by young artists such as Fabio Melosu, Frabianco, Sara Fratini, and Make. The courtyards host permanent or temporary installations.

FAVARA[R]T // EXPLODE THE ENERGY

Dario De Gregorio, Raphaela Djalili, Lisa Iglseder, Giuseppe Mammo Zagarella

"FAVARA[R]T—Explode the energy" suggests that spatial aspects of different sectors (manufacturing, agriculture, society, and culture) be incentivised along four steps: choosing, spotting, combining, zoning. With a highlight on sustainable mobility and new quality of urban space in the inner zone of Favara, the project argues for a step-by-step transformation of mobility activities and spaces, connected to impressive storytelling.

The Project FAVARA[R]T counteracts the local problems of weak economic activities and building vacancy. It aims to emphasize underrepresented usages of arts and crafts in order to create a new image for Favara. This idea is explained with help of the story of Gianni, a fictive person and an owner of a steel mill, who wants to make the city safer for pedestrians and cyclists after an accident. He establishes the brand FAVARA[R]T with light-weight steel frames, open workshops, and cycling tours. Additionally, bike sharing stations are installed. These stations are marked by cultural or artistic installations to be recognizable as part of the "FAVARA[R]T" brand. In this way, Favara becomes a cyclist- and pedestrian-friendly city with a new sustainable image that can also be translated to other typical Favara products afrom others sectors such as railings, tiles, marzipan, pistachios, wine, or oil.

Figure 5. FAVARA[R]T. Graphic: authors

[RE]SOURCE IT! // A SOURCE FOR FAVARA

Laura Bornickel, Elena Hellmuth, Alberto La Mantia, Gabriele Vassallo

"(RE)source it! A source for Favara" suggests that we work on the idea of connecting and branding by water: in the valley, in linkages to larger networks along waterways as new routes across the territory and to the coast, and as new perceptions of ecological and cultural connections. The theme of water in the city is shown to have a strong potential and spatial force in the open small channels, collecting points and basins, and water terraces in the valley as a water machine for purification, storage, protection, and visibility, thus enhancing new productivity in gardens and agriculture. This idea has its origin in the Arabian word *Fawwara* which means source of water. The aim is to use the river Naro and retransform it into a new life vein connecting all the hotspots of the region—for example the city of Favara itself, which can be enriched and restructured with the help of secondary canals. A new system collects water in case of rainfall from the roofs and balconies, and directs it with partially opened canals through the city into the valley. Therefore, the citizens automatically take part in reshaping the empty valley. The valley becomes an attractive place due to the creation of the terraces and seasonal and temporary lakes. The terraces are wedge-shaped to use the existing conditions of landscape and to give the water a specific direction when rain is flooding the streets. Due to the diversity of the given functions, the different platforms gain a range of amenity values, such as micro agriculture, playgrounds, sport fields, and recreational areas. Plants with filtering abilities contribute to a healthy ecosystem and emphasize water as the continuing theme.

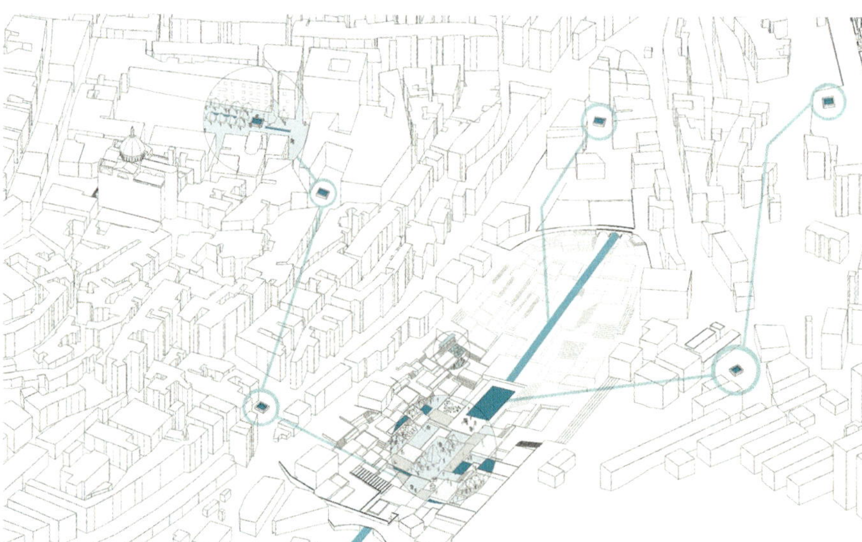

Figure 6. A Source for Favara. Grapic: authors

PATH TO NETWORK

Giulio Cellura, Flora Hagedorn, Magdalena Jackstadt, Federica Tognetti

"Path to network" sees the city in an artistic sense and develops the idea of connecting single nuclei of transformation in order to transform them into nodes of a network: the air-horizon of the streets becomes a free space for artistic intervention, advancing network-systematics and processes, facilitating the identification of additional nodes, and linking the centre to open space in valley and across the valley to the hillside in the east. In order to revitalize the city centre of Favara and to strengthen the local industries, the valley is used as an entrance for connecting the residential areas to the centre and to the surrounding countryside. The southern part of the valley is dedicated to the use of local agricultural production. Small industries can settle in the unused buildings along the valley, where they produce and sell their individual and local products. On the northern side of the bridge a public park is provided for local residents and visitors. It is highlighted by street art at the ground floor of the already-existing entrance building, which can be reused as a cafe or shop that sells local products and also informs about the project. An interactive and educational tour through the city is created that informs visitors about the history and future of Favara. Information signs along the stops will give information about important buildings and projects. Accompanied by interactive street art such as street chess and graffiti, people will begin to actually use the spaces along the path and thereby create a reason for local enterprises to settle there.

Figure 7. Path to Network. Graphic: authors

INSIDE OUT // REACTIVATION OF PUBLIC INTERACTIONS

Lisa Freke, Valentin Zellmer, Giovanni Viola, Sofia Nocera

"Inside out—Reactivation of public interaction" addresses the interface between the valley and the historic centre, while also crossing also the main road along the valley, with a spatial and programmatic matrix of interventions. The concentration on the elements of houses, as active changers of urban space, explores interface elements between inside and outside: façade, intermediate spaces, private gardens, public entrance; it also enhances in a larger frame the interweaving and activation of urban spaces, especially open spaces. Activating principles from FARM are transferred to façades outside of courtyards, turning the success factor of hidden transformations into public domains. Inside-Out faces not only the reactivation of the valley itself, but also of the whole historic centre of Favara. On a larger scale the urban life inside the city is intended to spread outside to the valley. For this, the valley has to be made an attractive, open escape from the density of the town. But first, the valley needs to be made visible! The houses and spaces facing the intersection points show the qualities of the other side and therefore include their own improvement. For example, by confronting us with openness density is relaxed, making it possible for these spaces to raise their profile as a hot-spot for social life, or by confronting us with a density of life, gardens shape our perception of them as an oasis. Starting from small single implementation in colonisation-phases, clusters of implementation and intensive transformation shape the process in consolidation-phases, while development-phases realise transformations that reach out further into town.

Figure 8. Inside Out. Graphic: authors

FAVARA CRAFT // COLOR IT

Morgane Alonzo, Christian Corral, Matti Hänsch, Beatrice Rezzani

"Favara Craft—Colour it" proposes a spatially initiated branding concept of social innovation, for multiple roles and connectivity of the historic centre with the valley space. Economic productivity in manufacturing and agriculture, new ecological paradigms in building, and citizens' activation, are addressed with nuclei of transformation that establish new networks in the city. Qualities and possibilities are hidden in the narrow streets of Favara, and places create qualities through the heterogeneity of their different constructions. The integration, the active participation, and the voice of the society serve as catalysts for the project. It was conceived as a "step by step-project", so that the changes, not only from its urban part, create a natural image oft the city Favara. This image is able to change slowly in order to favour economic references. A new network is created that is spread over the whole area and will create a new system. The chosen buildings are defined as info points and can be used as space for various activities, such as exhibitions related to Favara Craft. The colours serve as an analogy to the corresponding function of the building, so that the system is legible from the outside and inside. These places become active organisms of the city and have the ability to change appearance and function as required. Each of them features a different theme, a specific quality, and can be identified by a colour: education, agriculture, temporary living, food, and art. These spaces serve as signs to lead people in Favara. The valley: the new filter area, the periphery, becomes the centre along the edges.

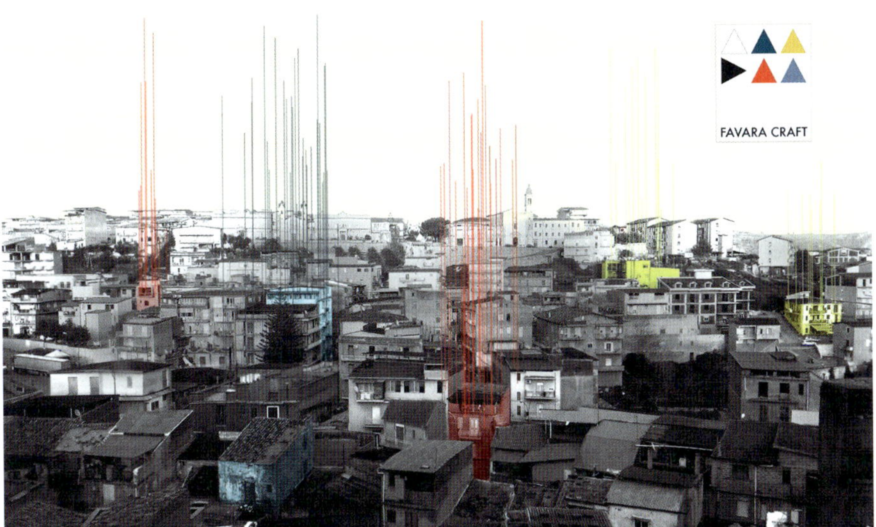

Figure 9. Favara Craft. Graphic: authors

Figure 10. Workshop in Favara. Photos: LUH

Figure 11. Site workshop Favara. Photo: UniPA

Figure 12. Favara. Photo: Emanuele Sommariva

Figure 13. Favara. Photo: Emanuele Sommariva

Figure 14. Gibellina. Photo: Sarah Hartmann

Figure 15. Gibellina. Photo: Sarah Hartmann

DYNAMICS OF PERIPHERY

ATLAS INTRODUCTION

In-Transition Processes

Barbara Lino

As products of in-transition processes and of a haphazard transformation "model", dynamic and in evolution, peripheries are muscling their way in as landscapes laden with ambiguity and problems, but also at the same time with possibilities and latency.

1. Processes of Structural Change

Peripheries appear as spaces of destabilisation and transformation—not as "an immutable institution but [as] a set of interactions" (Ippolito). They are "landscapes in crisis and potential hubs of innovation where the city and territories become propulsive and active in change" (Sgaramella). "Constant changes here are discernible in material and social aspects, as well as in persistent shifts of uses, dynamics and densities" (Diesch). "The peripheral conditions in relation to the morphology of the territory" need "a holistic perspective, combining economic, social, cultural and mobility aspects with the precise geographical condition" (Hartmann).

In 1961, Lewis Mumford described the American peripheries as "a multitude of uniform, unidentifiable houses, lined up inflexibly, at uniform distances, on uniform roads, in a treeless communal waste, inhabited by people of the same class, the same income, the same age group, witnessing the same television performances, eating the same tasteless prefabricated foods, from the same freezers, conforming in every outward and inward respect to a common mould" (Mumford 1961, p. 486). The dull image of unidentifiable houses, at uniform distances on uniform roads, single-class social groups, and standardized lifestyles describes a very different suburban scenario from that of Europe during the same years and is even more different when compared to Europe today. Now, the most macroscopic outcomes of the social and spatial trajectories of transformation are evident in the narratives dominating the media and political arenas, which describe urban peripheries as problem spaces, where issues of safety and social inequality are intensified. In the periodic uprisings of the Parisian banlieues and the episodes of violence, intolerance, and complicated civil coexistence in the peripheries of Marseille, Brussels, Munich, and the many districts of Rome, Milan, or other Italian cities, social inequalities are establishing themselves as a "new urban issue" (Secchi 2013, p. 59). They remind us of the city's role as a selection and separation machine for integration or social exclusion, in which the temporal nature and ways of using the urban space by various social groups are not only articulated by the effects of social and economic policies, but also by the stratification of infrastructural and urban planning choices. "The city has always been a machine regulating idiorhythms: using physical, spatial, legal, and institutional devices, it has

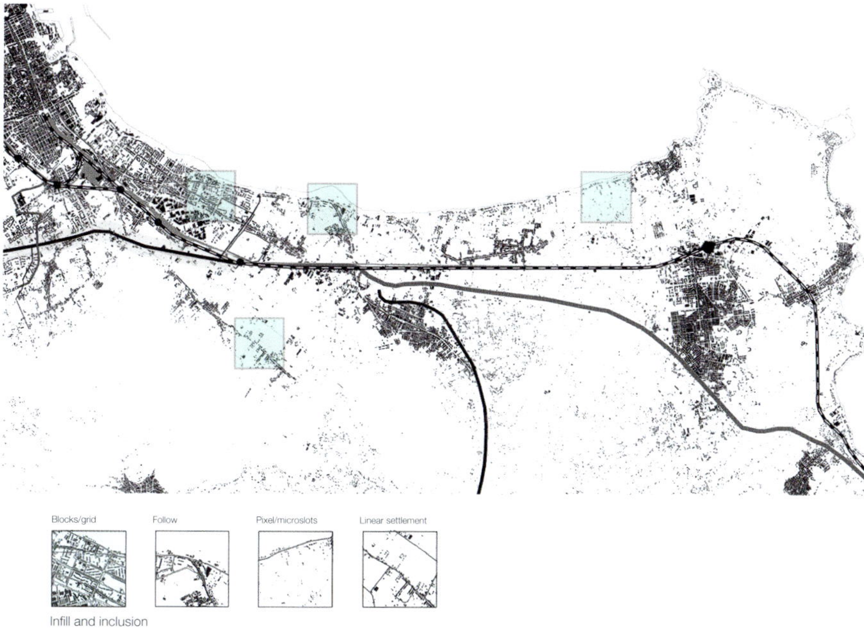

Figure 1. Dynamic processes in Palermo's periphery: Infill and inclusion. Image: author

constantly turned the various idiorhymths into articulate and often very complex spatial, economic, and social relations" (Secchi 2013, p. IX). Separated by infrastructure belts, the fences of industrial areas, or large unused green spaces, peripheries carry out their own daily activities and social rhythms among unsold property, large business districts, overspecialized enclaves of consumption and leisure time, outlets, factories, service stations, and playgrounds, separated by in-between spaces, such as clearings, car parks, debris areas on the fringes of infrastructure, viaducts, and interchanges. They are liminal landscapes (Turner 1969), on one hand due to the conflictual conditions generated by the market and by the formal and informal stakeholders pushing for transformation, and on the other, due to the sense of indeterminacy of border spaces and, at the same time, their potential and suspension between the past and future. In peripheries micro and macro forces collide, driven by order and disorder; formal pushes for transformation result from planning processes and informal pushes result from the new routines and lifestyles of the communities that inhabit them.

2. Flexible Spaces and Creative Patterns

Peripheries appear as "areas open to experimentation ... most open to innovation and innovative processes ... It is a matter of activation rather than integration" (Betta). Peripheries are "a laboratory of experimentation in which together environmental patterns and communities plays a key role"

Figure 2. Palermo's periphery-landscape.
Photo: Jessica Smeralda Oliva

(Caruso), where "complex dynamics and the current revolutionary phenomena" are in place (Tucci). "The processes involving peripheries are increasingly connected to an innovative vision of the territory" (Torrisi). Peripheries are "a result of new processes that demobilize and relocate resources through and across a variety of sites and disciplines" (Garbarini).

Investigating the suburbanisation phenomenon at a global level in "Suburban Constellations" (2013), Roger Keil has attempted to define what is global in a phenomenon that is one of the most "shared" experiences on the planet and which occurs "globally", but is structured "locally" as a function of specific consumer choices, the real estate market, production, and the distribution of goods. Specifically, according to Keil, three interrelated components should be governed to guide the way outskirts form: the land market; the governance dimension, where the ability of public action to regulate the market is crucial in counteracting forms of spatial and social segregation; and infrastructure, which has a clear consequence for the spatial structure of the territory. Keil's most interesting theoretical contribution, however, lies in the formulation of a new urban theory.

By shifting the focus from a taxonomic and defining problem to the building of a new theory, Keil invokes the "urban revolution" that Lefebvre spoke of in the seventies, and talks about a "suburban revolution", recognizing in suburban settings the creative potential traditionally attributed to more central areas, which instead emerge exponentially in the activities and different lifestyles that occur there. Overturning a dominant view, which identifies in the more central areas a level of creativity capable of producing innovation, Keil highlights the rapid change that the social "factory" of the outskirts is undergoing and draws attention to the huge potential for social innovation contained in the various lifestyles that suburban settings produce as innovation hot spots.

3. Collaborative Networks

Peripheries call for policies that can support "the modelling process covering the processes of initiation, involvement, intervention and implementation" (Listen Prima). "The interrelation between recycling and socially innovative practices creates an innovative process" (Scaffidi), "mobilising power and creative potential of peripheral contexts as trading zones ... a co-creation perspective that recombines the territorial capital providing a competitive advantage to overcome the inequalities" (Massari). "Processes should be based on the integration between the initiatives arising from communities, local stakeholders, even those facilitated by local administration, and the creation and activation of more structured strategies" (Oliva).

In an era of serious crisis and the contemporary progression toward zero of public budgets, in many territories we witness the spread of practices of more or less temporary uses of neglected areas through informal processes of transformation and reappropriation such as community gardening operations, movements of occupation of abandoned spaces, or forms of urban art. The concepts of "care" approach the opposition between a public space "designed", intended as a vehicle for institutional representation, and a "lived space", as amended by the uses and practices of everyday life. Creative processes of urban innovation propose new ways of decision and action, using forms of coordination and collaboration, sharing spaces and co-design practices.

In this kind of "second hand urbanism" the recovery of brownfield in urban spaces and small scale transformations of public abandoned spaces introduce new temporal and low impact features in a process of recycling and reentering waste into the metabolism of the city; urbanisation stimulates the revival of peripheral neighbourhoods to become an expression of a renewed sense of belonging and community.

Collaborative networks, advanced models of city-making, and social innovation initiatives are expressed in a rediscovered adaptive capacity of urban communities and, as a sort of "local resilience", involved in bridging the dramatic gap of public welfare by offering a view of sharing and circularity as an alternative to the slowness and rigidity of institutional processes of transformation. This Urbanism is, unexpectedly comprises questions about how to "enable" cocreation processes as part of the traditional linear decision-making process, considering the strength and opportunity of activating transformation processes based on collaboration, incrementality, and flexibility.

Bibliography

Keil R. ed. (2013) *Suburban Constellations: Governance, Land and Infrastructure in the 21st Century*. Berlin, Jovis.
Lefebvre E. (1970) *La Révolution urbaine*. Paris, Gallimard.
Lino B. (2013) *Periferie in trasform-azione. Riflessioni dai "margini" delle città*. Firenze, Alinea.
Mumford L. (1961) *The City in History: Its Origins, its Transformations, and its Prospects.* New York, Harcourt, Brace and World.
Secchi B. (2010) "A New Urban Question". In: *Territorio* 53/2010, pp. 8–18.
Secchi B. (2013) *La città dei ricchi e la città dei poveri.* Roma-Bari, Laterza.

Place: Managing the Change

Maddalena Ferretti

In one of the last scenes of *Il Gattopardo*, Tancredi, addressing the prince of Salina, says: "If we want things to stay as they are, things will have to change". That is what constantly happens to places. No matter what we do to keep them "in place", they constantly get transformed and transform themselves under the influence of different factors: environment, economy, aesthetics, etc. But the major changes of places are related to transformations that have to do with people's changing needs and uses. Understanding these flows, learning how to govern and design the inevitable change and to address transformations to real needs and desires for more resilient and smart habitats is the major task of architects and planners, especially in unstable and dynamic places like peripheries.

Identity: Making the Place

Special characteristics, such as traditional buildings, historical settlements and pattern, specific sceneries and special geographic locations, must be considered a significant potential for local development (Listen Prima). The potential of a century-old plaza for local identity and further development is a prolific source for future configuration of the suburban space, with new uses within established structures (Diesch). Physical places in the flat, inner-city periphery are a resource for the future development and reintensification of cities. Places, as urban formations of public spaces, have the capacity to actively shape the public domain and to physically express collective identity in an increasingly digitalized world (Hartmann).

In the early 2000s, the digital revolution put places into crisis—not only because of the loss of use, which, especially in Southern European countries, meant the abandonment of built structures and settlements, but also because of an identity crisis. The counter-effect of this trend, nowadays, is a "return to the ground", to the real space, to the local qualities of places. The negative side of this development, connected especially to the recent major migration movements, is that communities and societies are progressively affirming their identity as a form of protection from "otherness": "in the warm clothes of identity, the urban society preserves itself against what's new, stranger or changing. As positive and necessary this self-certitude is, it equally entails some qualities of stagnation and rigidity" (Wolfrum 2016, p. 62). Together with this discussion, it might be observed that peripheries manifest a special and perhaps more interesting idea of identity, even though the sense of belonging to the place, in these contexts, may appear not so evident. In his most famous book, *Place and Placelessness*, the American geographer Edward Relph investigates how places are experienced and how they are changing. One interesting result regarding "people's sense of place" is that "the kinds of dystopian cityscapes most reviled by social critics or authors are not necessarily experienced as "placelessness' by the inhabitants of such environments" (Relph 1975, p. 80). Nevertheless, this perceived identity-crisis had the effect that "place-making" became central to the disciplinary debate concerning city transformation, although this approach showed also weaknesses, especially in the implementation phase, due to its top-down approach. Indeed, the scarcity of resources in the era of the financial crisis and people's participation in a time dominated by a democratic and horizontal approach to the decision-making process, contributed to a progressive loss of significance of "place-making", at least as conceived ten years ago. On the other hand, the downside of participation is often related to the inability to engage complex problems, if the transformation process lacks experts. The concept of "place-making" needs perhaps to be reinvented by putting the accent on "making" the place. Place then is not anymore linked to a static idea of identity; on the contrary, it is a physical space continuously transformed by the creativity of people and communities and by an act of design. In this line of thoughts, periphery can be understood as a place of new identity.

Dynamism: Boosting Place

Peripheries are an interesting and complex urban phenomenon. Their role can be fundamental for economic opportunity and innovation (Ippolito). The richness of the territory is connected to the ability to renew, activate, or reactivate existing spaces and resources, creating opportunities for cultural, social, and economic growth (Torrisi). Territorial capitals located in peripheral areas have an essential role in the reactivation of these places … they have to be recognised and developed. This would create new possibilities to enhance the region and generate new flows, new physical, and intangible connections between polar sites and peripheries (Scaffidi).

What is observable in the complex territorial systems discussed in this book is a progressive fragmentation of places, due to years of sectorial policies more preoccupied with defending and stressing the autonomy of their disciplinary knowledge than creating real spaces of living. This approach not only lacked the capacity to establish new relationships between diverse elements of the territory, but also to establish a real connection with the material heritage of places. In recent years a renewed interest towards territorial configurations arose in debates, research, and practice all over Europe. This attention influences policies and actions at a European, national, and local level, and it implies a multi-disciplinary, multi-sectoral, and multi-governance approach in order to manage such complex contexts. In a wider perspective, looking beyond growing metropolitan centres, polycentric and reticular territorial systems are receiving deeper consideration, especially in the European context.

It is nevertheless still necessary to strengthen this approach in architectural and urban fields, in order to allow a new understanding of hybrid territories (between rural and urban) as interwoven systems of relationships where natural and built structures meet (Schröder, Ferretti, Hartmann,

Figure 1. Rural-urban contexts in the Metropolitan Region Hamburg.
Survey and analysis developed within the trans-disciplinary project Regiobranding.
Photo: Chair for Regional Building and Urban Planning LUH

Sommariva 2017). Especially in peripheral areas this dynamism is noticeable on a social level, but also on a spatial one, where innovation and creativity provokes a quicker and more effective physical transformation of space (e.g., in operations such as the Favara Cultural Farm in Sicily). Peripheries are test fields where these dynamics are not "passively experienced", due to the external intervention of top-down processes. Here, it is the place itself that cultivates the gems of transformation—in its concealed material and immaterial qualities—and becomes an enabler and a booster of transformation. Place thus represents the frame for new dynamics of territorial development, and the pattern of larger systems of relationships with new aesthetic values. Periphery is the place of this new dynamism.

Action: transforming the place

We need to change our viewpoint on peripheries, leaving the stereotyped image that commonly marks them as places of social conflicts and troubles, of mono-functionality and economic depression, of aesthetic poverty and physical degradation (Oliva). This combination of technology, adaptation strategies, and social attention could transform a place into a meaningful site for its inhabitants (Garbarini). A crucial need to rethink territorial models has been encouraged by the boosting of new practice-based innovation environments, which are often located in marginal places and able to provide a context for new modes of social activism (Massari).

Peripheries are sensors of change. They condense innovation forces, which in these loose contexts are freer to find a place of expression. The "marginal" condition of peripheries paradoxically makes them extremely central in the debate about social inclusion and sharing. It is in such peripheral spaces that empty pockets for action can be detected and reactivated. In recent years this phenomenon of space occupation has been recognised in several experiences worldwide. It is from this action of appropriation that the culture of participation arose, in response to a new call for quality from the people's side. More recently, this trend got stronger as a result of the combination of two important phenomena: the vast migration waves that led to the necessity of new approaches towards social inclusion, and the culture of recycle, resulting from the progressive abandonment and marginalisation of physical spaces.

The action of "makers", "urban pioneers", activists, engaged in the transformation and reactivation of "peripheral" contexts (inside or outside the urban fabric), contributed significantly to a new awareness concerning the importance of the social layer in the "production of space". The downside has been a misunderstanding or a lack of control from administrators and public actors that has often missed the chance to make good use of these energies, or even hindered them. More recently, though, new forms of integration in the decision-making process are noticeable, as well as larger and more conscious sharing and inclusion approaches, which are particularly successful especially in socially problematic contexts. New modes of co-design and co-planning are being tried out, overcoming rigid regulations about space usage and testing more flexible activities and processual approaches, in order to allow peripheries to increasingly become places of inclusion.

Bibliography

Janson A., Wolfrum S. (2016) *Architektur der Stadt*. Stuttgart, Kraemer Verlag.
Relph E. (1976) *Place and Placelessness*. London, Pion.
Schröder J., Ferretti M., Hartmann S., Sommariva E. (2017) "ReCycle: A Territory-Based Approach". In: Fabian L., Munarin S. eds. (2017) *Re-Cycle Italy Atlante*. Siracusa, LetteraVentidue Edizioni. pp. 385–387.

Narrative: Stories from the Periphery

Maddalena Ferretti

Narrative as Reading Tool

"By analysing the local capacities and potential, the demand of local communities can be better addressed, in order to draw a scenario based on local values, through adapted analytical and conceptual methods" (Listen Prima). "Narrative has a fundamental role in redrawing our perception of fringe areas ... and not conceiving of them [anymore] as in a relation of dependence with elements of centrality" (Betta). "Thus—as in the time of the Cantino planisphere—the urban discipline is prevented from seeing the rural differently, since the rural is not even in the visible field as is the urban, then consequently impossible to rethink the rural" (Pereira).

Narrative has always been a tool for analysing and understanding the city. Architecture and urbanism use the stories told by communities, handing over traditions and memories, to unveil concealed characteristics and values of places. In urban disciplines, narratives have not only been "passively" heard and collected, but evidently, and with major success, also invented and told. Narratives, as related to urban studies, play a crucial role in the construction of imageries (a change of perception), in the manifestation of the necessity of new instruments (in order to read, for example, changing contexts such as peripheries), and in the consequent conceptualisation of new models for urban and territorial transformations.

In spatial disciplines, there has been a long dispute between narration and description. In the article "Descriptive City Planning", published by Casabella in 1992, Secchi criticizes the descriptive drift of planning over the previous fifteen years, where long text documentations accompanying plans and projects for the city didn't really bring progress to the understanding of the dispersed city. He reasserts the need of a more subjective perspective, as the one that in his view is provided by narration. This is quite a contemporary position, which just a few years later was criticised by Corboz (2001), who took a position in defence of scientific and objective description in urban sciences.

Corboz claimed that narration, in the sense of a subjective understanding of the spatial context, is already inherent in description. Indeed, description entails at the same time "reading" and "writing" of an urban context, conveying the idea of a subjective and constructive interpretation of the city. Mapping and representation are also forms of description, but they are at the same time a narrative, as they are always "fiction": "Représenter le territoire c'est déjà le saisir. Or cette représenta-

Figure 1. "Pocket Utopias", new narratives for the abandoned islands of the Venice lagoon. Models realised during the Biennale Session 2016, Venice. Organised by Chair for Regional Building and Urban Planning LUH, with IUAV Venice and Politecnico di Milano

tion n'est pas un calque, mais toujours une construction [Representing the territory is already understanding it. This representation is not a cast, but always a construction]" (Corboz 2001, p. 46; Binotto, Gerber 2010). In this same direction, one could read Corner's position: "Mapping is a fantastic cultural project, creating and building the world as much as measuring and describing it" (1999, p.213). This "cultural construct" is the effect of city's representation in literature, urban history, critical sociology, literary studies, and it is narrowly bound up with the description (or narration) of the city through metaphors. In architecture and urban design, the city is described more often than not in metaphorical terms, e.g., the "city as a text" (Eisenman), "the city as a body" (Ungers).

Metaphors have been used to describe dichotomy and ambivalence, two characteristics that have been intrinsically connected to city narration and imagination since the Middle Age, when Saint Augustine spoke about the indistinguishable character of the city of God (Jerusalem) and the city of the world (Babylon). And perhaps this ambivalent and changing nature of urban space is what makes the city so attractive and charming. In narratives of cities, we might include the traces left by the inhabitants who customise their space, recomposing on a daily basis their urban fragments in different trajectories and stories, as Wirth-Nesher argues (1996). And if there exists "the Boston that everybody knows", as Lynch claims (1960), there are also many different mental maps, all telling a diverse narrative about different perceptions and uses of the space.

Qualitative instruments, such as perception maps and interviews collected in the field, have recently catalysed new attention in urban design and planning, as they enable a new perspective on places. Indeed, when the object of analysis changes—as it is the case with dynamic peripheries and new territorial configurations—and when new paradigms arise, descriptive tools must consequently adapt. But, coming back to Secchi, it is not only a matter of description. What is especially needed is "a different strategy of attention on the part of city planners" and perhaps a repositioning of the role of design within this debate.

Narrative as Design Tool

Narratives are meant as design-projective tools, being able to build sense and identity, to make visible intangible elements and dynamics, to generate sharing of stories and values (Oliva). Narrative enables the overcoming of implicit labelling, based on the postulate of peripheries=degradation; it enables a shift to a vision where challenges are opportunities, giving the inhabitants the capacity to co-generate public arrangements (Massari). Narration is not a solution, but rather is the starting point for generating debate ... through the sharing of values, knowledge, and actions in communities, making them a resource for change (Sgaramella). Narratives can become a tool for immaterially and materially describing inner-city peripheries, in order to unveil their capacity for social inclusion and collectivity (Hartmann). It was greatly to Lefevbre's credit that cities' symbolic representations were drawn into the processes of the "production of space", gaining a crucial position also in these fields of study and application (Ameel 2013). It is significant to observe the meaningful role that metaphors, for example, have played for architects and planners: "metaphors are also part of the very creative process of architectural design. It is undeniable that architects invent metaphors in order to progress in design and to create particular unforeseen combinations" (Gerber 2013, p.21). This is transferrable also to narrative, as an instrument for enabling diverse perspectives on a specific context. Indeed, sometimes it is not about changing the object, but telling a different story in order to look at that same object with different eyes. This quality is embedded in design. Every project is actually a story that, through the reassembling capacity of design, which is a more intuitive and direct approach, manages to transcend a static and traditional interpretation, to grasp concealed qualities, and to activate a new key for reading, for example, of a degraded context. In this sense, design is a tool of knowledge. But the narrative inherent in design is also a strong instrument of communication, for generating generate public debate in a shared process of city transformation. Narrative is therefore a crucial instrument of social inclusion and participation.

Narrative as Strategic Tool

The regenerated vision of peripheries creates new dynamisms that improve the quality of the space and define new habitats (Scaffidi). Population has to narrate local population needs not only through participatory planning ... but also with an operative role linked to the economic aspect (Torrisi). Prospective storytelling as part of a scenario strategy could be a valuable approach bridging the wide gap of local dynamics and top-down planning (Diesch).

The recent development of spatial disciplines shows an increasing use of narrative in participation processes. In a society that is (or claims to be) more and more horizontal and democratic, where the individual recognises himself as part of the community and aims to have a major voice in the transformation process, storytelling has revealed itself as a useful tool for sharing. Especially in complex processes of transformation of regions and territories, and particularly in the last decade with a renewed political and economic push toward regional development, the use of scenario-building has increased significantly. Scenarios are stories of the future. Inhabitants and local communities are called to share these future visions and to contribute by providing feedback and being involved in dialogue with public actors.

This communication happens often through the means of narratives that accompany the proposed scenarios of transformation, the so-called storytelling. The latter functions as an instrument both for simplifying the complex structure of the envisaged territorial future and for drawing the attention of the audience, stimulating debate. Sometimes, though—as Matthey (2011) warns—behind the honest façade of a right and fair participatory process, the use of storytelling in planning processes masks a double hidden goal: it provides a powerful instrument of political control, and it contributes to the "spectacularisation" of urbanism, "based on the assumption that a good story is better than boring facts" (Matthey 2011). According to this thesis, a sort of "fictional urbanism" has arisen in the last years, where despite the progressive trivialisation of places, what counts are the shiny futuristic visions of urban transformations. Storytelling could be an effective tool for sharing and perhaps even an instrument of co-design. But the precondition for this to happen is avoiding the trivialisation of technical expertise in favour of a simplistic communication that, besides being offensive, reduces the possibility of people taking active and critical position in the transformation of their future habitats. Narrative can help change perspective on marginalised areas, telling the different stories of the many people and actors living in a place and transforming their territories. Especially in the complex contexts observed and collected in this book, narratives have provided an original key for the reading of dynamic places, an instrument that has contributed to the development of local qualities and future potentials of peripheries.

Bibliography

Ameel L. (2013) *Moved by the City: Experiences of Helsinik in Finnish Prose Fiction* 1889–1941. Helsinki, Unigrafia.

Binotto J., Gerber A. (2010) "Narration/Non-Ville/Description". In: *Le Journal Spéciale 'Z*, pp. 32–39. Posted at the Zurich Open Repository and Archive, University of Zurich ZOR. Available on line at: https://doi.org/10.5167/uzh-45960. [Accessed 5.12.2017].

Corboz A. (2001) "Le territoire comme palimpseste". In: Corboz A. (2001) *Le Territorie comme palimpseste et autres essais*. Besançon, Les Éditions de l'Imprimeur.

Corner J. (1999) "The Agency of Mapping: Speculation, Critique and Invention". In: Cosgrove D. (1999) *Mappings*. London, Reaktion. pp. 213–252.

Gerber A. (2013) *Introduction*. In: Gerber A., Patterson B. eds. (2013) *Metaphors in Architecture and Urbanism: An Introduction.* Bielefeld, transcript Verlag. pp. 13–30.

Lynch K. (1960) *The Image of the City*. Cambridge. Technology Pr.

Matthey L. (2011) "Urbanisme fictionnel: l'action urbaine à l'heure de la société du spectacle". In: *Métropolitiques*. Available on line at: www.metropolitiques.eu/Urbanisme-fictionnel-l-action.html?lang=fr. [Accessed 1.12.2017].

Secchi B. (1992) "Descriptive City Planning". In: Casabella 588/1992, pp. 61–62.

Wirth-Nesher H. (1996) *City Codes: Reading the Modern Urban Novel.* Cambridge, Cambridge University Press.

DYNAMICS OF PERIPHERY

A HABITAT VISION

Envisioning the Baltic

Maddalena Ferretti

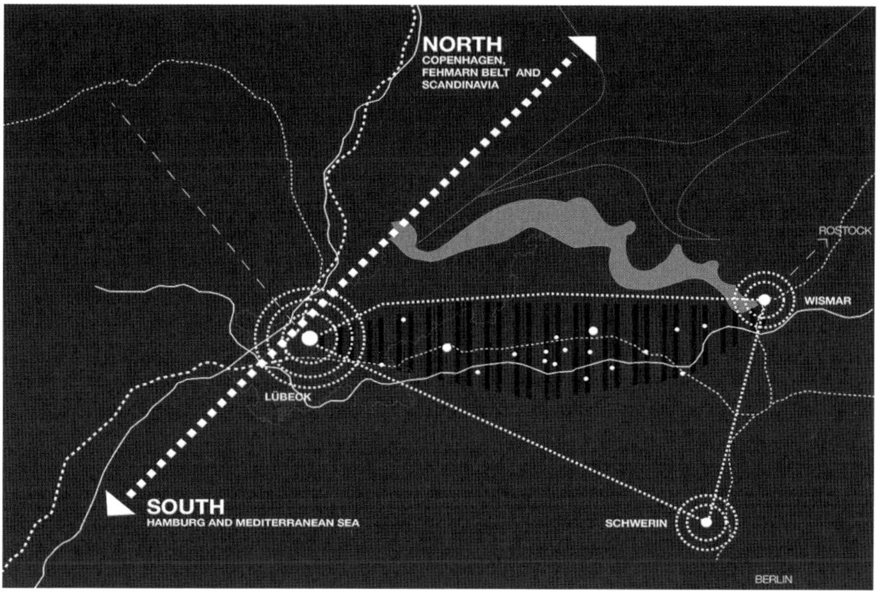

Figure 1. Explorative scenario for the Focus Region Lübeck-Nordwestmecklenburg. Realised for Regiobranding by the Chair for Regional Building and Urban Planning LUH. Graphic: M. Ferretti

1,700 km of Coastline

In the collective imagination, the word "periphery" is still generally associated to a marginal, underdeveloped context, where a scarce quality of living is often combined with social inequalities, economic setback, lack of services, and insufficient infrastructure. This contribution aims to propose a change of perspective, addressing peripheries as motors of innovation and as test-fields for impulses and new dynamics of development. The focus is the German Baltic Coast, a territory in a "peripheral" position with regard to the growing metropolis of Hamburg and, as a coastal region, also part—and periphery—of another space: the Baltic sea region. Coastal regions in Europe host circa 205 million people (2008), namely 41% of the European population, spread over twenty-two member states and six maritime basins, the Baltic Sea being one of them (EU 2011). Moreover, despite sharing the common trends of European "peripheral" areas (negative or neutral demographic trends, more or less significant economic and structural stagnation, ageing population etc.), the German Baltic Coast is recently witnessing a boom in the touristic sector. In 2016, Mecklenburg-Vorpommern was the third top holiday destination for Germans (FUR 2017), and already in 2014, it reached the highest touristic intensity in Germany, with more than 17,000 overnight stays per 1,000 inhabitants (Statisches Amt MV 2015). Most of the tourism in Mecklenburg Vorpommern is concentrated along the coastline. For example, in 2016 the travel destinations along the Baltic Coast (Mecklenburgische Ostseeküste, Rügen/Hiddensee, Vorpommern) scored more than 80% of the overnight stays in the whole State of Mecklenburg-Vorpommern. The German Baltic Coast shares

Figure 2. "A new architecture for the Baltic Coast", Design studio class for master students, summer 17, Chair for Regional Building and Urban Planning LUH

In 2016, Europe defined strategic priority themes for urban development (Urban Agenda 2016). In a holistic view focused on territorial systems, "peripheral" contexts such as coastal regions acquire new centrality and—especially in connection with tourism, which strengthens circular local economies—become an important element of European competitiveness on a global scale. A systematic process of thorough analysis is basic for such areas, in order to propose meaningful transformations that comply with European strategic assets. At the same time, a closer look at real contexts is needed to preserve the special qualities of places. This multi-scalar approach relies on the idea that strategic territorial goals can be addressed through design interventions. For the German Baltic Coast, for example, transformations have been suggested, focusing on the capacity of architectural and urban design interventions, to function as a motor for larger impulses. This process does not aim to reduce the importance of strategic territorial visions, but rather to connect together different scales and disciplines to achieve innovative, resilient, and smart living habitats. Research on field and qualitative instruments, such as interviews, are also part of this approach, enabling a deeper understanding of complex "peripheral" and dynamic territories. Using traditional data such as GIS, the study of literature, and analysis of development trends, but also focusing on the spatial, urban, and architectural features of the place, this approach leads to the identification of qualities and potentials that become crucial in the design phase. In this analysis process, design itself is an indispensable instrument for the knowledge of the territory.

with the other member countries the EU Strategy for the Baltic Sea Region, which defines objectives and policy areas for the region. Evidently, specific contextual conditions of the Baltic Region, related for example to ageing population, determine a major attention of the strategy on new financing models of social welfare and on changing urbanisation patterns. Tourism, especially along the coastline, represents an essential voice of this economy, even more today, as a consequence of the insecurity in the Middle-East, and it is thus an important element within the macro-regional strategy (EUSBSR 2017). These dynamics and trends constituted the starting point for reflecting on the future of this 1,700 kilometre strip, running from Lübeck, in the west, to Szczecin (Stettin) in Poland, in the east. This area is characterised by interesting and very diverse settlement conditions: from small and medium cities to rural areas; from secondary homes to developing cities and towns; from natural spaces connected to the rich water system to industrial sites connected to harbours. In this challenging context, some questions arise. How can the touristic impulse become a leverage of a more structural development? How can spatial transformations, even at micro-scale, contribute to improving qualities of settlements and territories? How can a strategic approach to territorial development be effectively combined with the anticipatory quality of design to realise more liveable and resilient habitats? How can local development be interfaced with tourism, environmental issues, sustainable mobility, etc.? These questions have been addressed within the framework of some teaching activities in the year 2016-17.[1]

New Architectures

The design projects developed along the Baltic Coast cover a broad range of topics and places, from Lübeck to Stettin, encountering very different habitats. Using architectural designs and urban interventions as motors of change, the goal was to develop strategic assets for the region and, programmatically, to expand and distribute the positive economic effects of tourism across the territory towards a deeper, more rooted, and long-lasting local development, involving also the residents as the main target group of the transformation. The proposals work in different contexts along the coast, adapting to local conditions and profiting from local resources. The area is mostly known for health tourism and sport-holidays. Water tourism is also a very relevant sector, although seasonal. In compensation, the cultural tourism offering is expanding, making use of heritage and historical sites, such as the noble castles and palaces in the stretch between Lübeck and Boltenhagen. Cultural activities and events, also related to education, tradition, cooking etc., are also increasing, especially in bigger towns and cities. The region is also known for the wide range of diverse natural spaces, both along the coast (sand beaches, rock coastlines, lagoons), and in inner areas (rivers, lakes, woods, regional or national parks). On the other hand, economic sectors related to innovation and creativity do not yet represent a significant factor in the region. A strengthening of these fields is desirable. The analysed regional features represented the starting point for giving shape to very different works, both with Bachelor's theses, and during a master's design studio class. The "Hafen Campus" is a research and knowledge harbour in Prerow, between Rostock and Stralsund. The project is an innovative campus for education and research, that aims to bring the different administrative and governance bodies of the Baltic Sea Region into contact with each

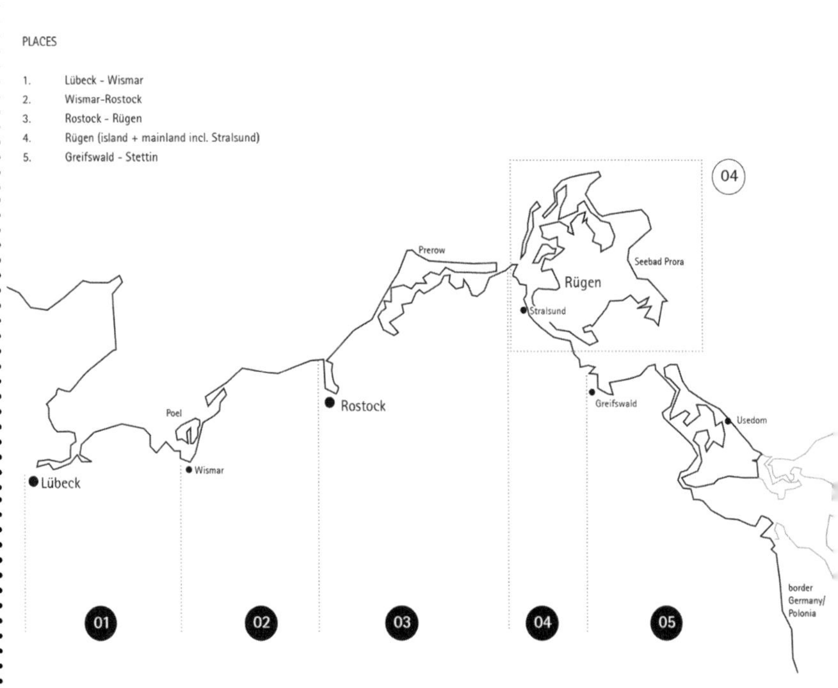

Figure 3. “A new architecture for the Baltic Coast”, Design studio class for master's students, summer 17, Map of the 1,700 km of German coastline along the Baltic Sea, Chair for Regional Building and Urgban Planning LUH

When speaking about place, the risk is to end up in a rhetoric and senseless discussion about identity, falling into a sort of “commonplace of the place”. Sometimes “identity” loses its reference to the “genius loci” and is used to “greenwash” the failures of regional development strategies. The trivialisation risk is even higher for peripheries, which are often perceived as banal and monofunctional places that need a strong branding strategy in order to be revived. However, what is often missing in this kind of approach, is the link to the real place, to its spatial qualities, to the natural spaces constituting its exceptional value, to the small cities, towns, and villages that make up its fine fabric, its vernacular and new architectures, built with local techniques and materials, its traditions and dialects, conveyed over the centuries by the communities, and finally to the values embedded in its uniqueness. And perhaps this uniqueness depends exactly on a constantly changing character, which is ultimately the most interesting aspect of dynamic peripheries, such as for the German Baltic coastline, where booming trends like tourism and territorial innovation are boosting regional development and, consequently, pressing this territory to adapt and transform. Here efforts must be channelled into the creation of new synergies between the dynamism of global impulses and the very specific qualities of this place.

other and foster a more efficient cooperation. Next to the village, but also detached through the wood and the beach, difficult to reach by feet, but easy to reach by boat, the squared building is a new landmark, although it recycles an existing port infrastructure. It is made of a modular system of boxes under a common roof, with conference and meeting rooms, co-working spaces, and accommodation facilities. The new architecture is a clear and recognisable figure, that aims to envision a new image for the Baltic Sea. Indeed, a transfer process is also being imagined to further implement the "Hafen Campus" in other similar conditions in the Baltic Region: along the coastline, in similar spatial configurations; in capital cities, occupying open public spaces, to complete missing or insufficient cultural and educational services; in the middle of the Baltic Sea, e.g., next to an oil platform, to stress its independence from political control.

Explorative Scenarios

In line with this trans-scalar approach the Chair for Regional Building and Urban Planning, within the project "Regiobranding", has envisioned different scenarios to test the dynamics of development of the Baltic coast.[2] The scenario-building methodology proposes explorative scenarios that show self-consistent plausible conditions/situations, together depicting a likely future. The methodology doesn't aim to boost one particular scenario, or to create alternative and concurrent "futures". It rather suggests a possible superimposition of different likely situations, in order to detect similarities and contradictions and to lead towards a sharable future vision. Developed with a trans-disciplinary co-planning approach, and built up through the participation of regional actors and specific target groups of interest who share their local knowledge with the academic partners and who provided feedback on the outputs of this process, the scenarios can be synthesised into the following three development paths:

1. Development along the north-south axis of the Scandinavian-Mediterranean Corridor, under the impulse of the "TEN-T Transport Infrastructure Policy", defining the "Core Corridors" of Europe (EU 2016b). In this scenario, the project of the Fehmarnbelt (the eighteen kilometres of immersed tunnel for trains and cars connecting Germany to Denmark) acquires a major strategic importance for the region. A reconnection along the former GDR's border, dividing western (Lübeck) and eastern (Nordwestmecklenburg) Germany, is another essential topic to be debated. The reconnection could have positive influence in the whole region. Also thanks to the connection to the planned north-south axis, the west-east connection could help overcome structural issues such as suburbanisation along the former border, and provide new areas of possible development to counterbalance the otherwise overly high pressure in the area of Lübeck.

2. Development of polarities, especially of Lübeck, but also of Wismar and Schwerin. The polarities could be positively influenced by the metropolitan centre Hamburg. The connection to Hamburg and the Baltic region strengthens the role of these poles within a larger area of relations (including also Rostock and Berlin). The poles are also providers of services and infrastructure for the surrounding areas. The connection west-east runs parallel to the coastline (regional rail), where

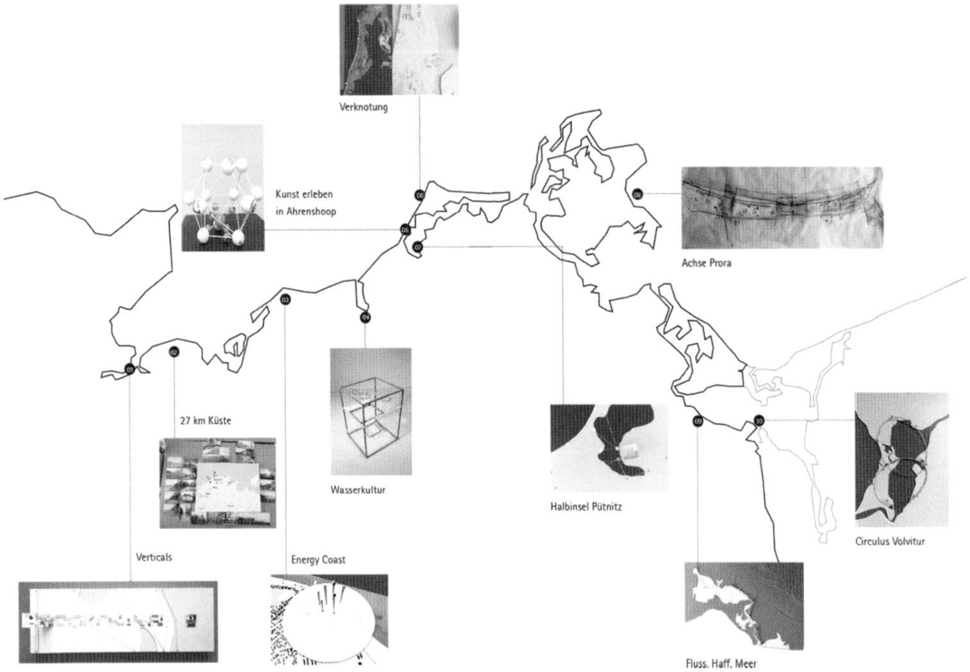

Figure 4. "A new architecture for the Baltic Coast", Design studio class for master' students, summer 17, Projects matrix. Chair for Regional Building and Urban Planning LUH

At a first glance, looking at the "Map of the coastal regions in the European Union, by sea basins and by NUTS 3 regions", coastlines seem to be peripheral contexts, because, from a geographic point of view, they are positioned at the outer borders of Europe. They are also thinly stretched territories, often no more than fifty kilometres wide, that, compared with the European inner core, does not seem to play a crucial role in dynamics of development. We could narrate this story and make it more convincing through the aid of maps and data. But we could also tell a different one, based on other—also significant —numbers, such as the strong increase in tourism, for example in the German Baltic coast. This narrative could be also supported by relevant maps, showing the density of activities along the thin coastline, the intensity of relationships and exchange established with the inland, and, most importantly, the countless connections taking place every day between coastal regions and the rest of the globe. On the Baltic Sea, the perspective is directed to a different centre than inner Europe, and the sea itself builds the common ground and the "identity" for the cooperation of different countries on the implementation of a common strategy of development for the region. The synergic combination of scenarios of territorial development and design interventions at the local scale enables the creation of a new perspective, envisioning a completely different narrative for "peripheral" coastal regions.

suburban settlements and rural areas can profit from this development impulse and possibly for a renewed cooperation among each other and with other small and medium cities.

3. Development towards the east (Mecklenburg), specifically in the inner rural areas and along the Baltic Coast. Touristic and natural resources along the coast are combined with the potentials of small cities and villages along the linear connection between Lübeck and Wismar. The highway A20, running parallel to the coastline, provides connection along the east-west axis, and has already caused suburbanisation effects in this segment. But the major connecting potential, also in terms of sustainable mobility, is offered by the regional train running east-west. The triangle Lübeck-Wismar-Schwerin is strengthened in terms of infrastructural linkages and of cooperation, with new governance models and tools, in order to activate new spatial configurations, economic impulses, and innovative energies.

In conclusion, crucial aspects of a future vision of development for the German Baltic area are a linear development along the north-south axis, a networked development in polarities, and a development towards Mecklenburg to the East and along the coast. This perspective can rely on several, not yet fully valorised, potentials, namely: a) the trans-European connection along the Scandinavian-Mediterranean corridor, which could positively influence the suburban and rural areas in Lübeck South; b) the polarities (Lübeck, Wismar, Schwerin, etc.) as a strong territorial background for envisioning an enlarged development perspective connected to the metropolitan region Hamburg, relying also on innovative impulses in smaller towns around the poles; c) inner rural areas and small towns in Mecklenburg, as well as natural and economic resources along the Baltic coastline, that can be understood as a premise for major cooperation between Lübeck and Nordwestmecklenburg, fostering tourism but also—in line with a new "habitat vision"—possibly turning this "peripheral" territory into an innovative living and working model for peripheries.

Notes/Bibliography

1 During the academic year 2016–17, the Chair for Regional Building and Urban Planning of the Leibniz Universität Hannover organised a Bachelor's Thesis with the title "Sommerfrische Ostsee" and an Urban Design Studio Class for Master's students, with the title "Baltic Coast". Both activities were centred on the German Baltic Coast.

2 The Chair for Regional Building and Urban Planning of the Leibniz Universität Hannover is a partner in the trans-disciplinary project Regiobranding, funded by the German Ministry of Education and Research in 2014–19 and coordinated by the Institute for Environmental Planning of the Leibniz Universität Hannover. The project aims at a branding of urban-rural regions through valorisation of cultural landscape characteristics. Case studies are three urban-rural areas in the Metropolitan Region Hamburg (MRH). Within the project, the Chair is leading the expertise in settlement development and building structures (www.regiobranding.de).

EU (2011) *Eurostat Regional Yearbook 2011*. Available online at: http://ec.europa.eu/eurostat/en/web/ products-statistical-books/-/KS-HA-11-001-06. [Accessed 05.12.2017].

EU (2016a) *Urban Agenda for the European Union. Pact of Amsterdam*. Available online at: http://ec.europa.eu/ regional_policy/sources/policy/themes/urban-development/agenda/pact-of-amsterdam.pdf. [Accessed 05.12.2017].

EU (2016b) *Scandinavian-Mediterranean*. Second Work Plan of the European Coordinator Pat Cox. Available online at: https://ec.europa.eu/transport/sites/transport/files/2nd_workplan_sm.pdf. [Accessed 05.12.2017].

EUSBSR (2017) *Action Plan for the European Union Strategy for the Baltic Sea Region*. Available online at: http://balticsea-region.eu/action-plan?task=document.viewdoc&id=17. [Accessed 05.12.2017].

FUR (2017) *Reiseanalyse 2017*. Available online at: http://www.fur.de/fileadmin/user_upload/RA_2017/ RA2017_Erste_Ergebnisse_DE.pdf. [Accessed 05.12.2017].

Statisches Amt Mecklenburg-Vorpommern (2015) *Statistisches Jahrbuch Mecklenburg-Vorpommern*. Available online at: https://www.laiv-mv.de/static/LAIV/Abt4.Statistisches%20Amt/Dateien/Publikationen/Statistisches%20Jahrbuch/ Z011%20 2015%2000.pdf. [Accessed 05.12.2017].

Palermo Metro-Peripheries: The Role of Peripheries in a Metropolitan Perspective

Barbara Lino

Hybrid Dynamics: Theoretical Framework and Strategic Questions

An extensive and varied literature has dislodged the established idea of urbanised space (Dematteis 1988 and 2005; Lanzani 1991), altered the terms of the urban issue (Secchi 2010 and 2013), interpreted new post-metropolitan settlement forms (Balducci 2015; Soja 2011), and pointed out images of transformation (Carta 2017) and new theoretical approaches to traditional terms such as "urban" and "scale", arguing that urban/rural distinctions are no longer meaningful where capitalist networks reach to every corner of the globe: a multidimensional morphology in witch the distinction between inside and outside of a city no longer makes sense. The features that most deeply affect the disarticulation of the organisational and socio-spatial forms by unhinging the urban operating model as we have traditionally known it are social and economic fragmentation; the accelerated movement of people, goods, and information; and the building of new networks (Balducci 2015). The spatial dynamics in place are actually the result of a combination of border crossing by the central city into other municipal areas, true conurbation between adjacent centres, and phenomena characterised by variable geometry. If we do not distinguish an inside and outside, an urban and a countryside, peripheries are spatial and relational phenomenon, the result of the way in which we read the space depending on the social, economic, and functional relationships that determine it.

Territorial forms are modelled by social and economic forces but also by institutional arrangements and political strategies. The updated governance model of the territorial phenomena being experienced as much in various European urban contexts as nationally, within the scope of defining new metropolitan cities, is radically changing the governance system at a metropolitan scale and is subjecting the outskirts to significant further transformative tension, with repercussions on spatial and functional relationships, especially between suburban areas of the city core and the municipalities of the first belt. In Italy, at a national level, legislative innovations regarding the reform of metropolitan cities introduced by the Delrio Law have opened a new theoretical and political context that calls for, on the one hand, a general rethinking of the administrative and governance system and a testing of a decision-making system that is as participatory as possible and capable of engaging the multiplicity of the territory's stakeholders, and, on the other, a profound cultural, social, and disciplinary challenge aimed at shaping new tools for responding to the spatial dynamics of territorialisation and cross-scale urban phenomena affecting new metropolitan cities. Omitting the extensive debate underway regarding both the political dimension, relating to the formation and operation of the metropolitan government, and the administrative dimension, on the suitability of the border configuration of the metropolitan city which, by law, includes the municipalities of the former province of the same name, it is good to note how the complex future action of the metropolitan city is not facing new phenomena, nor completely new administrative boundaries (the phenomena involved are already underway and the administrative boundaries coincide with the previous borders of the province), but, rather, requires renewed instruments of action for new visions. Can the new metropolitan city determine spatial modification processes that work on centre-peripheral polarization processes? Can it contribute to the generation of a more inclusive settlement model capable of rebalancing existing asymmetries by relocating now peripheral areas to a new centrality?

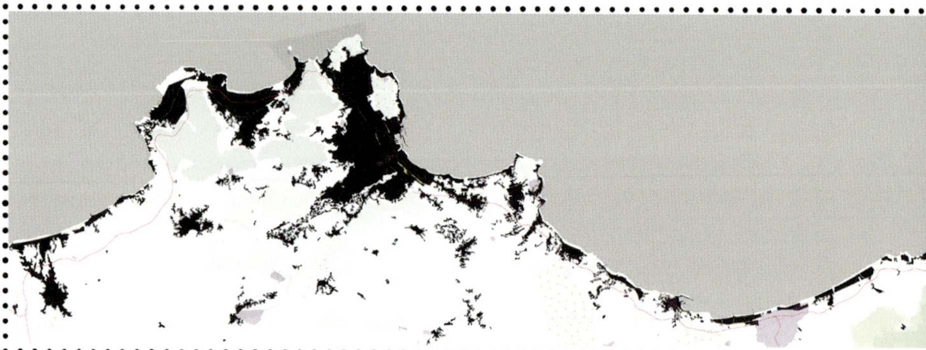

Figure 1. Palermo Metropolitan City linear polycentrism. Graphic: author

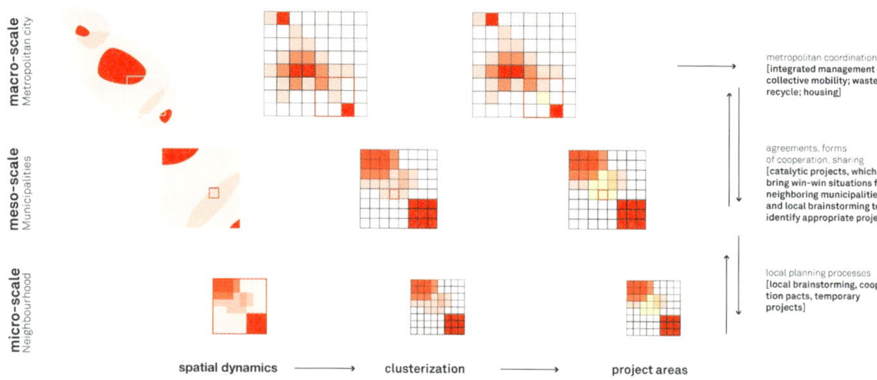

Figure 2. Metro-peripheries multilevel governance matrix. Graphic: author

The deep change in functional, political, and symbolic relations between core and peripheries in European metropolitan dynamics has blurred the current categories of "periphery" and "core". The periphery is no longer a homogeneous reality, but a dynamic and fragmented urban landscape. The institution of new territorial bodies in Italy, with the metropolitan cities and new forms of institutional collaboration between territorial bodies, is a new political framework that calls for new solutions in regional policy-making in order to overcome the radial (core-centric) urban model: peripheries are not longer satellites of core cities' development but realities that, in a wider view, have a new spatial and relational centrality in a metropolitan perspective. The challenges of metro-peripheries can only be successful if all tiers of planning and decision-making are willing and committed to cooperate in strategic development processes: a "multilayered" governance, as balanced combination of bottom-up and top down processes, acting at micro/meso and macro scales.

XL Palermo: The New Metropolitan City and the South-East Corridor

In order to explore theoretical questions, the dynamics of transformation of Palermo metropolitan city and its South-East corridor have been analysed. Consistent with legislative innovations affecting the national territory, whereby metropolitan cities supplanted the provinces of the same name from the 1 January 2015, in Sicily, Law no. 15 of 4 August 2015, established the breakdown of Sicilian metropolitan cities, making them coincide with the territorial extent of the corresponding regional provinces. In addition to being the capital of the Sicily Region, with approximately 656,000 inhabitants (ISTAT, 2011) and a municipal area of 160 square kilometres, Palermo is the city with the greatest concentration of inhabitants. Indeed, the city has a population density of 4,278 people per square kilometres, while Catania has a density of 1,731 people per square kilometre and Messina 1,193 people per square kilometre. The Palermo territory corresponds to the province of the same name, on whose perimeter the metropolitan city is based. It has a population of about 1,300,000, extends over a surface of around 5,000 square kilometres, and includes eighty-two metropolitan municipalities. Based on these data, Palermo is the fifth largest Italian metropolitan city in terms of population and the third largest in size. An analysis of the demographic trend highlights the attractive role of the metropolitan city territory. While the city of Palermo hasn't grown since 1981, the area of the metropolitan city of Palermo grew by over 10% between 1971 and 2011 (ISTAT, 2011). While it was originally an archetype of monocentrism in the 1960s, the contemporary metropolitan configuration delineates a settlement layout we could define as "linear polycentrism", which extends beyond the municipality administrative boundaries and in which the coastal axis unfolds linearly through polarized aggregations. The result of this process is an urbanised system of first-belt municipalities characterised by a settlement continuity along the coastal axis where the main infrastructure is concentrated, forming a multimodal transport "corridor" (highway, motorway, and railway) that serves the most populated municipalities gravitating to the capital.

The South-East Corridor

The study area of this research is a marginal area that is part of a group of municipalities (Palermo, Bagheria, Ficarazzi, Misilmeri, Villabate), the so-called south-east corridor, situated close to the coastal railway route and the highway connecting Palermo with Catania. The greatest concentrations of marginality have been caused by settlement processes that, over time, have pinpointed the southern suburbs with two clear dividing lines—the Oreto River to the south of the city and the ring road to the west; here, "Oltre-Oreto" (Orlando 2015) is an area which can, more than others, exemplify the potential strategic role defined by the new geography of the metropolitan city. The gradually encroaching Palermo metropolitan development has overlaid the original rural structure by inserting new elements, as result of random additions and substitutions rather than implemented plans (Lino 2015). If we observe more recent on-going transformations, the percentage of population growth shows how all the municipalities of the south-east corridor have grown between 2001 and 2011 with the exception of Palermo (Ficarazzi 21.94%, Bagheria 6.69%, Villabate 7.88%, Misilmeri 19.3%). Looking at governance and transformations processes, coordinated action to reorganise the mobility system to serve the entry system into the city and to reorganise the urban

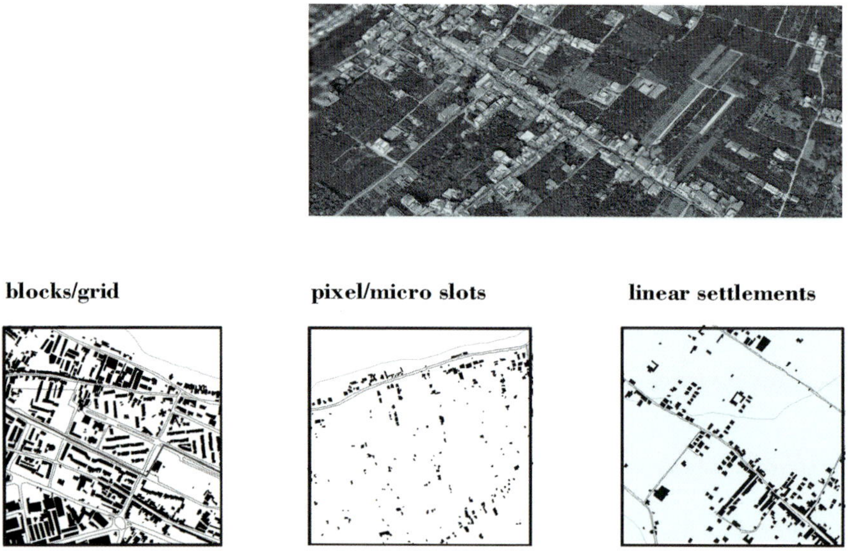

Figure 3. Palermo, South Coast. Spatial patterns. Graphic: author

The emerging territory model facing metropolitan cities and its peripheries is characterised by very complex phenomena already in place, which suggest overriding the image of a city traditionally described as a compact urban structure that develops around a centre and thins out (in density, functions, and urban values) along centre-outskirts trajectories. The spatial dynamics are actually the result of a combination of border crossing by the central city into other municipal areas, true conurbation between adjacent centres, and phenomena characterised by variable geometry. As a effect of these dynamics, peripheries are morphologically, functionally, socially, and relationally fragmented urban landscapes. In terms of quality transformations and dynamics and spatial matrixes, if we observe the ways in which the urbanised land has grown from a qualitative viewpoint, urbanisation has often originated mainly from the welding of adjacent centres and the inclusion of pre-existing urbanised fabrics. The peripheries are candidates for playing a key role in the rebalancing of settlement weights, in response to the challenge of urban quality and social equality, becoming valuable stakes for the construction of poly-nuclear and reticular residential and productive patterns.

connections is radically redefining the role this area can play as an urban gateway from the south. Various redevelopment initiatives have already begun in the area: the Urban Duty-Free Zone for economic activities; the reconversion of the San Paolo Palace Hotel—confiscated from organised crime—into a residence for university students; a huge investment of 130 million euros allocated by the National Funds for Metropolitan Cities (PON Metro) (European Programme 2014/2020), approximately half of which relates to the technological innovation of existing buildings and urbanisation, and the other half to social inclusion.

At the level of the city level, the 2025 strategic scenario for Palermo has been set up with the purpose to provide orientation for and coherence of territorial transformations and of the future spatial governance of the city, involving communities through voluntary agreements. The plan, while acting within the municipal boundary (at the current state of administrative boundaries of reference), due to its large-area vision has effects on the metropolitan scale and on the potential role of the south-east corridor. The strategic plan for Palermo Capital[1] "that is not just metropolitan (the belt of municipalities or the former province), but overtly "metapolitan" (for a broader regional area stretching from Cefalù to Marsala), [has] to guide the processes of regeneration and development" (Carta 2017, p. 71). The plan introduces a vision of the city as a "metropolitan super-organism, that is, a geo-eco-system of urban and rur-urban settlements of sub-provincial dimensions, organised as a single cohesive community, in which each settlement and productive system has a clearly defined role and in which all parts—as the components of a perfect mechanism—act in unison, contributing in a differential and incremental manner to the pursuit of the development of the organism" (Carta 2017, p. 78).

In terms of transformations, dynamics, and spatial matrixes, if we observe the ways in which the urbanised land has grown from a qualitative viewpoint, urbanisation has originated mainly from the welding of adjacent centres and the inclusion of pre-existing urbanised fabrics. The housing development is characterised by a densification of plots over a block grid and mass-produced housing in the 1970s and in the 1980s. In this pattern we can also recognise new taxonomy elements as results of infill and inclusion dynamics: blocks/grid, mirco slots, linear settlements. In-between building spaces there are often empty spaces or "micro-landscapes". In the end, the centrifugal forces of urbanisation that have influenced the geography of commercial and production spaces at the municipal level also act in this area where we find an industrial site, the so-called Brancaccio ASI, and a big commercial spaces: using an interpretation of Brenner definition, "micro-operational landscapes".

Challenges of Metro-Peripheries

Although simple and partial, the data relating to emerging dynamics, both on the metropolitan scale and on the scale of suburban areas, show the extent of the flows and relations that the arising metropolitan city must be able to steer and govern. The definition of a metropolitan territorial agenda will require us, on the one hand, to consider phenomena already in place and pre-existing

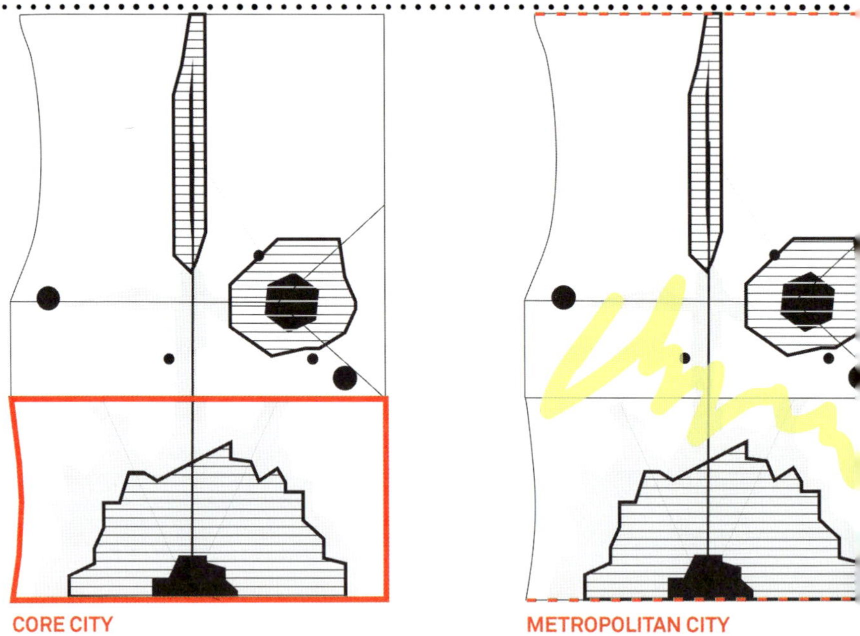

Figure 4. The new centre is in-between. Graphic: author

If we do not distinguish an inside and outside, an urban and a countryside, peripheries become spatial and relational phenomenon, and spaces depending on the social, economic, and functional relationships that determine them. The definition of periphery and its conceptualization should be linked to the processes that produce it, as a result of relationships with other places and territories: marginalization and polarization, decline, territorial inequality. The growing problems of social inequality and polarization of the "new urban question" (Secchi 2013, IX) require us to field social cohesion strategies and place-based initiatives targeted at aggregate community around shared projects. In last years, we have recognised "future signals", different "stories of change-makers" transforming neglected and abandoned building and peripheral areas by delivering services to the community. They are the figure of the change being made, the production of public services, in our daily care strategies for individual and collective wellbeing, cultural practices, and mobility. From this different narrative perspective—the creative perspective of urban innovation—peripheries offer themselves as a privileged field of potentials, and not only for commuting and rent containment, but also as an experimentation field for new policies for co-creation, co-production, and co-management of common resources, accordingly with a renewed instance in social cohesion and an awareness of the right to the city.

areas with high functional interdependence, and on the other, to radically redefine the system of planning and local authorities in favour of greater coordination, solidarity, and collaboration between neighbouring players, also beginning with solutions that can find greater localization opportunities in the outskirts of the core city as a result of a new spatial centrality and their potential role as overly thin joints between neighbouring areas. In the metropolitan perspective, the challenges of metro-peripheries can only be successful if all tiers of planning and decision-making are willing and committed to cooperate in a strategic and "multilayered" development processes able to loosen the dependence of gravitational centres on the city core and an overall rethinking of the territorial imbalances (Lino, 2013), counteracting de-concentration phenomena, reorganizing the mobility system, counter-balancing dispersive phenomena, and differentiating and promoting of local contexts: a system of multilevel governance that allow nodes and networks of development to be standardised in distributive forms (Carta 2017).

Metropolitan cities need to test "a new approach to decisions and actions regarding the numerous flows and cycles involving metropolitan systems. An approach that effectively uses scale crossing, flexibility, and circularity as paradigms/instruments of new large-scale territorial policies rather than traditional gravitations that are no longer able to represent the complex metropolitan relations" (Carta 2017, p. 71). At the metropolitan city level, a metropolitan coordination may lead to integrated management of collective mobility, integrated waste recycling or social housing policies. At the "meso-scale", at the municipality level, agreements, forms of cooperation and sharing, and carefully selected catalytic projects, which bring win-win situations for both, may be an appropriate means for building up strategic alliances from which both the central city and the surrounding municipalities can only benefit (e.g., common services, commercial spaces, etc.). At the "micro-scale", at the neighbourhood level of local planning processes, local brainstorming, cooperation pacts, and temporary projects, are perfect learning grounds for promoting local learning and and for continuously qualifying local planning and decision-making processes.

Note/Bibliography

1 The strategic plan for Palermo Capital has been set up from November 2014 to November 2015 by the Municipality of Palermo, with the scientific advice of Creta srl, Maurizio Carta, Stefano Stanghellini.

Balducci A. (2015) "Le trasformazioni post-metropolitane e il modificarsi del legame tra spazio, forme dell'urbano e confini amministrativi". In: Lodigiani R. ed., *Milano 2015 Rapporto sulla città. La città metropolitana sfide, contraddizioni*. Milano, Ambrosianeum Fondazione Culturale, FrancoAngeli pp. 41–54.
Carta M. (2017), "Hyper-metropolitan Palermo. Unconventional strategies and mapping for circular metropolitan scenarios". In: Carta M., Lino B., Ronsivalle D. eds., *Re-cyclical Urbanism. Visions, paradigms and projects for the circular methamorphosis*. Trento, ListLab. pp. 70–91.
Dematteis G. (1988) "La scomposizione metropolitana". In: Mazza G. ed., *XVII Triennale, partecipazioni internazionali*. Milano, Electa.
Dematteis G. (2005) *La città nell'era della conoscenza: un sistema territoriale irragionevole*. Pisa, Irme.
Lanzani A. (1991) *Il territorio al plurale*. Milano, FrancoAngeli.
Lino B. (2013) *Periferie in trasform-azione. Riflessioni dai "margini" delle città*. Firenze, Alinea.
Lino B. (2015) "Vecchie e nuove visioni per Palermo: uno sguardo rivolto a Sud". In: Carta M., Lino B. eds., *Urban Hyper-Metabolism*. Roma, Aracne Int.le. pp. 170–79.
Orlando L. (2015) "Oltre Oreto". In: Carta M., Lino B. eds., *Urban Hyper-Metabolism*. Roma, Aracne. pp. 15–17.
Secchi B. (2010) "A new urban question". In: *Territorio* nr. 53. pp. 8–18.
Secchi B. (2013) *La città dei ricchi e la città dei poveri*. Roma-Bari, Laterza.
Soja E. (2011) "Regional Urbanisation and the End of the Metropolitan Era". In: Bridge G., Watson S. eds. (2011) *The New Blackwell Companion to the City*. New York, John Wiley & Sons. pp. 679–89.

Mapping the Transformation of Bogotá's Periphery

Alissa Diesch

Figure 1: Hybrid landscape in Usme. Photo: Alissa Diesch

Due to the extreme growth of Bogotá in the second half of the twentieth century, the city has incorporated six villages. These former rural sites demonstrate a long settlement history similar to the historic centre of Bogotá—initially indigenous settlements, later reshaped as colonial *pueblos de indios* by the Spaniards, and during the twentieth century, administratively and morphologically connected to Bogotá. Up to the nineteen-fifties, the former villages were clearly recognisable in the territory because of their independent urban layout. Today, connected to the city by a continuous fabric, they are knots within the city's complex periphery. Currently, village traditions hardly play a decisive role in everyday practices, but their rural origin can be traced back in architecture, urban patterns, and memories. In spite of sharing the same genealogy, the former rural sub-centralities have transformed into very different parts of the city (Fig. 4, Fig. 5).

The places have experienced not only a spatial-architectonical shift, but also a social transition to urban neighbourhoods. Both transformations will be analysed in the doctoral thesis *The Rural Heritage of Bogotá* using different types of cartographies, based on on-site studies and the analysis of historic maps. The general idea of critical cartography will be applied to all cartographic materials, taking into consideration the fact that mapping is closely related to "specific relations of power" and that maps are not "neutral scientific documents" (Crampton, Krygier 2005, p. 12). To describe this phycial transformation, existing maps and photo documents are analysed, digitally traced and presented in a graphically unified style. The "dance" (Solà-Morales, M. 1997) of urban growth and transformation of the territory is made visible through maps in the scale of 1:10,000 of the six villages at three different moments. The elements to be analysed, based on Solà-Morales, are "parcellation", "urbanisation" (including infrastructure but also the modification of geographical

Figure 2. Bogotá in 1950 and 2016: the emerging periphery. Graphic: Alissa Diesch

Emerging nations such as Colombia can be seen as dynamic global peripheries, as their political and economic power on an international level is rather secondary, although they have presented vivid processes of transformation, often away from the spotlight. In a condensed form this is true in the suburban fringe of Latin-American metropolises, which have emerged as a product of rapid urbanisation in the last sixty years (Fig. 1). Constant changes here are discernible in material and social aspects, as well as in persistent shifts of uses, dynamics, and densities. Makeovers triggered by different, mostly non-formal, stakeholders persist and continuously transform the space, hence people of multifarious origins are also generating new socio-cultural hybridisations.
In this drive lies a great potential for urban peripheries as a breeding ground for a change that leads towards new and sustainable urban networks, enhances life quality, and adapts to future challenges. In order to influence these transformations, it is necessary to understand the processes of alteration and to recognise the change agents behind these forces. Participatory action research methods can not only help to identify these actors, but also serve as starting points for action and empowerment of underrepresented populations. The unexplored value of historic centralities as persisting knots in the transforming territory bears an underestimated potential for these centres to become places of new impulses.

elements) and "buildings", which form the spatial aspects of the rhythm of the urban project. The three historical moments are 1950, just before the administrative incorporation; 1980, in a phase of conurbation, and 2016, the current state, as physically part of the city. On the one hand, these years mark similar intervals since the annexation in 1954, and on the other hand the exercise depends on the availability of maps of the six sites in the same periods.

Applying the mind-set of critical cartography that assumes that maps are never neutral representations of a territory, but that "they exercise power and they can be a powerful means of promoting social change" (Crampton, Krygier 2005, p. 15), the question of why and in which representation we will find the complete map material of the examined zones of the Bogotá area in these moments is crucial. This leads us to presume that the precise and unified mapping of the area that is currently the Capital District of Bogotá had the implication of analysing this area with a cartographic base for the political decision-making before its creation as district. Undoubtedly, Le Corbusier also had these maps as a basis for his proposal of the "Plan Piloto" for Bogotá in 1951, a plan that was never implemented, but which clearly includes a regional strategy for the circumjacent villages. In fact, the political-administrative annexation was executed during the government of General Rojas Pinilla, a representative of autocratic rule, who entirely ignored Le Corbusier's recommendations, which underscores the correlation of map-making and power. The plan material around the year 1980 is not homogenous, the creation dates fluctuate between 1978 and 1982 and are presented in different styles and scales; in one case there isn't even a map available but an aerial photo. One can interpret this as an advanced de-territorialisation or as a vanishing coherence of the relation of the former villages to Bogotá, as in this phase the former villages are mostly no longer traditional rural settlements but in different stages of becoming part of the city. The current maps, based on GIS datasets, stick strictly to the administrative limits of Bogotá and even include most of the informal settlements. But they omit the continuing settlement fabric towards neighbouring communities (Calderon 2016), which expresses a disputable representation of the territory and also hinders integrated planning.

However, the standardised plan synopsis of each site depicts the phases and principles of the urbanisation processes, determining similar developments and peculiarities of the transformation of the six villages. This will prove how and when the almost completed process of morphological union of each village with the city of Bogotá occurred. The conurbation has not followed the same scheme in the different cases, regarding the moment of connection, the size and character of the village at the time, and the use and morphological patterns and (non-)formality of the linking barrios (Cortés 2006). However, there are still many similarities in use, interconnection, and spatial configuration of the village cores that can be traced back to their common history. The reiterating generic spatial configuration of each *plaza* with its surrounding *cuadras* (Calderon 2016) proves the colonial origin of the villages and links them to the central *plaza* of Bogotá, as all of them were erected in the same period, according to principles that were later taken down in the *Leyes de Indias* (Salcedo 1996). Also, their function as poles of urban development can be identified in the consistency of connecting roads that later have been transformed into highways or elements such as cemeteries,

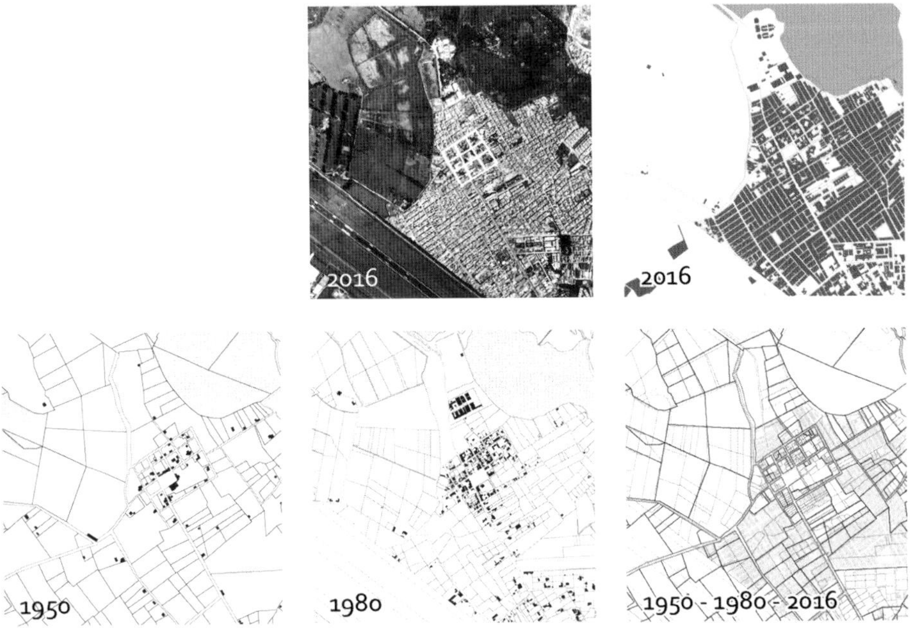

Figure 3. The *plaza* of Engativá, constancy in a changing environment. Graphic: Alissa Diesch

"Significant places do not lose their importance. Rather, we are interested in squares because they offer an open tableau for constantly changing social and urban use. They are at the same time places of conciseness and contingency" (Wolfrum 2014, p. 18). The peripheral fringe of the metropolis is not a homogenous compound of faceless neighbourhoods: it has structure and history, as well as places where this is shown in a condensed way. If the current city is based on former agricultural patterns, the previous rural places of concentration are still present within the now urbanised structures. In a process of reterritorialization, Europeans in Latin America often adopted existing indigenous habitat structures, interconnections, and positioning towards geographic features; places that had been proven to be smartly chosen and loaded with identity. On the same sites, colonial foundations altered the place by a generic spatial framework present in the central plaza, which has been crucial to its symbolic inauguration and following use. This spatial code makes them highly recognisable, three-dimensional signs of centrality and gathering that are still installed even in new residential areas. Every *barrio* has its tangible *plaza* (Fig. 2) that comes with its own imaginaries, formed by its usage and history. The potential of a century-old *plaza* for local identity and further development is a prolific source for future configuration of the suburban space, with new uses within established structures.

market halls, and railways stations, often still recognisable and sometimes even still in use. The origin of current street orientations and names of barrios can be explained by this exercise as well as the influence of former (hydro-)geographic features on the present morphology. The analysis of how land use and tenure structures have been transformed in use and subdivision, and of how settlement patterns have been adapted in their interrelation to geographic and hydrologic settings, can show and retell the "cultural aspect of the village system" (Reichenbach-Klinke 2010, p. 303) and its contribution to cultural landscape considerations. This knowledge could be used further on to propose a sustainable future urban development based on past structures that have proven their purpose for centuries.

To complement the study of social space, methods of Participation-Action-Research (PAR) and inventive methods are applied. These methods are qualitative and empirical, and no quantitative results will be obtained. The main characteristics of PAR are that the people express themselves as "active" protagonists and not "passive" research objects; their implicit knowledge is made explicit in a process that also empowers them to understand and consequently address their situation (Leal 2009). One methodology, mainly applied in Latin-America, is social cartography: inhabitants make maps, elaborated without specifications, of a site that expresses the subjective perception of their territory. They decide what and how to portray their habitat, which generates space to express meanings and ideas that cannot be transmitted with codes, techniques, and conventions offered by traditional maps (Corner 1999). This can be considered an inventive method, as the research approach is originating, open, and explorative and no hypothesis is to be proven (Wildner 2015). It is naturally another manifestation of critical cartography, expressing visions of "situated knowledge" (Haraway 1988) and contesting obsolete relations of power in cartography.

An interesting aspect concerning the rapid shift from villages to urban neighbourhoods, is how the past and the transforming processes can be made visible through this kind of mapping (Diez 2012). The inhabitants can express their "social significance" (Byrne 2008, p. 152) through cartography, including memories that are attached to material aspects that may have already vanished. Maps do not only have the potential to represent a territory, they are able to "[uncover] realities previously unseen or unimagined" (Corner 1999, p. 213), revealing new layers and aspects. The question is which aspects and meanings are represented in the final map. So expert-made maps are "true" and show measurable elements of the geographical and constructed territory, but a social cartography of the same site that expresses subjective "territorial data" that is "internal, not external" (Diez 2012, p. 18), is also "true".

In the PhD project presented here, social cartography will be conducted in combination with photography during a documented collective creation and selection process with community members of different generations in the former villages. Just like cartography, photography has for a long time been considered an "objective" method for reproducing reality, a fact that visual anthropologists have strongly questioned in the last fifty years, emphasising the influence images and photographs have on the construction and production of knowledge in social science (Casasbuenas, Diesch

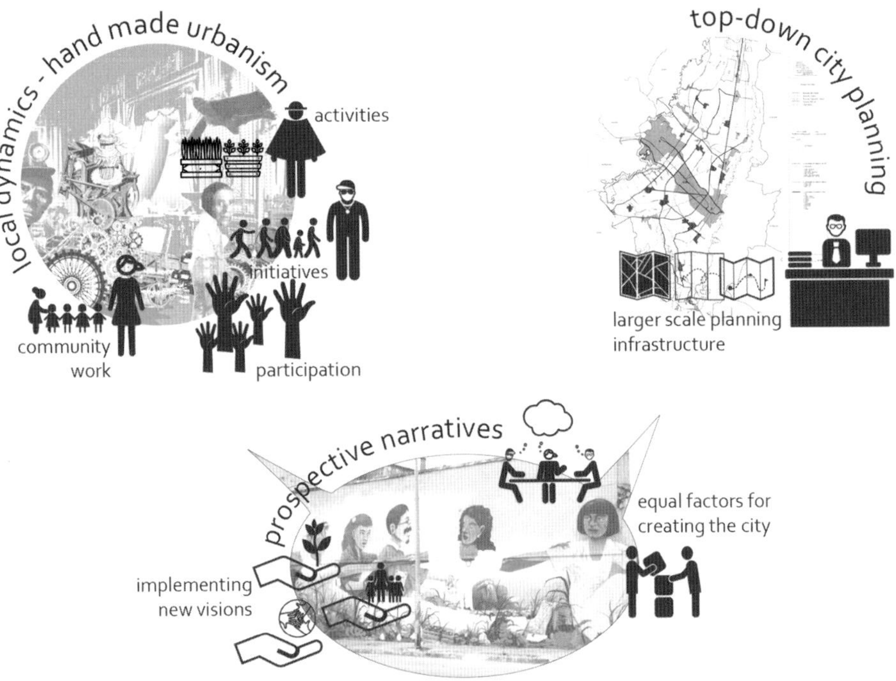

Figure 4. Connecting different agents in process of making the city.
Graphic: Alissa Diesch

The agency of imaginaries and narratives in Bogotá is strongly recognisable and for the urban development at least as powerful as official city planning. Prospective storytelling as part of a scenario strategy could be a valuable approach bridging the wide gap between local dynamics and top-down planning (Fig. 3). In an initial step, the challenges and driving forces on a very local level must be understood and visualised to develop, later on, a story addressing all actors. Inhabitants from working class neighbourhoods in Bogotá's periphery may thus have never heard of "public space" and "participation", but may nevertheless exercise it on a daily base with no official recognition. There are also countless initiatives and activities in the fields of youth, cultural, and ecological work in the communities, which in their majority are not interconnected on a larger scale or higher level of organisation. To make use of this underrated potential of local knowledge and organisation, the creation of scenarios allows the possibility of visualising these dynamics, for instance, through cartographies. Furthermore, they allow us to understand these dynamics as equal factors in creating the city by presenting them side by side with official territorial resources. As an outcome, prospective "change agents" can be identified and help spread and support a conceptualised narrative by strengthening and making the best use of ongoing processes. This also provides for territorial planning a tool set and a base for building new visions in order to direct transformations.

2017). Both methods have the ability to visualise things but also to make other aspects invisible (Giordano, Reyero 2011), thus questioning these osensibly "neutral" and positivist methods in a collective process which is part of this way of knowledge production.

Already established photo-social cartographies with students from two universities in Bogotá[2] prove the viability of this methodology (Casasbuenas, Diesch 2017) and demonstrate that an artistic and participative approach to representing the challenging or even impossible "objective representation of the metropolis"[3] (Solà-Morales, I. 2002, p. 73) by displaying "subjective cartographies"[4] (Solà-Morales, I. 2002, p. 74) is worthwhile, especially in the given context which does not provide any prior scientific material or documentation of the examined sites. It is also clear that this process needs documentation of the selection of materials, as well as interviews and written statements accompanying the visual materials.

Bibliography

Byrne D. (2008) "Heritage as Social Action". In: Fairclough G. et. al. eds. (2008) *The Heritage Reader*. London/New York, Routledge. pp. 149–74.

Calderón A. (2016) *Territorios simultáneos. Formas de territorialización de la Sabana de Bogotá*. PhD thesis. Barcelona, Department of Urban and Territorial Planning, UPC Universitat Politècnica de Catalunya.

Casasbuenas M., Diesch A. (2017) "Fotografía y cartografía social. Aproximaciones al patrimonio urbano de Bogotá". In: León P., Troya M. eds. (2017) *Mapear no es habitar*. 4° encuentro iberoamericano de arte, trabajo y economía (4EIATE). Quito, Arte-actual FLACSO. pp. 185–204.

Corner J. (1999) "The Agency of Mapping: Speculation, Critique and Invention". In: Cosgrove D. ed. (1999) *Mappings*. London, Reaktion Books. pp. 213–51.

Cortés M. (2006) *La anexión de los 6 municipios vecinos a Bogotá en 1954*. Bogotá, Universidad Nacional de Colombia.

Crampton J., Krygier J. (2005) "An Introduction to Critical Cartography". In: ACME: An International E-Journal for Critical Geographies, 4 (1). pp. 11–33.

Diez J. (2012) "Cartografía Social. Herramienta de intervención e investigación social compleja. El vertebramiento inercial como proceso mapeado". In: Diez J; Escudero B. eds. (2012) *Cartografía social. Investigación e intervención desde las ciencias sociales, métodos y experiencias de aplicación*. Comodoro Rivadavia, Universitaria de la Patagonia. pp. 13–25.

Giordano M., Rayero A. (2011) "Introducción". In: Giordano M., Rayero A. eds. (2011) *Identidades en foco. Fotografía e investigación social*. Resistencia, Universidad Nacional del Nordeste. pp. 13–24.

Haraway D. (1988) "Situated Knowledges: The Science Question in Feminism and the Privilege of Partial Perspective". In: Feminist Studies, 14 (3). pp. 575–99.

Leal F. (2009) "La Investigación Acción Participación, un aporte al conocimiento y a la transformación de Latinoamérica, en permanente movimiento". Revista de Investigación (Caracas), Nr. 67. pp. 13–34.

Reichenbach-Klinke M. (2010) "Cultural Landscape 1: New Farm Models in Agriculture". In: Schröder J, Weigert, K. eds. (2010) *Landraum*. Berlin, Jovis, pp. 300–303.

Salcedo J. (1996) *Urbanismo Hispano-Americano: Siglos XVI, XVII y XVIII, el modelo urbano aplicado a la América española, su génesis y su desarrollo teórico y práctico*. Bogotá, Pontificia Universidad Javeriana.

Solá-Morales I. (2002) *Territorios*. Barcelona, Gustavo Gili.

Solá-Morales M. (1986) "Las formas del crecimiento". In: Solá-Morales M. ed. (1997) *Las formas del crecimiento*. Barcelona, Ediciones UOC. pp. 19–22.

Wildner K. (2015) "Inventive Methods. Künstlerische Ansätze in der ethnographischen Stadtforschung". Ethnoscripts (Hamburg), 17. pp. 168–85.

Wolfrum S. (2015) *Squares: Urban Spaces in Europe*. Basel, Birkhäuser.

Peri-Cities

Nicola Valentino Canessa

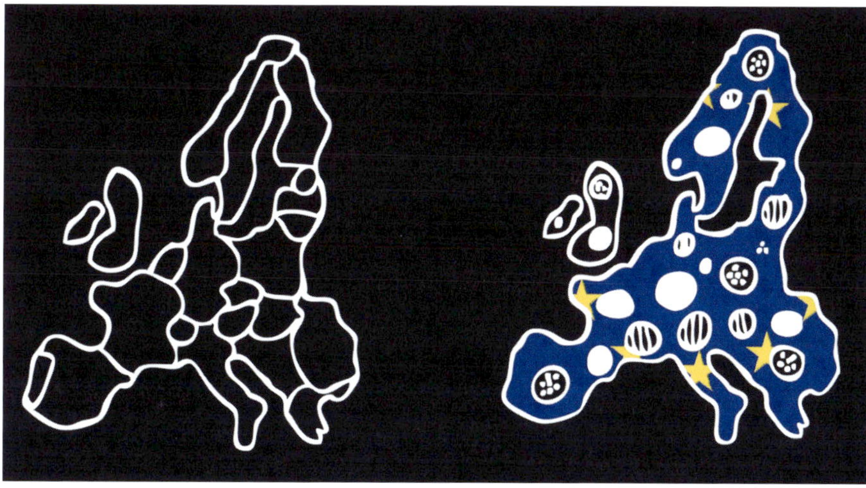

Figure 1. Reflection on the Peri-City in the European future: out of limits or new enclave?
Graphic: Nicola Canessa

The city of the future is in the suburbs: in fact, urbanisation should be in an implosive phase (not a decrease) that should connect and bring out the human and social potential of the city of today. Suburbs have garnered increasing international attention over the last few years, especially in light of the discontent of the youth in European peripheries that, in recent years, has resulted in social tension with often tragic consequences (consider, for example, the Parisian banlieue. Throughout history, cities have been at the centre of change, from the spread of Greek and Roman civilisations, through the Italian Renaissance, to the industrial revolution in the United Kingdom. Over time, Europe has slowly transformed from being a largely rural and agricultural community and, according to the United Nations, more than half of the European population was living in an urban area by 1950; this was also the case in North America and Oceania.

According to the United Nations (World Urbanisation Prospects, 2014), approximately two-thirds of the world's population will be living in an urban area by 2050. This rapid pace of change is projected to be driven primarily by changes in Africa and Asia, as the focus of global urbanisation-patterns continues to shift towards developing and emerging economies. The pace of change in Europe will likely be slower, with the share of the population living in urban areas projected to rise to just over 80% by 2050. Aside from the considerable differences in shares of urban populations across continents, there are also widespread differences between countries.

UN also provides information on the share of the urban population in 2016, which peaked (among those countries shown) in Argentina and Japan (2010 data) at over 90%. Just over half (54.3%) the population of China was living in an urban area in 2016, while the urban population in India (2011

Figure 2. World City Population 1950-2030. Source: UN World Urbanisation Prospect 2014

The United Nations defines a megacity as having in excess of 10 million inhabitants. According to this criterion, there are only two megacities within the European Union (EU), Paris and London. Of the top thirty global agglomerations in 2015, all but one of these—the Peruvian capital of Lima (9.9 million inhabitants)—are classified as a megacity.

Of the twenty-nine megacities in 2015, Tokyo (Japan) was the world's largest city; its agglomeration numbered 38.0 million inhabitants. This was followed by Delhi (India) with 25.7 million; Shanghai (China) with 23.7 million; Mexico City (Mexico), Mumbai (India), and São Paulo (Brazil), each with around 21 million; and Beijing (China) and Osaka (Japan), each with just over 20 million inhabitants. The populations of Paris and London were—in global terms—relatively small, as each had less than 11 million inhabitants; in other words they were less than one-third the size of Tokyo. There were two other European cities in the ranking, the Turkish city of Istanbul (14.2 million inhabitants) and the Russian capital of Moscow (12.2 million inhabitants).

data) accounted for less than one-third (31.1%) of the total number of inhabitants. The spatial distribution of cities varies considerably: Europe is generally characterised by a high number of relatively small cities and towns that are distributed in a polycentric fashion. This reflects, to some degree, its historical past which has led to a fragmented pattern of around fifty countries being spread over the continent. By contrast, in some parts of Asia and North America, a relatively high proportion of the urban population is concentrated in a small number of very large cities.

Urban areas in the EU are often characterised by high concentrations of economic activity, employment, and wealth with the daily flow of commuters into many of Europe's largest cities suggesting that opportunities abound in these hubs of innovation, distribution, and consumption. However, cities in the EU are also characterised by a range of social inequalities, and it is commonplace to find people who enjoy a comfortable life living in close proximity to others who may face considerable challenges, for example, in relation to housing, poverty, or crime—herein lies the "urban paradox". These polarised opportunities/challenges are often in stark contrast, as patterns of inequality in cities are generally more widespread than those observed for countries as a whole.

There are considerable differences in the size and spatial distribution of urban developments across the EU member states: for example, The Netherlands is characterised by a high level of population density and a high share of urban land use, whereas in most of the Nordic member states and the interior of the Iberian Peninsula much lower levels of urban land-use are common. Each of the EU member states has a distinctive history of territorial developments: for example, centrally-planned economies and the lack of a market for land/property resulted in compact urban developments across most eastern and Baltic member states. Since the middle of the last century, most of Europe has been characterised by spreading cities and increased population numbers, with people choosing to move out of inner cities to suburban and peri-urban areas (hybrid areas of fragmented urban and rural characteristics); this has resulted in the divide between urban and rural areas becoming increasingly blurred.

Capital cities have the potential to play a crucial role in urban developments within the EU; they are often hubs for competitiveness and employment, and may be seen as drivers of innovation and growth, and as centres for education, science, and for social, cultural, and ethnic diversity. A comparison of European cities' economic performance indicates that the major cities—and in particular, the metropolitan regions of EU capital cities—generally outperform the rest. In some EU member states, capital cities exert a form of "capital magnetism", through a monocentric pattern of urban development which attracts investment/resources so these are concentrated in the capital. Whether such disparities have a positive or negative effect on the national economy is open to debate, as capital cities that dominate their national economies may create high levels of income and wealth that radiate to surrounding regions and pull other cities/regions up.

Smart cities may be defined as those which seek to address public issues via ICT-based solutions involving multi-stakeholder partnerships. Smart cities have the potential to improve the quality of

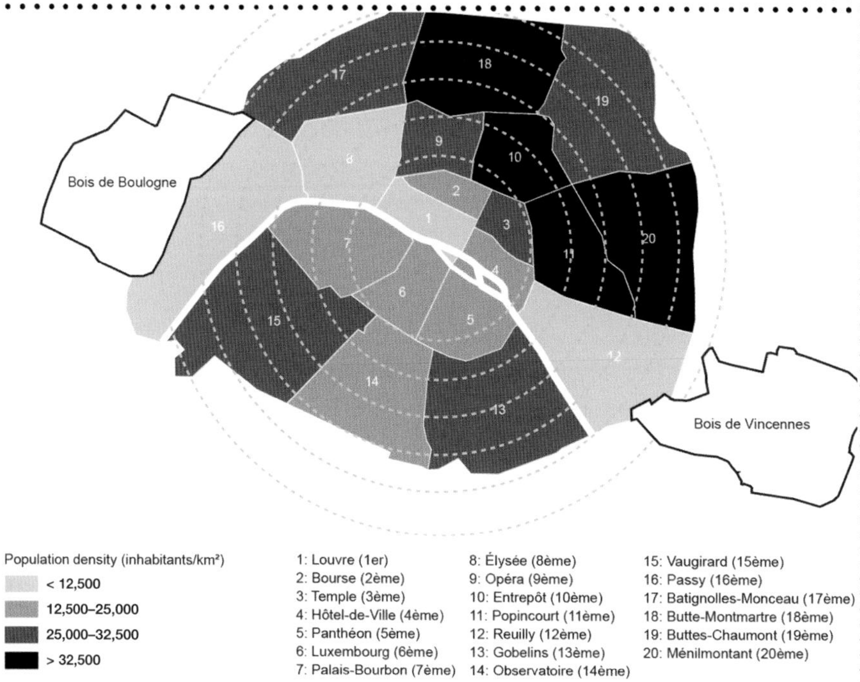

Figure 3. Paris: population density. Source: Eurostat

Considering the highest levels of population density for local administrative units in each of the EU member states, significant differences across the states and within the same state can be noted. For example, the most densely populated local administrative unit in France was the eleventh *arrondissement* of Paris (42,138 inhabitants/km^2 in 2014), where population density was more than forty times as high as in the most densely populated area of Slovenia, the capital Ljubljana (1,044 inhabitants/km^2 in 2015).

In a majority of the EU member states, the highest level of population density, by local administrative unit, was recorded in (part of) the capital city. There were however a number of exceptions of non-capital cities with higher population density ratios: Plovdiv (Bulgaria), Munich (Germany), Emperador in the northern suburbs of Valencia (Spain), Rijeka (Croatia), Casavatore in the northern suburbs of Napoli (Italy), Esch-sur-Alzette (Luxembourg), 's-Gravenhage (the Netherlands), Legionowo to the north of Warszawa (Poland), and Košice (Slovakia).

The population in the eleventh arrondissement of Paris (to the north and east of the Place de la Bastille; see Fig. 3), was almost twice as high as the average for the whole of the city, and was at least four times as high as in four arrondissements running along the right bank of the river Seine.

life: they are innovative, making traditional networks and services more efficient through social innovation and the use of digital technologies, creating more inclusive, sustainable, and connected cities for the potential benefit of their inhabitants, public administrations, and businesses. Smart cities are generally characterised by very high concentrations of people having completed a higher education, while statistics on innovation activity confirm that they also record a high propensity to patent.

In keeping with many aspects of urban development, tourism is a paradox, insofar as an increasing number of tourists in some towns and cities has resulted in congestion/saturation which may damage the atmosphere and local culture that made them attractive in the first place; Venezia (Italy) and Barcelona (Spain) are two of the most documented examples. Furthermore, while tourism has the potential to generate income which may be used to redevelop/regenerate urban areas, an influx of tourists can potentially lower the quality of life for local inhabitants, for example, through: higher levels of pollution and congestion, new retail formats replacing traditional commerce, increased prices, or increased noise.

Migrants have historically played an important role in demographic and economic developments within the EU, particularly in some of Europe's largest cities. However, the selective nature of migratory patterns is such that migrant destinations are often restricted to relatively few, large cities, which tend to receive a disproportionate number of immigrants. These patterns are often accentuated as first-wave migrants who establish themselves in a particular part of a city subsequently encourage relatives and friends to follow them.

The metropolitan regions of capital cities have often recorded some of the highest rates of net migration, with Greater London having the highest number of foreign-born inhabitants, at almost three million. Foreign-born populations living in urban regions were typically of working age and a majority were born outside of the EU, although in Luxembourg almost one-third of the total population was born in another EU member state.

Young people tend to live in the suburbs of some of the largest cities in the EU. Aside from attracting (potential) business investment, cities also need to attract individuals: this can be done through the quality of what they can offer in terms of education, jobs, social experiences, culture, sports and leisure facilities, environment, or urban safety. The results suggest that a high proportion of Europe's ageing population lives in relatively small towns and cities (with a preference to live on the coast), whereas younger people are more likely to live in the suburbs within close proximity of capital or other large cities. But the suburbs today are not only the encoded spaces; today we have suburbs beyond the suburbs and peripheral enclaves within the urban core. We could almost say that the periphery is everywhere.

Many areas are being abandoned and, with new European funding, people are moving towards the reactivation of the peripheral areas, with incentives to agriculture, culture, and creativity. And this

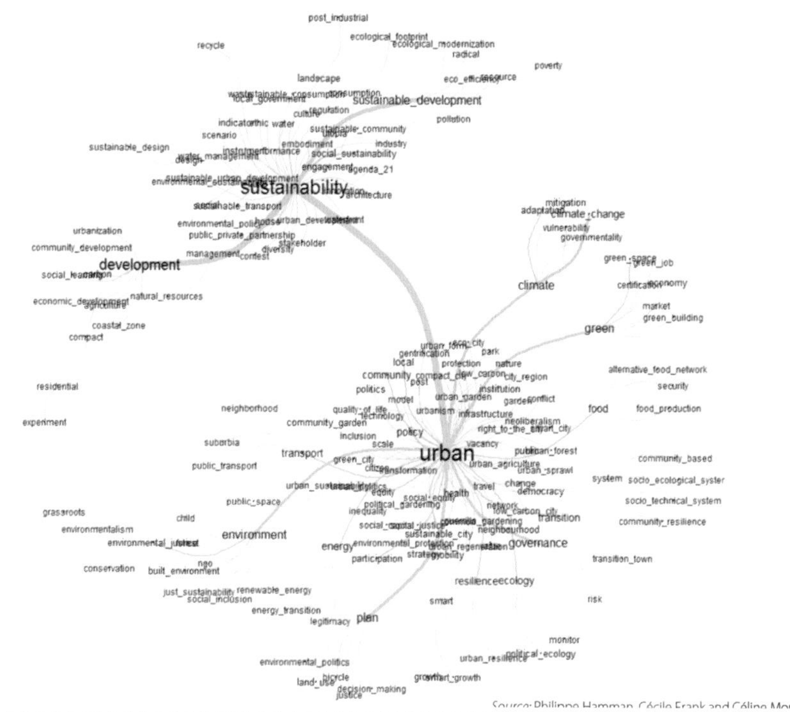

Figure 4. Strength of ties between terms associated with the "sustainable city". Graphic: author, based on Ph. Hamman et.al.

Given the growing number of people who are living in cities and the fact that cities are often the source of and can potentially provide the solution to many of today's economic, social and environmental challenges, these urban territories are increasingly under the spotlight of policy makers. The revised 2014–20 cohesion policy framework introduced a set of eleven thematic objectives to support growth.

European structural and investment funds were reassessed, and additional recognition was given to the role that urban territories can play in economic development, as well as the linkages that exist between urban and rural regions. Some ten billion EUR of European Regional Development Fund resources were foreseen for initiatives linked to sustainable urban development, covering areas such as urban mobility, the regeneration of deprived communities, improving research and innovation capacity, or tackling climate change.

The European Union's urban agenda involves cities in the design of policies, so they may play a key role in translating national and EU policy objectives into specific actions. Signed during the Dutch presidency in 2016, the Pact of Amsterdam established the operational framework for the EU's urban agenda and it also set-up four thematic partnership projects relating to: air quality; migrants and refugees; housing; urban poverty.

also binds certain actions in progress that foster the relocation of migrants in the smaller centres, in a sort of repopulation.

Revitalising the suburbs through the action of the young and the voluntary sector is a positive initiative, which goes precisely in the direction of the effort to be undertaken by Europe to recover the long delay in the support and enhancement of the redevelopment of peripheries. After meeting in the last century the great challenge of the preservation of the historic centres of our cities, the suburbs and all contexts that seem peripheral are the great challenge of the next twenty years.

Bibliography

Angelini A. (2007) *Mediterraneo. Città, culture, ambiente, governance, migranti.* Bologna, Franco Angeli.
Boeri S. (2003) *USE: Un viaggio nell'Europa che cambia*. Milano, Skira editore.
Carta M. (2014) *Reimagining Urbanism*. Trento, List editore.
Eurostat (2016) *Urban Europe Statistics on Cities, Towns and Suburbs*. Luxembourg, Publications office of the European Union.
Gausa M. (2010) *Open*. Barcelona, Actar.
Leonitidou L. (1990) *City in Transition. Social Change and Urban Development*. Cambridge, Cambridge University Press.

Matera-Basilicata 1950–2019

Chiara Rizzi

The purpose of this article is to provide some aspects of dynamics of periphery starting from the case study of the city of Matera. This will provide a vantage point to observe the contemporary city in a perspective towards territorial creativity and in relationship to the processes of gentrification in cities characterised by a high concentration of historical assets and local traditions. Over the years Matera was transformed in a field of urban tests in which different images of the city were superimposed. These images have undergone a process of hybridisation and have characterised the different meanings of "laboratory city" that Matera assumed: from the laboratory of modern architecture and urbanism in the 1950s to the laboratory of a culture city of today. During the last years Matera has been living a "new renaissance" based on its cultural heritage. This is a great opportunity for its development, but at the same time it could prove to be a failure if the city is not able to elaborate a comprehensive vision beyond 2019, when Matera will be European Capital of Culture.

The Periphery Doesn't Exist

In common imagination Matera coincides with its Sassi, a specific form of houses caved into rocks. If you search on google images using the key word "Matera", you will get only images of Sassi. Panoramas, monuments, souvenir photos, movie locations, hotel or b&b advertising—everything is conveyed through the image of the Sassi. This is a compelling imagination that though is evidently constructed. If we look the Sassi from the top, time seems to have stopped. Matera seems to be a static city, where nothing has changed over the years, a "beautiful nativity scene" and nothing more. It is not only a question of how you direct your view, but it is the consequence of a concept and of an idea of the city. In the last two decades, more or less since the Sassi of Matera has been declared a UNESCO World Heritage Site, the city has undergone a mutation of its DNA. It has quickly transformed from a farming town into a touristic town. This process has been accelerated by the recognition of Matera as European Capital of Culture. In the past seven years the number of Matera's visitors has increased of 152.4%, more than of Rome (+30.6%), Florence (+25.2%), or Venice (22.3%) (Source: Centro Studi Turistici di Firenze). From 2015 to 2016 the number of tourist arrivals increased from 353,645 to 409,421, almost equivalent to a rise of +16% in one year. In the same period the number of accommodation establishments increased from 301 to 482, almost equivalent to a rise of +60%. Only by comparing this data with that of a few years ago is it possible to measure how this phenomenon is deeply influencing urban dynamics. In 1999, the number of tourist arrivals was approximately 88,000 (Source: APT Regione Basilicata). This is a phenomenon of enormous dimension if we consider that the city has little more than 60,000 inhabitants and that,

Figure 1. "Racconto di un popolo di statue". Exhibition by Pietro Guida, Sassi, Matera 2016. Photo: A. De Sanctis

The urban history of Matera represents a unique chapter in the history of the modern urban age in Italy. Over the last decades the urban processes have been strongly influenced by two main socio-anthropological issues: the caves and the agricultural nature of the area.

After the Second World War, the great success of Carlo Levi's book *Christ Stopped at Eboli* disclosed to Italy and to the world the "case of Matera". According to a definition of Palmiro Togliatti, an Italian politician, Matera became "the shame of Italy". The debate prompted by the case of the Sassi runs through the whole recent history of the city and is the main issue to outline its perspectives for the future.

Over the years, Matera was transformed in a field of urban tests in which different images of the city were superimposed. These images have undergone a process of hybridisation and have characterised the different meanings of "city lab" that Matera assumed: laboratory of modern architecture and urbanism (the master plan by Luigi Piccinato and architectural competitions for new neighbourhoods); anthropological laboratory (research projects of Friedmann and De Martino); socio-territorial laboratory (working group of the sociologist Aldo Musacchio *Il Politecnico* and the regional planning initiative by Adriano Olivetti); socio-political laboratory (the journal "Basilicata" and the association *Circolo la Scaletta*); cultural laboratory of Matera 2019 (Mininni 2017).

since 2014, its demographic balance is negative (Source: ISTAT, 2016). The effects are evident. The Sassi, once the shame of Italy, a neglected and inhospitable place, have become the centre of economic interests of the city and the region. Almost all activities are organised connected the tourist product "Sassi". From this point of view, Matera as the city of Sassi, periphery do not exist. But this is obviously a provocation and a simplification. Extending our view and considering the complexity of the physical and social structure of the city, we soon discover that the two correlative concepts centre-periphery constitute an unsuitable paradigm for describing and interpreting Matera's reality. It is precisely the city's urban history that puts it in crisis. Moreover, the Sassi were, at alternate stages, centre and periphery and today they include both definitions. The process of contemporary "colonisation" of the Sassi creates a large number of dysfunctionalities that dissolve the geographical, social, and political boundaries that characterise and legitimize the dichotomy between centre and periphery. It is not necessarily a sign of courage to say that the periphery is gone, at least as we knew it. It has simply disappeared because it shows no longer the connotations and the characters that have allowed us to recognise it (Ciorra 2010).

The Periphery is Everywhere

It is no longer possible to recognise the periphery because it is everywhere. This statement only apparently stands in contrast to the previous observations, and it shifts the reflection from a physical-geographical perspective to a socio-cultural one. The Sassi are peripheral if we consider their emptying of any function that is not specialised for tourism. The modern neighbourhoods are central if we replace the parameters of distance, difference, and dependence with those of dynamism, innovation, and action. The modern Matera was born with the help of the law on "Reconstruction of the Sassi" of 1952. This law marks the beginning of an organic intervention on the city guided by a polycentric view that identified the Sassi as a great void, as an absence. The master plan of Luigi Piccinato in 1953-56 established the *damnazio memoriae* of the "shame of Italy". The plan marked a turning point of meanings, new neighbourhoods became the new centres in which farming communities can find new identification. The new city, organised through two connective spaces characterised by infrastructure and green networks, is designed as the sum of the neighbourhoods that were called "Scandinavian" for wide range of collective and green spaces and for the quality of detailling in urban design.

"Paradoxically, this ideal city was unsuitable to host the former habitants of the Sassi. Rural villages in the Sassi were soon abandoned. The new neighbourhoods, called *rioni* assume the connotation of neighbourhood-ghetto, places of a humanity eradicated from its natural habitat. The emptied Sassi entered into a progressive physical-structural deprivation and partly began to serve as a degraded residential fringe for recent urban immigrants and for the poor" (Rota 2011). Already in the early nineteen-seventies, in Matera the periphery was everywhere. In the following decades, urban development followed this direction even if it had different trajectories and shapes. The contemporary city inherits, from the past, this situation of uncertainty and of an inability to orient toward the several socio-economical changes it has experienced. Moreover, the complex sequence of events

Figure 2. Spring in Lanera, Matera 2017. Photo: A. De Sanctis

Each of these iterations of "city lab" added or transformed parts of the city and modified landscapes. In particular, the framework of the master plan of Piccinato from 1954 is based on the development of new and organic neighbourhoods and on the completion of rural villages with the realisation of La Martella, Borgo Venusio, Torre Spagnola, and of two areas for services, Picciano and Timmari (Aymonino 1959). The new neighbourhoods called *rioni* were developed as new centralities. The particular condition created by the evacuation of Sassi was the opportunity to develop a new urban design based on a polycentric model. The Sassi became the periphery of new city centres, no planning framework was set up for this area before the 1990s: in fact, in the master plan of Piccinato the area of the Sassi was "marked off" with a grey pattern. Today, Matera has about 60,000 inhabitants, of wich only 1,491 live in the Sassi. About 30% of the population lives in the parts of the city built between the 1950s and the 1960s. Two more quarters are a sort of buffer zone between the Sassi and the *rioni* in which most public services are concentrated. Built with a very strong social aspiration, the quarters of the *rioni* have undergone a long period of "peripheralisation" that has reduced collective services to a state of semi-abandonment. It is an important available asset for reimagining a more creative and adaptive city, a new urban culture, starting from the opportunity of Matera 2019.

of the Sassi's renewal started with the controversial International competition of 1975, highlighting an inherent weakness: a total incapability of "being a city". In 2010, the architect Luigi Acito wrote that "the Sassi are once more part of the 'city'. Their ancient fabric, now in two-thirds rehabilitated, as well as a fair number of housing units recovered (about 600) is teeming with activities linked to enhancing the urban and historical-cultural heritage. Today, Matera lives an exciting adventure as a city that has transformed the protection and the enhancement of its past into a key, perhaps the most important one, for its future" (Acito, 2010). Well, the future has come, but the Sassi are no longer a city.

Beyond Matera-Basilicata 2019

The future in Matera came with a new big challenge: its proclamation as the European Capital of Culture in 2019. The new fame of the city is producing an effect comparable to that of Sassi's rehabilitation law: the emptying of the Sassi and the expulsion of its inhabitants to other areas of the city. No residential activity seems to be able to compete with an older law than that of 1952: real estate rent. New types of "colonisation" overlap with historic fabric transforming it into a sort of fetish for touristic consumption.

Souvenir shops replace craft shops and neighbourhood shops are replaced by fast food in a local version. For each living room you will find a plaque advertising a b&b or of a holiday home. An interesting study of the Laboratory of Socio-Geographical Research of the University of Siena, based in the Department of Political and Cognitive Sciences (LADEST), reveals that the phenomenon of economic sharing is expanding this process. It aims to examine "the 'airification' of cities: towards a qualification of the impact of peer-to-peer short-term letting for urban functions and economy" and states critically that "Italians also seem to be ignoring the controversy which the fast rise of Airbnb has generated around the world: accusations of driving up rents, depleting the residential housing market, and, as is the case in Barcelona, turning entire neighbourhoods into twenty-four-hour party zones, to the bewilderment of residents". In a comparison of the data concerning housing stock devoted to short term rentals (STR) in thirteen Italian historic centres, Matera had the highest quote with 25%—more than Florence (18%) and Rome (8%) (Picascia et al. 2017).

This phenomenon should not be stigmatised but analysed with the aim of developing a more comprehensive strategy for the future of the city beyond 2019, the year as Cultural Capital of Europe. Once again, it seems obvious that Matera is considered to be a sum of specialized parts, or worse, as a great setting. The opportunity of 2019 would be missed for the city if it gives up on a real renewal of its urban and social fabric. Some of the processes implemented by the Foundation of Matera-Basilicata 2019 go in this direction, but they still seem too shy. "Gardentopia", for example, aims to regenerate some abandoned or underused spaces of modern neighbourhoods with recycling processes and shared urban practices of designing and management. However, resources and projects are totally inadequate for outlining a strategic vision for the future city. Consistently with its history, Matera should take this opportunity to start a new season of its identity as "city lab"

Figure 3. Agoragri, Matera, 2017. Photo: Rocco Giove

"Gardentopia" is a strategy for Matera 2019. It belongs to a cluster called "The Caring City". This cluster belongs to the theme "Utopias and Dystopias". Utopias and dystopias refer to the history of Matera, from Rocco Scotellaro's poems to Ludovico Quaroni and Giancarlo De Carlo's urban experiments. According to the dossier of candidature, Matera 2019 aims to test radical new models that challenge assumptions—the assumption that tourism is the only viable path towards economic stability for southern cities, that technology is the only possible mediator for relationships, that industrial monoculture is the only path to affluence, and that gourmet food and wine are the main identity-generating factors in a given area. Gardentopia is a strategic view of regeneration for abandoned areas. It focuses on underused, degraded, or abandoned green areas of the *rioni*. By now, the following projects have been carried out: "The Garden of Moments" (Lanera), "White Ears" (Spine Bianche) and Agoragri (Serra Venerdì and S. Giacomo).

"Agoragri" is a public urban park with a synergic vegetable garden, a theatre of straw, family gardens and a wooden pavilion for events. It is a project of the association Agrinetural and was designed by Meson-ro studio and studio GRRIZ with the collaboration of artist Alex Wilde. It has been realised in collaboration with experts, volunteers, and citizens, with the support of students from the University of Basilicata (from the course of landscape, environment and urban green), with many technical partners, and with the economic contribution of public and private sponsors.

from its cultural heritage. Creativity, innovation, and sharing should be the three key words of this urban programme. All resources should agree on it, from the regeneration project of the Piccianello district that was recently funded by the government with thirteen million Euro, within the national regeneration programme for the periphery. There are many design proposals for the neighborhood of Piccianello. For example, "Boulevard Matera 2019", "La via del carro", is a proposal by the Nature-City Lab of the University of Basilicata that focuses on Piccianello and its connection with the centre. The proposal aims to redesign the main street, from "La fabbrica del carro" to the core of the city, transforming it into a pedestrian street and regenerating its proximity areas.

Every year, on 2 July, this route becomes a triumphal avenue of access to the city. It is here, in fact, that the traditional ritual of the "Triumphal Chariot" has been renewed for more than six centuries. After that day, the city comes back to its ordinary rhythm of life. In the light of everyday life, it is possible to read all the contradictions of an urban narrative often made of isolated and fragmented episodes, characterised by casual juxtapositions of degraded and abandoned open spaces. "Boulevard Matera 2019" an experimental research started during the process of applying for the city as the European Capital of Culture. "Fare strada Matera" is "a design activity in the part of the city once called the periphery" that recognises the road as the space in which it is possible to reset three different periods of the city: "'the 'cyclic' time of nature regeneration; the 'scopic' time of techniques of ecological reconversion of city life (and work); the 'eschatological' circulation of a common" (Sichenze, Macaione, 2016). The proposal addresses critically urban emerging issues and considers 2019 as the beginning of a new cycle and not its ending.

Bibliography

Acito L. (2010) "I sassi di matera. Storia di un restauro urbano". In: *Urbanistica,* nr. 141/2010. pp. 9–14 (translation by the author).
Aymonino C. (1959) "Matera: mito e realtà". In: *Casabella Continuità,* nr. 231/1959. pp. 9–10.
Ciorra P. (2010) "La fine delle periferie". In: *Dizionario del XXI secolo*. Roma, Treccani.
Mininni M. (2017) *MateraLucania2017: laboratorio città paesaggio*. Macerata, Quodlibet. pp. 43–44.
Picascia S., Romano A., Teobaldi M. (2017) "The Airification of Cities: Making Sense of the Impact of Peer to Peer Short Term Letting on Urban Functions and Economy". In: *Proceedings of the Annual Congress of the Association of European Schools of Planning*, Lisbon 11–14 July 2017.
Rota L. (2011) *Matera, storia di una città. Matera*, Edizioni Giannatelli (translation by the author).
Sichenze A., Macaione I. (2016), "Ischia 2012, fare stradanel tempo della città-natura: tracce, tracciati, traiettorie". In: Macaione I. (2016) *Città Natura, visioni attraverso l'architettura italiana*. Trento-Barcelona, ListLab. p. 191 (translation by the author).

Hybrid Alps: Sustainable Strategies for Alpine Peri-Urban Areas

Alessandro Betta

Statistics and studies show clearly how the world's population is constantly moving from rural to urban areas and how cities around the world are steadily increasing their inhabitants and their footprint. More than half of the world's population is now living in urban areas compared to 30% in 1950. Moreover, according to a recent study from the World Bank, forty-six of the so-called global cities are ranked among the first hundred areas according to their GDP. Cities as Tokyo, London, or São Paulo each produce more GDP than countries like Mexico or Switzerland; plus they contribute to a huge share of their national GDP. Apparently then, we are living in the age of cities, in an age when urban areas are at forefront both in theoretical and political discourse. It has to be said, though, that there are many shadows and weak points in such a vision of our globe. It is at least an oversimplification of the reality.

Towards a Critic. The Peri-Urban Revolution

Since the seventies, cities have faced fast and radical changes in their structure all over the world. Since the French philosopher Henri Lefebvre wrote his books on the anthropological dimension of the urban phenomenon (or urban revolution as he called it) the term “urban” became more and more central in theoretical and political discourses. This term has to be used (as Lefebvre did) not only in a spatial sense but more as a socio-economical feature of territory (Lefebvre 1970). One of the first research questions posed by this work is whether it is still possible to use the category “urban” to describe current situations of the territory. It is only an apparent paradox to say that while more and more people are moving towards urban areas the very idea of urbanity is disappearing. UN statistics showing that population is moving to cities are in some way of “artefacts” and even that they are incoherent (Brenner 2014).

I would say that both booming and shrinking cities around the world are becoming borderless amoebae; collections of hybrid and fluid spaces without edges rather than coherent urban entities. “Nature” infiltrates spaces while cities are shrinking as in Detroit, or formless growth leaves empty “natural” spots while cities are booming as in China, India, or Africa. Research tries to sustain the idea that the world is becoming peri-urban rather than urban, that urban cores are losing importance compared to their hybrid peripheral surroundings. Such territories call for different paradigms to be investigated and, moreover, these paradigms need to not originate from those used until now by urban theories and planning (Jakob 2008).

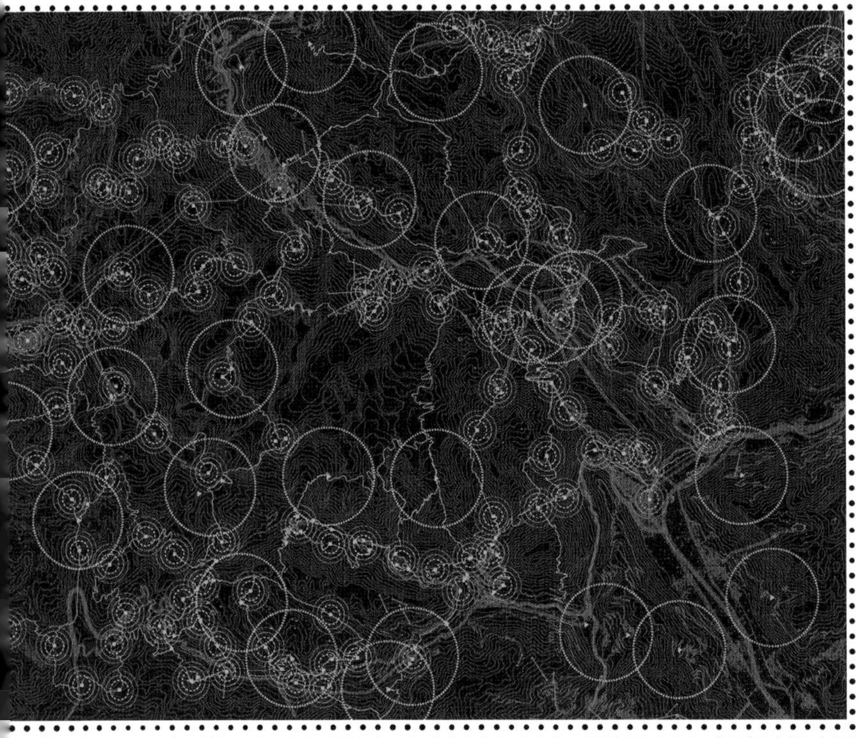

Figure 1. Strategical energy master plan for Mont Blanc territory. Graphic: Alessandro Betta 2015

Peripheral areas could be described as "unstable" territories, as areas open to experimentation. Due to their instability these areas are the most open to innovation and innovative processes. Ecological paradigms, if properly adapted, could be starting points to transform peripheral areas and to make them into "motherboards" for activating social and environmental energies. The search for a different logic has to overcome several typical paradigms of modernity. First, the role of architecture and architectural objects; in peripheral areas patterns of small scale interventions are much more effective than single strong figures that stand out of the ground (Fig.1). Another paradigm that should at least overlap with planning strategies for peripheral areas is the "industrial" approach to infrastructure seeking for maximum efficiency of single elements rather than the performativity of the overall territorial system. Administrative boundaries and functional divisions have to be erased in order to release the potentialities of fringes, resulting in heterogeneous, continuous, and performative morphologies. Moreover, as an open field, peripheries can welcome transformations related to complex urban green infrastructure requirements that will merge some parts of the urban with "techno-natural" elements. Participation of citizens is here fundamental to catalyse transformations, as willingness to change is stronger than any other part of the city. It is a matter of activation rather than integration.

Previous Experiments: Agrarian Urbanism

What has been called the "peri-urban revolution" in the previous section traces its roots back to some theoretical models proposed during twentieth century by architects like Frank Lloyd Wright, Ludwig Hilbersheimer, or Andrea Branzi. All of them pursued the idea of dissolving the city into nature following paradigms that art and science were pursuing at that time (Cattaneo 2014). The three models cannot be considered exactly as evolutions of each other but rather as reconceptualisations of the same idea.[1] Wright's Broadacre City is probably the most similar to what today has become typical western suburbia of single-family houses. It has to be said that in his case plots were thought as agricultural land for families' self-consumption rather than as gardens. Hilbersheimer went beyond this concept in proposing a pattern rather than a model for a city that would overcome boundaries between urban and nature ("ruralizing the city and urbanizing the nature").[2]

Neither of the two was able differentiate themselves from an industrial logic of space production, as the proposals were based on the role of grey infrastructures and industries as backbones for urbanisation. Years later Italian designer Andrea Branzi, drawing from previous experiments, explored a possible new model adapted to the post-industrial contemporary age. In the Agronica model, Branzi conceptualises an urban pattern at the intersection of agriculture, technology, and mobility to form territories beyond urbanity. Being part of Branzi's search for models of weak urbanisation, Agronica began as a theoretical investigation of the possibilities for less rigid territorial devices that would allow for the realization of more intermediate and flexible zoning. In this case urban grey infrastructure is not the backbone of the settlement's pattern since the intention was clearly to explore post-industrial territories (Waldheim 2010). Both Branzi and Hilbersheimer chose to represent their models more like systems of flows and relations rather than with figurative elements in order to express this change of paradigm. It is impossible not to recognise the role that these models have had in the development of recent theories on urbanism and landscape, and therefore it is not possible to set up a discourse on "peri-urbanity" and new strategies for urban areas without considering such proposals. To sustain what will be said later, it is important to recognise the assumption of a constant decentralisation of cities (which is a current phenomenon on a global scale) and landscape becoming a category used to determine interventions on urban areas.

Proposition

The research questions proposed by this article move from the consideration that a different approach to peripheral areas is needed. As the urban paradigm entered a deep crisis in spite of its apparent popularity within technical and political discussions, a different perception and glossary have to be introduced to face this complex situation. It is ot only a matter of redefining the concept of periphery to consider it as something different and capable of generating its own paradigms, but it is also a matter of finding possible categories of intervention, given the unstable and hybrid nature of peripheries. This very special nature of peripheral areas requires me to specify several terms in order to frame this research.

Figure 2. Alpine and peri-alpine settlement density. Image: Alessandro Betta 2015

Fringes are by-products of “a capitalist mode of production of space”, spaces of an incomplete colonisation by infrastructure and industries. There is an apparent contradiction in saying that peripheral areas are able to become reserves of resilience for future changes. Pressure by infrastructure and settlement is at its limit and calls for a radical change in planning approaches (Fig. 2). As the relation between artefacts and nature is blurred and becomes more open, it leaves a large space for establishing different systemic relations based on ecological paradigms. In terms of biodiversity and ecological connectivity, fringes represent fundamental bypasses and infiltration axes for nature into the urban fabric. They work as urban ecotones where ecological elements are connected with social and economical activities in a mutually positive relation. Once, these areas were symbols of a kind of development without any regard for soil and resources consumption; this is why nowadays they are fundamental as the "last line of defence" to avoid urban settlement to completely destroying agricultural and natural lands. As ecotones are something different from the simple sum of surrounding ecosystems, peripheries are more than simple intermediaries but rather fields of exploration for experimenting with different urban forms and capable of combining ecology and artificial environments.

Weak Fringes

Even if the two words in my title apparently have a "bad" meaning, I use them here in order to strengthen the role and importance of peripheral areas. The term "weak" could be explained in a spatial sense meaning territories which are undefined, in-between "nature" and "urban" and therefore without a precise definition and perception of use. But if we consider the term in a broader sense, it is linked with philosophical approaches claiming more trans-disciplinary and less self-confident research and projects able to cope with multiple realities of our peripheries, and which therefore go beyond dual, dogmatic, and positivist theories (Vattimo 2010). As the meaning of "weak thought" is related to the need to overcome a sort of dialectic structure of reality, research attempts at the same time tries to push forward the idea that these areas have their own structure and are not simply something "different" from "cores" or "centralities". For a long time, projects on peripheries looked at peripheries as places to be transformed into new centralities or to be connected to existing urban cores—to somehow iterate a process moving by-products and hetero-topic spaces a bit further from the nucleus. This process led the concept of periphery to be extended to a geographic scale, defining seamless territories characterised by hybrid, weak, and fluid models of urbanisation. The proposition is to start to use the word "fringe" to indicate "spaces of negotiation rather than edges" (Borden 2001); "thick" transition spaces following their own logic and not related to an inside or outside.

Urban Ecotones

As fringes are spaces of negotiation between artificial, semi-natural, and natural factors, the question becomes which kind of strategies and devices have to be implemented to act on such fluid spaces. Disciplines such as landscape ecology have already faced similar issues while working on fragmented ecosystems (Farina 1998). The term "ecotone" has been introduced to mean a boundary area whose characteristics are not simply a mix of those of the surrounding ecosystems but present peculiar elements of its own.[3]

Fringe areas can therefore be considered as urban ecotones, connective tissue between different man-made environments. The interesting condition of being at the same time a typical by-product of an industrial mode of production of space and fundamental reservoirs of resilience for a post-industrial society is why they are considered so important to explore within this research.

Even if the role of fringes as ecological corridors and pathways has yet to be fully demonstrated, their relation with existing grey artificial infrastructure plays a key role in the overall system. This relation is often conflictual but at the same time very rich in terms of potentiality. Performative environments must improve these relations in order to achieve true resilience in a way that will "redistribute population, industries, wealth, capital, culture, technology, and complexity" in a territory of cross-scalar fluxes where "density gradients are flattened" (Odum 1973).[4] Nature as strongly influenced by humans thus becomes techno-nature; a new kind of agricultural ecology able to act not only

Figure 3. For a new narrative of alpine peripheral spaces. Image: Alessandro Betta 2015

Narrative has a fundamental role in redrawing our perception of fringe areas. One of the first goals of the research to be pushed forward is to set a different narrative for peripheries in order to not conceive them in a relation of dependence with elements of centrality. Until fringe areas are considered as something opposed to a core and therefore as areas to be "integrated" (or better colonised), they will never realise their own potential. The most probable result in such cases is that peripheries will remain as incomplete leftover spaces of urbanisation. In terms of spatial perception, fringes have to be experienced through different means of transportation as the dominance of grey infrastructure contributed a great deal to a sort of "tunnel effect" that made such areas blank, unnamed parts of cities and megalopolises. Transversal connections and narratives have to be built in order to create a "self-consciousness of the fringe". Even if apparently out of context, human scale is one of the main features of fringes (Fig. 3). Years ago Foucault spoke about heterotopias and the fundamental role of what he called "espace autre"; a space able to collect what was refused by "mainstream society" but which was at the same time the most creative and open.

on perception but also on the performance of territories. In the end, processes of decentralisation are not only an answer to "modern" planning theories but also a more equal and efficient answer to the problems of the contemporary age. Dispersion is an answer to fragmentation and hybrid morphologies—or seamless geographies—will have to replace the traditional distinction between centre and periphery.

Case Study: Alpine Metropolis

The Alps are a very interesting case study as in this territory, as in many other "extreme" landscapes around the globe, interdependence between humans and nature is much deeper that in other metropolitan areas. Here topography plays a fundamental role in drawing both physical and "mental" geographies of inhabitants. Many areas in the Alps will face strong changes in the near future due to climate and related social changes (Graham 2016), therefore becoming experimental areas to investigate. Paradigms of energy production, touristic economies, and "pure nature" have been the driving forces modelling the Alps for decades; the question now becomes what to do or how to build the "Alps after the Alps", as this development model is entering into a deep crisis.

Notes/Bibliography

1 Bevz E., Papoulias G. (2014) "Dissolving the Urban Figure into the Domesticated Landscape: The Search for the 'Nature' of Natural City". ETH Zürich research paper (not published). The authors propose a reading of the relationship between city and nature considering it as "a profound reconceptualization of the city—a radical decentralization and dissolution of the urban figure into a productive landscape ... The dissolution of figure into field rendered the classical distinction between city and countryside irrelevant, replacing it with a conflation of suburb and region—a suburbanised regionalism."

2 Diego Barajas, Marisol Rivas Velazquez (2008) Hilberseimer: Radical Urbanism. Published on the web magazine of the Innsbruck University of Architecture under the mentorship of professor Bart Lootsma (www.architekturtheorie.eu).

3 An ecotone is generally described in landscape ecology manuals and theories as a boundary area or buffer zone between two adjacent ecosystems. Although the borders can be marked by abrupt changes in ecological character, they are most commonly zones of transition in which overlapping and inter digitation lend the ecotone some of the characteristics of both of its contiguous ecosystems".

4 Odum 1973. Regarding performativity and constant redistribution of fluxes and matter, it is important to quote this American scientist, as he was the first to introduce a shift from closed systems to open systems ecologies which was later translated into urban thinking by authors as Pierre Bèlanger. To quote Odum: "Systems in nature are known that shift from fast growth to steady state gradually with programmatic substitution, but other instances are known in which the shift is marked by total crash and destruction of the growth system before the emergence of the succeeding steady state regime."

Borden I., Rendell J. (2001) *InterSections: Architectural History and Critical Theory.* London, Routledge. pp. 221–46.
Branzi A. (2006) *Modernità debole e diffusa. Il mondo del progetto all'inizio del XXI secolo.* Milano, Skira Editore.
Brenner N. (2014) *Implosions/Explosions: Towards a Study of Planetary Urbanization.* Berlin, Jovis Verlag.
Cattaneo E.C. (2013) *Loaded Void: City Theory Since 1956.* Santarcangelo di Romagna, Maggioli Editore.
Farina A. (1998) *Principles and Methods in Landscape Ecology.* New York, Springer.
Graham J. (ed.) (2016) *Climates: Architecture and the Planetary Imaginary.* Zurich, Lars Müller Publishers.
Jakob M. (2008) *Il paesaggio.* Bologna, Il Mulino.
Lefebvre H. (2003) *The Urban Revolution.* Minneapolis, University of Minnesota Press [Original in French, 1970].
Odum H. T. (1973) "Energy, Ecology and Economics". In: *AMBIO* 2, nr. 6. New York, Springer. pp. 220–27.
Rovatti P.A., Vattimo G. (2010) *Il pensiero debole.* Milano, Feltrinelli.
Waldheim C. (2010) "Weak Work: Andrea Branzi's 'Weak Metropolis' and the Projective Potential of an 'Ecological Urbanism'". In: Mostafavi M, Doherty G. eds. (2010) *Ecological Urbanism.* Zurich, Lars Müller Publishers.

Digital Technologies for Pro-Active Landscapes

Giulia Garbarini

The guiding principle of the projects that are examined in this article lies in the combination and correlation between two thematic and disciplinary areas. One the one hand, "landscape"—with its conceptual evolution; and on the other, "smartness"—overused and almost omnipresent in various cultural and social spheres. The purpose of this contribution is to illustrate how cities and peripheries are currently integrated into a single network of interrelations that can lead to a concept of "smart landscape".

The landscape, which has been facing the new millennium with a new interpretation, with a new "mission" and function, is no longer just a field of experimentation for visual arts, a beautiful garden, an urban green area within a city. Landscape from the early 2000s up to present is seen as "everything", and, unlike geographical "place", it is not composed of things but is only a way of seeing and representing objects in the world (Farinelli 2003). In fact, the power of this discipline resides precisely in its generic nature; it is strong to a point that it leads to being "matched" with a multitude of disciplines that approach and enter the landscape, redefining it successfully, due to its generic features, which in turn becomes its potential. Declining various material from other disciplines within the landscape, it occasionally acquires its own specificity, accurately transforming and projecting new landscapes in relation to the characteristics and needs of the site under consideration and no longer imposing conventional and standardised practices from above.

On the other hand there is "smartness", in the current debate made up of technologies, and also of new social and cultural models. It seems difficult to identify (at least in the view of the present work) a unique and somewhat shared definition of "smart" and even less so that of "smart city", "smart land" ,and "smart landscape". The intelligence that should be found in our landscapes, however, can not only be tied to a technological factor or "big data" when we are talking about its ability to leverage these devices and tools and link them together into a vision that functions by combining points and successful interventions, as it was already anticipated in the "No-Stop City" of Archizoom.

By using smart grid architecture as a network on which we can draw a smart landscape, we can exploit its rigidity as a potential. This allows us to no longer work with master plans and plans dictated from above, but with an approach of "weak (urban) diffused structure" (Branzi 2006), which in this case functions with points and with the connection of these points, which are triggered by a combination of energy, technology, environmental and social interests, and applications.

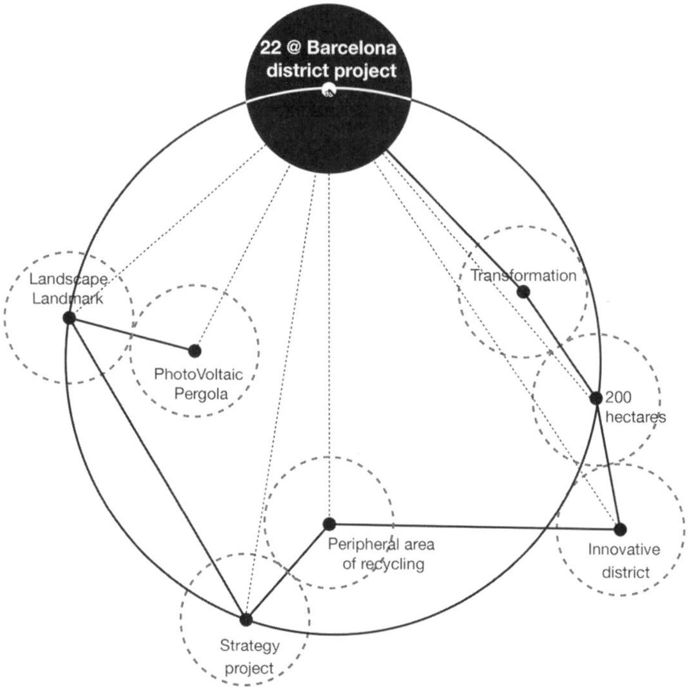

Figure 1. Scheme of transformation in 22@ Barcelona district. Image: author

Speaking about processes, it could be interesting to mention the spatial and social processes of the project of Photovoltaic Pergola that was placed within the 22@ Barcelona district project. The project has led to the transformation of 200 hectares of industrial area into an innovative district that offers modern spaces for a strategic concentration of intensive activities based on education, training, and knowledge.The value of this new project might be estimated by the fact that it has become one of the most important urban transformation projects of Barcelona in recent years. Within the project, the device of PhotoVoltaic Pergola was located in a peripheral recycled area, where a tool such as the photovoltaic panel, in correlation with an image-strategy project (the Universal Forum of Cultures in 2004), not only generates a successful landmark but also offers the city a great opportunity to position itself on the international scene and show itself at its best. Seen this way, the project can be defined as a device that might be included and used in smart landscapes (where the smart landscape works with and uses transdisciplinary characteristics to link European policies, energy smart grids, and energy devices with different places), since it relates to energy potential and landscape recognition (landmarks), which makes it a true enabler of technologies. During the Forum of Cultures (2004), it became evident how transformation and services that the project 22@ Barcelona had conducted led to photovoltaic installation as an unmistakable symbol of landscape in which a strong urban transformation process was built.

Peripheral locations such as the Parisian banlieue, Skt. Kjelds District, Outter Østerbro in Copenhagen's neighbourhood and the 22@ Barcelona district project can regain a new centrality and value when they are networked by applying devices or processes that trigger changes or provide a new context of service. The concept of network is therefore fundamental, and it is possible to extract a theoretical position that concerns cities as networks from a range of theorists, such as Stephen Graham, Saskia Sassen, and Ann Markusen. A network is to be seen as a concept of contemporary urban condition rather than a as concrete planning method. This concept encourages the redefinition of the perception of a city and its urban districts in the age of globalisation, a society of networks, and virtual technologies. This position thus represents a larger discussion that is relevant not only for architects and planners with their innovative understanding of cities in all aspects, be it architecture or planning. Multiple contemporary projects start to indirectly grasp this understanding to different degrees, even if they do not yet advocate directly for the concept of network city.

The main focus of the network city is concentrated on network infrastructure (transport, telecommunications, capitals, energy, water, and streets), which make up cities and urban regions; thus, contemporary urbanism emerges as a complex and dynamic socio-technical process. These urban complexes or dynamics are therefore viewed as ecosystems of competing networks (Graham 2000) which could be extended onto concepts of landscape. The integration of information and communication technologies in urban areas is much more than a technological matter (Graham, Marvin 1999; Graham 2000). Considering the strategies adapted in Paris, Copenhagen, and Barcelona, it becomes evident that cities and landscapes aspiring to become smart should proceed with caution and adopt an approach that looks beyond technology and considers other non-technical yet crucial factors: human factors that are less discussed; collaboration between organisations of various sectors and citizens (Public-Private-People Partnership); a long-term general overview and specific objectives; communication and promotion; availability of financial resources; capability to select the right combination of projects to develop in the short and medium terms.

If our era could be defined as one of smart cities, the first action, as Maurizio Carta (2009) argues, would be to adopt an urban life-cycle planning and management model that is capable of constantly integrating ICT components with governance and local urban decisions. However, if we follow this path we will find ourselves in a "relational pathology" (Carta 2009), resulting from a pseudo-integration between residential and production contexts, buildings and public spaces, knots and nets. Thus, if the "relational pathology" resides in these places, in the cities and in their suburbs, it is there that we should find conscious solutions, which should also take into account the socio-economic change in action and tend to adapt a wider concept of a "smart landscape". To do this, the era of networks comes to our rescue, as it consists of nodes and streams of connections that keep our cities linked through infrastructure (material) such as roads, railway lines, smart grids, and also energy, communication, Internet, and aviation networks (immaterial). This will lead to the creation of new interactions, new European contexts, and new paradigms. In this new paradigmatic configuration, landscape could be defined as a network, which can be intepreted as the beginning of a "smart landscape", seen and understood as a primary resource that need not

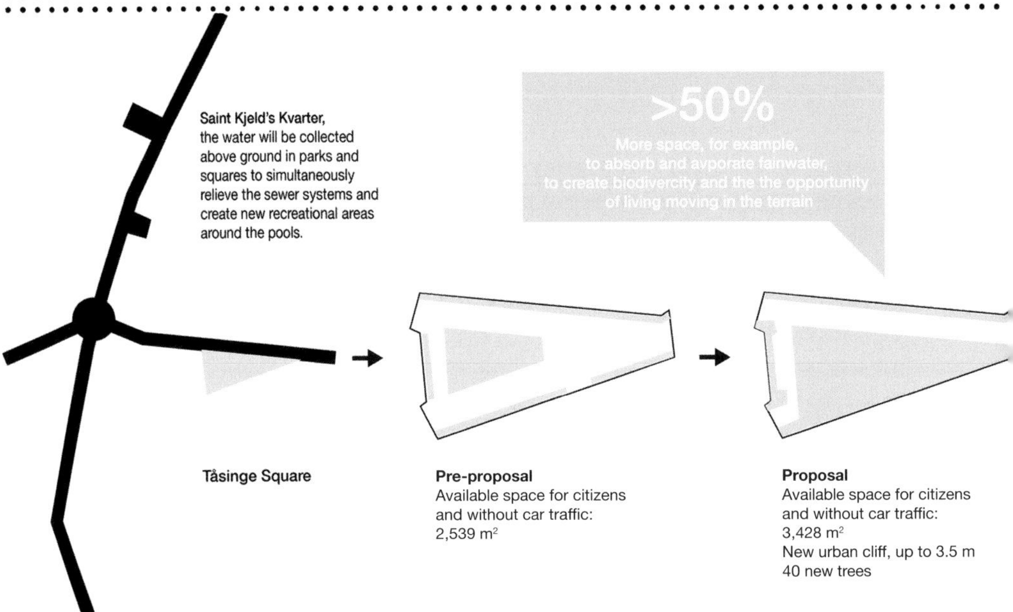

Figure 2. Scheme transformation Stk. Kjelds district, Copenhagen. Image: author

Speaking about places, it would be approapriate to share some ideas about a project that represents a spatial resource for the future development of habitats, and that works both on weaknesses (site pertinence and environmental problems) and potentials. This initiative is the project of Tåsinge Square.

There is a plan to develop Denmark's first climate-adapted neighbourhood, which would transform Skt. Kjelds District, Outter Østerbro, into Copenhagen's greenest neighbourhood. This comprehensive urban development project seeks to demonstrate in what way the city can be arranged so that rainwater can be managed in a more natural and effective way (Furuto 2012). Earlier, Tåsinge Square used to be a gathering point for the entire neighbourhood; it was similar to a "smart" park, which uses local weakness as a future driving force, where the final design of the square is decided with the help of the area's residents. This combination of technology, adaptation strategies, and social attention could transform the place into a meaningful site for its inhabitants. Tåsinge Square is an urban habitat, where the city's rhythm meets nature's cycles, and the logic of rainwater collection forms urban environment. The activity of citizens, water flows, and the precise geometry of the district are all combined with the natural and self-sufficient approach to vegetation and water. The topography creates an urban space where edges, transitions, and connection between inside and outside are essential (GHB 2014).

only to be preserved, but that first and foremost promotes development. A resource defined as a network is a new physical structure that creates new forms of socialization. Rather than getting lost in multiple processes of past urban dynamism, while it is better while working with a network to adapt the view of integration of advanced technologies to urban contexts in order to improve conditions of soil and energy on the planet. It could be possible here to use the term "smart landscape". Landscape, beginning with what has just been said, can be considered as a system of infrastructural-technological, social-cultural, economic- and information-exchange network. The nature of the connections that influence the material conformation and specific operations in the territory determines the morphology and the way we occupy the landscape of our urban and sub-urban contexts (Lyster 2006).

New interchange processes are then recognizable as a result of new processes that demobilize and relocate resources through and across a variety of sites and disciplines. From an object / site connection, this process proceeds to an organisation of higher complexity, which is created through multiple sites. From singularity to plurality: this observation gives rise to the territorial interpretation of the new exchange processes (Lyster 2006). James Corner takes up the concept of the exchange network system in *Landscape Urbanism: A Manual for the Machinic Landscape* (Mostafavi, Najle 2003). Every element of the system is connected with all the others in co-dependence and interactive connections through soft systems that are evolving and sensitive to any change in stimulus, which allows information to be absorbed, transformed, and exchanged with the context, and the stability and robustness of which stem from its ability to handle dynamic differential motion processes (Corner 2003). Our view of the territory is therefore nourished by an ecological interest in environmental sustainability not solely linked to the balance between energy production and usage, but to harmonious integration in time and to various scales of rural and urban landscape.

Nowadays, we are already in a landscape as a network—a technologically advanced landscape that profits from new technologies and in which these technologies are taken as a slogan for big industries or environmental policies. Nevertheless, the expression "smart landscape"—proposed in the current work—does not only mean the simple integration of landscape with a technological surface. Landscape here is considered "smart" because it exploits technological, political, and social advamcements that occur in society to become a "responsive" landscape. The actors who inhabit and transform this landscape have to be conscious about the fact that there is a need to work and build different landscapes, which in a symbiotic way are able to use utterly advanced technologies to make the system "sentient", i.e., they are able to cope with the limits of sustainability and to overcome these limits.

By contrast, I would like to argue that, as it can be seen in the three projects described in this article, within the concept of landscape we can propose an articulation for knots that are able to become drivers of a regenerative catalytic process both of the sites in question and of the surrounding objects. In a place where we exploit the wide scale of landscapes, we can work with different surfaces, devices, and policies, creating a kind of realignment in which landscape replaces

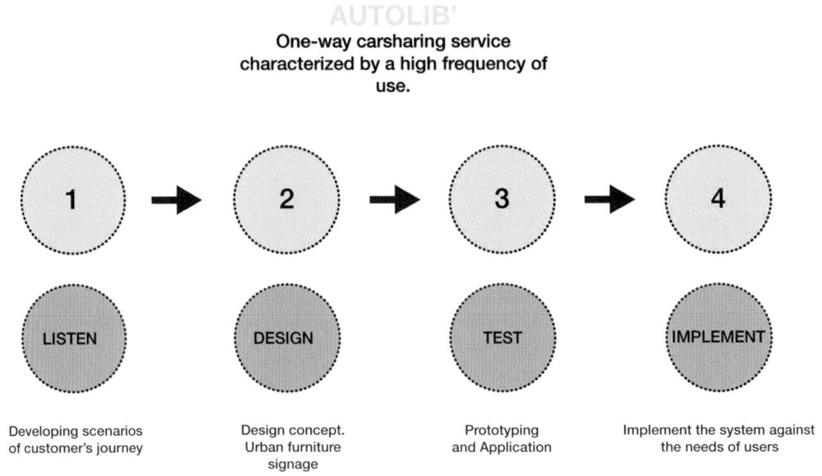

Figure 3. Scheme Autolib' project narrative. Image: author

A vision of Autolib' project—which aims at developing a new ecological mobility system for the city of Paris—was well illustrated by Sylvain Marty, the director of *Syndicat Mixte* Autolib' (Marty 2010), who described its birth, evolution, and concept. Everything was born from the ambitious vision of the Mayor of Paris, who proposed a mobility solution covering a coherent territory in terms of density, variety of use, and travel needs. Forty-one municipalities of *Île-de-France* decided to cooperate in a public institution, the Joint Association Autolib', and to launch a mobility union between city centre and periphery.

The narrative that this project provided to the participants, even if it is often summarized only in terms of its environmental benefits, was proven to be the vision of a more dynamic connection. In fact, the project was included in a more dynamic system, the main benefits of which are expected in terms of changing mobility patterns of users. By changing the traditional borderline between individual movement and transport, Autolib' provided a new type of fluidity in the design of mobility. The aim of Autolib' and the general vision guiding the project, are primarily related to the choice of electric vehicles with reduced greenhouse-gas emissions. At the same time, Autolib' promotes the rethinking of services provided to users in connection to their placement within the urban fabric.

In today's landscape, mobility is mainly based on a vision of social inclusion, which implies giving citizens and users of a city an easy access to sustainable modes of transport. Autolib's mobility service can also be seen as a result of combining various dynamics, which are served and also increased by the aspect of mobility.

urbanism and architecture (Corner 2006). Due to the combination of a wide range of disciplines, the concept of landscape has become an instrument through which a contemporary city can not only be represented, but also be built, modified, and reactivated. Thinking of landscape as a network, the use of new technologies becomes part of a network of actions to enhance the landscape and to provide a new vision for transforming it.

Bibliography

Branzi A. (2006) *Modernità debole e diffusa. Il mondo del progetto all'inizio del XXI secolo.* Ginevra-Milano, Skira.

Carta M. (2009) "Creative City 3.0. New Scenarios and Projects". In: Scaglione P. ed. (2009) *Monograph.it 1*. Trento-Barcelona, ListLab. pp. 160–185.

Corner J. (2003) "Landscape Urbanism". In: Mostafavi M., Najle C. (2003) *Landscape Urbanism: A Manual for the Machinic Landscape*. London, AA Press. p. 63.

Corner J. (2006) "Terra fluxus". In: Waldheim C. (2006) *The Landscape Urbanism Reader*. New York, Princeton Architectural Press. p. 29.

Farinelli F. (2003) *Geografia. Un'introduzione ai modelli del mondo*. Torino, Einaudi. p. 232.

Farinelli F. (2015) "La capriola del paesaggio, quindici anni dopo la Convenzione Europea del Paesaggio 2000–2015". In: *Sentieri urbani* 17/2015. Trento, Bi Quattro Editrice, pp. 18–22.

Furuto A. (2012) "Climate Adapted Neighbourhood / Tredje Natur". Available online at: http://www.archdaily.com/266077/climate-adapted-neighbourhood-tredje-natur/. Accessed: 7 July 2017.

GHB Landskabsarkitekter a/s (2014) "Taasinge square: rainwater management". Available online at: https://www.ghb-landskab.dk/en/projects/taasinge-square. Accessed 10 July 2017.

Graham, S. (2000) "Introduction: Cities and Infrastructure Networks". In: *International Journal of Urban and Regional Research*, 24/2000. Oxford, Blackwell Publishers. pp. 114–119.

Lyster C. (2006) "Landscapes of Exchange: Re-articulating Site". In: Waldheim C. (2006) *The Landscape Urbanism Reader.* New York, Princeton Architectural Press. pp. 219–237.

Marty S. (2010) "Autolib' - Prêt-à rouler sur les rues de Paris". Available online at: https://worldstreets.files.wordpress.com/2010/12/autolib-sylvain-marty.pdf. Accessed 17 July 2017.

The Neighbourhood Tamburi in Taranto between Visibility and Invisibility

Antonio Ippolito

Figure 1. TamburiCircolare. Graphic: Antonio Ippolito

Since 2012, Taranto has been characterised by many events related to urban development. Every actor wants a clean and healthy Taranto and desires a new identification with the city. However, although there is a common interest in changing the city, the actions that individuals take to accomplish this goal differ. In any case, the future of the city is linked to the future of ILVA, the largest steel factory in Europe. The new owner of ILVA aims to change the factory and implement actions towards a more sustainable environment. Meanwhile, people continue to have health problems as there is a lack of concrete actions. The Sustainable Development Agenda implies objectives of equality, dignity, quality of life, and sustainability—goals that for many aspects of the situation in Taranto seem to be a merely utopian dream. The conflict between the right to work and the right to health is still a question to be solved. The emblematic case of this great paradox is the district of Tamburi, an area located next to the ILVA where almost twenty-thousand people are living. Its presence has influenced the whole territory and the main problem is related to the pollution, which represents the cause of its degradation. The high presence of pollutants is the reason for the high mortality rate and illness of the residents (Pirastu 2014). This is a physical degradation that has a direct influence on social deterioration, making Tamburi one of the least liveable areas in Italy. The actual conditions need utmost attention by national, regional, and local governments, from environmental bodies responsible for the protection of the territory, and from the health agency (Ippolito 2017). According to the data from national control bodies, this terrible condition results in an increasing incivility of citizens, who believe that they are living in an anarchic state.

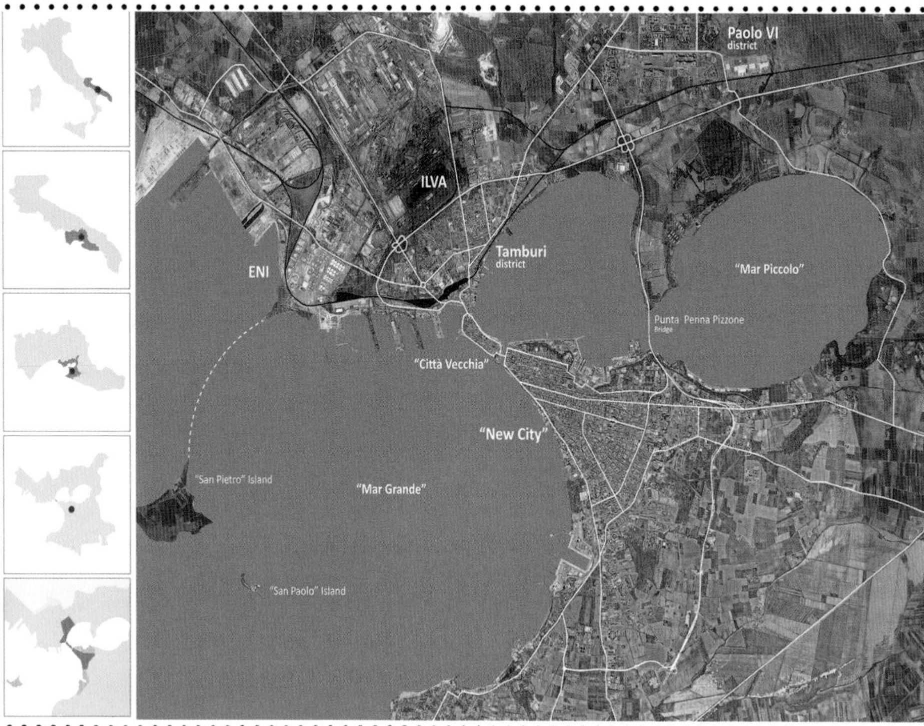

Figure 2. Taranto and ILVA. Graphic: Antonio Ippolito

Peripheries can evolve into new centralities. They cannot be compared to an "immutable institution" but to a set of interactions that are able to create a change of state. "Places, temporalities, and processes are the product of social interactions ... a plurality of heterogeneous paths and narratives" (Cremaschi 2008). Enhancing human and social capital is one of the objectives that can move peripheries towards more resilient communities (Macaione et al. 2016) and in this regard, the Nature_City theory (Sichenze 2000) represents a new key for the city towards dynamic processes. Taranto is an interesting example of this concept, caugth between the right to live and the right to work. Its status of degraded city, due to ILVA (the largest steel factory in Europe), is difficult to change. No urban planning projects can be started, and actually the city is in a static condition. Studies show that citizens citizens who become participant actors are modifiers of their built environment (Macaione 2016). "The production of the city through socio-environmental changes results in the continuous production of new 'urban natures'" (Cronon 1991), and in this moment, Taranto needs to rethink itself according to this concept.

In fact, the neighbourhood has been completely abandoned by social and political institutions, and its situation is completely run-down. In Tamburi and Taranto there is a lack of ethical rights. That is because the state preferred to focus on economic development without considering the people who live in the area. In this context, the question is: is it possible to undertake a new course towards change?

The emergence of environmental issues due to the steel industry is a sad reality that has become a matter of global concern for the health of citizens and the protection of the environment. Among industries, steel factories are those that cause most problems (Nicotra 2016). To solve these problems, it is important to find solutions that will either eliminate the identified risk or at least reduce it to an acceptable level, not only through physical actions but also with a holistic approach able to think of the city from a social and economic point of view. Regenerating a city means satisfying urban, socioeconomic, and environmental needs expressed by the population through actions and reversible processes that are able to influence the development of the city. In this context, it is important to recall the definition of resilience provided by Cutter. Resilience "is the ability of a social system to respond and recover from disasters and it includes those inherent conditions that allow the system to absorb impacts and cope with an event, as well as post-event, adaptive processes that facilitate the ability of the social system to reorganise, change, and learn in response to a threat" (Cutter et al. 2008). Thinking about this concept and its application to Tamburi it can be useful for introducing the paradigm of Nature_City (NC) that aims to expand the definition of resilience in new ways.

The change of Tamburi could become an important experience as it could be linked to the concept of an open laboratory in which the relationship between actors can help create a resilient community. This idea relies on the definition of "new beginnings of cities" that aims at reading the built environment in relationship with nature and history (Macaione, Sichenze 2013). Through an intelligent system and responsible actions, and through make-thinking-creation, it is possible to use the concepts of recycle, reduce, and reuse for the strategy. Tamburi needs to be rethought to create opportunities and change its status. According to Carta, "we must be the main protagonists of a structural change in which cities are called to (re)activate their territorial capital, guided by urbanism able to guarantee new forms of convergence between cultural, economic, environmental, and social sustainability. ... Especially through the effectiveness of the decisions, the quality of the projects and the efficiency of the processes" (Carta 2014).

The NC theory is based on a match of qualitative values—such as mutual dependence, diversification, complexity, the cyclic nature of processes, and streams of information, contextual conditions, etc.—with human experience and cultural heritage; the NC theory is linked to new ways of reading in order to understand the eco-cultural urban phenomena. This theory allowed us to create a scenario which represents a possible solution for Tamburi. The aim of the strategy is not to create a new form of urbanism but rather to offer an integrated and dynamic perspective of the future. The use of new paradigms aims towards a more dynamic territorial development, able to reconnect the

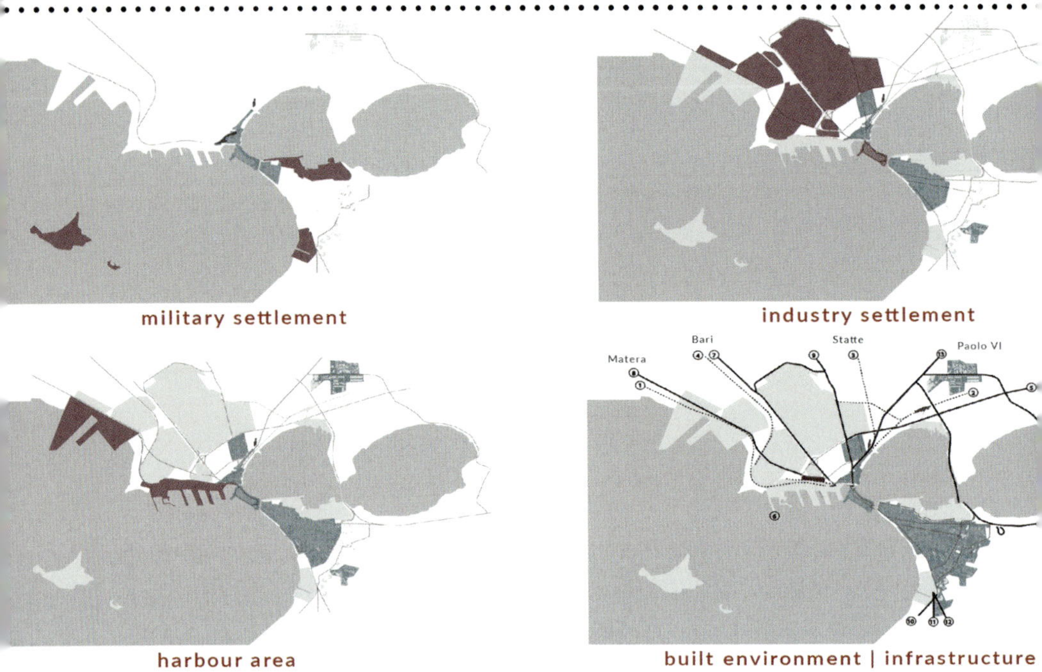

Figure 3. Urban development of Taranto. Graphic: Antonio Ippolito

Life in urban peripheries is characterised by unevenness in economic and political terms and access to infrastructure. Peripheries are an interesting and complex urban phenomenon, because they are characterised by multiple factors in which physical and non-physical infrastructure tends to evolve, creating new kinds of centralities. In fact, as Renzo Piano has stated (2015) "the peripheries of the cities are not beautiful, of course; they are not treated well. But they are the future of the city, or they are the city of the future. Places where energy is in the city" (Poggioli 2015). Their role can be fundamental for new economic opportunities and for innovation. Following this concept, Tamburi, a district of Taranto, should change starting from the community through to the creation of a cultural framework. It should become a "project" in which it is necessary to have the presence of a "permanent laboratory" able to create a communication system between citizens and institutions. In this sense, "it is important to guarantee a local shared design, focusing operations for interventions that could relaunch local economy through the involvement of inhabitants, in a transformation process that stimulates the sense of belonging" (Prinsi 2015). Only in this way will the transformation be able to renew the territory.

fragmented territory through the (re)generation of a new urban and social settlement. In a process of such magnitude, the role of flows is fundamental as they represent the territorial dynamism. The prefix "re" aims precisely to help identify the approach of this strategy. (Re)naturalise identifies the need to take action on the environmental structure towards connection between built environment and naturalistic areas. In fact, the district is at the centre of a naturalistic context that needs to be reconnected. Through this process it is possible to link the "Parco delle Gravine", the coastal areas, the "Parco Cimino", and the "La Vela WWF Oasi" in a unique green system that converges on the area. (Re)vitalise is the paradigm of new life, able to bring efficiency to all portions of the territory and/or elements of the built environment that represent a new opportunity (Markwirth 2012). It means providing the new elements and tools for a new identity and giving new life; it means giving the opportunity to live in the city, promote socio-economic development, and create new forms of fluid urbanism.

For Tamburi it is about creating connections between the urban fabric and public spaces. Thinking in this direction means generating the idea of Nature_City in order to create "new beginnings of cities". (Re)generate means approaching the evolution of the urban structure through micro-actions able to lead renewal processes in its conformation. This vision is able to give Tamburi a new image of itself. (Re)configure means starting from criticality and opportunity of the territory. In Tamburi there are many degraded buildings and empty spaces. Through physical actions it is thus possible to give Tamburi a new urban configuration able to integrate the city into a dynamic relationship system. These kinds of forms are connected with the paradigm of "new forms" of living and urban communication. (Re)start the results from the others. It can allow the city to start with a new identity: relational, cultural, touristic, and economic. In all this, the community represents the key to success towards a new way of conceiving the city. Every factor seeks and guarantees sustainable development, and every element of the built environment becomes central to a new dimension. In this sense, the role of ICT is important because it can involve citizens in becoming more responsible and a fundamental element of territorial reconversion.

Change towards a resilient place represents a real opportunity for the district. The goal is to give a new light to Tamburi, and to do this there is a need to catalyse the paradigm of Nature_City into three macro objectives: centrality, attractiveness, and equity. To achieve this goal, it's important to implement a series of actions that can (re)activate the relationship between neighbourhood, health, and environment. In this process, an important role is played by actors that are called upon to put their skills into action. In this way, it will be possible to (re)think the district in a framework where concepts of quality and sustainability are fundamental for (re)building the future of Tamburi. In this regards the case of Molinay (district of Seraing in Belgium where a steel factory is located) is interesting. The project of Molinay is divided into two steps. The first is the master plan that left the Molinay neighbourhood almost completely untouched. The second is very interesting because, to respond to this lack, the local association launched a participative process called Molinay 2017. With the help of public and private sectors, new urban proposals were imagined. The main innovative aspects are the role of civil society and the duration of the process that is the result of

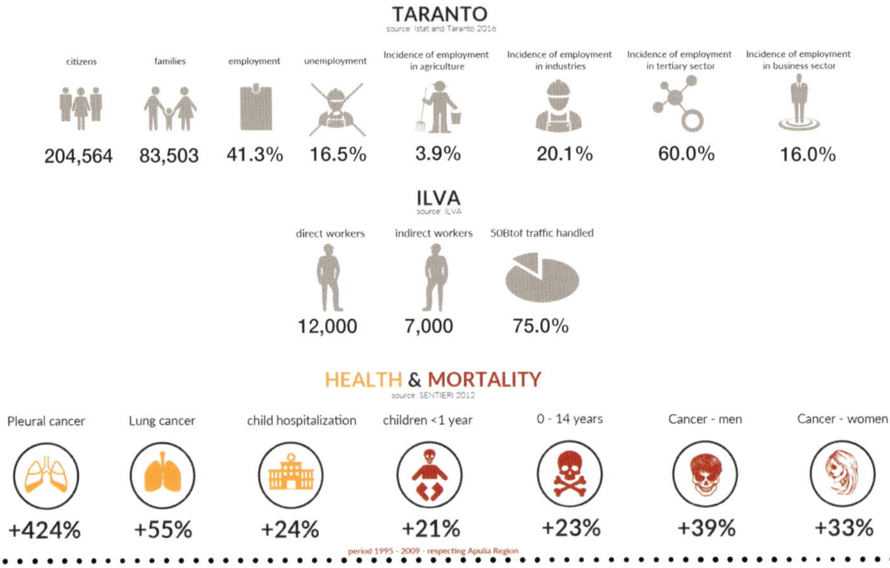

Figure 4. Taranto and ILVA. Graphic: Antonio Ippolito

Tamburi represents an emblematic case of a periphery in which there is a dichotomy between visibility and invisibility. It is a residential area very close to ILVA, where almost twenty-thousand people live. The presence of ILVA has influenced the whole territory, in particular with the pollution, that represents the cause of its degradation. A scenario for reconverting the "steel district" can be linked to the paradigms of Nature_City and of resilience. Through intelligent systems and ethically responsible actions, and through make-thinking-creation, it might be possible to merge the concepts of recycle, reuse, and reduce into two macro concepts: (re)connect and (re)vitalize. In this way, the territory could be (re)considered as a dynamic and resilient system in which new opportunities can arise. Making Tamburi a dynamic neighbourhood means catalysing its identity within a regional and national cultural tourism system. This is a change that will allow citizens to have a new "dimension" in which the quality of life, work, health, and education makes the difference. This will protect and enhance local resources for future generations in a sustainable way. It is a vision that assigns to the neighbourhood the key for its development and can make the neighbourhood a catalyst for new forms of urban dynamism.

cooperation between actors. This cooperation enabled the inclusion of ideas, projects, and proposals designed by the population, associations, and experts in the master plan, thus changing the original plan (Institute Destree 2017).

Learning from this case study, it is possible to start a similar process in Tamburi. Beginning in 2012, the association "Comitato Cittadini e Lavoratori Liberi e Pensanti" started process to bring a great visibility to Taranto and to become the element of connection between all territorial actors. A permanent laboratory can be the first physical action for this change because it can become a catalyst of identity for the activation of a cultural infrastructure. In this way, the great paradox of a city where there is a dichotomy between visibility and invisibility can be overcome through the theory of NC. As Sichenze and Macaione claim, cities need to change starting from identification, and when people become resilient the "new beginning of cities" will represent a new starting point towards a sustainable future.

Bibliography

Carta M. (2014) *Reimagining Urbanism*. Trento, ListLab.
Cremaschi M. (2008) *Tracce di Quartieri: il Legame Sociale nella Città che Cambia*. Milano, FrancoAngeli.
Cronon W. (1991) *Nature's Metropolis*. New York, A.A. Norton.
Cutter S. L., Barnes L., Berry M., Burton C., Evans E., Take E., and Webb J. (Forthcoming). "A Place-Based Model for Understanding Community Resilience to Natural Disasters". In: *Global Environmental Change*, 18(4). pp. 598–606.
Ippolito A. (2017) "Nature-City. Matera and Taranto Two 'Resilient' Cities". In: *S.Arch*. The 4th International Conference 7–9 June 2017.
Lefebvre H. (1968) *Le Droit à la Ville*. Paris, Anthropos.
Macaione I., Sichenze A. (2013). *Scrivere architettura. Multiscalarità e Progetto*. Milano, FrancoAngeli.
Macaione I., Sichenze A., Anello E., Ippolito A. (2016). "Cross Phenomena. The Nature_City Matera (Italy): From National Disgrace to European Culture Capital 2019". In: *Youth in Conservation of Culturale Heritage*. YOCOCU 2016 Conference. Madrid, MNCARS.
Pirastu R., Comba P., Conti S., Iavarone I., Fazzo L., Pasetto R., Zona A., Crocetti E., Ricci P. (2014) *SENTIERI Epidemiological Study of Residents in National Priority Contaminated Sites: Mortality, Cancer Incidence and Hospital Discharges*. Milano, Edizioni Inferenze.
Poggioli S. (2015) "Architect Renzo Piano: The Future of Europe's Cities is in the Suburbs". Available online at: http://www.npr.org/sections/parallels/2015/03/10/390981452/architect-renzo-piano-thefuture-of-europes-cities-is-in-the-suburbs [Accessed 24.5.2016].
Prinsi E.U. (2016) "Senator Renzo Piano's G124 Team Is Poised to Transform Italy's Cities, One Shipping Container at a Time". Available online at: https://architizer.com/blog/renzo-piano-g124/ [Accessed 10.10.2017].
Sichenze A. (2000) *Città-Natura/nature-city in Basilicata*. Milano, DeAgostini.

DYNAMICS OF PERIPHERY

RESERVES OF RESILIENCE

Riverside Resilience

Emanuele Sommariva

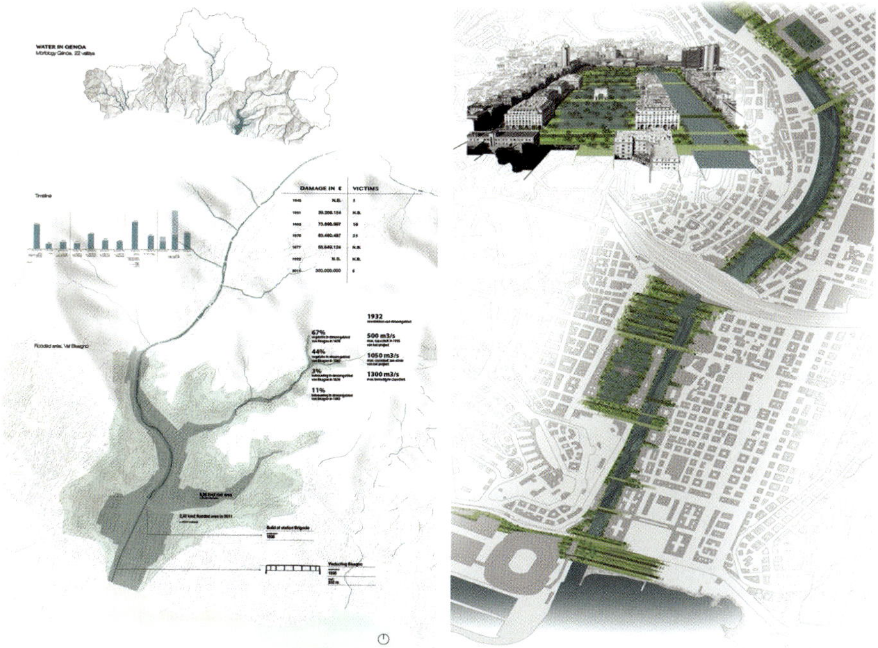

Figure 1. Urban riverbank regeneration with landscaping strategies and diffuse soil permeability.
Graphic: F. van Zuilekom 2013, A. Zampichelli 2014

The prevention of natural disasters linked with the contingency/recovery planning disciplines has been recognised as crucial for the future of Europe. With respect to risk management related to watercourses, urban open spaces are often identified as areas prone to natural hazards rather than structuring components of the territory able to implement mitigation infrastructure and reduce the exposure to flash floods and other calamities. Alternative mitigation strategies combined with a regional planning approach are needed, which this paper addresses by describing innovative urban design concepts that focus on flood resilience. By applying resilience theory, this contribution aims to explore in particular an alternative framework for urban flood hazard management in peripheral contexts, such as the Bisagno River Valley in Genoa.

The disciplines of recovery planning and urban design traditionally appear to be disconnected. Recent studies suggest how much open space is required for egress or refuge, but the debate about structural qualities or strategical re-arrangement of urban riverfronts and mitigation landscapes has still had little impact on communities and territorial stakeholders (Geis 2000). Whether or not rivers have always played a crucial part in the emergence of human society, it's also true that most cities tended to be founded near a continually available water source and with notable events along the river course chosen for their location, such as confluences, sharp bends, high-points, islands, lagoons, river mouths (Kostof 1992, Valena 1990). But today, the metropolitan dimension

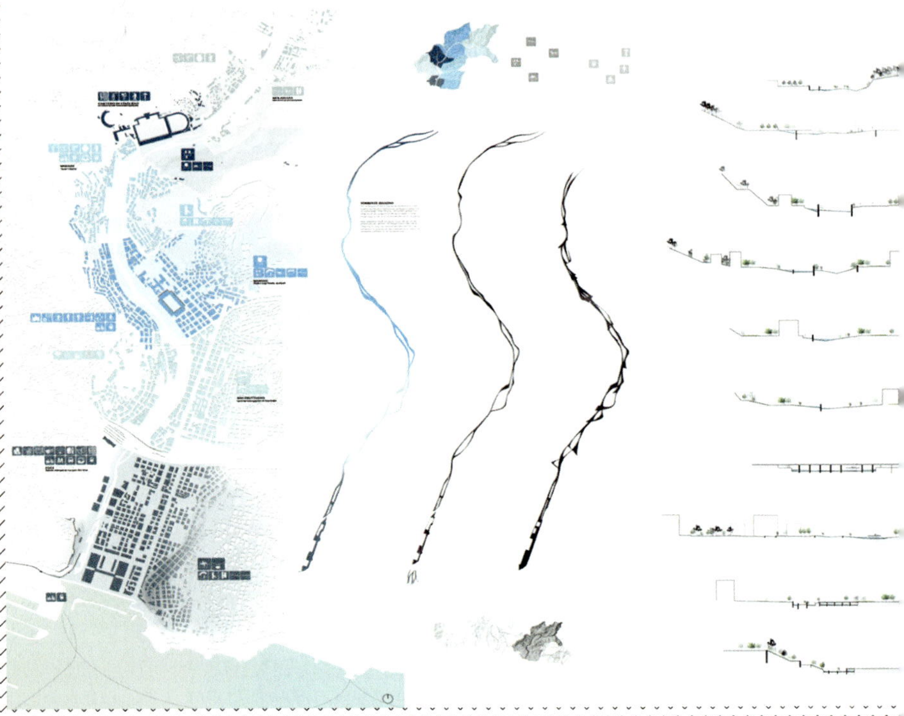

Figure 2. Territorial and hydro-morphological analysis for Bisagno River Contract proposal.
Graphic: F. van Zuilekom, 2013

Negotiating land and water use: integrated River Contracts (RCs):

The success of sustainable and integrated territorial planning is based on both production and conservation as fundamental parts. Using negotiation to resolve conflicts regarding land-water management strategies, the River Contracts (RCs) responds to the 2000/60/EU Directive (Water Framework Directive, WFD) inspired by international experiences (i.e., Belgium, France, Italy). River Contracts defines watersheds as geo-morphologic dynamic systems in order to generate new urban and rural territoriality, set up a network of local initiatives, and create integrated enhancement policies for the active conservation and development of a particular region.

The plan adopts a cross-sectoral approach (soil-water safeguarding and uses, environmental improvement, landscape valorisation, regional development, payment of ecosystem services, multifunctional agriculture) through the concept of building a "River Community" as an interactive platform of partnerships between local actors, governments, and stakeholders.

Moreover, the implementation of a methodology for the qualitative and quantitative monitoring of the contract results, could help to evaluate the congruence of current and future planning decisions and the environmental and strategic objectives established by other territorial programmes and measures such as the Regional Water Protection Plans (WPP), Hydrographic District Plans (HDP), and Rural Development Programmes (RDPs).

is confronting territorial complexity as the unique meta-system in rapid evolution (Gausa 2010). Different types of urban agglomerations characterised by diversified and contradictory spaces can be found in extremely intertwined natural landscapes, such as river basins, in which metamorphism and dynamics emerge as basic factors for understanding the spatial and stress conditions of these contexts. In fact, every year geo-hydrological hazards challenge more and more costal and river cities despite the fact that many of them are protected by extensive flood/water control infrastructure.

A recent UN survey entitled *The Human Cost of Weather-related Disasters* revealed that in the last 20 years, 2.3 billion people in the world suffered the consequences of geo-hydrological damage. More than 3,000 flood events (43% overall) have been counted, in some cases with extreme consequences such as in New Orleans, USA (2005); Guangdong, China (2007); Genova, Italy (2011, 2014); Elbe River, Germany (2013); and Seine River, France (2016); with a frequency that will increase in the next future. However, flood-control infrastructure is not always a reliable mitigation approach, especially in the face of uncertainties resulting from climate change. In fact, most of these systems are designed to operate under an obsolete assumption that the pattern of flow variability remains unchanged over time, underlining how much mitigation strategies have focused on protection and resistance rather than resilience.[1]

One way to put resilience application into practice is to look for the contextual properties that alter resilience over time (processual alteration). For coastal and river cities, a property defining vulnerability to flood would be one that reflects the physical and hydrologic changes of the floodable lands[2], over which urban and market-driven interests conflict with natural flood processes, giving rise to the most critical focus areas for geo-hydrological disasters (Criss, Shock 2001).

The assertion that cities and floods cannot coexist shows a lack of imagination, resulting from being too accustomed to the kind of built environment not adapted to floods. With a shift in perception and creative planning and design open spaces can become multifunctional to convey and store floodwater during wet seasons; Infrastructure can be redesigned into a collection of diverse functional elements that are flexible in operation; Buildings can be remodeled to be elevated, floatable, or wet-proofed (Guikema 2009).

According to its operative perspective, urban resilience to floods can be defined as a city's capacity to tolerate flooding and to reorganise physical damage, in a balance between prevention and coexistence, by learning opportunities to emergency quick response in a multi-equilibria set of structures and processes (Godschalk 2003). Adaptive capacity can increase resilience over time, as it is associated with the pro-active learning capability of the territory, while redundancy provides insurance against total system failure. These basics principles could integrate both systemic strategies and site-based interventions in order to balance new internal demands (responsive services, smart infrastructure and new living concepts) and external shocks (risk prevention, hazards mitigation, ecological performances). This is the backdrop against which the cities in Southern Europe and, in particular in the Italian peninsula, are described as a focus of scientific interest due to susceptibility

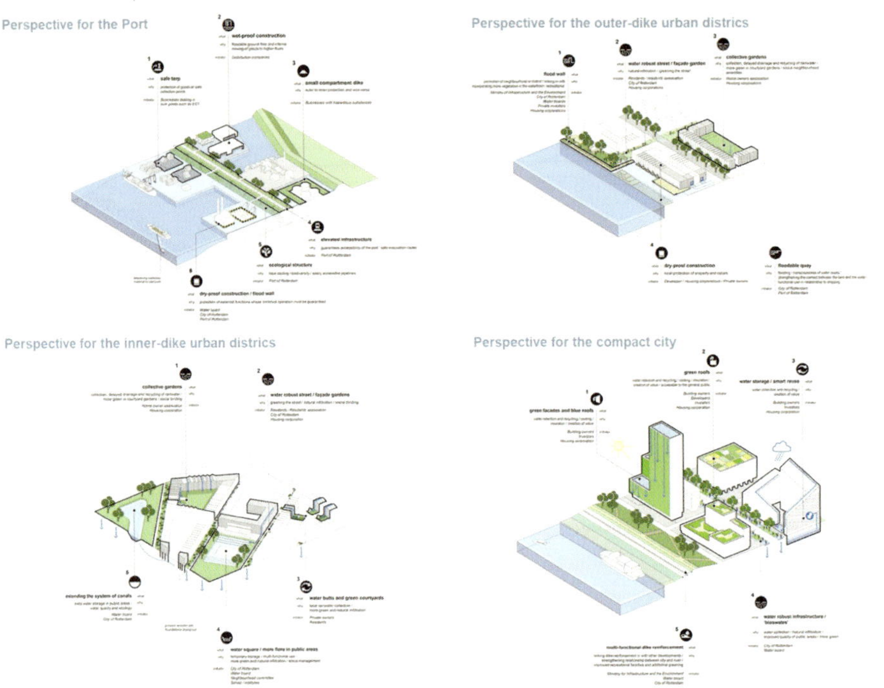

Figure 3. Perspectives for the climate proof and adaptation strategies of Delta City.
Graphics: Rotterdam Climate Initiative, 2013

Water Squares for Rotterdam 2050:

Rotterdam is a strategic hub for Northern Europe located within the Rhine–Meuse–Scheldt river delta, which provides excellent access to the hinterland upstream reaching to Basel, Switzerland and into France. But the city is also doomed to get afflicted by growing amount of heavy rainfalls, raising sea levels and widespread reduction of soil permeability due to urban and infrastructural sprawl. The lack of space below ground, the absence of canalizations like in Amsterdam and the huge spaces devoted to logistic and port facilities, create many problems to the sewer system. With the new policy agenda for urban water management, designed by the agency De Urbanisten, Rotterdam Metro Region calculated a new retention capacity of 750.000 m^3 (equivalent to 94 ha of new basins and lakes), upcycling underused or vacant plots, outer-dike urban districts, leftover pockets of land in the suburbs or in the port authority areas.

In 2012, using some testing grounds the Municipality explored the possibility to create different full-scale water squares in Benthemplein, hosting green infrastructure and open space sport facilities, fully accessible in the dry season and able to prevent floods during the rainy season. Similar interventions have been initiated also in the Schieland and Krimpenerwaard District Water Board.

and frequency of geo-hydrological processes (landslides, debris flows, flooding, coastal erosion), affecting different areas of the territory (Luino 2005). Among these, the metropolitan area of Genoa (with a surface of 4.000 km^2 and 1.5 mil inhabitants) has become an international case study for geo-hydrological risk, mainly due to the predisposing conditions of climate changes in the rainfall regime and urban development. Genoa reflects the impacts of flooding and other weather-related disasters as exemplified by significant events in all its history and especially some remarkable flash floods dated back the last forty years.[3] Due to complex topography and lack of empty floodplains areas, the geo-hydrological fragility of Genoa's river valleys compared to urban development processes can be grouped into four main morphological – environmental issues:

- modifications in land use (rural to urban areas) mostly evident with the widespread urbanisation of valleys and the covering of the watercourses to open new streets;
- variations in the flood channel width of the streams with a narrowing of the effective discharge section;
- extension of the urbanisation process in coastal plains and towards the sea with new embankments;
- total diversion of the natural riverbed and concentration of surface runoff in more restricted areas.

Whether resilience is a concept that provokes varied reactions across the design and technical disciplines engaged in evolving the practice and cultural debate on water landscapes, the combination of this approach with climatic analysis and the evaluation of urban sprawl through historical maps could be useful to understand better the impacts of recent geo-hydrological risk in complex system like Genoa Therefore, the concept of recycle applied to urban landscapes, infrastructure, and hybrid systems (Ricci 2016) is the base of the diverse design interventions collected in two master graduation projects on the Bisagno River valley in Genoa, within the didactic and research experience led into the Recycle Genoa Lab (PRIN Recycle Italy 2012–2016). The proposal developed by F. van Zuilekom, in partnership with the Academy of Architecture Amsterdam, analysed the progressive urbanisation of floodplains and hills, which had led to the reduction of flow sections, soil waterproofing and a rise in runoff velocity especially in relation to most consolidated urban areas. The work has been structured on a research by design methodology about the rediscovering of 22 side valleys within the watershed of Bisagno River. The main territorial strategy defined the rehabilitation programme of large portions of urban riverbanks, combining landscaping actions with punctual demolition of buildings/obstacles close to water bodies; the enhancement of soil permeability and the water drainage/catchment areas working on green rooftops, open paving and new buffer zones. In the same area, the proposal of A. Zampichelli tackles the emergence of environmental issues and urban sustainability goals related to the regeneration of public spaces and alternative mobility system in the Bisagno river park. The projects deals with mitigation strategies, especially connected to flash flood events, by developing new detention basins (former cement quarries) water squares (Piazza della Vittoria) and studying the territorial impact of blue infrastructure (ecological, social, economic and aesthetic values). Reducing risk posed by future

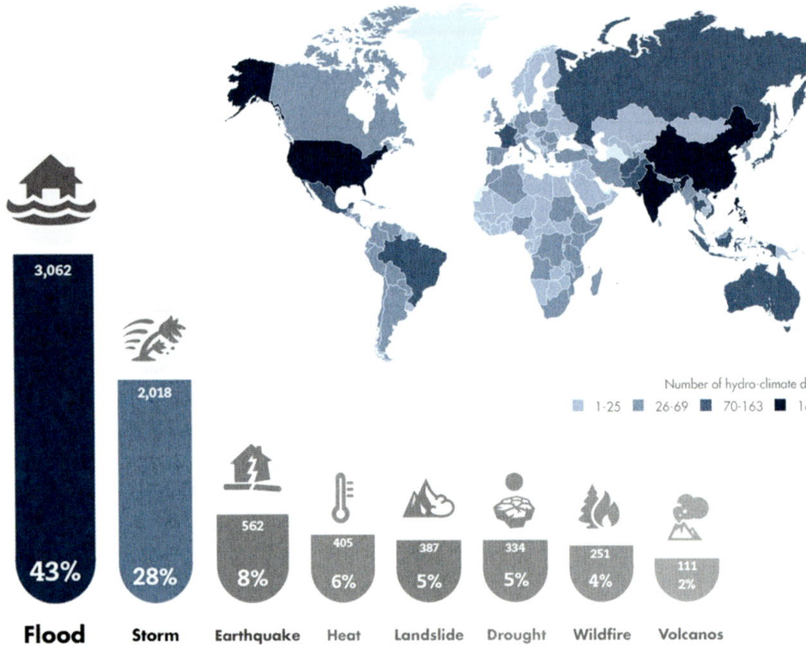

Figure 4. Global perception on water-related problems compared to disasters incidence.
Graphic: COP 21 Report UNISDR, 2015

Water Eurobarometers: the social perception of water-related issues:

In close connection to EU 2020 Strategy, the *Blueprint to Safeguard Europe's Water Resources* (2012) has been developed to survey the current attitude of European population towards water-related issues. The increasing demand by citizens and environmental organisations for cleaner rivers, lakes and coastal beaches has been evident for considerable time in EU programmes and reconfirmed recently by a representative opinion poll named Eurobarometer in all 25 EU countries, focusing on the following questions:

- level og knowledge about water-related problems facing climate changes;
- seriousness of perceived changes in the quality of drinking water;
- health check and current policies on groundwater,rivers,lakes and coastal waters;
- impact of various sectors and activities and main threats to the water enviroment;
- price of water and the measures to be implemented to tackle water availability.

In this particular framework, water reuse has been recognised as a significant strategy to improve the status of river basins and reduce territorial pressures. At present, about 1 billion m^3 of wastewater is reused annually (2.4% of the treated urban effluents) but the EU potential has been counted as six times the current volume. Moreover, when compared to alternative sources of water supply such as desalination or water transfer, water reuse often turns out to require lower investment costs and energy, also contributing to reduce greenhouse gas emissions.

geo-hydrological events requires not only knowledge about the hazards, but also taking actions to use that knowledge. Future development needs to incorporate actions that maintain the natural river channel, limit further coastline progradation, avoid the constriction of the width of the river channel and counter the effect of more impervious urban surfaces. The intent would be to reduce vulnerability by increasing the community resilience to future hazardous events, resilience being «the ability to prepare and plan for, absorb, recover from, and more successfully adapt to adverse effects» (CINR 2012). The move towards creating resilient cities to floods and natural hazards is a research frontier.

Notes/Bibliography

1 The idea of resilience has a long history in ecology and engineering, but its application to natural hazard management is relatively recent (Berkes 2007). In engineering, resilience is concerned with disturbances that threaten the functional stability of infrastructural systems (Wang, Blackmore 2009). In ecology, Holling (1973) uses resilience to describe an evolutionary process of ecosystem dynamics towards different forms of stability. The two concepts have been used in hybrid systems theories, such as socio–ecological systems (Berkes, Folke 1998), but in relation to water hazards, they concern mostly a tolerance regime that an urban context can maintain when experiencing a flood event, involving socio–spatial and environmental changes (Walker et al. 2004).

2 Floodable lands contribute to the city's water-related tolerance, by storing or conveying floodwater and sediments without incurring damage locally and elsewhere. These areas can be of any land use and cover, and thus do not exclusively refer to undeveloped or green areas such as wetlands. If organised in a network of adaptive open spaces, these areas can lower flood peaks and impact by integrating new paradigms for susceptibility and complex territorial dynamics (Peterson et al. 1998; Adger 2006).

3 In 1970, Genoa suffered one the most catastrophic flood events with serious damage to infrastructure, railroads, and houses (2000 evacuated people) especially in the peripheral areas of Voltri and western Riviera (Tropeano, Turconi 2004). The sequence of destructive events continued in 2010, 2011, and 2014. Multiple landslides and intense flash floods have caused casualties and diffuse collateral damage within the consolidated areas of the city that are connected to the main important river basins of Bisagno (95 km^2) and Polcevera (140 km^2) as well as the minor streams that were covered over during the last 50 years.

Adger W. N. (2006) "Vulnerability". In :*Global Environmental Change*, vol. 16. pp. 268–281.

Berkes F. (2007) "Understanding Uncertainty and Reducing Vulnerability: Lessons from Resilience Thinking". In: *Natural Hazards*, vol. 41, pp. 283–295.

Berkes F., Folke C. (1998) *Linking Social and Ecological Systems: Management Practices and Social Mechanisms for Building Resilience*. Cambridge, Cambridge University Press.

CINR (2012) *Disaster Resilience: A National Imperative*. Washington D.C., National Academies Press.

Criss R., Shock L. (2001) "Flood Enhancement through Flood Control". In: *Geology*, vol. 29, pp. 875–873.

Faccini F., Luino F., Sacchini A., Turconi L. (2014) "Flash Flood Events and Urban Development in Genoa: Lost in Translation". In: *Engineering Geology for Society and Territory IAEG 2014 Conference Proceedings*, vol. 5. Berlin, Springer, pp. 797–801.

Gausa M. (2010) *Open, Espacio Tiempo y Información*. Barcelona, Actar.

Geis D. (2000) "By Design: The Disaster Resistant and Quality of Life Community". In: *Natural Hazards Review*, vol. 1, pp. 151–160.

Godschalk D. R. (2003) "Urban Hazard Mitigation: Creating Resilient Cities". In: *Natural Hazards Review*, vol. 4, pp. 136–143.

Guikema S. D. (2009) "Infrastructure Design Issues in Disaster-Prone Regions". In: *Science*, n.323, pp. 1302–1303.

Gunderson L., Holling C.S, Lance H. (2002) "Resilience and Adaptive Cycles". In: Gunderson L., Holling C.S. eds. (2002) *Panarchy: Understanding Transformations in Human and Natural Systems*,. Washington D.C., Island Press.

Kostof S. (1992) *The City Assembled: The Elements of Urban Form through History*. London, Thames & Hudson.

Luino F. (2005) "Sequence of Instability Processes Triggered by Heavy Rainfall in the Northern Italy". In: *Geomorphology*, n. 66, pp. 13–39.

Peterson G., Allen C., Holling C. (1998) "Ecological Resilience, Biodiversity, and Scale". In: *Ecosystems* vol.1, pp. 6–18.

Ricci M. (2016) "The Recyle GOA Pro-Active Manifesto". In: Ricci M., Schröder J. eds. (2016) *Recycle Book 16: Towards a Pro-Active Manifesto*. Rome, Aracne. pp. 20–29.

Tropeano D., Turconi L. (2004) "Using Historical Documents for Landslide, Debris Flow and Stream Flood Prevention, Applications in Northern Italy". In: *Natural Hazards*, vol. 31, pp. 663–679.

UNISDR (2015) *The Human Cost of Weather-Related Disasters 1995–2015*. COP 21 Technical Report. Brussels, ed. CRED.

Valena T. (1990) *Stadt und Topographie*. Berlin, Ernst & Sohn.

Walker B., Holling C., Carpenter S., Kinzig. A. (2004) "Resilience, Adaptability and Transformability in Social-Ecological Systems". In: *Ecology and Society*, vol. 9.

Wang C., Blackmore J. (2009) "Resilience Concepts for Water Resource Systems". In: *Journal of Water Resources Planning and Management*, vol. 135, pp. 528–536.

Zevenbergen C., Gersonius B. (2007) "Challenges in Urban Flood Management". In: Pasche A. ed. (2007) *Advances in Urban Flood Management*. New York, Taylor & Francis. pp. 1–11.

Foodsheds and the Role of Public Food Markets in the Province of Girona

Fava Nadia, Romà Garrido, Marta Carrasco Bonet

Figure 1. Salt periphery. Photo: Nadia Fava

In the new era of food systems, European cities are experiencing a growing interest in urban public spaces, urban fringes, rural-urban areas, green corridors, and suburban areas dedicated to the supply, commercialisation, and consumption of food (Parham 2015, Marino 2016). Academic research on the “food issue” from the different perspectives of urban planners, sociologists, anthropologists, ecologists, and economists is increasing. Research specifically on alternative food production seems to be a key issue for solving questions of identity, gender, poverty, social inequality, health, rural-urban links, and the climate change problem, even if, until now, this has meant small segments of real food consumption. The debate seems to focus on what the alternatives or possibilities are and what their impact would be for supplying the growing population. This, however, is all within the frame of social, economic, and environmental sustainability, resilience precepts, or the principles of the circular economy. The main question seems to be not just to decide between either the mass production food or locally produced food, but rather to study, understand, and accommodate the nuances of both of these. There are all types of logic that can help one express nuances to enlarge the spectrum of possibilities and develop innovative projects. The word alternative, which in some contexts is still seen as an element haunting established society as subversive tendencies and forces, now represents the constellation of choices which focus on the disjuncture between current and possible multiple alternatives (Brenner 2009). The Alternative Food Network, alternative economies, and alternative pedagogies encompass approaches that differ from the

Figure 2. Geographical provenance of food in Salt Market Hall. Graphic: Laura Plana

In Europe, "peripheries" is often a synonym for external and marginalized areas, areas neglected by the central city and to where the problems have been moved. Not all challenges for cities are homogenous within their territory; for instance gentrification and unaffordability are mostly present in the core of a city, while segregation and inequality seem to affect the outskirts more. Nevertheless, in the current situation where the mainstream economy, and social and culture spheres are in crisis and being questioned, the so-called "alternative movement", (i.e., an alternative economy, food network, and culture), would seem to suggest an innovative and creative alternative—a field of exploration for the territory. The interface between city development and food production on the periphery is important because the nature of its production, distribution, and retailing signify a territorial and societal resource. Thus, the peripheries become a complex system encompassing the interlinking between rural and urban entities, where the interactions on an urban level suggest different dimensions for the urban study and project. The social and economic crisis of the beginning of the twenty-first century and, more importantly, the problem of food safety, price, and sustainability is changing the rural-urban link and food has been returned to the agenda.

The new practices for the production, distribution, and consumption of agri-food in the peripheric and marginal areas call for research able to understand the resulting social, economic, and environmental potentiality. The issue of food was often absorbed by the gastro-gentrification debate in the heart of the city core, whereas the periphery assumes other connotations linked to the problems of equity and integration. The periphery seems an ideal testing ground for food policies based not only on the lessons learned from alternative practices, but also on the nature-based solutions for tackling societal challenges such as climate change, food security, human health, and management.

mainstream and that have already been tested in different historical and cultural contexts. Risk society and reflexive modernisation seem to mirror these perspectives, supporting a criticism of the economy of scale and globalisation. The increasing number of food markets, consumption cooperatives, the Alternative Food Network, Community Supported Agriculture (CSA), and other food movement are signals that the food system may be entering a new era and will play a deeper, more differentiated role in the construction of society and territory. The food question is difficult to enclose within narrow barriers; on the contrary, it focuses on the interplay between the physical form and social sphere, and on economic and cultural practices that are looking for a response to the threat of climate change (Parham, 2015).

Foodshed: Application of Urban Studies

In a globalised food system, increased distances between production and consumption areas are often connected to social disconnection and loss of identification, owing to a hegemonic agri-industrial model that fails to respect the specific nature and value of local landscapes, agricultural practices, and of associated cultural practices. Monoculture agriculture that is technologically and chemically dependent has a huge impact on the environment, whereas the management of sustainable territory development involves economic, social, and environmental dimensions that rely on the short food supply chain as a tool for improving the economic and social resilience of the territory. Food production, processing, exchange, and consumption is an intricate web which is hard to capture theoretically given its complex interweaving of players, interests, and spaces: urban territory, peri-urban and rural realms. In Europe, spaces are framed in the city as a spatial condition characterised by co-penetrating rural and urban realms, beyond a simplistic centre/periphery opposition. The traditional notion of periphery linked, on the one hand, to the physical placement far from the centre while, on the other hand, to conditions of degradation and marginalization that often characterise suburban areas, today reveals a complex and contradictory concept, no longer attributable to just one clear and unambiguous definition. The Greek etymology of periphery is "to move around" and also points to the complex system and networks for supplying citizens. The movements of food are more economic than physical (Peters et. al. 2009), and for this very reason they are very complex to understand.

The analysis of food movement and its impact on the effects of climate change is multifaceted, but if we focus on the geography and processes of short food chains, the concept of the foodshed elaborated in the 1990s by Artur Getz will be meaningful when applied to urban studies. There are now several definitions of the foodshed which are focused on different aspects such as the foodshed representing a more locally reliant food system, or a geographic area which supplies the population. The mapping of the foodshed often has a projectable aim or is looking for the project of the alternative.

Mapping the Food Movement: the objective of the food movement is to individualize a nearby area from which the food arrives to the urban area and protect it as a "fresh food reservoir". Furthermore,

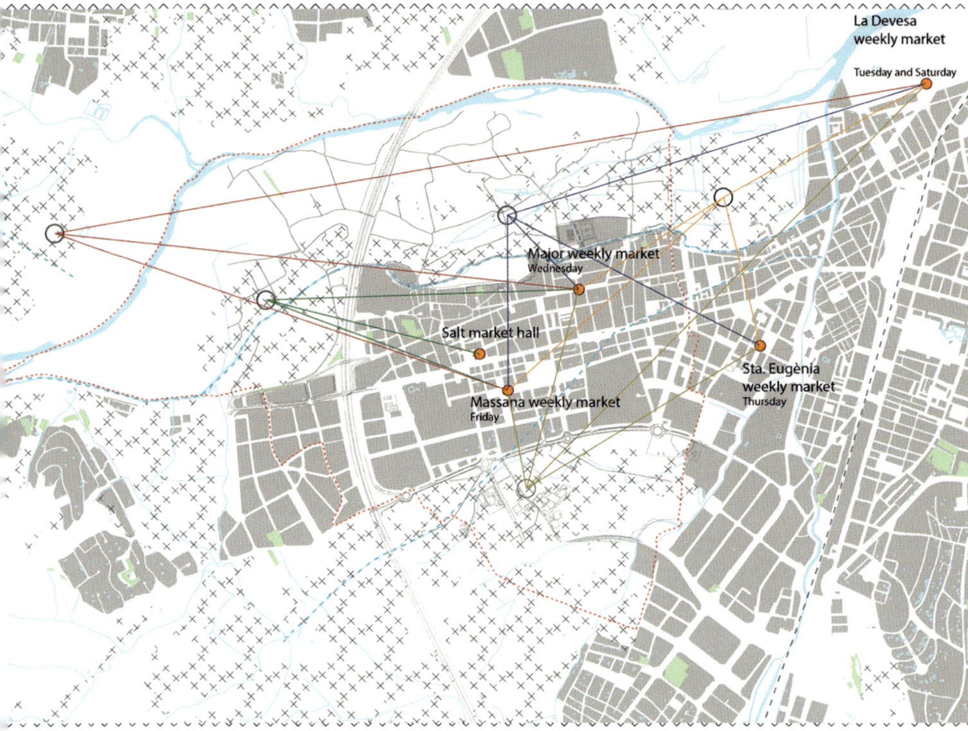

Figure 3. Provenance and circuits of food producers of the stall holder in weekly markets.
Graphic: Romà Garrido

The periphery embodies a complex system of space which is an archipelago of different uses, practices, and processes and matched to correspondingly diverse landscapes. The periphery is composed of both open and built-up spaces, green, grey, and blue spaces, as well consumption and agri-food production spaces which are, at the same time, educational and recreational places. As Viganò stated (2014), the redefinition of natural and social territories in the periphery and their dynamics inspire less abstract and more situated approaches. Tools and methodologies are required that are able to understand the "new modernity" in which the agency of natural elements is integrated into the social space and social space is integrated into the ecological frame. Looking at the territory of food is a means of directing or redirecting attention towards what constitutes support in the contemporary rural-urban territory. It focuses attention on the flows of food and energy, the meaning of the landscape form and image, lifecycles and citizens' empowerment, and social relationships to question what it means "to develop". The spatial and social quality of the peripheries are more often the result of the intense use of land, but if we shift their value onto their green, open, and agri-food productive areas, the meaning of development would change according to the theory of "degrowth" and sustainable principals.

it aims to understand the food journeys and the relationship with the transport system and the impact on the CO_2 footprint.

Mapping the Food Spaces: the aim of mapping the food spaces is to correlate the spatial distribution of food supply and food demand at the local scale in order to understand up to what point food spaces can create urban and collective spaces of socialisation and proximity. Moreover, the analysis of the types of food sold (local, ecological, from a cooperative, etc.) will help to identify the category of consumers and the market and food retailing threshold.

Mapping Networks of the Food Players: the aim of mapping the network of food players could represent the topological (not always spatial) relationships between some elements of the territory related to food like players' network maps used in food studies in an almost metaphoric, non-geo-referred sense, capitalising on the power of mapping as a conceptual tool for organising facts (Dansero & Pettenati 2015).

The Salt Foodshed: Nourishing the Periphery

The role public markets in European cities play in the modern period has been studied by integrating different perspectives and looking at their role in what is called gastro gentrification. Less relevant are investigations that explore public markets in small provincial towns or marginal suburban areas and the role they play not only in nourishing the urban-rural relationship, but also as a public service able to improve and manage food policies in the quest for social cohesion and integration and to reduce poverty. Our case study area is the municipality of Salt, Catalonia (Spain), which is located on the outskirts of the more major town of Girona. Salt has about 30,000 inhabitants of which 37% are immigrants. Salt also has a higher population density and a lower GDP than Girona. Historically, Salt was not only the food supplier of Girona, but also the neighbourhood of immigrants and the poor. Nowadays, because of urbanisation, the land used for cultivation has been reduced but is still a valuable space. The municipality has one food market hall and two weekly markets where food and other merchandise are available.

The analysis was conducted according to two main assessments: 1) that the markets need to be analysed in relationship to local food retailing, and 2) that the food markets are seen as the connectors of urban and rural areas, whatever they may be. The main concern was the local foodshed analysis used to comprehend which landscapes are related to the food distributed by the local market, which movements are connected to food, and what active social roles could be ascribed to the food issue. The analysis was conducted by embracing different dimension and methodologies. In other words, by mapping the local food retailing and the empty floor space close by the market, by surveying the type of food seller-producers or retailers, the type of products and their provenance, how the food was transported, and, finally, by interviewing the main players as well the director of the market and the public administration. The results were not unequivocal, but what emerged was that the impact the indoor market hall has on the physical and social dimension of

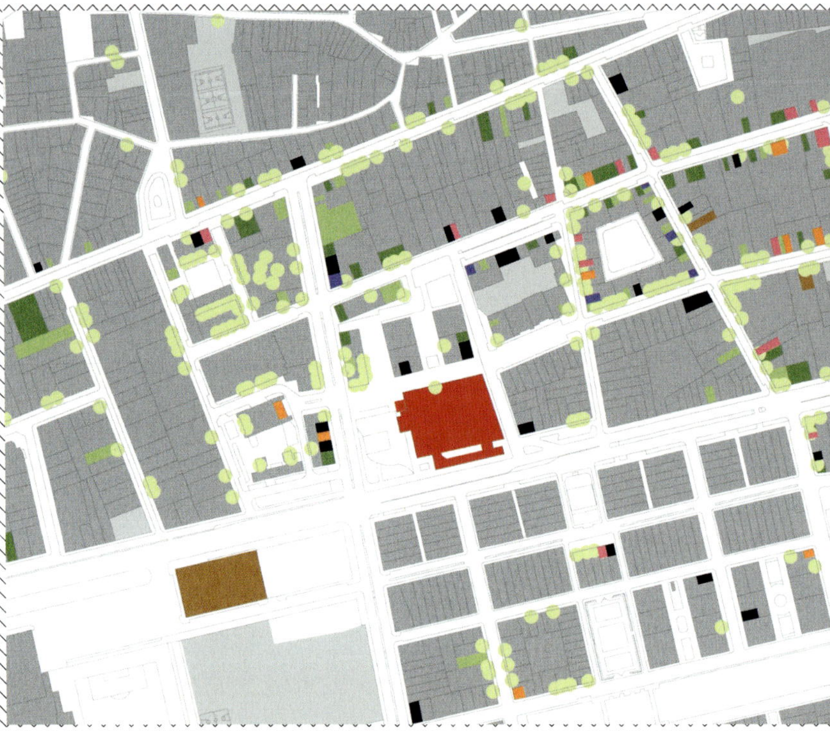

Figure 4. Commercial activity and empty ground floors around Salt Public Market Hall.
Graphic: Laura Plana

Food discourse and narratives are multiple and embrace different segmented dimensions as well as "food sovereignty, safety, equity and security". That said, their narrative with respect to territorial transformation could be synthetised into two larger scenarios:

Narrative 1: Proximity and short food chain

Growing concern about climate change and, above all, the social and economic crisis resulting from an obsolete model that has extended beyond its beginnings from 2007, has led to a paradigm shift in the product consumption system, with an increasing trend towards a more responsible consumption based on proximity and a short food chain. Through the understanding of these new opportunities, food policies able to respond to players involved in the short food chain can be encouraged.

Narrative 2: Food and social opportunities and equity

Worldwide and nationally, policies are formed and implemented to meet challenges to attain city -based policies, including social cohesion and inclusion, by working with bottom-up governance. The periphery is traditionally considered as marginal space. However, from both the economic and social dimension, it is a potentially innovative and experimental productive territory. It is an opportunity to develop long-term social resilience while creating positive economic effects by promoting business entrepreneurship in neighbouring businesses simply because of their proximity. Small-scale initiatives, such as selling agri-products at farmers' markets or establishing learning communities about gardening or gastronomy, result in communicative, instrumental, and emancipatory learning, thus enhancing the social capital of the participants.

the city is quite different from that of the weekly markets. The market hall was built in 1985 and renovated in 2004. During this renovation, the objective was to introduce a one-stop shop inside the market and cut the number of food stalls from nearly sixty to ten by focusing on the high specialization of the product being sold. The 2010 economic crisis, and maybe also the opening of a supermarket inside the market, caused the surrounding area to be affected by what is now recognisable as the phenomenon of a "food desert", visible in the presence of closed food stores. The director of the market hall is now encouraging the purchase of some of these shops to promote a social project linked to the food issue, a consumer cooperative, or multicultural gastronomy space to reactivate Salt's economy, and, furthermore, to promote integration and solidarity.

The situation in the weekly markets is completely different. The municipality does not see their potentialities for the city. In this case, the stall holders are divided between producers and food retailers. Food retailers work five to six days a week, while the producers, who are sometimes food producing cooperatives of whom most have land just within the municipal area of Salt, are used to going to the market just two or three times a week because they need to dedicate time to cultivation. The impression is that producers and retailers belong to two different economic and social models, which are in conflict, but the municipal adminstration has been unable to act as mediators. These two models respond to the different needs of Salt's consumers whose demand swings between low-priced food for the poorest population and higher-priced and higher-quality goods for the food-conscious consumer.

If it is true that local production and distribution is only a small segment of all food commerce and that it is difficult to completely change our nutritional system, then the study of the foodshed allows us to understand these spaces and their possibilities which could be translated into public policies and actions directed towards nourishing and learning from the periphery.

Bibliography

Brenner N. (2009) "What is Critical Urban Theory?" In: *City,* 13 (2–3), pp. 198–207.
Dansero E., Pettenat G. (2015) "The Atlas of Food. A Space of Representation, a Place for Policies, a Methodology of Territorial Analysis, 1–14". Retrieved from http://www.fao.org/fileadmin/templates/ags/docs/MUFN/CALL_FILES_EXPERT_2015/CFP1-05_Full_Paper.pdf (accessed 02.12.2017).
Marino D. (2016) *Agricoltura Urbana e filiere corte*. Torino, Franco Angeli.
Parham S. (2015) *Food and Urbanism: The Convivial City and a Sustainable Future*. London, Bloomsbury.
Peters C. J., Bills N. L., Wilkins J. L., Fick G. W. (2009) "Foodshed Analysis and its Relevance to Sustainability". In: *Renewable Agriculture and Food Systems*, 24(1), pp. 1–7.
Viganò P. (2014) *Territorialism*. Cambridge, Harvard University Press.

The Peripheri-City of the Inner Areas: Local Development in the Sicani Territory

Annalisa Contato

The Concept of Peripheri-City of the Inner Areas

The post-war territorial systems, characterised by the phenomenon of polarisation and by subordination in the relations between the centre and the periphery, between rural areas and urban poles, represent a spatial projection of the economic and social relations of a territory, from which the localisation of patterns of living, mobility, and services depends.

Polarisation initially produced the delocalisation of productive systems, the impoverishment of local economies, and a gradual depopulation of small centres due to the lack of adequate services and infrastructure, generating two-speed territories. Today, the dense and differentiated network of rural-urban poles disconnected from each other and characterised by a widespread micro-economic tissue—still of molecular type, but with a high potential of cultural, natural, agricultural, and zootechnical resources—can be interpreted as the ability and resilience of the peripheral territory that is reacting with the strength of its territorial and human capital by expressing the value of its uniqueness, and that arises as more than what cannot can be eradicated from its place of origin, thus adding the value and strength of territorial rooting to the concept of globalisation (Corrado 2005; Bighi et al. 2010).

In recognition of the current territorial metamorphosis—or rather recognition of the fact that the territory is back to being the main subject of economic and social processes, where the conflict of flows occurs—it can be stated that these processes should be anchored, rooted, and deployed in the territory as a reticular system through which local economies face the challenge of the global economy with the strength of what is called "horizontal society", which places the territory as the organisational principle of production and inclusion (Bonomi et al. 2016). Hence, it is possible to affirm the importance of the recent definition and identification of the Italian Inner Areas, a deeply heterogeneous territorial dimension in geographical, economic, social, cultural, and eco-systemic terms that expresses different basic needs and requirements from those of urban poles. This definition, in Italy, found in the national strategy *Strategia Nazionale per le Aree Interne (SNAI),* and through the ordinary funds of the Stability Law and the Community Funds 2014–2020, the opportunity to boost development, reduce disparities, and strengthen cohesion. The Department for Development and Economic Cohesion *(Dipartimento per lo Sviluppo e la Coesione Economica DPS)*, starting from a polycentric reading of the territory, identified the level of peripherality of all Italian municipalities (identifying three different levels: ultra-remote, remote, and intermediate) through the

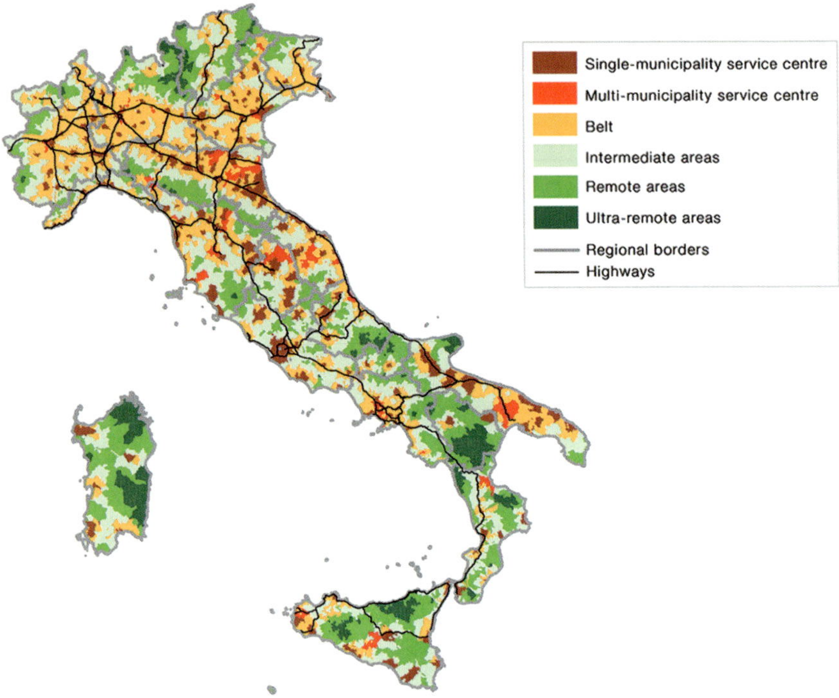

Figure 1. The level of peripherality in Italy. From this identification started the individuation of the Inner Areas and the processes towards a new form of local development. Source: DPS

The dense and differentiated network of rur-urban poles disconnected from each other and characterised by peculiar identities and a widespread micro-economic fabric has been defined and identified by Italian national policies with the term Inner Areas.

Innovation in the process introduced in Italy by the *Strategia Nazionale per le Aree Interne (SNAI)* concerns not only the recognition of the value of these vast territories, their variety and complexity, but above all the elaboration of an approach with a constant interaction between national and local levels (with the intermediate transition of the regions), thus urging participatory processes and elaboration of shared local strategies (Lucatelli 2016). Hence, the role of municipalities—in the form of associations of municipalities and as a basic unit of political decision-making (DPS 2014)—emerges in the construction process of local development strategies and for the realisation of projects: the associative capacity of territories becomes a crucial element for the feasibility of development.

Other important innovative elements of SNAI are constituted by providing support for development (in a market perspective) and citizenship (facilitating access to services), particularly as regards citizens' quality of life, and the elaboration of a medium to long-term area strategy in order to prevent this developmental opportunity from being transformed into a set of fragmented projects that fail to recognise the existing polycentric system.

use of a set of indicators based on the assessment of the distance, in terms of time, of a settlement from a "service centre", meaning to a kind of service centre that only a municipality or an aggregate of neighbouring municipalities can simultaneously offer: all secondary schools, hospitals of the first level DEA sites,[1] and platinum, gold, or silver railway stations (DPS 2012).[2] Subsequently, the DPS conducted further analyses that showed that areas with a level of peripherality equal to or greater than "intermediate" are characterised by low population density (about 25% of the national population on a territorial dimension of about 60% of the total), a significant demographic decline below the critical threshold (Istat 2011a), a high rate of elderly population, a decrease of the economy mainly linked to the agricultural-productive system (Istat 2011b), and a gradual reduction of local public services. It is thus assessed that this structural situation influences strongly economic and social development processes (Mantino, Lucatelli 2016). SNAI's attention to "peripherality" aims to highlight above all the distance in terms of socio-economic and political connections, a "relational peripherality" which can also occur near to or even within central areas (Copus, Noguera 2016). This method of territorial characterisation, in fact, overcomes the classic contrast between city and rural areas, as it finds that a gravitational centre can be both a small municipality and a set of neighbouring municipalities capable of offering basic services, while "peripheral" may be a large urban pole that is unable to provide adequate basic services (Lucatelli 2016).

The definition of the term "inner periphery", used for the first time in the European document *The Territorial State and Perspectives of the European Union*, describes well the characteristics of the Inner Areas: "Internal peripheries are unique types of rural peripheries in European terms. The vast majority of these areas are located in Central and Eastern and in Southeast Europe and most of them have serious problems. Their peripherality comes primarily from their poor accessibility and paucity of real urban centres where central functions can be concentrated. These problems derive from the historical under-development of these territories and they are often compounded by specific features of the settlement network or social characteristics. The main problems of these areas are their weak and vulnerable regional economies and their lack of appropriate job opportunities. In these circumstances negative demographic processes, notably out-migration and ageing of the population, are getting stronger and stronger. These trends create the conditions for social exclusion, and even territorial exclusion from mainstream socio-economic processes and opportunities" (Ministry of National Development of Hungary, Váti Nonprofit Ltd. 2011, p. 57).

With the term "inner periphery", the spatial concept of peripherality—attributed to sparsely populated areas and placed on the margins of great urban centres—has therefore been accompanied by a new reading of urban-rural contexts where peripherality is more linked socio-economic characteristics than to geographic ones, recognising a propensity to change rather than staying in a state of decadence. Even if weaknesses are acknowledged—as the lack of access to services and to other opportunities, insufficient infrastructure interconnection with repercussions for productive development (due to the difficult supply of raw materials and the connection to logistical nodes to access markets), poor quality of life in terms of social disadvantages and social exclusion—Inner Areas are subject to a reverse gradient compared to the negative centre-periphery definition, which

Figure 2. The Sicilian Inner Area "Terre Sicane". View from Giuliana's Castle. Photo: Gino Pira

Peripheral territories are in fact characterised by poor infrastructural endowments, by a constantly decreasing population, and by rur-urban settlements in precarious state of maintenance. But they are not only this. The peripheral territories, or rather the inner peripheries, are dense with landscape, natural, and cultural resources, and values related to artisan and agricultural production. They are places intent on change and experimentation that are capable of generating extraordinary interrelations between innovation and tradition, where human capital—especially in recent years—is demonstrating its potential and ability to adapt to the challenge imposed by global processes. The inner peripheries are places that offer a different quality of life than that offered by the large urban poles, where it is possible to establish more healthy relations with the territory and with the inhabitants, and sense of relation and sharing strengthens the human aspect of settlement. In these places, the "middle territories" of the urban centres assume a new role as they have the potential to become an interface space, connected and porous, which generates the transition from a reticular system formed by lines and points to a "territorial archipelago" (Carta 2017) where the force of the network creates new plots to share identities, roles, and hierarchies, creating a new urban metabolism.

highlights the value of identity, high heterogeneity, high levels of territorial rooting, low anthropic pressure, unique and diversified cultural and landscape resources, quality of agri-pastoral production systems, and a lifestyle that is alternative to that of great urban poles. Moreover, today, as these territories are characterised as places for bottom-up experiments and for new innovative economies that cope with discomfort in infrastructure systems, a potential of economic and human capital is attributed to them linked to the quality of life and welfare of the population (Espon Geospecs 2014). In their complexity and variety, therefore, the Inner Areas represent areas in which a rethinking of the rural/urban, society/territory, society/economy, and territory/production relationship is increasingly urgent for stopping the process of abandoning; empowering and networking small innovative experiences (start ups, living lab, "makers", active associations, etc.) that are demonstrating that it is still possible for the Inner Areas to become cosy and functional places through the realisation of new local centralities of global attractiveness (Carta 2016).

The Sicani Archipelago

The "SicaniLab"[3] has recognised the existence of a strong territorial coalition formed by twenty-four municipalities (Contato, Orlando 2015) in the Sicilian Inner Area "Terre Sicane"—formed by twelve towns of rural character and by villages in the hillside and the mountains, immersed in a vast agricultural area—which led to the identification of a wider territory on which to define development strategies in the medium to long-term.

The qualitative and quantitative analyses carried out on this territory have allowed it to be defined as a "territorial archipelago" and recognised as "an urban and rural settlement system connected by landscape, production, and mobility infrastructure that act as connective interfaces. The connective system of the territorial archipelago consists of a perimeter belt landscape around urban areas with different ecosystem-functions: agricultural/productive, river corridor, renaturalisation fields, sports facilities, slow mobility, etc. … The territorial archipelago … uses the power of its reticular relations, sharing identities, roles, and hierarchies" (Carta 2017, p. 44). Therefore, the Sicani archipelago is characterised by cultural, agricultural, and landscape islands of excellence and by a wide area between the various nodes/cities which through the use of the territorial device of "interface" will become a connective and relational space. Therefore, the territorial strategy for the Sicani Archipelago will have to identify strategies, policies, planning devices, and specific actions necessary for reducing the infrastructural gap, for enabling networking processes, generating connective functions, and acting on territorial metabolism, thus acting on different levels of connection.

A first level is inside of the area—the "connective interfaces device"—where new relationships between the parts are to be created to generate new metabolisms and flows, reinforcing the structure of the archipelago and the internal connections through active networking processes (Dematteis, Guarrasi 1995; Bighi et al. 2010). Connections between the different territorial components will not only have to be infrastructural but above all cultural, functional, and connected to landscapes, in which the interface space becomes an infrastructure of porous spaces and dense resources,

Figure 3. An example of bottom-up urban and social regeneration. The premises of the former convent of Sant'Antonio in Cianciana have been restored (after almost 60 years) thanks to the Oops Association, "makers", and artists who voluntarily contributed. The site was inaugurated with the initiative "Artemidee il Festival del pensiero creativo", and today it is a site for cultural and social events. Photo: Oops Association.

The inner peripheries are now subject to territorial and social metamorphosis in the sense that they are returning to be attractive places for younger generations through the rediscovery of the potential that they offer in terms of resources and propensity to change. Characterised by an evergrowing number of bottom-up innovation experiences of both traditional crafts and agricultural production, and with abandoned sites in social and cultural places having been recovered, thus allowing the rediscovery the sense of sharing and conviviality typical of these places in the past to be rediscovered, these sites presently need to be discussed, described, and thought of in a new way. The experience of tourism, for example, is a new way to make these territories known and to increase talk about them (especially on social networks) through images and stories that transmit not only the beauty of the territories but above all the sensations of living there, known and rediscovered local traditions, their different quality of life, their sense of hospitality, and their strength in constantly innovating.

The inner peripheries are formed not only by territorial resources, but above all by the human capital that inhabits them, which is connected to history and is also experiencing new and different forms of development. It is from the story of the latter that we can work to create a new image of the inner peripheries, to increase their attractiveness, in terms of investments and for new inhabitants.

identities, and innovation that will have to modulate communication between the different spatial entities, and between different nodes and connectors, creating new places and new identifications for a constant innovation of the archipelago. The second level is the regional one, networking the five Sicilian Inner Areas, building a network of local identifications and production chains rooted in the territory, in which heterogeneity becomes a network of polycentric ecosystems and multiple multifunctional opportunities. Finally, the third level of connection concerns the construction of relationship with those urban poles that can act as a gateway city in order to create a multilayer network territory (Clementi 2007), in which the different layers are held together by internal and external structured connective bundles, ensuring that the externalities produced by the network reach all levels and that each node becomes an attracter and flow generator.

Notes/Bibliography

1 Represents a functional aggregation of operational units that, in addition to the benefits provided by Emergency Rooms, provides observation, short-term stay and resuscitation functions, and diagnostic-therapeutic interventions of general medicine, general surgery, orthopedics and traumatology, and intensive cardiology therapy.
2 A classification of Italian train stations based on the number of passengers and the frequency of the trains.
3 The research project on the "Terre Sicane" Inner Area is conducted in the Local Development Laboratory of the "Polo Universitario di Ricerca di Bivona e Santo Stefano Quisquina per l'energia, l'ambiente e le risorse del territorio". The Research Centre began in 2011 through the renewal of an agreement between the Region of Sicily, the University of Palermo, the Province of Agrigento, and the cities of Bivona and S. Stefano Quisquina. The Laboratory (SicaniLab) is coordinated by Professor Maurizio Carta and is composed of B. Lino, A. Contato, M. Orlando, D. Ronsivalle, M. Marafon Pecoraro, G. Mortellaro, A. Carrara, and M. Buondonno.

Bighi S., Cotella G., Rota F.S. eds. (2010) *Torino e Piemonte fra locale e globale. politiche di rete e ancoraggi territoriali. Tre percorsi per la ricerca*. Working Paper 32/2010. Politecnico e Università di Torino, Dipartimento Interateneo Territorio.
Bonomi A., Masiero R., Della Puppa F. (2016) *La società circolare. Fordismo, capitalismo molecolare, sharing economy*. Roma, Comunità concrete.
Carta M. (2016) "Innovazione, circolarità e sviluppo locale". In: Carta M., Lino B., Ronsivalle D. eds. (2016) *Re-cyclical Urbanism. Visioni, paradigmi e progetti per la metamorfosi circolare*. Trento, ListLab. pp. 92–103.
Carta M. (2017) "Planning for the Rur-Urban Anthropocene". In: Schröder J., Carta M., Ferretti M., Lino B. eds. (2017) *Territories: Rural-Urban Strategies*. Berlin, Jovis Verlag. pp. 36–53.
Clementi A. (2007) "Un avvenire possibile del territorio italiano". In: Ministero delle Infrastrutture, Dicoter eds. (2007) *Reti e territori al futuro. Materiali per una visione*. Roma, Ministero delle Infrastrutture. pp. 11–34.
Contato A., Orlando M. (2015) "Il territorio dei Monti Sicani. Il sistema delle risorse territoriali per l'attivazione di politiche di sviluppo locale". In: Carta M., Ronsivalle D. (2015) *Territori interni*. Roma, Aracne. pp. 84–103.
Copus A., Noguera J. (2016) "Le 'periferie interne'. Che cosa sono e di quali politiche necessitano?". In: *Agriregionieuropa*, 45/2016. pp. 10–13.
Corrado F. ed. (2005) *Le risorse territoriali nello sviluppo locale*. Firenze, Alinea.
Dematteis G., Guarrasi V. eds. (1995) *Urban Networks*. Bologna, Pàtron.
DPS Dipartimento per lo sviluppo e la coesione economica (2012) *Nota Metodologica per la definizione delle Aree Interne*. Roma.
DPS Dipartimento per lo sviluppo e la coesione economica (2014) *Strategia nazionale per le Aree interne. Accordo di Partenariato 2014–2020*. Sezione 1°. Roma.
Espon Geospecs (2014) *Inner Peripheries: A Socio-Economic Territorial Specificity*. Final Report. Luxembourg, Espon.
Istat (2011a) *Censimento della popolazione e delle abitazioni*. Roma, Istat.
Istat (2011b) *Censimento dell'agricoltura*. Roma, Istat.
Lucatelli S. (2016) "Strategia Nazionale per le Aree Interne: un punto a due anni dal lancio della Strategia". In: Agriregionieuropa, 45/2016. pp. 4–9.
Mantino F., Lucatelli S. (2016) "Le aree interne in Italia: un laboratorio per lo sviluppo locale". In: *Agriregionieuropa*, 45/2016. pp. 1–3.
Ministry of National Development of Hungary, Váti Nonprofit Ltd. (2011) *The Territorial State and Perspectives of the European Union*. Background document for the Territorial Agenda of the European Union 2020, presented at the Informal Meeting of Ministers responsible for Spatial Planning and Territorial Development on 19th May 2011 Gödöllő, Hungary.

The Role of Blue Infrastructure for Urban Metabolism

Daniele Caruso

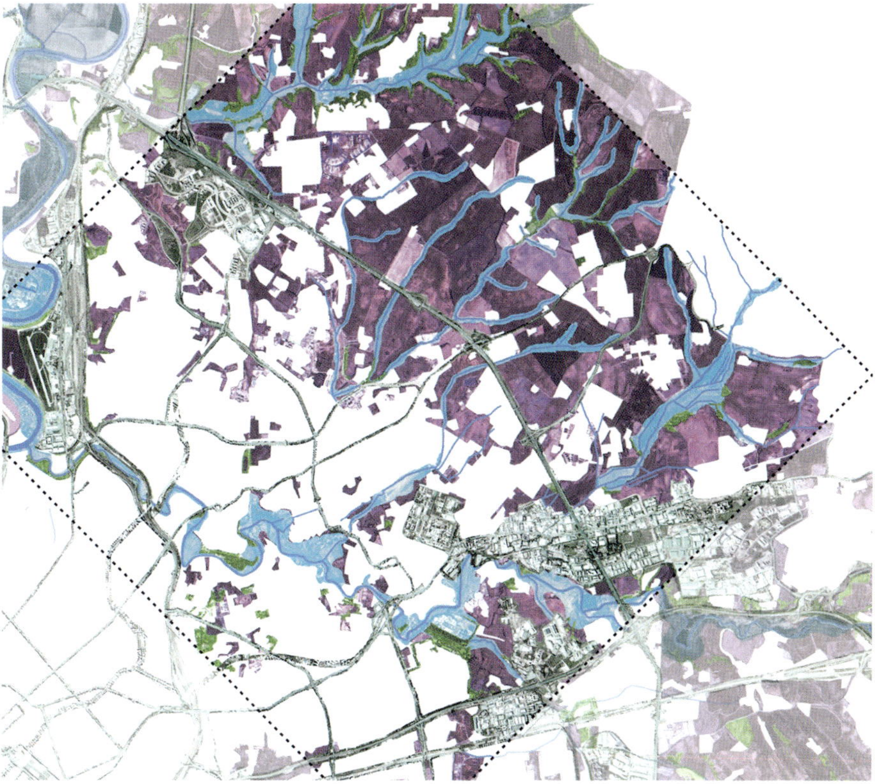

Figure 1. The construction of the blue network in the north quadrant of Rome.
Graphic: Daniele Caruso

In the avant-garde culture the role of blue infrastructure is occupying an important position that demonstrates how the vision of the future of cities is changing and how it increasingly depends on natural resources. However, each country is characterised by its own political framework and by own visions, and this also reflects different declinations of these countries intend for blue infrastructure, as well as for its ecological, social, material, or immaterial components. Looking at the European context, it is easy to find a widening spectrum of differences corresponding to the economic, political, and environmental priorities that the numerous countries have, which determines the development of several instruments that are the result of the necessary expectations these countries hold. When the concept of resilience is applied to water, it also produces different interpretations in different countries of the European Union. The city of Rotterdam's Resilience Strategy (2013), for example, proposes an integrated approach to the water: "From the laying of the first foundations of the city, the spirit of resilience has been engrained in our psyche. Instead of fighting the water, we used it to our advantage, creating land, establishing a new waterway (Nieuwe Waterweg) and promoting our city and world–class port as the main gateway to Europe."[3]

Figure 2. Vacaresti Park in Romany is a former dyke near Dambovita river which is presently undergoing a renaturalisation process. Photo: Daniele Caruso

As is well known, the concept of periphery is undergoing a process of redfinition that widens the field of work in which this term is used. These aspects have generated a cultural change and a great awareness on the part of planners and architects who are tackling more complex situations that are bound up with environmental issues. These planners need to transform those parts of the city that are usually considered to be remainders of past activities (brownfield, landfill, dump, etc.) into more complex catalysts capable of ensuring the future of cities and responding to climate change effects. "Any rational organisation of territory produces a remainder" (Clément 2004). Furthermore, it is questioned what is happening to the municipalities which also require a role as protagonist in those scenarios of transformation that are initially conducted by a top-down approach. "Europe is a union of cities and towns; around 75% of population of the EU have chosen urban areas as their place to live."[1] In this respect, it becomes more important to understand periphery as an urban dimension that simultaneously considers themes such as energy, technologies, optimisation in the resource control, mobility, safety, logistics, and also agriculture, resilience, climate change. In this way objectives as welfare, well-being, and safety make way for protection and control networks, and for social inclusion networks established by active citizenship. In this perspective the periphery changes its aspect and moves from an area of expectation toward dynamic processes that transform it into a laboratory of experimentation in which environmental patterns and communities together play a key role.

By comparison, at present in the south of Italy, some cities are unfortunately fighting draught and emergencies, which is a problem that is frequently linked not only to climate change but also to the management of water resources. Depending on the factors, these dynamics could highlight, in a different way, different situations according to the economic and political stability and the development level of these countries. Looking within the same European continent, there are different ways to approach water resources within inhabited territories, and these depend on a series of articulated parameters that are identifiable in cities. This point of view transforms the peripheries as places where blue infrastructure comprises landscape networks, meaning a field of work characterized by the presence of several layers, some material and some immaterial, that coexist and cooperate harmoniously.

Despite this, defining blue infrastructure has proven very difficult. The definition that the European commission has proposed for blue infrastructure is not clear, for example, because this infrastructure is frequently included within related functions of green infrastructure and so lacks a fully autonomous description.[4] "GI (green infrastructure) is a strategically planned network of natural and semi-natural areas with other environmental features designed and managed to deliver a wide range of ecosystem services. It incorporates green spaces (or blue if aquatic ecosystems are concerned) and other physical features in terrestrial (including coastal) and marine areas. On land, GI is present in rural and urban settings" (European Commission 2013). This represents one of the crucial issues that has emerged in the first studies on the role of water in the future of policies. This research question, in particular, is divided in two parts: the first is an overall study/exploration phase that aims to define a theoretical framework of what is currently considered blue infrastructure, what policies are intend for it, what scenarios they foresee for an ecologically oriented development of cities in order to tackle effects of climate change and to ensure sustainable development. In order to respond in the first phase and summarise the criteria through which these countries[5] define blue infrastructure, the study envisions the realisation of six levels of interpretation that have been used to describe blue infrastructure and to articulate its field of work:

1. Landscape networks and conformed technical infrastructure for the dynamic coexistence of water and cities, mitigation and risk adaptations, but also of water cycles management.

2. Permeable and highly qualified vegetated landscape networks for the improvement of microclimate and air quality in cities.

3. Waste sites and drosscape networks (polluted water basins and their marginalised, abandoned spaces) to be recycled and converted into public spaces for collective, social, and productive uses.

4. Road infrastructure and sewage system adapt to respond to the new water treatment issues through energetic and digital networks.

Figure 3. The nature reserve of Aniene River crosses the periphery of Rome. Photo: Daniele Caruso

For a long time, the periphery has been imagined as a planned or spontaneous spatial container in which people live in an informal manner. Frequently, projects for these territories have not considered the specificity of their sites or the presence of a historical track. "The public periphery has frequently been considered to be the result of a finished project that is impermeable to procedural modification and expresses a planning culture inclined toward big and complex architectural machines" (Gasparrini 2006).[2] However, a greater acquisition of awareness by citizens at a global level around some important themes--including climate change effects, economic crisis, and many other factors—induce us to find a common field of orientation for different research. In fact, different ways of thinking the periphery reflect different cultural approaches in countries in regard to certain issues that can be observed separately. "The periphery is everywhere"; it is where socio-economic and environmental issues converge, where scientific communities are faced with ensuring liveable conditions in the present moment and for new generations. The themes of "green and blue infrastructure" work, in different ways, as a network that negotiates economic opportunities, social integration, and bottom-up actions, and which stimulates and encourages general involvement. Each territory develops a local strategy because of their local specificity which is at the same time nevertheless situated within a shared field work.

5. Highly qualified public spaces as networks for the improvement of local identity, for better uses, and safety of the communities.

6. Sites of convergence of multiple actors to be appropriated by citizens, recycle resources, enter into new collaborative agreements for the common good, and develop the circular economy.[6]

These six levels represent a starting point and a key for achieving multidimensional and multi-scale interpretations that go beyond the traditional natural field, thus offering ecological and socio-economic declinations that aree more complex and useful for describing the metabolism of contemporary cities, their multiple risks and dynamics, and new landscape forms with their economies.

The second part of research is focused on the role of river corridors in peripheral areas and, starting from landscape ecology approaches,[7] which currently engage new dynamics in order to describe this new ecosystem. This work aims to develop a new key that understands these natural components as elements that are facing a progressive migration within urban contexts that are increasingly fragmented and characterised by human factors. In this perspective, the river corridors not only interact with large areas but also with fragmented and complex settelements that are above all characterised by the presence of artifical water networks (underground, sewage systems, artificial basins, etc.) and open spaces, thus constituting infrastructure that regulates urban metabolism.

The use of these six level of interpretation (also through a set of indicators) allows us to realise new interpretative maps that construct an important framework of information—as combined quantitative and qualitative analysis that supports policies and collects detailed information on the mapping of these ecosystems. In this perspective peripheral areas are considered part of urban ecosystems.[8] Mapping qualitative data allows us also to monitor the informal actions carried out generally by local communities and to observe the behaviour of citizens. The possibility of mapping and of documenting these data improves our awareness of them and transforms ordinary places into intelligent territories. "An intelligent territory can apply adequate information and communication technologies within its perimeter in order to maximise efficiency: it can increase competiveness while reducing resource consumption."[9]

The case study of the periphery of Rome represents, in this sense, one the first interpretations that is concentrated on very select choices, in which the crucial figure is a multi-scalars blue network capable of adjusting to the changing climate conditions and creating an innovative network of public spaces focusing on certain commons. At the geostrategic scale, the hydrological system--together with large floodplains and the infiltration of blue networks--aims to overcome the mono-functionality and impenetrability of urban fabrics and industrial/commercial clusters. In this perspective, in addition to the design of blue network as public space and as technical and smart network, there exists a constellation of local initiatives produced by associations—for example,

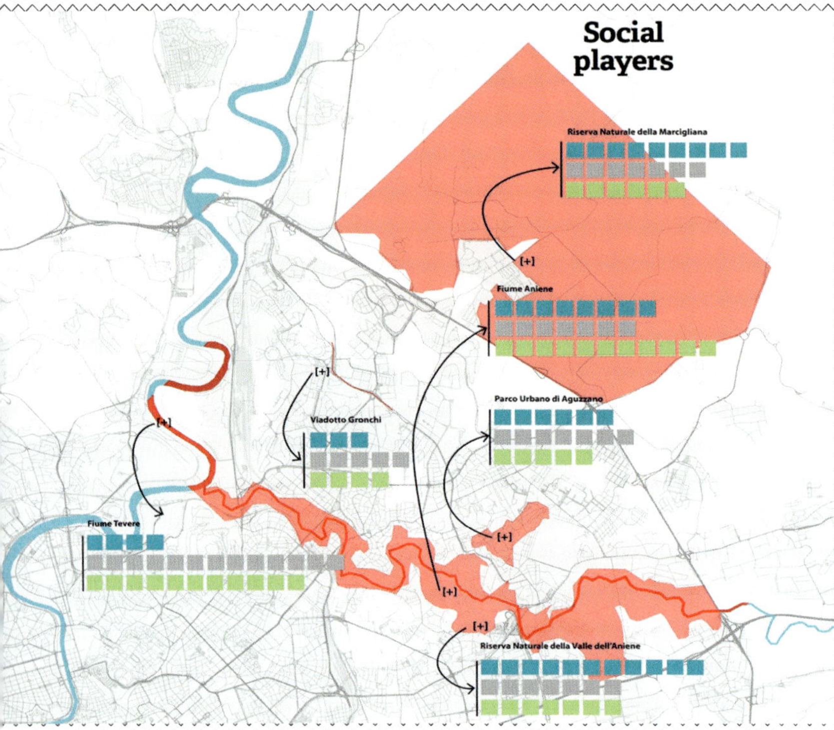

Figure 4. Social players (local communities and associations) active in the point of confluence between Aniene and Tiber rivers. Graphic: Daniele Caruso

The construction of a narrative of place has emerged in the research work, beginning with the ability to explore the context of communities. Narratives try to transmit context awareness. "The territories as a palimpsest" is constituted by material and immaterial layers, and the its knowledge becomes the starting point to construct collaborative maps that are capable of imagining the future of the city through an overall vision as collection of a small actions that generate flows and networks. However, the paradigm has changed and the meaning of periphery needs to be turned by new interpretations that consider important spatial dynamics, as well as socio-economic ones, and even those that the public action does not control. In some cases this involves social innovation that produces a bottom-up approach in urban regeneration processes.

At the same time, the EU Urban Agenda aims at smart and sustainable cities created through the empowerment of key concepts that include social inclusion, stakeholder involvements, and urban intelligence. Public institutions as mediators and groups of communities as the principal actors modify the way to conceive urban policies. These concepts applied to blue and green infrastructure explain how they contribute not only to the environmental balances but also how they concieve ecosystem services that influence natural and also socio-economic development.

ZappataRomana association[10]—, by citizens, and projects realised by public institutions. These initiatives define a new map of actors that can be flexible and adapt to socio-economic dynamics and be monitored for a long time. In this sense, the possibility of flooding may be utilized as a resource for changing the forms of the landscape and to heighten the contrast to the further build up of defensive structures. At the same time, other measures can be undertaken such as the recycling of white and grey waters, the safeguarding of permeable soils through compatible uses (for example, urban agriculture and small pleasure gardens at the local level), or the setting up of energy devices to be managed in the urban clusters. In addition, these spaces demand appropriate opportunities for social life and urban centrality to which blue infrastructure should respond.

Notes/Bibliography

1 See the data given by the European Commission in a publication by the European Environment Agency: "Europe is a union of cities and towns; around 75% of the population of the EU have chosen urban areas as their place to live. But the impacts of urbanisation extend beyond city borders. Europeans have adopted urban lifestyles and they use city amenities such as cultural, educational, or health services. While cities are the motors of Europe's economy and creators of European wealth, they depend heavily on resources of outside regions to meet their demand for resources like energy, water, and food, and to accommodate waste and emissions" (EEA 2011, p. 5).

2 The traditional image of public periphery is described by Carlo Gasparrini (2006).

3 In this consultation document Arnoud Molenaar, chief resilience officer of Rotterdam, claims that the city will be better prepared for the future, and he states: "This document is Rotterdam's first Resilience Strategy. Our primary goal is to make resilience–thinking common practice in our city and part of our DNA" (City of Rotterdam 2013, p. 9).

4 In the studies and publications reported in the text there are different definitions of what is considered Green Infrastructure, including water resources (European Commission 2013).

5 For more insight, the first phase of the research considers case studies from all over the world and not only in EU countries.

6 The circular economy aims to renew water management in order to achieve an efficient system. This produces an important innovation in the urban context, also in terms of social and cultural impacts, increasing the awareness of the scarcity of resources. The circularity applied to water represents an important challenge for the future of cities, starting from the improvement of the sewage systems, the reduction of water loss, the improvement of water quality, and the recycling of resources and their treatment.

7 The contemporary dynamics reverse the situation and the approach of landscape ecology deeply, by transforming and seeing the city as an ecological and environmental pattern.

8 In the fourth report of *Urban Ecosystems*, "Mapping and Assessment of Ecosystems and their Services", urban ecosystems are defined as socio-ecological systems which are composed of green infrastructure (GI also includes water resources) and built infrastructure.

9 Paolo Fusero (2009) wrote about four different ways of applying intelligence to territories, one of them is obtaining intelligent information from territories.

10 "ZappataRomana" is an association that is transforming degraded and abandoned spaces into new forms of collective use including urban agriculture, involving local communities, and transforming them into economic actors.

Berger A. (2006) "Drosscape". In: Waldheim C. ed. (2006) *The Urban Landscape Urbanism Reader*. New York, Princeton Architectural Press, pp. 197–217.

Bonomi A., Della Puppa F., Masiero R. (2016) *La società circolare. Fordismo capitalismo molecolare, sharing economy*. Roma, DeriveApprodi.

City of Rotterdam (2013) *Resilience strategy. Ready for 21st century*. Rotterdam, Veenam+.

Clément G. ed. (2005) *Manifesto del terzo paesaggio*. Macerata, Quodlibet.

EEA (2011) *European Environment Agency*. Yearbook. Copenhagen.

European Commission (2013) "Green Infrastructure (GI). Enhancing Europe's Natural Capital". In: *Communication from the Commission to the European Parliament, the Council, the European Economic and Social Committee of the Regions*. Bruxelles, European Commission. pp. 2–3.

Fusero P. (2009) *E-ity: Digital Networks and Cities of the Future*. Barcellona, LIST Lab. Gasparrini C. (2006) "Mestieri e Misteri del progetto urbano in Italia: un dibattito ordinario e una prassi straordinaria". In: Belli A. ed. (2006) *Oltre la città pensare la periferia*. Napoli, Edizioni Cronopio, pp. 71–82.

Waldheim C. (2006) *The Landscape Urbanism Reader*. New York, Princeton Architectural Press.

Mobility Infrastructure: Connecting Tools of Peripheral Areas or Techno-Ecologial Services?

Gaia Sgaramella

Figure 1. View from the Autogrill bridge on the motorway A4 Milan–Venice. Photo: Gaia Sgaramella

Are motorways only a connection tool or could they become something new? Nowadays, when motorways are mentioned, our attitude is to visualise asphalt surfaces, roadways, guard-rails, and large road axes that lead us through unlimited territories toward multiple destinations. This simple description feeds the modern vision of the motorway, which instead is more complex than what we can see. Influenced by temporal, social, and technological dynamics of each period, motorways have assumed different meanings and roles in time. Starting from the "stone age" of infrastructure, the first motorway ante litteram was the Royal Way of Persia from the fifth century B.C., followed by Roman roads, the Silk Road and so on. All these examples differ from modern motorways in their form, but not in their objectives. They are basically governed by three principles: to connect different territories, to exchange resources and culture, and to define a link between people and territories, reinforcing power and wealth. These paths share the change of shapes and spaces they cross, rather than the change of tools for travelling. After the first technological and industrial revolution, the motorway became the consequence and the outcome of the development of communications technology, the cultural perception of space, and the development of urban forms over time. From this moment, the motorway started its genealogy, following three principal steps. From an initial stage 1.0 concerned with the need to move, through a 2.0 level concerned with the development of the motorway between innovation and standardisation, we arrive to a 3.0 stage related to the unexpected ecological impact that motorways have had on territories, including those

Figure 2. Roma. Mural of Chekos "Ventrem feri imperium", Tor Vergata, viale della Sorbona. GRAart project, street art under Raccordo Anulare, promoted by Anas. Photo: Gaia Sgaramella

Peripheries are places where change is possible. They are indefinite, hybrid, and transition spaces. Processes that activates them are dynamic and never deterministic. In these urban poles, through improvisation and necessity, creative and unplanned dynamics come to fruition, creating new and different spaces. The process is in progress, activation tools can be assigned, but the results are unpredictable. As Marcel Proust said, "An hour is not just an hour, it's a jar full of scents, sounds, projects, climates", as is the time of the peripheries. Over time, they activate adaptive and incremental urban recycling dynamics, connecting into an activating polycentric system that instantly uses resilience and pragmatism to change places that are waiting for a destination. Each action is not an end to itself, but defines other actions, and transformation takes place in a slow or fast way, in response to the reaction time of society and to the kind of need it manifests. The peripheries are landscapes in crisis and potential hubs of innovation where city and territory become propulsive and active in change. Infrastructure could be a tool to implement these processes.

that are now on-going. The first period (M 1.0) started with the first industrial revolution and finished in 1913 with the spread of mass-produced cars in the US. The network systems were built without a plan, to respond and solve practical problems caused by the transportation of resources from the countryside to the city and technological development. The second period (M 2.0) started in 1913 with the mass production of the Ford T-model and lasted until 1963. This step was characterised by the succession of destruction and reconstruction periods between the two world wars, where the network system was a tool of development, engine of economic process, and link for peripheral areas through a planned system. The third period (M 3.0) started in 1963 with the publication of the book *Silent Spring* by Rachel Carson and it is still on-going. This book opened an ecological period, which influenced the environmentalist perception of the Anthropocene in relationship to nature, as well as the design process with an ecological approach.[1] Here the motorway assumed a role of impact, a symbol of negative actions of the artificial world on the natural environment. Over the last decades, the motorway has been critisised for impacting natural ecosystems, driving territorial fragmentation, and diminishing the quality of landscapes.

Starting from this perception and from an ecological approach to design and to management, targets were approved in Europe that were to be achieved within precisely specified periods. For mobility infrastructure the most important goals into the European policies are TEN-T and the EU Targets for 2020, 2030 and 2050 related to climate change and energy. One may argue that constructing new infrastructure will no longer be a priority, in particular for motorway networks. We are a liquid society (Bauman 2011) in which boundaries and reference points (in this case physical and not social) are lost and no longer need to exist in the digital interconnection systems of information and communication technologies (ICT). This underlines the relativity of the concept of marginality. If infrastructure is created as the engine of economic development for peripheral situations, then the result is a scenario in which boundaries have no reason to exist. Inevitably infrastructure arrives at a state of obsolescence, due to the inability to keep pace with time and society, which changes between the design and the execution phase of the works.

In the ESPON 2020 European cooperation programme, one priority objective is marginal areas affected by the inaccessibility of priority services of general interest. Accessibility has also been the key element in the ESPON 2013 project TRACC (Transport accessibility at regional/local scale and patterns in Europe). In the analysis of its study case in Northern Italy, which involves the entire Alps, it becomes clear that accessibility is not actually necessary for the economic development of peripheral areas. Another key aspect is the impact of new road and rail infrastructure, planned in the European programme TEN-T. Locally, the potential accessibility of infrastructure to the population is significant; but modifying the current access model, which is significantly influenced by the distribution of the population in the territory, does not have a decisive effect. Given the problems facing marginal areas, large infrastructure will not accomplish much; it will bypass rather than connect peripheral areas. The potential acccessbility of peripheral areas is less than average and takes into account only 6% of the population.[2] The solution most likely does not always lie in strategies for connection. According also to Aiscat data, in the Adige valley the role of the motorway will change

Figure 3. TechnoEcosystemic Motorway as interface between landscapes, Motorway A22.

Peripheries are interface sites or islands in an unlimited territory. The archipelago, that they constitute, is a system of dynamic sites, where the clash between different landscapes blends and re-invents the available resources. Peripheries produce creativity and innovation where there is a crisis; this generates a crash that actives an enrichment of places. The versatility of the dimensions of space and time feeds these seemingly empty, abandoned, and closed spaces, but they actually potentially enclose a range of options inside themselves. The archipelago is osmotic, does not remain closed within its limits, but becomes a porous sponge, an interface, capable of spreading and balancing the processes in progress, of binding them to the surrounding sites. The connection can be digital, straightforward, physical, or osmotic but never static and always in progress. Peripheries are shaped based on the needs they meet, becoming the missing link between the definite and indefinite space, between technological and natural ecosystems, defining a range of opportunities regulated by changes and needs.

because of the construction of the high capacity train line to complete the TEN Scandianvian-Mediterranean Corridor.[3] If we take the last six months of 2016 into account, there could be a reduction of 30% of traffic, if the transportation of goods will happen in the future mainly by train. In this specific framework, but also according to the general Italian[4] and European strategy, what will be the future role of this motorway in the Adige valley?

Periphery is related to the contexts and to the territory in which it is situated. So every place can be considered peripheral and central at the same time (Ricci 2012). This point leads us more and more towards the idea that these areas are saturated both for need and contingency. Therefore the strategies to be applied must turn to a more careful use of existing infrastructure, both obsolete and not, through tactics that aim to reuse and increase ecological and technological capacity, to provide services locally.

Now the motorway will move to a 4.0 stage. The complex vision seems to have completely disappeared due to the implementation of performance techniques aimed at solving specific localised problems rather than working on a general scale through different level of design. According to this point, a new generation of motorway infrastructure is to be defined, through a new vision, which responds to current social, cultural, and ecological demands and which will guide strategies toward the future. Reaching a 4.0 stage is crucial. As technology is making giant steps, at the same time infrastructure should be able to react quickly to the dynamics of the innovation that is active in urban and suburban contexts. Now, the motorways are a symbol of a change that did not happen. Motorway 4.0 will be the answer to the need for a new generational change for mobility infrastructure, which over time has remained the same, limiting its propulsive and visionary objectives for the surrounding areas.

In this frame, the research project Reinventing A22, promoted by the enterprise of the motorway, Autostrada del Brennero S.p.A., and developed by the University of Trento, defined a concept of the motorway that goes beyond the present, through the combination of ecology and technology. Starting from ecology, as a medium between nature and the anthropocentric sphere and technology as a medium for innovation toward the future, the research defines the concept of TechnoEcoSystem as a tool to select design strategies for next generation motorways.[5] Like a backbone, the motorway in this concept holds a fragmented, dispersive urban structure together, and, like an osmotic surface, absorbs everything around itself. The concept, which was developed in the first part of the research and is made more experimental in this second step, is to design osmotic devices that can establish energetic and functional relations with the landscape. The aim is to rethink traditional elements such as noise barriers, overpasses, underpasses, rest areas, and tollbooths in accordance with a landscape-sensitive design approach and materialising the potential services that a TechnoEcoSystem could offer.[6] In the end, aiming at a variable, adaptive, and perfectible approach to natural changes in the environment, the motorway finds its place inside the Ecosphere, obtaining an active and propulsive position in relationship to the other natural and artificial ecosystems, assuming a role that goes toward the future.

Figure 4. Autostrada del Brennero. "Memory on the road". Photos: Arianna Scaglione

Telling to inform, telling to test, telling to transform. Narrative about the dynamism of peripheries increases the identity of places in a range of time. The story of the places encloses the change in frames of possibilities that are put into effect in the activation processes. Narrative often becomes the only way you have to leave a trace, a message. Often urban action does not leave physical signs, but it actives communities, feelings of affection, hope, and desire to act, which is often revealed only by a story of process and not by the description of an outcome. The community and the convivial moment are often decisive. For this reason, they must not only describe but retell. The knowledge and values that the narrative of a process tells us are useful for spreading messages that feed a contamination effect within the peripheral archipelago. Telling to transform and to feed a widespread of the fermenting phenomenon of a bottom-up process, is central in projects of social and cultural innovation. Narration is not a solution, but rather the starting point for generating debate and comparison with the processes that take place in peripheries through the sharing of values, knowledge, and actions in communities, making them a resource for change.

Notes/Bibliography

1 In this period the design approach changed. In 1969, Ian McHarg published *Design with Nature* and followed an ecological point of view with the use of an overlay mapping technique, based on values of territories.
2 ESPON 2013: TRACC Transport Accessibility at Regional/Local Scale and Patterns in Europe.
3 Data from January to June 2016. Aiscat (Associazione Italiana Società Concessionarie Autostrade e Trafori).
4 "Connettere l'Italia, Ministero delle infrastrutture e dei trasporti", Ministero delle Infrastrutture e Trasporti, Conference on 14 June 2016, University of Sapienza, Rome.
5 TechnoEcoSystemic Motorway. Techno, that is smart, innovative, and artificial, in a permanent state of relationship, networking, "glocal" and resilient to changes in the context and for the context; Eco, that is ecological, ecosystemic, and energetic, in a state of perpetual and dynamic metabolic exchange, which acts in the environment and for the environment; System, that is the structure, function, and ensemble, in a state of interacting support, articulated and constant in the territories and for the territories. In summary, the TechnoEcoSystem is a motorway that works within the landscape and for the landscape.
6 For the 2006 Millennium Ecosystem Assessment (MA), ecosystem services are the benefits that people obtain from ecosystems. These are: provisioning, cultural, regulating, and supporting. Can design process follow these services as a strategy for the technoecosystemic motorway?

AISCAT Associazione Italiana Società Concessionarie Autostrade e Trafori (2017) *AISCAT in cifre, anni 2009–2016*. available online at: http://www.aiscat.it/pubb_cifre.htm?ck=1&sub=3&idl=4&nome=pubblicazioni&nome_sub=aiscat%20in%20cifre (accessed 15.12.2017).
Bauman Z. ed. (2011) *Modernità liquida*. Bari, Laterza.
Brown H. (2014) *Next Generation Infrastructure. Principles for Post-Industrial Public Works*. Washington, Island Press.
Carta M. (2013) *Reimagining Urbanism*. Trento, List Laboratorio Internazionale Editoriale.
Favargiotti S. (2016) *Airports On-Hold. Towards Resilient Infrastructures*. Trento, List Laboratorio Internazionale Editoriale.
Forman R.T.T., Sperling D., Bissonette J. A., Clevenger A. P., Cutshall C. D., Dale V. D. (2002) *Road Ecology: Science and Solutions*. Washington DC, EditorelsIand Press.
Naveh Z., Lieberman A.S. (1990) *Landscape Ecology, Theory and Application*. New York, Springer Science.
Reed C., Lister N.M. eds. (2013) *Projective Ecologies*. Chambersburg, Actar Birkhauser Distribution.
Ricci M. (2012) *Nuovi Paradigmi*. Trento, List Laboratorio Internazionale Editoriale.
Ricci M., Scaglione G. eds. (2012) *Nuove ecologie per infra/strutture osmotiche*. Trento, List Laboratorio Internazionale Editoriale.
Rizzi C. (2014) *Quarto paesaggio*. Trento, List Laboratorio Internazionale Editoriale.

Resilience in City-Core Peripheries: Flexible, Creative, and Dynamic Urban Regeneration Processes

Jessica Smeralda Oliva

Figure 1. ZoHo, Rotterdam. Graphic: Jessica Smeralda Oliva

Resilience thinking in urban planning and design has arisen in recent years as a compelling means to foster research and innovation both in theory and practice, also stimulating collaboration between different disciplines. As a result of the consciousness about global change and the new challenges that cities are facing, the concept of urban resilience has increasingly appeared in the last few decades in scientific research and planning discourse. In fact, inhabiting an urban world, cities are home to most of the world population. Due to this concentration, risks and effects coming from global change are intensified in urban areas. Thus, global change and uncertainty ask for new ways of thinking and acting, granting the extraordinary opportunity to deeply innovate and reimagine our standpoint and behaviours towards a possible, respectful, sustainable, and better way of living (identifying challenges and tools for a new urbanism; see Carta 2014). The global change is a radical metamorphosis, a transition, that requires us to consider a non-equilibrium perspective. It is no longer possible to think about fixed solutions; on the contrary we have to imagine new approaches and new strategies.

When uncertainty is recognised as the dominant condition, new questions arise, for example reframing the question of sustainability from the identification of an ideal spatial form to the organisation able to strengthen and raise the resilience capacity of the city (Ahern 2013), including flexibility

Figure 2. Evolutive processes in peripheries based on co-design, incrementality, flexibility, and collaboration. Graphic: Jessica Smeralda Oliva

The transition that we are experiencing, characterised by a non-equilibrium perspective, offers us the possibility to reconsider peripheries and to replace them at the centre of the discourse about new dynamic processes of transformation. In fact, peripheries are by nature dynamic and in evolution, and can be understood as transitional spaces, areas of potentiality for change, between action and transformation, “peripheries in transform-a(c)tion” (Lino 2013). Between public policies, new social and civic activist networks, and private interests, in recent times the regeneration processes of peripheries have frequently been communicated as bottom-up. Actually more often it is about a mixed approach based upon collaboration and co-design. Relying on the transitional potential of peripheries, processes should be based on the integration between the initiatives arising from communities, local stakeholders, even those facilitated by local administration, and the creation and activation of more structured strategies. It is no longer the case that we should think and act following top-down or bottom-up models, but it is important to rethink planning tools in order to fill the gap between those two approaches, activating transformation and development processes based on incrementality, flexibility, and collaboration.[1]

both in planning processes and projects. In many contexts, it has been the rise of the concept of resilience that has guided recent changes in processes, transformations, and policies. Incrementality, collaboration and flexibility emerge as key-characteristics for resilience in/of processes and projects of urban transformation and regeneration. Following the considerations by professor Maurizio Carta (Carta 2013), in the context of cities in rapid evolution in which we are living, peripheries can constitute "precious reserves of resilience" or "resilient avantgardes", provided with greater elasticity, evolving from the status of criticalities and marginalization producers into active components of urban transformation within a new paradigm based on flexibility, diversity, fluidity, and perturbation. Thus, as spaces of opportunities, peripheries are proposed as favoured contexts for design experimentation aiming to build resilience in cities.

Starting from the premise that peripheries are everywhere, this contribution aims to discuss the experience of ZoHo, a district in Rotterdam, Netherlands, that has been chosen as a case study for the doctoral research of the author. Located in the Noord borough of Rotterdam and characterised by a mixed social environment with the presence of a very multicultural and multi-ethnic population—with the predominance of Turkish and Moroccan communities—today ZoHo is a district in transition. In recent years it has been the object of an incremental process of urban regeneration that is still going on. It could be considered a city-core or inner periphery. Actually, although it is located very close to the city centre, the area never got a good reputation, due to its geographical position and limits—between the central station, a disused railway viaduct and a channel—that contributed to the perception of the area as an enclosed fringe zone. But despite the marginalisation, the area could still benefit from its position as an opportunity.

Characterised by mono-functionality—mainly a residential area—in the past, ZoHo is now becoming more and more a mixed use and interconnected area through a progressive urban regeneration process, started with a public-private agreement for the use of neglected office buildings and the revitalization and reactivation of public spaces. This process has been boosted and enriched with the themes of climate change, water resilience, and adaptation over the past four years, thanks to the realisation of an urban catalyst as the well-known Benthemplein watersquare, but also because the area of ZoHo has been chosen as a pilot experimentation area for the implementation at the district scale of the "Rotterdam Climate Change Adaptation Strategy" (RAS).

In 2011, due to the economic crisis, the social housing corporation Havensteder, owner of certain low-value and disused commercial properties in the Zomerhofkwartier area, found it impossible to implement two residential complexes, in place of the industrial buildings as was planned. However, it was in the interest of the company, which holds many residential properties in the adjacent area of Agniesebuurt, was to act, albeit with limited resources, to avoid a further degradation process of the area. An agreement was therefore signed between Havensteder and the municipality for the temporary use of those unused properties. The agreement envisaged the company's commitment to the use of low-rent buildings for activities primarily related to creative industries, with support from the municipality that acted as a facilitator and co-ordinator of initiatives and interventions,

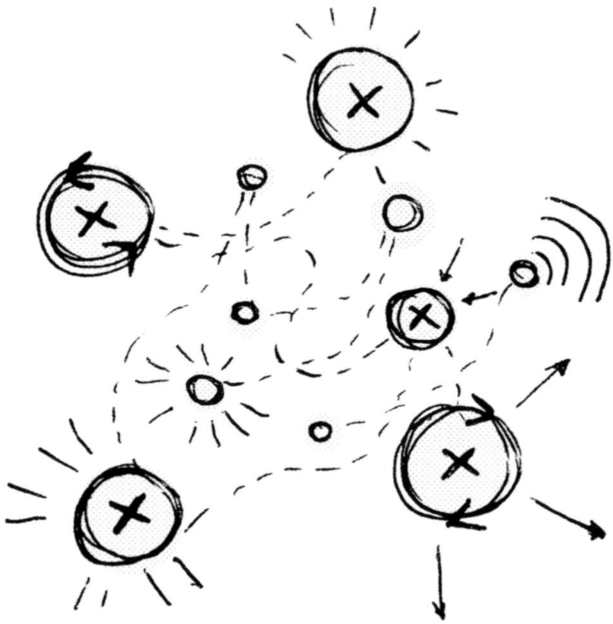

Figure 3. Peripheries as new treasure troves, spaces for experimentation and creative recycling. Graphic: Jessica Smeralda Oliva

We need to change our viewpoint on peripheries, leaving behind the stereotyped image that commonly marks them as places of social conflicts and troubles, of mono-functionality and economic depression, of aesthetic poverty and physical degradation, even if these characteristics are often present. But peripheries are to be intended as the new treasure troves of future human settlements, recognizing in their criticalities and transformation potential the opportunity to rethink a new relationship between city and landscape, between humans and nature. Far from being spaces of anonymity, possibly labelled as "non-places", peripheries are precious places of identity formation, offering space for experimentation. Often denoted by a more transformable and mouldable fabric, peripheries are meant as spatial resources to explore and tackle social, environmental, ecological, and economic challenges of our urban time. Post-crisis and global change peripheries make room for creative recycling of unused buildings, activating new productive cycles and relational landscapes, creating new co-managed green spaces, using the existing underused surfaces for urban agriculture, transforming derelict buildings through physical retrofitting and functional densification, providing services and accessibility, giving new sense and identity to public space, valorising open space as integration place for communities, and interconnecting the human and the natural habitat.

streamlining the bureaucratic steps and applying a flexible approach. In 2013, thanks to the collaboration between Havensteder and Stipo, a "city maker" office working in ZoHo's Yellow Building, the area became a field of experimentation of a so-called slow urbanism. Slow urbanism is described as an organic process in which traditional public planning actors give space to other people who collaborate and support urban development (Laven, de Velde, Elleswijk 2016). The transformation of the area evolves through an incremental process that works on the small scale, initially without a predefined final goal or a pre-packaged configuration, but with the aim of making ZoHo an attractive neighbourhood by capturing the opportunities that emerge during the process and activating a continuous learning mechanism. A steady point is that all interventions and initiatives must bring added value to the community and to the stakeholders.

During the development and evolution of these dynamics, after the realisation of the Benthemplein watersquare and the release of the RAS, in 2014 the design office De Urbanisten—who had already worked on the RAS and the design of the watersquare—proposed to the municipality to use ZoHo as the first experiment to implement the strategy at the neighbourhood scale, feeding on the energies that already animated the area. The area is characterised by the limited presence of public green spaces, as well as experiencing the consequences of climate change, being particularly subject to flooding events due to heavy rainfall.

Thus, the "ZoHo Climate Proof District" project interprets adaptation to climate change and climate proofing as an added opportunity to create a quality and attractive public space. Given the catalyst role played by Benthemplein watersquare, the incremental implementation of climate adaptation measures, following the slow urbanism approach, is pursued as a means to improve the multidimensional resilience of the area. So, in 2014, the office De Urbanisten organised a series of workshops in collaboration with the city and Stipo, initiating a co-design process with entrepreneurs and residents, identifying local opportunities for climate adaptation and at the same time improving the quality of public space, by sharing a systemic vision of the future of ZoHo and Agniesebuurt, to be implemented through green acupuncture interventions, soil de-sealing, separation of sewage and rainwater systems, slowdown of runoff, and microclimatic regulation thanks to the creation of green roofs and rain gardens.

The first initiative has been the realisation of a small demonstrative zero-budget rain garden made in collaboration between local government, professionals, businesses, and residents. Two parking lots and a part of the sidewalk in front of the Yellow Building have been depaved, subtracting grey surface and increasing permeable surface, planting a small garden that has the power to be a concrete example of the possible transformation for climate adaptation of public space in ZoHo. This is a small intervention that, for the process in which it is inserted, has the potential to facilitate the creation of a sense of belonging to the urban space in those who work and live in the area and which is essential for the sustainability of actions. In addition, the maintenance of the pocket rain garden has been entrusted to the guest of a former addict centre that is located in ZoHo, generating an appreciable social outcome.

Figure 4. Narratives as design-projective tools for peripheries. Graphic: Jessica Smeralda Oliva

Narratives are meant as design-projective tools, being able to build sense and identity, make visible intangible elements and dynamics, and generate sharing of stories and values. Urban storytelling can be used both as research instrument for reading phenomena and processes, as an interpretation tool, and as a communication device able to produce changes. Urban storytelling could also contribute to deconstructing negative stereotypes, modifying the perception of places, and enabling actions in that vibrant environment that frequently characterises peripheries. So, as analysis and design-projective tools, narratives can not only be used by researchers and designers, but they can be an instrument to be integrated in formal planning processes involving institutional actors. In the regeneration process of peripheral areas narratives acquire multiple purposes: interpreting the present condition and giving voice to otherwise invisible phenomena and dynamics, for instance highlighting the human face of neighbourhoods; fostering scenarios for the future of those areas, supporting better quality of life, economic and ecological improvement, treasuring analysis, interpretation, and design—mostly co-design—thereby producing a vision that can be shared. Nonetheless it is important to draw attention to likely knotty aspects of this tool, using it in a critical way, being aware of its viewpoint-based nature, thus avoiding the risk of a reduction of the complexity of reality and a biased use of stories.

Following the success of this initiative, as the first demonstrative experiment, financial resources for the implementation of the climate adaptation project have been set up, and the city of Rotterdam has received an EU Life+ subsidy for ZoHo initiative development. Throughout the process, an element that appears to be fundamental is on the one hand the awareness of a situation of uncertainty and on the other hand the openness to novelty while maintaining a shared sense of responsibility and a common goal among the various actors involved. The incrementality has enabled both of these efforts to make small-steps visible transformations and to learn from each action, activating a continuous learning process, literally learning-by-doing.

Not only did the owner company have to put in place a new way of acting, but the administration also had to develop its own flexibility in making ZoHo's initiatives feasible. As pointed out by Jacco Bakker, district manager of Noord district and ZoHo facilitator for Rotterdam, "you have to find a new way to deal with all these changes in the outside world. So that's quite an interesting time!" Another success factor is that climate adaptation has not been introduced as an additional and end-to-end measure but by integrating climate resilience interventions into an integral resilience vision of the area. Then, the complementarity of ecological, environmental, social, and economic resilience becomes evident. Creating new relationships, imagining and realizing new practices and initiatives, creating new opportunities that were not imagined before—that is what is happening in ZoHo, from the crisis to the generation of what has been termed as the "resilience dividend" (Rodin 2014).

Note/Bibliography

1 An effective process of this kind has been theorised in detail by Maurizio Carta (see the Cityforming© Protocol: Carta 2015).

Ahern J. (2013) "Urban Landscape Sustainability and Resilience: The Promise and Challenges of Integrating Ecology with Urban Planning and Design". In: *Landscape Ecology* 28/2013. Dordrecht, Springer, pp. 1203–1212.

Carta M. (2013) "Prefazione. Periferie, riserve di resilienza per le città in evoluzione". In: Lino B. (2013) *Periferie in trasform-azione. Riflessioni dai "margini" delle città*. Firenze, Alinea, pp. 9–16.

Carta M. (2014) *Reimagining Urbanism. Creative, Smart and Green Cities for the Changing Times*. Trento, LISt Lab.

Carta M. (2015) "Iper-strategie del riciclo: Cityforming© Protocol". In: Carta M., Lino B. eds. (2015) *Urban Hyper-Metabolism*. Ariccia, Aracne, pp. 157–169.

Laven J., de Velde G.J., Elleswijk P. (2016) "Take Action #2 – District: Bottom-up Meets Top-down at Eye Level". In: Karssenberg H., Laven J., Glaser M., van 't Hoff M. eds. (2016) *The City at Eye Level. Second and Extended Version*. Delft, Eburon Academic Publishers, pp. 301–304.

Lino B. (2013) *Periferie in trasform-azione. Riflessioni dai "margini" delle città*. Firenze, Alinea.

Rodin J. (2014) *The Resilience Dividend. Being Strong in a World Where Things Go Wrong*. New York, Public Affairs.

New Relationships between Urban and Rural Areas: The Case of Agri Gentium Landscape Regeneration

Luca Torrisi

Figure 1. The connection between urban and rural system is evident in the relationship between the Agrigento archeological park and the Kolymnetra garden. Source: reworked version by Luca Torrisi

Rural areas are currently gaining increasing interest, as they present different development opportunities (productivity, qualification of the territory, and attractiveness) compared to metropolitan areas. The relevance of these areas is connected not only to productivity, but also to activities and services which already exist in the territory. Moreover, territorial conformation has changed over the last decades because urban processes do not seem to meet quality expectations. Over the years, some cities have suffered from the phenomenon of abandonment, because the number of existing buildings in the urban network is now too large compared to the population. These cities are affected, consequently, by an ever-growing economic deficit, lower quality of life, and increasing decay in urban areas. These areas are conditioned first of all by a change of territory dictated by diffused cities, sprawl (Ingersoll 2004), increase in social inequalities (Secchi 2013), unused areas that characterise drosscape both in peripheral and historical areas (Berger 2006). This phenomenon reveals the effects of a planning connected to growth, accumulation, and development without a focus on strategies.

At the moment, although rural areas are perceived as potential spaces for the development of the territory, they are characterised by hydrogeological risk, often due to abandonment. The disappearance of agricultural activity is highlighted by increasingly worrying data on the decline in employment[1] and the consequent decline in farming and used agricultural areas:[2] this is a sign of the lack of planning strategies for the development of rural areas in connection with the evolution of

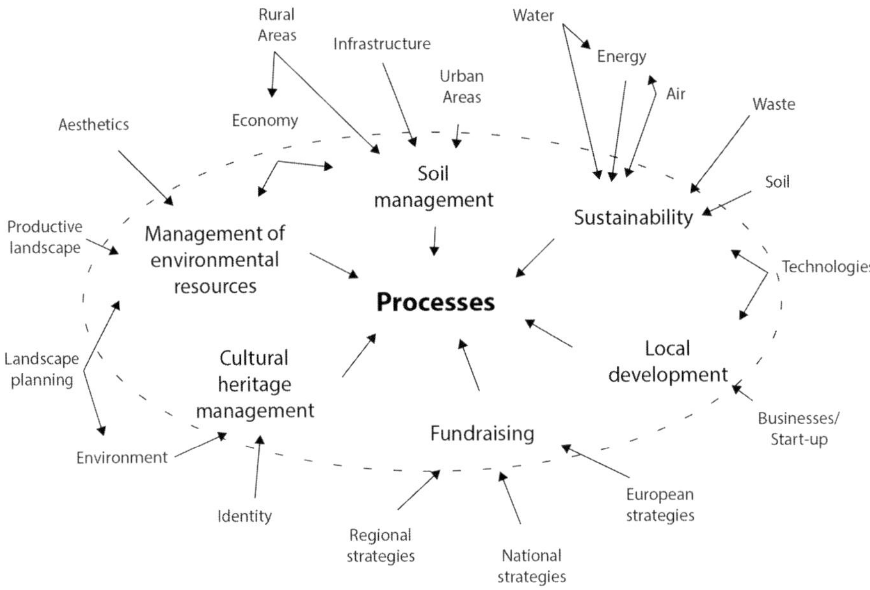

Figure 2. The new processes that affect urban strategies are connected to sustainable development. Graphic: Luca Torrisi

The processes involving peripheries are increasingly connected to an innovative vision of the territory. New principles that look at the territory in its uniformity are being developed. In this territorial context, there is a cooperation between urban and rural areas. The territory, therefore, should not be conceived only as a concentrated conformation, but also as an archipelago. In this concept, connections have to determine relationships between parts of the territory that could be different and unique, but at the same time related to each other. The concept of the "rur-urban archipelago" is capable of combining new, extensive, connected, and multipolar functions (Carta 2017 B, pp. 36–53). In this vision of the territory, landscape does not have an aesthetic value but it has a productive role. Particularly, in rural areas there are innovative companies and start-ups that promote new business models and the development of new technologies. These activities build a dense network of relationships between urban and rural areas that overcomes the separation between peripheries and cities. The Edison Pulse prize for sustainable innovation concerns production, energy efficiency, storage, and electricity consumption. "Orthoponics" (hydroponic cultivation and agricultural cultivation in the consolidated city) and "Acquaplus" (water management to reduce irrigation consumption, saving environmental resources) projects have been rewarded. The Rural hub hackspace promotes social innovation in rural areas, events, rural start-up incubators, agri-food labs, and activation projects for rural communities.

technological processes. It is not enough to consider rural areas as mere production sites and urban areas as attractive places. There is a holistic territorial system that works through connections, similar to an "archipelago, ... which is able to combine new, extensive, connected and multipolar functions" (Carta 2017b). The theme of the archipelago works through these connections and can generate an attractiveness similar to that of a condensed form of the territorial system. Relations between cities and rural areas give the latter a new centrality in economic, productive, environmental, landscape, recreational, cultural, and social terms, to build self-sustainable local development models. Rural areas thus become "laboratory sites of new productive, environmental, and fruitful relationships involving urban and rural areas" (Magnaghi 2012).

In the interpretation of the territory as a unitary system, landscape action should be considered. In fact, the European Landscape Convention (approved on 20 October 2000 in Florence and adopted by the Italian State in 2006) changed the idea of landscape policy. The Convention states that landscape is a public good, and this concept is no longer limited to situations of excellence. The Convention also introduces a new idea of landscape, going beyond its merely aesthetic value. Sereni's teachings are still valid: landscape is linked to the relationship with humans, who transform it through their activities (Sereni 1961). The relationship between human and landscape exists because society has evolved by establishing physical, symbolic, and ecological relationships with the territory. Today, these connections need to be revised through less defined ways of making communities (Donadieu 2001). We need to replace the "aesthetic" landscape (to look) with the "ethical" landscape (to live) (Settis 2013), able to operate on monitoring, communication, accessibility, management, and marketing (Carta 2007, pp. 9–16).

Landscape is not a visual issue but a multidisciplinary system that does not only involve images, but a continuous regeneration process brought about by the interaction between landscape and community and between communities and the environment (Rizzi 2016). This concept is most evident in landscape urbanism, which focuses not only on environmental issues, but above all on the interrelations between human activities and the natural landscape (Waldheim 2016). An example of the quality of the relationship between urban areas, rural areas, and landscape is Agri Gentium Landscape Regeneration.[3] This project is being implemented in the Archaeological Park of the Valley of the Temples of Agrigento. The relationship between the Archaeological Park and the city was blocked, especially in the second half of the twentieth century, by the construction of new buildings both inside the park and in the surrounding agricultural areas, culminating in the landslide of 1966 which caused the collapse of several buildings.

This continuous building process was partially stopped in 1997, when the valley was first included in the Unesco World Heritage List (WHL), because the importance of the archaeological area was recognised. Besides the importance of the valley, the environmental value of the surrounding area has been investigated. This could allow Agrigento to become a polycentric system (Scavone 2016, pp. 89-101), because of restrictions affecting the area around the valley. In fact, the presence of a large area not capable of being developed near the urban area of the Municipality of Agrigento has

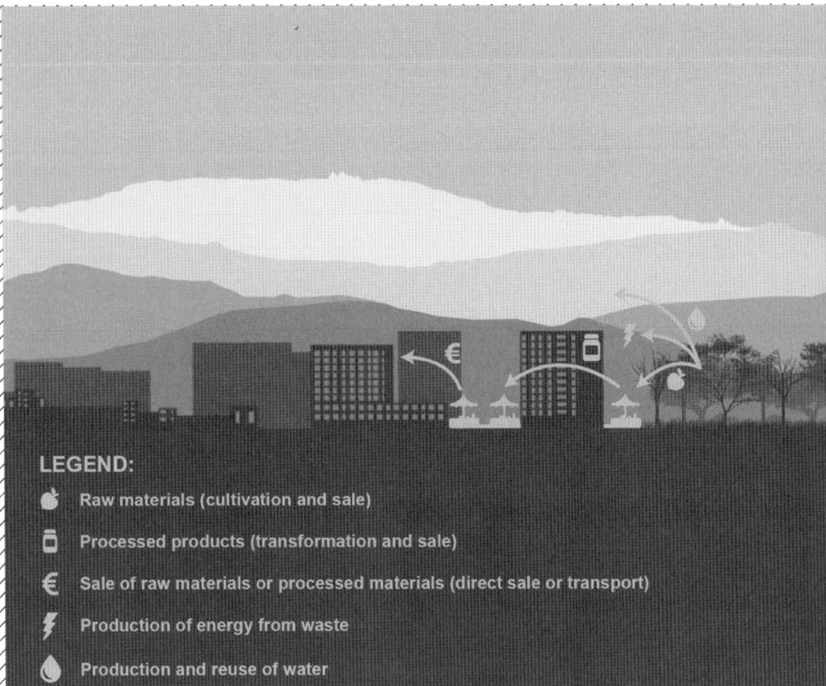

Figure 3. Urban strategies related to sustainable development use territorial resources and transform them to increase and differentiate production. Graphic: Luca Torrisi

In a polycentric territorial system, peripheries play a fundamental role in the territory, starting with their peculiarities. A conscious use of the resources that identify a territory leads to local, sustainable, and environmental development, starting from new strategies related to social and economic development.

The richness of the territory is connected to the ability to renew, activate, or reactivate existing spaces and resources, creating opportunities for cultural, social, and economic growth (Carta, Lino 2015). Resusing raw materials permits a reduction in the consumption of territorial resources. In this way, in agricultural production, waste as crops, tree cuttings, and animal waste allow the production of biogas for energy sustainability; forest residues can also be used in the reuse of waste, while soil drainage and water purification reduce water consumption, because water can be reused in production processes. These strategies work together to qualify the territory and, consequently, landscape through human action. In fact, rural landscape is the form that human impresses on natural landscapes, for their agricultural production activities (Sereni 1961). The landscape is therefore a representation of nature and not scenery. This idea becomes a dynamic concept of a part of the territory that follows the needs of the population according to different historical periods and often becomes the representation of the identity of the territory.

the potential to change the compact composition of the city through new functions and services that can generate additional and different attractiveness. There may one day be a park system in the territory between the Archaeological Park and the towns of Montaperto, Dune, Giardina Gallotti, and Cannatello, in which the relationship between the city and the rural areas is very strong. In the Agrigento Town Plan, which was drawn up in 2012, the built-in reduction forecasts are not implemented. On the contrary there is an increase in soil consumption.

Initially the Agrigento Town Plan also included the demolition of state roads 118 and 640, but in the end both were maintained. State road 118, in particular, divided the Archaeological Park into two parts; this situation has been resolved by the construction of a bridge, designed by architects Cottone and Indelicato, which connected the two parts of the valley again. The Park Plan aims to increase the landscape quality of the park through the use of original crops and a greenway system that runs through the entire park, reusing the abandoned buildings within the valley to implement the services.

This is the background for the Agri Gentium Landscape Regeneration project. The project aims to promote public-private collaboration through the reuse of the ancient railroad that passes through the park. Other actions expected in the framework of this project include: the breeding of the typical "Girgentana goat", the "Museum of historic almonds and almond seeds", which are at risk of extinction, the revival of ancient cultivation techniques, and the inauguration of social gardens. The importance of the project is to recover the identity and quality of the landscape in the relationship between archaeological heritage and rural areas. The issue of citizens' involvement through participatory processes is addressed; in fact, social farms and agricultural management initiatives are planned: they aim at rehabilitation and social reintegration.

In this context, regulations have an important role in the implementation of the European Union's rural development policy, regulated by laws that include a strategic approach connected to both European structural funds and policy strategies of the Common Agricultural Policy. This system results from the drafting of technical documents by the European Commission capable of providing guidelines to the regions and member states involved in the programming and implementation of various aspects of the policy. At the national and regional level, however, rural areas need to be seen as more than just productive areas. Renewed attention should be given to the emergence of new connections between rural and urban areas, between services and production, between compact and scattered settlements. The guidelines from the National Strategy for Inner Lands and the Rural Development programmes are a helpful tool in this sense. The Common Agricultural Policy aims at improving the competitiveness of agriculture and a development of rural areas.

Community strategies also include fundraising actions that promote a relationship between urban areas and rural areas, but these actions are actually limited to their economic potential. An example of community fundraising is Horizon 2020, which contains calls for proposals for rural renaissance in terms of fostering innovation and business opportunities, with a specific focus on

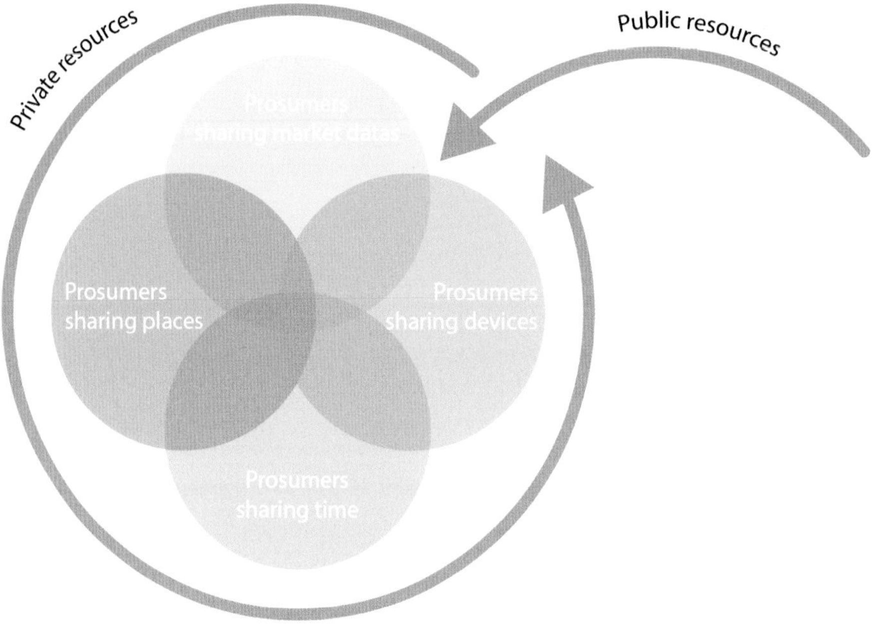

Figure 4. The relationship between public and private resources involves prosumers. They share not only money, but also time, places and tools to increase territorial development. Graphic: Luca Torrisi

In a possible future scenario, the inland areas, and especially the rural ones, will have to strengthen their values and identity in order to be better integrated into their territorial systems, so that the territory is "augmented" (Carta 2017a) according to a holistic system. In this scenario it is important to actively engage all users. In fact, the action of public administrations is not enough, because in addition to the economic resources it is necessary to actively engage the human resources that live continuously in the territory.

The regeneration of peripheries is a dynamic process that has to start from the bottom and has to develop networks not only through infrastructure but, above all, with the involvement of citizens. In fact, a new way of describing the territory is needed involving administrations, designers, and citizens in planning strategies. Population has to narrate local population needs not only through participatory planning and therefore involvement in choices but also with an operative role linked to the economic aspect and, in particular, the identity of the territory. Citizens are not confined to the passive role of consumers, but actively participate in the different phases of the production process: users become producers ("prosumers") that combine the two aspects. This new economic dynamism is only possible through a business and financial system that benefits from public and private resources for territorial development. This can be achieved if the public administration gives impulse to territorial development, directly involving citizens in this process.

policy framework and governance models for rur-urban connections. The increase in urbanisation and the transformation of rural economies and communities has generated new modes of interaction between rural and urban areas, to which government policies still need to be fully adapted. Rural development strategies are not constrained by legislation, but they should address a variety of issues alongside agricultural production. There are innovative solutions for rural areas, such as businesses and new technologies developed by start-ups. Start-ups are growing fast in rural areas, where they seek to promote sustainable growth, technological development, and employment.

These issues are discussed by the Institute for Services for the Agricultural Food Market, which is dedicated to project financing for agro-industry, guarantees and insurance in the field of agro-food, services to the public administration, and to monitoring of agricultural markets, start-ups, and enterprise development. In addition to the traditional agricultural system, the "Rural Hub" searches for innovative systems of economic development related to rural businesses, working on social and market problems associated with these areas. The "Rural Hub" promotes co-living and co-working. Over the years, territorial policies will have to address questions related to urban and rural areas, based on the needs of the population. They will also need to develop strategies in order to give new values (related to quality of the production and rural-urban connections) and new identities (characterised by production, culture, territory, and landscape) to those areas which are considered marginal in traditional development processes.

Notes/Bibliography

1 Data source: http://www.istat.it/it/lavoro-e-retribuzioni (accessed on 9.11.2017).
2 Data source: http://www.istat.it/it/agricoltura (accessed on 11.11.2017).
3 Project selected by Italy for the European Landscape Award (accessed on 10.11.2017).

Berger A. (2006) *Drosscape: Wasting Land in Urban America*. New York, Princeton Architectural Press.
Carta M. (2007) "Prefazione". In: Ronsivalle D. (2007) *Ri-generare il paesaggio*. Milano, Franco Angeli, pp. 9–16
Carta M. (2017a) *The Augmented City: A Paradigm Shift*. Trento, List Lab.
Carta M. (2017b) "Planning for the Rur-Urban Anthropocene". In: Schröder J., Carta M., Ferretti M., Lino B. eds. (2017) *Territories: Rural-Urban Strategies*. Berlin, Jovis Verlag, pp. 36–53.
Carta M. Lino B. eds. (2015) *Urban Hyper Metabolism*. Ariccia, Aracne editrice.
Donadieu P. (2001) *La société paysagiste*. Arles, Actes Sud.
Ingersoll R. (2004) *Sprawltown: cercando la citta in periferia*. Roma, Meltemi editore.
Magnaghi A. (2012) "Politiche e progetti di territorio per il ripopolamento rurale". In: *Storicamente* 1/2011.
Rizzi C. (2016) João Nunes: progettare paesaggi. Trento, List Lab.
Scavone V. (2016) "Un gioiello tra la città e il territorio". In: Carta M. ed. (2016) *Patrimonio e creatività. Agrigento, la valle e il parco*. Trento, List Lab, pp. 89–101.
Secchi B. (2013) *La città dei ricchi e la città dei poveri*. Roma-Bari, Laterza.
Sereni E. (1961) *Storia del paesaggio agrario italiano*. Bari, Laterza.
Settis S. (2013) *Il paesaggio come bene comune*. Napoli, La scuola di Pitagora editrice.
Waldheim C. (2016) *Landscape as Urbanism: A General Theory*. New York, Princeton Architectural Press.

DYNAMICS OF PERIPHERY

TERRITORIAL CREATIVITY

The Power of the Young Town: An Itinerary for Palermo

Luciana Macaluso

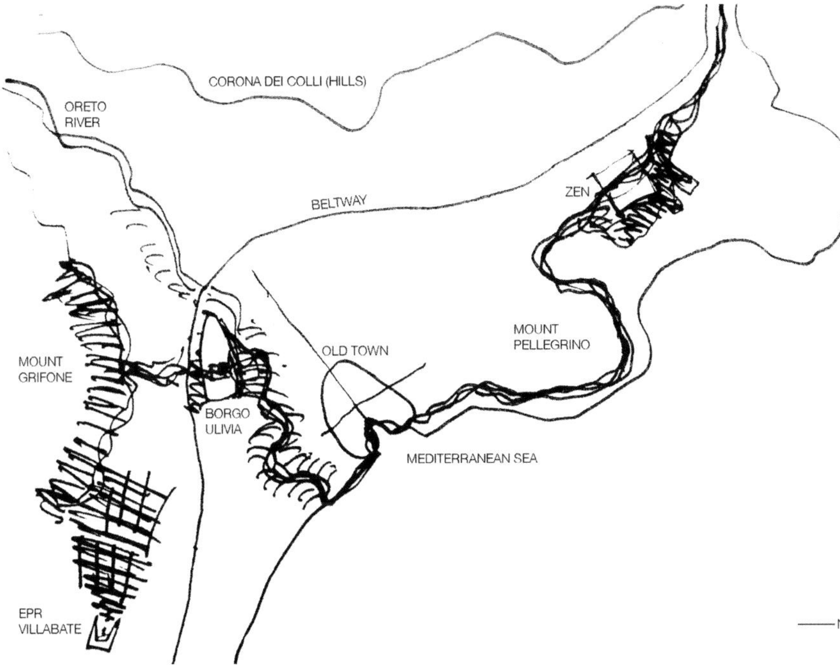

Figure 1. The power of the Young Town, map of Palermo. Graphic: Luciana Macaluso

> Kids wanna be so hard.
> But in my dreams we're still screamin' and runnin' through the yard.
> And all of the walls that they built in the seventies finally fall.
> *Arcade Fire, The Suburbs 2010*

Since the end of the Second World War, in Europe, an urban renewal has started gathering people's enthusiasm and the commitment of many entrepreneurs and public administrators. In Palermo (Sicily), the agricultural lands began to include new neighbourhoods that quickly merged with the historic and nineteenth-twentieth century centre. In the fifties, between the town and its geographic limits (Corona dei Colli), a beltway has been hypothesized and, in a few years, will become manifest as a founding board (Culotta 2005) for a "new town" made of peripheries. In the seventies, it was the spine of an expanding urban fabric that absorbed citrus and olive groves, vineyards, field of flowers, gardens, rural buildings, warehouses, villas, and historical villages in a complex and dynamic "rural-urban" fabric.

Figure 2. The power of the Young Town lies in its lymph-tissues and possible graft.
Graphic: Luciana Macaluso

Peripheries make the great part of our contemporary metropolis: hybrid and changing territories in which rural and urban traces are combined in a complex palimpsest of different times, identities, and stories. This town is more alive, more unfinished and younger than a historic centre. It needs flexible, adaptive programmes of transformation able to include the motion of heterogeneous factors in a higher order, not imposed top down but built starting from the same places, in accordance with their social and environmental peculiarities. The metaphor of the graft can clarify this process. Every plant can be combined only with some others. The plant continues its growth but it produces new flowers and fruits. In an urban transformation, the project of architecture and landscape can be a core of trans-disciplinary studies, in its multiple scales of representation and investigation. It is, by its own nature, an imperfect (it needs other disciplines, it does not immediately work except step by step) and optimistic instrument that helps us to trust in the potential of peripheries. From the small scale to the big scale, and vice versa, it makes us see and recognise "sleeping" values also in neglected or disadvantaged places; these values become the main ingredients whose "pertinent combination" can take new meanings. Within the experimental design the analysis develops and refines its results; analysis and proposal are not really divisble into different phases. On the contrary, the process continuously moves back and forth between reality and possibilities. This experimental design activity should be fed by seminars, visits, research, and collective parallel events following the more innovative method of participatory planning.

This continuous town is about fifty years old: it is very "young", considering the ancient core of Palermo was founded in the fifth century BC. "Young" is intended as especially dynamic, heterogeneous, creative and, potentially, ecologic, unlike the compact city. Its inertia against physical changes is slighter, indeed human action is very powerful, and consequently also possibly dangerous. The risk is a cancellation of identities and human, historical traces: sometimes those are weak or hidden, but in Palermo always present.

In the sixties and seventies abstract plans often prevailed over the rural heritage. However a cultural change, in which the progressive awareness of pre-existing environmental condition had an important role, made architects and planners more and more sensitive to the marks of the territories (Rogers 1958). Two previous studies[1] focused on how some of these suburbs "tell stories" (Secchi 1992), about their origins and current state through sketches, technical drawings, and texts to thus propose their future development. Those studies are the starting point for emphasising the dynamism of three neighbourhoods in Palermo—Borgo Ulivia, and Zen—that include significant interpretations of the Modern Movement's lesson in "Nucleo Sperimentale in Borgo Ulivia", in the Zen 2, and the Public Housing of Villabate (ERP). Equally considering assumptions coming from those works, we could imagine an itinerary for Palermo from north (ZEN) to south (ERP) and vice versa, between "rural-urban" parks, along the seaside and the riverside, up to citrus groves and orchards from the plain to the hills.

The Zen 2 was born "among the rural and urban world" as a combination between a compact and modern town where the ground floors should have been permeable, opening paths towards the countryside and the geography (Gregotti, in Macaluso 2016). This plan has been partially constructed (without facilities); Palermo grew to the north, up to it, and the villages around it also expanded. This boom produced a lot of buildings independent from the streets and enclosed with fences step by step. Also the *insulae* (blocks) in the Zen 2 have been closed. Pedestrian crossing in the ground floor failed to effect a special domestic character of the courts that are an extension of the apartments according to the tradition of living in Palermo (Sciascia 2003). Inhabitants take care of these spaces by maintaining them, they clean and place plants, chairs, tables, and small religious *aedicule*. This is where the neighbourhood relationships and activities develop.

Referring to other texts for a complete description (Sciascia 2003), the attention can be focused on those parts of the Zen not built because of the protection of historical fragments, from south to north: villa Pensabene, Cortile Gnazziddi, Fondo Trapani, villa Mercadante, Case Buffa, and villa Raffo, comparable to what in the imagination of the child of Michelangelo were "abandoned house[s] that belonged to a duke, a count, a prince, or maybe, why not, an emir" surrounded by "lemon groves like baobab, conifers that seemed to come directly from the Tierra del Fuego, giant sequoia, strange plants with primitive roots and so much water!" (Sciascia 2012). After all, the Arabic aqueduct (*qanat*) crosses the underground of the Zen. In a narrative approach, quantitative data about these places also show their qualities. In the district (including Borgo Pallavicino, Zen 1, and Zen 2) there are about 22,000 inhabitants of which only 1,495 are more than sixty-five

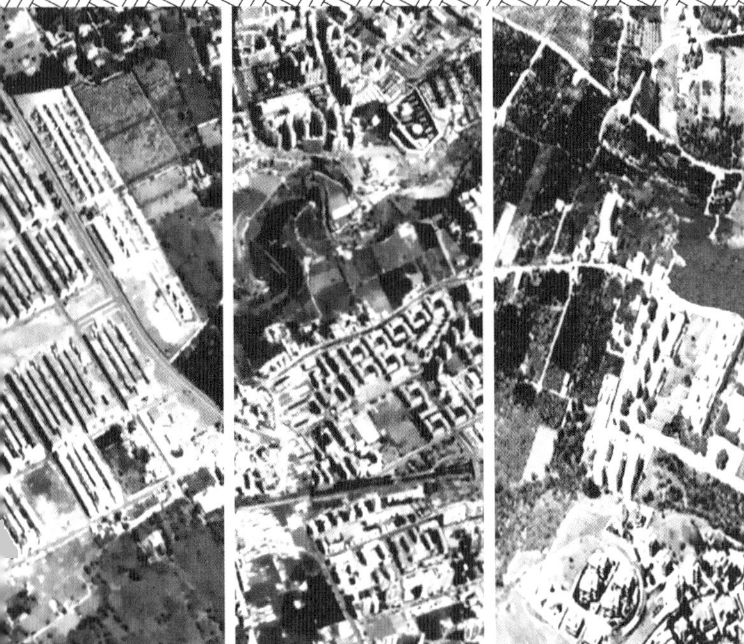

Figure 3. The power of the Young Town is in its intersection with the rural areas, Zen, Borgo Ulivia, ERP Villabate in Palermo (Sicily). Graphic: Luciana Macaluso

In Palermo, in the surrounding of the beltway, the "peripheries" shape a continuous town hardly held back by its geographical limits (the sea and the mountains) and the historical centre. "Peripheries" include an area about seven times larger than the old town, pushing their living force towards small villages and rural fields, absorbing those and dominating, at the end, the whole urban system: the town is "peripheries". We consider three neighbourhoods in different conditions:

- Surrounded by a prestigious sprawl area and important sport facilities: Zen 2 (Zona Espansione Nord) is situated in the northwest of the old town, in the core of the Piana dei Colli, between the villages of Mondello, Cardillo, Partanna and Pallavicino. F. Amoroso (head of the team), S. Bisogni, V. Gregotti, H. Matsui, and F. Purini planned it in 1970. It is a compact fabric made by *insulae* (blocks). As if a seed of the old town fell out its wall in the countryside (Tafuri 1982) growing with modern characters such as permeable ground floors and wide perspectives towards the territory.
- Between Oreto river and the beltway: Borgo Ulivia is located in the south of the old town, merged with the villages Barone della Scala, Santa Maria di Gesù, Villagrazia and Ponte Rotto. In 1959, G. Samonà (head of the team), A. Bonafede, R. Calandra, and E. Caracciolo designed the "Nucleo Sperimentale" where self-referential blocks were placed to shape a street and a square.
- Where the countryside is still luxuriant: Public Housing of Villabate (ERP) is in the southeast of Palermo, between the villages of Ciaculli and Villabate. A. Bonafede, R. Calandra, B. Colajanni, S. Incorpora, G. Pirrone, N. Vicari designed it in 1975. The core of the neighbourhood is a square "out of scale" compared to the housing.

years old (Municipality of Palermo, Statistic Office). Therefore not just the town is "young" but also its inhabitants in comparison with the Italian average: the potential for participating in bottom-up activities and place-making is strong. On-going processes of inhabitants' creativity (e.g., street art and other activities by the Comitato Internazionale per lo Sviluppo dei Popoli and by Zeninsieme), the dynamic of unfinished spaces, and the pre-existing historical conditions, lead to a new urban pedestrian continuity, which is not generally spread out but links existing important steps in a path that forms an almost oblique line crossing the neighbourhood from the southeast corner to the northwest corner, and which works at a different scale to also involve the surroundings (rich sprawl and villages) and beyond.[2]

Considering other studies carried out over the years at the University of Palermo on the urban design of Mount Pellegrino, the waterfront, and the Oreto River, our itinerary should reach the opposite side of the town, up to Borgo Ulivia, on the south border of Oreto River.[3] It includes sixteen different allotments characterised by linear blocks placed in open groups (among which the Nucleo Sperimentale is an interesting exception) or forming, in the east part, closed courts on the model of Sicilian type of the *baglio*.[4] A common character shared by these forms is the autonomy of their settlements from pre-existing elements of the place: via Villagrazia, a sinuous street along which a small village developed, the geometry of the rural fields, and the beltway.

The gap between the buildings, the streets, and the same different parts of the neighbourhood is fenced, private or privatised; if open, it quickly changes because of its mixed use (storage, parking, vegetable garden, football field, aggregation spaces with temporary pavilions). Sometimes, the functions have given almost a special identity to some interstitial areas, such as the weekly market in largo dell'Anitra. These spaces, apparently "void", are rich in vocations and previous traces waiting to be experienced; they have a hierarchy, although it is still in progress. Within the wave of the original intentions of the designers who worked between architecture and geography, we can look beyond the strong border of the neighbourhood to consider a territorial dimension including the Mount Grifone and the Oreto River. From this perspective a residual rural area along via Ponte Rotto plays an important role in a cycle-pedestrian route crossing the neighbourhood (Sciascia 2012). It should become a green core pushing and inhaling its lymph-tissue towards and from interstitial spaces and the wide parks of the Oreto River and Mount Grifone.

From the slopes of Mount Grifone, the itinerary leads to the luxuriant citrus groves of Ciaculli and the Public Housing of Villabate (ERP) where a regular settlement is compared with the trapezoidal shape of the lot, open towards the countryside. The big square of the neighbourhood (43 per 115 metres) is purposely "out of scale" if we consider the dimensions of the housing (two to four levels, with very horizontal façades). It should have been a territorial attraction more in proportion to the rural fields than only to its perimeter buildings. Nevertheless, the latest urban expansion followed other criteria and the access to the facilities is from the opposite sides, so that the school and other services back to the square favour their carriage entrances. Public space is just partially used, almost abandoned, as are the gangways that link it with the housing. The designers proposed a

Figure 4. The power of the Young Town is in its unfinished state. Graphic: Luciana Macaluso

"From an anonymous apartment for rent in downtown we moved to the new: our home in Michelangelo [a neighbourhood of Palermo]. ... Just that home in Michelangelo was not there yet. There was the skeleton, the base ... a concrete space with the rebar appearing to underline its condition of work in progress. A kind of stump. But we were already there. ... We spent the days sweeping, organizing, cleaning a construction site. ... The Michelangelo was still to colonise. It was nothing, a virgin territory. If someone had taken a photo of us we were like founding fathers. ... How beautiful nature in Michelangelo neighbourhood there was. ... We cooked and ate in what would become our dining room. And also the children were bustled, we were the sons of the founding fathers of Michelangelo. We built huts ... with those things that the workers left unused. ... In the back of the construction site, behind the Islamic garden, there was an abandoned house that belonged to a duke, a count, a prince, or maybe, why not, an emir" (Vetri 2015, pp. 9).

The phantasy of a child, who shared the enthusiasm of his parents constructing their home, in the 70s, well describes the current potential of a town, just thirty years old, where much is still to be done. Architectural and landscape projects, like stories, tell new optimistic perspectives for the young town. The comparison of different proposals will reveal the main impulses of a new development.

separation between pedestrian and carriage paths through articulate cross-sections, but walkability is not at all common because of the distance of the main services and the inaccessibility of the green areas. The return to the countryside, out of need or choice, and the quality of the nearby traditional rural fields (which are rarely so wide and productive in the town) make ERP in Villabate a paradigmatic case for exploring new relations between territorial and architectural dimensions, innovative rural-urban social practices and spaces. The itinerary has crossed anisotropic and very different "peripheries" where dynamism persists in resilient pre-existing elements, in open and informal spaces, in inhabitants' activities, to push against the fences: "all of the walls that they built ... finally [will] fall" (Arcade Fire 2010).

Notes/Bibliography

1 MIUR PRIN 2007 "Design and Updating of Public Housing in Southern and Central Italy", National Coordinator University of Rome La Sapienza Valle Giulia Prof. B. Todaro, "Peripheries and Contemporary Town. "Palermo: Neighbourhoods, Peripheries and Contemporary Town", scientific responsible University of Palermo Prof. A. Sciascia; Research Group: A. Sciascia, M. Beccali, D. Costi, F. Fava, A. Mamì, E. Palazzotto, F. Schilleci, A. Biancucci, V. Cannizzo, E. Davì, G. De Simone, V. Garofalo, I. Grassedonio, L. Macaluso, D. Roccaro. Published in Sciascia A. (2012) *Periferie e città contemporanea. Progetti per i quartieri Borgo Ulivia e Zen a Palermo*, Palermo, Caracol. "Looking for a Normal Town. The Role of the Public Housing in the Growth of the Italian Towns in the Last 50 Years" (15 April – 15 June 2016, State Archive, Rome). Dipartimento di Ingegneria Civile Design Edilizia e Ambiente (DIcDEA) of the Seconda Università degli Studi of Naples (Prof. Pasquale Belfiore). Direzione Generale Arte e Architettura Contemporanee e Periferie Urbane, Ministero dei Beni e delle Attività culturali e del Turismo (MiBACT). The research on Sicilian districts (Zen, Borgo Ulivia, Villaseta, Librino, ERP Villabate) has been coordinated by Prof. Andrea Sciascia and carried out by Andrea Sciascia and Luciana Macaluso. Published in *Cantiere Periferie. Alla ricerca di una città normale*, "Metamorfosi", n.1, 2016.

2 See laboratory of master's thesis *I frammenti della città in estensione,* Supervisor Prof. A. Sciascia, Tutor L. Macaluso.

3 Carried out since the end of seventies by the professors of the Department of Architecture of Palermo of Urbanism, Planning and Architectural and Industrial Design.

4 The buildings with courtyards were planned by A. Bonafede, R. Calandra, U. Di Cristina, S. Gelfo, P. Mazzacurati, M. Natoli, C. Scavuzzo, V. Ugo, L. Vagnetti, G. Verace, and V. Ziino in 1963.

Arcade Fire (2010) *The Suburbs*.

Biancucci A. (2007) *Giuseppe Samonà e le presenze del progetto. Il restauro del Nucleo Sperimentale nel Borgo Ulivia a Palermo*. Roma, Kappa.

Culotta P. et al. (2005) *Palermo il terzo asse di fondazione*. Palermo, L'Epos.

Forman R. (1995), *Land Mosaics. The ecology of landscapes and regions*. Cambridge, University Press.

Gregotti V. (1966) *Il territorio dell'architettura*. Milan, Feltrinelli.

Inzerillo S. M. (1981) *Urbanistica e società negli ultimi duecento anni a Palermo. Piani e prassi amministrativa dall' "addizione" del Regalmici al concorso del 1939*. Palermo, Quaderno dell'Istituto di Urbanistica e Pianificazione Territoriale della Facoltà di Architettura di Palermo, n.9.

Macaluso L. (2016) *Rural-urban intersections*. Parma, MUP.

Rogers E. N. (1958) *L'esperienza dell'architettura*. Turin, Giulio Einaudi.

Sciascia A. (2003) *Tra le modernità dell'architettura. La questione del quartiere Zen 2 di Palermo*. L'Epos, Palermo.

Sciascia A. (2012) *Periferie e città contemporanea. Progetti per i quartieri Borgo Ulivia e Zen a Palermo*. Palermo, Caracol.

Sciascia A., Macaluso. L. (2016) "Cantiere Periferie. Alla ricerca di una città normale". In: *Metamorfosi*, n.1, 2016.

Secchi B. (1992) "Urbanistica descrittiva". In: *Casabella*, n. 588, 1992.

Tafuri M. (1982) *Storia dell'architettura italiana 1944-85*. Turin, Einaudi.

Todaro B., De Matteis F. eds. (2012), *Il secondo progetto. Interventi sull'abitare pubblico*. Rome, Prospettive.

Vetri N. (2015) *Il Michelangelo*. Palermo, Sellerio editore.

Crossing Boundaries: People, Traces, Events Transforming Peripheries

Raffaella Fagnoni

Figure 1. Giardini Luzzati is a social association founded by Il Ce.Sto in Genoa, 2012. It has recovered an old agorà as meeting point and cultural fertilization centre, proposing activities for children, social inclusion, food services, and national and international cultural events. Images: author

Dialogues

Cities are the most successful, most versatile human artifact, changing continuously while remaining the same. They are complex devices, whose main function has always been to be a massive "communication factory", an immense "workshop of dialogues". Communication, dialogue, interaction—this is the essence of the "urbanity" concept. (D'Eramo, M., 2017). Peripheries are defined as the external boundary of any area, the edge or outskirts, such as of a city or an urban region. Talking about peripheries means talking about boundaries, borders. Borders are something that disappear as we get closser, which dissolve, making them easier to cross. However, peripheries are no longer boundary environments surrounding a centre and enclose it. We have to consider the city as a continuous entity that makes boundaries imperceptible, or even as a succession of centres, as hubs that each attract and radiate energies. To improve our outskirts, we need to place and keep the humanity of people at the centre: city surroundings become better places when the dignity of the people living there can express itself fully. To recover the full respectability of suburbs as places with their own recognisable identity, we therefore need to give meaning not only to their spatial but also to their temporal dimensions, and to thus overcome the forgetfulness of the space and recover remembered, experienced, and imagined time. Repossessing the future will happen by recovering a historical consciousness that is firmly rooted in the territory and renewed daily in the present. It will be able to motivate the inhabitants of suburbs to develop a sense of belonging to their territorial communities, thus encouraging them to participate actively and be fully engaged in the imagination and design of tomorrow.

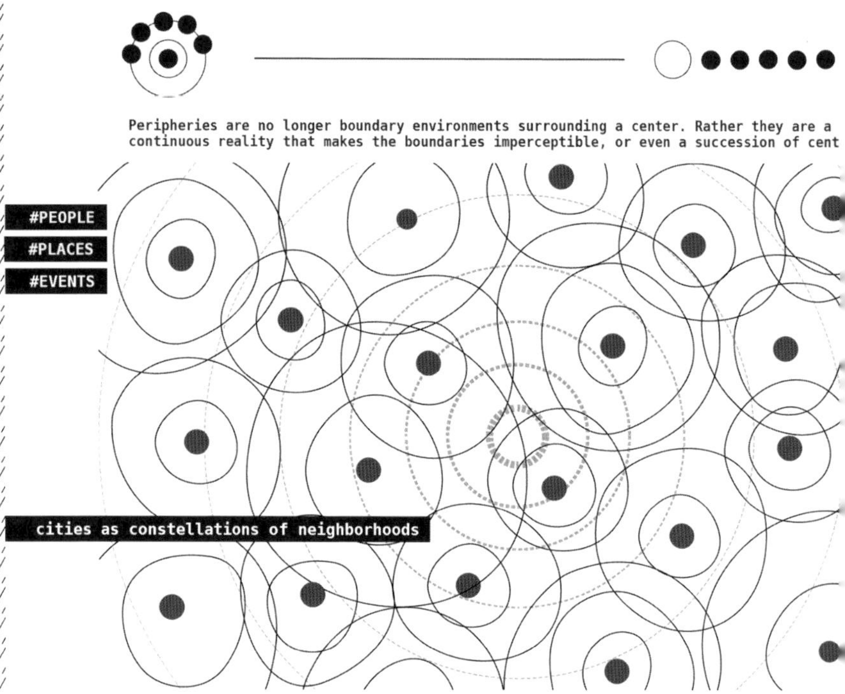

Figure 2. Processes. #Actionscapes. Cities can be conceived as constellations of neighbourhoods, each of which has "one of this places" as a reference, finding what is necessary within walking distance. Graphic: Raffaella Fagnoni

A people-centred design revolution is taking place. The "everyday people" (Sanders 2006) we serve through design are becoming proactive in their demand for better ways of living: they propose actions, events, temporary moments, and predictions, acts that are ephemeral but at the same time expressions of a community activating itself to recovery and rebuild. New design spaces are emerging in response to people's needs, developing environments that nurture learning, creativity, and human potential. They are spaces not only for consuming but also for experiencing, adapting, making, and creating, and the challenge is building an organisational capability. These events generate relational spaces and are going beyond the boundaries of the project's disciplinary categories (urbanism, architecture, design, landscape) where, more than the dimensional scale, the process counts. What typifies these interventions is not only the aesthetic, compositional, or narrative categories but the relationships they are capable of triggering, the performance features, the ability to enter the circular economy processes of their reference backgrounds. Citizen action is on the rise, more in the peripheries, and city governments are having trouble responding to it. The citizen's action level is higher in the situations where people have less choice and the government is weaker. Cities can be conceived as constellations of neighbourhoods, and each one of them has one of these event-places as a reference. Through these events and places, we create a social glue. The role of designers, citizens, and politicians is changing significantly.

Compared to other countries, Italy has an advantage due to the presence of monumental and historical frames even in the smaller cities and in the peripheries. Traces of the past remain in the present as evidence of previous times, often with a strong and emotional presence; and this influences the way we think about future. We are flâneurs moving among the signs of our history, acting, reacting, and interacting with them.

Actionscapes

Our cities are not just made out of buildings and streets, they are mainly built of events,[1] actions and practices, sharing knowledge. The set of small things happening in the neighbourhood make a difference. These events assume a social significance that meets representative and promotional needs. They are collective expressions of a will and an intention. They are a way to stage and test possible uses. They are a way to put spaces back into circulation by using installations—products, signs, and messages. They are tools to propose new cycles of life, give meaning, narrative and uses—even temporary uses—for underused or forgotten spaces, transforming them into central living hubs for a neighbourhood. A growing number of events and practices have been proposed in cities and villages as strategic and planned tools to achieve different aims. Their social role and their often bottom-up dynamics are fundamental inputs for breaking down the borders of the periphery, creating alternative centres. The activities of event design merge urban policies, social design, exhibit design, communication design, and storytelling with cultural and economic development.
Open source events aim to create something collaborative, social, culturally aware, sensitive to the context, multi-disciplinary, visionary, inspirational/motivating, inclusive, and transformative, using a bottom-up process. As Richards argues, in fact, "Eventfulness is intimately linked to the process of placemaking" (Richards, G., Palmer, R. 2010, p. 31). Different situations of our contemporary time describe possible futures for our living, propose different approaches, through a transition from conceptual to real, for crossing the borders of the peripheries and transforming them into a constellation of centres.

1. Crossing from Industrial to Digital

The city has changed, and with it the production systems, revolutionizing decisively our way of living, working, and communicating with others. The transition from the industrial to the digital production system affects all aspects of our daily life not only in the economy but in all disciplines and activities. Beyond the industrial context of the city, peripheries are becoming an informational context: while the industrial system is based on technological transfer, the informational/digital system is based on knowledge transfer. This phenomenon causes the multiplication of active citizenship initiatives, shared actions, proximity networks, and communities. At the same time, it leads us to rethink urban practices, as well as training and education, directly affecting the disciplines of the project. These are involved in shaping spaces and devices, and also in reflecting on future transformations through an innovative, rebellious optics aimed at investigating non-codified, but rooted, practices and tactics. As they transform industrial sites into knowledge places, we can talk about "cultural industries". Co-designing with citizens in order, later, to produce and manage with them is

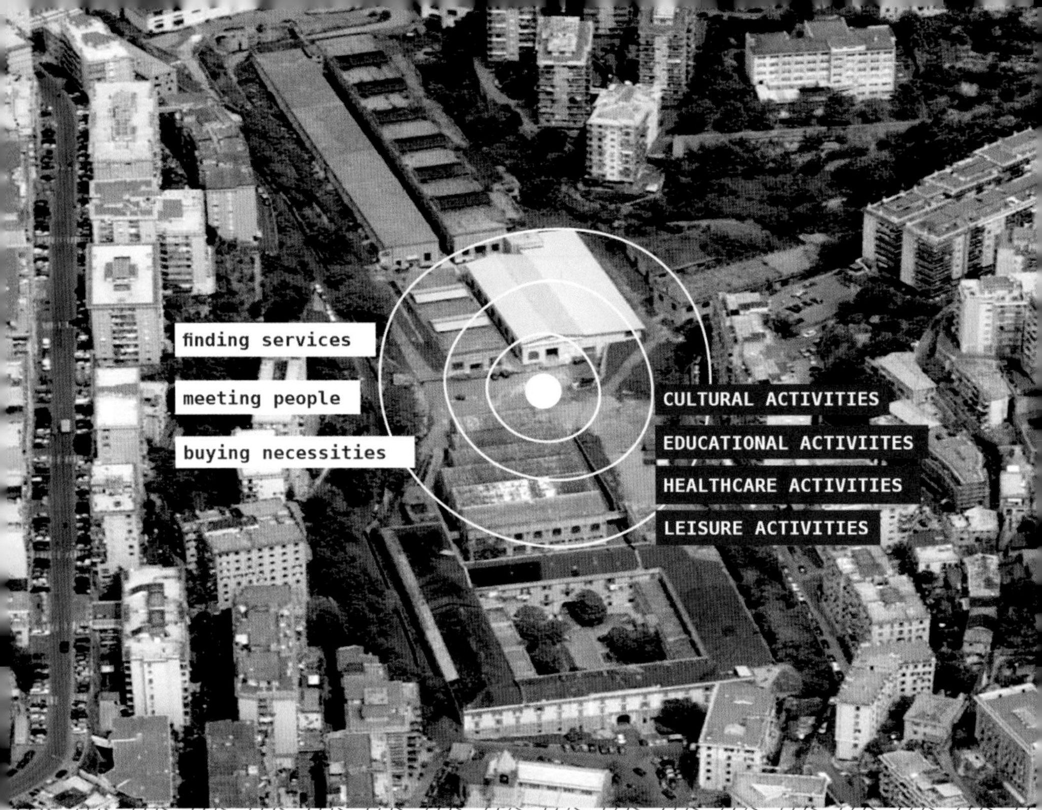

Figure 3. Places. #Plural-identities. From ex to next, the bottom-up practices create relational places, cultural centres, multi-purpose co-working, "makers' spaces", area services, gardens, different centres of gravity. Graphic: Raffaella Fagnoni

From ex to next. The historic city had a structure arranged in parishes. Today, by recovering this kind of sites, new urban polarities have to be set up, playing a role as poles around which episodes of everyday life revolve, identity drivers of the suburbs. The bottom-up practices create independent cultural centres, co-working, meeting venues such as multi-purpose bars or libraries, "makers' spaces", but also area services, gardens, play areas, often zero-consumption of soil and cement. Different centres of gravity, reference totems, new "taverns" are being formed, offering shelter to world travelers, creating plural identities. Sometimes these actions are supported by public funding. But there is still much to do in Italy, because there is a radical aversion, mainly political, for non-institutional paths. These places have developed thanks to independent movements that are often nurtured by the conflict, but then able to raise new interests, embryos of models that are now a reality even if still in search of affirmation. They are places such as the Ex Marseille Tobacco Factory, today La Friche Belle de Mai, one of the most active cultural centres born in a poorer district, or Giardini Luzzati Spazio Comune in Genoa, which grew rapidly as a cultural, leisure, and community centre. Many examples are emerging by challenging privileged relationships: public vs. private, non-profit vs. for-profit, often by colliding with established procedures. We need places shaping new forms of cooperation between public administrations, private property owners, and citizen initiatives.

in fact a revolution in its naive simplicity. It is a process that brings citizens to the centre of virtuous relationships, common values, and democratic politics. The tools that design's discipline offers in this process are articulated into different categories. This opens up several work possibilities, both on the field and on the didactic and experimental level of training.

2. Crossing from Functional to Convivial

Conviviality brings positive outcomes such as social cohesion, trust, and participation but meanwhile negative aspects can emerge when conviviality become an instrument of power relationships. The crossing from functional to convivial means, thus, that labour leads to well-lived moments. As described by Ivan Illich, there are two basic types of tools: "Convivial tools allow users to invest the world with their meaning, to enrich the environment with the fruits of their visions, and to use them for the accomplishment of a purpose they have chosen. Industrial tools deny this possibility to those who use them and they allow their designers to determine the meaning and expectations of others". The same action can be done in a functional or convivial way. Illich described eloquently how a balance between consumptive and creative activities is necessary for human survival. "People need not only to obtain things: they need, above all, the freedom to make things among which they can live, to give shape to them according to their own tastes, and to put them to use in caring for and about others" (1973, p. 20).

3. Crossing from Citizens to Users

Peripheries propound often a negative fashion, far from main interests, but if the confidence and the status of the people living there can express themselves fully, it will be possible to live them as beautiful places. This means adopting a new model of service co-development, designing events and practices in which those who have traditionally been individual end-users tend to become collaborative co-producers, in which people who have traditionally been considered only as parts of the problem become agents of the solution. Events and design practices are means of providing services, building a bridge between bottom-up social innovation and top-down public services. Furthermore, they need an appropriate use of design knowledge and skills, adopting a participatory and community-centred approach, focusing on and activating different actors, helping clarify their motivations and promoting their alignment towards a shared goal. In this context, community-centred design supports the consolidation of emerging ideas, making them more effective, accessible, and replicable.

4. Crossing from Linear to Circular

Circular means talking about performance, basing the economy on services more than products. We are moving towards a system that will not produce more products, but status of relationships, which appeal most to social design and interaction design. This means offering the services and availability of necessary products, preferably within walking distance. Peripheries are commonly considered as forgotten places of conflicts, but also as bottom-up laboratories. These are spaces that generate small original solutions that can be the basis for greater and replicable innovations in which the activist designers employ their skills and tools at the service of citizens to explore

STORY
designing the storytelling as part of the more intangible design elements.

SCALE
not only a physical size, but a collective, generative and participative dimension.

SHAPE
designing the servicescape, furniture, choosing materials and elements due to meaning, local history, circular economy.

EXPERIENCE
considering the experience design in each scenario's aspect, communication, food, services.

TIME
involving time and focus on the user experience.

SCHEDULE
programming activities, balancing ups and downs, and making picks involving people and stakeholders.

SET-UP
organizing each step in harmony, packaging and programming each activity.

Figure 4. Narratives. #Traces. We are flâneurs moving among the signs of our history. With these traces we act, react, interact. From “making city” to “being city”. Graphic: Raffaella Fagnoni

Once upon a time the territory was marked and protected by the presence of “genius loci”, a magical and mysterious involvement, typical of Latin culture, which could have various forms, often natural. These places today are different and not permanent; they tend to rotate, disappear, reappear elsewhere. They are made up of the fabric of the city: shops, bars, restaurants, meeting places, dynamic by their nature. They become theoretical sites, narrative experiments, provisional scenarios. Today there is a fairly circular, fluid time. Today we are flâneurs moving among the signs of our history, among traces of the past as evidence of previous times, often with a strong and emotional presence; this influences the way we think about the future, and we live in and with these traces. With these traces we act, by mapping and documenting; with these traces we react, by designing scenarios to rehabilitate places, defining goals; with these traces we interact, by involving people, creating platforms, collective actions, events to rehabilitate urban peripheries. To recover the full dignity of the suburbs as places with their own recognisable identity, we can therefore give meaning not only to their spatial but also to their temporal dimensions, to thus overcome the forgetfulness of the space and recover remembered, experienced, and imagined time. From “making city” to “being city”. If we are not going to be optimistic we will not solve problems, and we do need to solve them. We will also make it through the aesthetic component: ugliness is in fact a form of pollution and very serious degradation.

together new ways of inhabiting the city in a more sustainable way, both for an environmental and social point of view. In several regions, associations and organisations concerned with a circular-economy are emerging. The goal is to build a concrete "green" development accelerator for the territory and produce value, employment, and innovation.

5. Crossing from Reuse to U-rise

Peripheries are often places of dynamic becoming with a fragile identity. It is possible to create better conditions that place and keep the humanity of people at the centre of our thoughts and actions, with awareness and care for sustainability. This kind of activism—not a protest or political attitude—is an emergency reaction: citizens spontaneously organise themselves to give an immediate answer to their problems, starting from existing reality without waiting for top-down support and resources. According to Christian Iaione, (2015), the twenty-first century is the century of "COmmons, COllaboration, COoperation, COmmunity, COmmunication, CO-design…" This dimension facilitates the process of reusing not only waste, but spaces, materials, things, messages, cultures, thus transforming ways of living.

6. Crossing from Boredom to Fun

Peripheries are often boredom, and living is not a game. It's demanding, boring, and rarely fun. But it is possible to follow the aesthetic of play proposed by the philosopher and designer Ian Bogost in his book *Play Anything* (2016). Play isn't a mindless escape from boring reality. Instead, play is what happens when we accept limitations, narrow our focus, and, consequently, have fun. Which is also how to live a good life. Play cultivates humility, for it requires us to treat things as they are rather than as we wish them to be. If we let it, play can be the secret to contentment. Not because it provides happiness or pleasure, although it certainly can, but because it helps us pursue a greater respect for the things, people, and situations around us." After all, already in the fifteenth century, Marsilio Ficino, Accademico della Crusca, wrote: "iocari serio et studiosissime ludere" (joke seriously and play assiduously).

Note/Bibliography

1 About the concept of event and eventfulness: Hühn P. (2011) "Event and Eventfulness". In: Hühn, P. et al. eds (2011) *The Living Handbook of Narratology.* Hamburg University Press, open access publication cofunded by DFG. Hamburg. Available online at: www.lhn.uni-hamburg.de/article/event-and-eventfulness (accessed 1 Feb 2018); and Zizek 2014.

Iaione C. (2015) "La collaborazione civica per l'amministrazione, la governance e l'economia dei beni comuni". In: Arena G., Iaione, C. ed. (2015) *L'età della condivisione La collaborazione tra cittadini e amministrazione per i beni comuni.* Roma, Carocci, pp. 31–78.

Bogost I., (2016), *Play Anything: The Pleasure of Limits, the Uses of Boredom, and the Secret of Games*. N.Y. Basic Books.

D'Eramo M. (2017), *Il selfie del mondo, Indagine sull'età del turismo*. Milano, Feltrinelli.

Fagnoni R., Ricci M., (2016) "The Future is Backwards. Re-Cycle as Destiny". In: *Project Anticipation. When Design Shapes Futures in Architecture and Urban Design*, Proceedings of the First International Conference on Project Anticipation, session "Design and anticipation", Edited by D. Fanzini, Maggioli Editore, pp. 75–87.

Illich I. (1973) *Tools for Conviviality*. London. Harper & Row.

Manzini E., (2015), *Design When Everybody Designs. An Introduction to Design for Social Innovation.* Cambridge: MIT Press.

Mastrodonato A. (2013) EX ORDIUM. "Per un archivio della generatività sociale nelle periferie". In: *MeTis, Mondi educativi.* Temi indagini suggestioni, Anno III, Numero 2, 12/2013.

Richards G., Palmer, R., (2010) *Eventful Cities: Cultural Management and Urban Revitalisation,* Oxford, Routledge.

Sanders, E. B.–N. (2006) "Scaffolds for Building Everyday Creativity". In: Frascara J. ed. (2006) *Design for Effective Communications: Crating Contexts for Clarity and Meaning.* New York, Allworth Press.

Zizek S. (2014) *Event.* London, Penguin.

Infrastructural Axes as Urban Periphery and Fields of Potential: The Case Study of São Paulo

Sarah Hartmann

Figure 1. Urban Beach Minhocão. Photo: Sarah Hartmann

The principle of modernity consisted in separating functions and until today such areas—large housing sites or infrastructural canyons—even if now geographically central, are often perceived as "outer city", as periphery. The construction of the new capital in the hinterland of Brazil in the fifties, commonly referred to as the culmination of "Brazilian Modernity" and the monofunctional large infrastructural channels from the period of the military regime in São Paulo as well as Rio de Janeiro, bear witness to this attitude. Le Corbusier visited São Paulo already in 1929 and left an important sketch that "shows two gigantic buildings with straight motorways on the top, crossing at right angles in the very centre of the city, an urban vision that aimed to design the city through megastructures to dominate the territory" (Leite Rosa 2015, p. 45). Even though Le Corbusier's imaginations remained theoretical, São Paulo is organised according to the logic of functional production. Infrastructure, even if nowadays partly insufficient, is still the reason for São Paulo's economic strength and strategic position within the whole country. Planning and development responded to the cities' unforeseeable explosive growth and the focus on the automobile, with functional zoning and the implementation of massive infrastructures. Thus, public open space in a human related scale, in which people from different social backgrounds gather and encounter, is still scarce in the city. Fernando de Mello Franco goes so far as to say: "We can speak little of historical monuments or tissues. The main asset of this city is its network of infrastructure. ... Infrastructural networks

Figure 2. Topography, infrastructure and settlements: Different development processes in São Paulo.
Graphic: Sarah Hartmann

Iterative Dynamics: from Periphery to Centre to Periphery: "Centre" and "Periphery" are key terms of economic theories developed in the 1960s and 1970s in order to explain different processes of economic development and underdevelopment, rich and poor, countryside and city, all related to each other and proposing a geographical structure that is based on division. Still, urban development processes within the biggest agglomerations, especially if at the borders of the formal city and economically poor, are due to enormous growth rates and auto-constructions, often referred to as “Peripheral Urbanisations” (LSE 2014). The present statement proposes, instead, to conceive the process of peripherisation in relation to the morphology of the territory, in a holistic perspective, combining economic, social, cultural, and mobility aspects with the precise geographical condition. In fact, growing urbanisation has incorporated and integrated geographical periphery, as new spatial patterns, such as polycentricism, developed. But, due to the interest for the outer city, historic centres, like in São Paulo, were abandoned, economically degraded, and transformed into inner-city peripheries, lacking people and activities. In consequence, periphery became central, and the centre became periphery. Thus, periphery, seen from a process-related perspective and conceived as the process of re-integration of fragmented, lost, or undervalued urban places into the city fabric, regardless of their geographical position, can become the trigger for new and creative dynamics within the existing urban tissue.

are persistent elements, spatial and functional structures that, even obsolete, have a latent capacity for reactivation" (Franco 2011, p. 139). Accordingly, in contrast to the common interpretation of periphery, the present article proposes the hypothesis that peripheries exist also within highly urbanised areas and can become fields of potential for future developments. Nevertheless, the infrastructural canyons in São Paulo show that the urban approach to periphery is still ambivalent.

For one part of the citizens—the daily commuters with private automobiles—these infrastructural axes symbolize limited channels within the central areas of the Megacity (around 8 million car journeys a day). Limited, because these enormous open spaces have been implemented to provide the connection from A to B, without serving any other demand for a vital urbanity and cutting through the existing urban tissue. They are made out of concrete, are sometimes underground, sometimes elevated—but are always disconnected from the surroundings and almost everywhere exclusively reserved for the car. Hence, even if they are located centrally in the expanded centre, they unfold a peripheral condition within the everyday life outside the private automobile.

But due to a programme called *ruas abertas* (open streets) that officially opens up specific streets on Sundays and holidays to the people, some of these channels have become linear places were vibrant urbanity is triggered and where practices of everyday life are happening. These formerly peripheral axes became commercial-free zones of creative appropriation, manifold uses, and extraordinary collectiveness, condensed in a spatial interplay of architecture, infrastructure, and the city. The ability of the same physical structure to host various programmes, alternately or concurrently, is seen as significant spatial potential, which has the capacity to turn the peripheral infrastructural axes into central urban open spaces.

One important infrastructural axis, part of the east-west tangential, is the Minhocão: The 3.5 kilometer-long elevated Highway Elevado Presidente Costa e Silva, nicknamed Minhocão (big worm), which cuts through the central part of São Paulo, is emblematic for the era of heavy infrastructure investments of the military dictatorship, when there was no chance for opponents to protest. It was opened in 1971 to relieve the traffic in the underlying Avenue São João. Due to its negative impacts on the surrounding neighbourhoods its actual presence is as polemic as its nickname: Minhocão (big worm). It has drawn public attention and provoked plans to demolish it since it was built. Already in 1976 it was decided to shut it down temporarily for cars in the night, in 1992 additionally on Sundays and since 2015 additionally on Saturday afternoons. In the eighties, the area was conceived—due to the decrease of the real estate market resulting from the construction of the highway—as socially poor, highly dangerous, and unsecure. But in the last ten years, an occupation started on this modern monument that turned the meaning and role of the infrastructural artefact upside-down—into the so called "Parque Minhocão". In 2016, the highway was officially named a park, as people found that this ordinary and yet also unique public open space offered the opportunity to be used for both ordinary and extraordinary street-life activities.

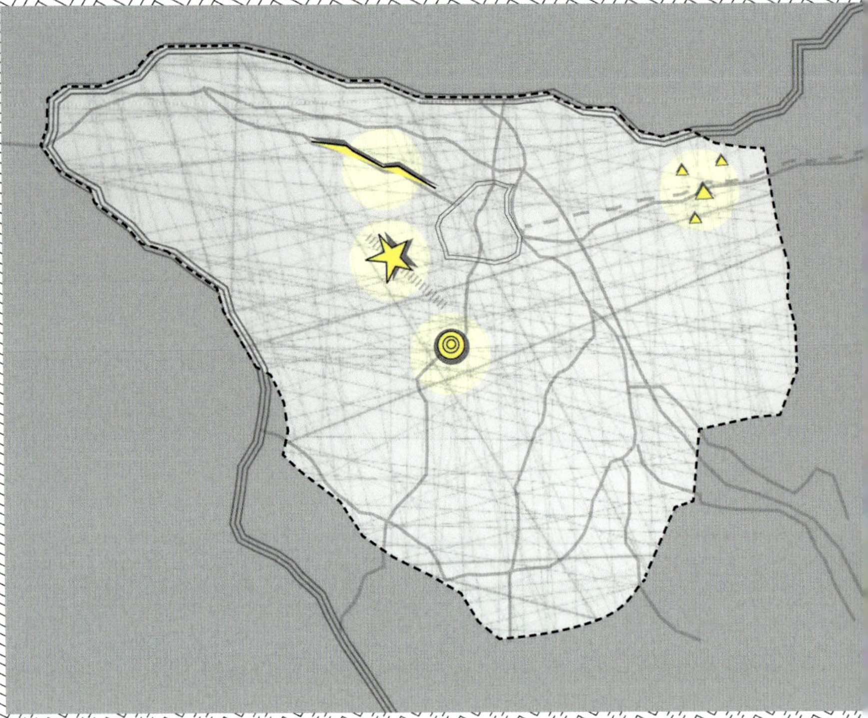

Figure 3. Places of intensification in the expanded centre of São Paulo. Graphic: Sarah Hartmann

Intensifying the Periphery: Ghettoization, depopulation of downtown areas, sprawl at the urban fringes, the fading of the cityscape, and the increasing privatization of public space are just some of the slogans among which urban space in São Paulo, but also the "crisis of the city" in general, are discussed. Moreover, as Tom Avermate explains, in the 1990s, Michael Sorkin's well known book *Variations on a Theme Park* was given the subtitle *The End of Public Space*, Rem Koolhaas spoke of the "evaporation of the public realm" in his essay about the "Generic City" and Bruce Robbins named his book *The Phantom Public Sphere* (Avermate 2007, p. 2). The spatial reference for this discussion is still the morphology of a historical city with clear borders, and an imaginative ideal of publicness and public places. Consequently, debates often note a loss of the material places and structural form and observe a loss of hierarchies in contemporary urban contexts. Peter Sloterdijk refers in his book to a kind of "neutralization" and "flatness" that effected spatial thinking in modern times (Sloterdijk 2013). Against this background, physical places in the flat, inner-city periphery are a resource for the future development and reintensification of cities. Places, as urban formations of public spaces, have the capacity—different from social structures that underpin the collective sphere—to actively shape the public domain and to physically express collective identity in an increasingly digitalized world. Periphery therefore has the potential to intensify strategic places.

Even though the implementation of the Minhocão is generally "seen as authoritarian act, which privileged the circulation of cars over pedestrians, and efficiency over socialization, its construction could by no means be considered a good solution for the area" (Barbosa 2012); neighbours and citizens re-interpreted this infrastructure as a new platform for practices of everyday life.
The case study of the Minhocão is only a small part of the infrastructural network of São Paulo, but it points nevertheless to a higher relevance of the topic of infrastructural peripheries in general. The present paper aims to explain their innovative dynamics and to formulate their potentials according to two spatial concepts:

Urban Beaches

Fernando de Mello Franco explains that important urban spaces are those where the exchange between different social groups is possible and does happen, and where conflict is negotiated in the way the space is used. According to him there are "two archetypes of Brazilian Culture where we find this venue: street soccer and the urban beach" (Franco 2011, p. 143). Aquino and Shanski's concept of the urban beach differentiates between the beach, as a physical space and the concept of "beachscape", which they define as an attitude, a method of observation, reflection, and work with the public space. "The beach reveals the image of a pleasure field. Yet that same territory can be identified as a place where differences are negotiated. The beach as a model can be extended to all kinds of urban spaces, producing multiple sites of encounter and release. Its accommodating infrastructure encourages multiple occupations, an open framework in support of urban life" (Aquino, Shanski 2014). São Paulo is located at a distance to the sea, nevertheless its affection to beachscape is rooted in cultural values. Franco highlights that "the urban beach conforms to a succession of programmatic features that look toward the horizon, interspersed with streets, sidewalks and surfaces of sand and water. One after the other, these tracks are the ground for ordinary actions such as walking, parking, driving, cycling, running, flirting, playing, trading, sunbathing, strolling, swimming, contemplating" (Franco 2011, p. 143).

This space between the sea and the houses, embodied by the streetscapes, opens up a mediating surface between the technical system of daily traffic and the playful activities experienced at the seafront. Thus the interrelation of the ambiguous programmatic contents defines the power of this network. In none of the places is there the beauty of the seaside or the shore, but the specific spatial situations provide new perspectives towards the unique landscape of the city. The infrastructural network provides the potential to observe the urban spectacle of passers-by, skaters, cyclists, chance encounters, and street traders. And at the same time one can be observed and seen, from passing cars, by joggers, or from the nearby windows. In view of São Paulo's ubiquity of infrastructure, its characteristic mobility channels, this article argues that precisely these relations to infrastructure—formerly a peripheral condition—provide an important contextual frame which triggers collective practices and everyday life activities.

Figure 4. Interpretation of the expanded Centre of São Paulo as Archipelago. Graphic: Sarah Hartmann

Explaining Peripheries: Mark Childs argues that narratives in urban design are able to inform and condition the design of places in multiple ways: "Urban designers can curate the narrative landscape of a town in ways that support designers' engagement with place stories, [they can] nurture a virtuous cycle of interactions between stories of place, built form, and the emergent form of a settlement, and [they] create formats for the inclusion of multiple designers and a diverse set of independent stories rather than master narratives" (Childs 2008, p. 172). Accordingly, narratives of inner-city peripheries can create a deeper understanding for the places which are essentially shaped by the relationship of centre and periphery conditions, past and present as well as durability and change, which can not be fully comprehended in complex situations at first sight. Cultivating narratives and rooting periphery in time, both in the past but also in the present, is extraordinarily relevant to establish a continuity of urban spaces, especially in highly transformative urban contexts. Narratives can become a tool to immaterially and materially describe inner-city peripheries, in order to unveil their capacity for social inclusion and collectivity.

Linear Belvedere

Within the dense urban tissue of São Paulo, which is marked by the presence of seemingly endless high-rise buildings, the Minhocão formulates a fraction. It marks a linear viewpoint, whose morphological quality is derived from the elevated position of the highway that hovers between eight and ten meters over the ground and provides—for the drivers, as well for the pedestrians—scenic views along its three kilometres of length. The Minhocão is not a punctual platform, like a belvedere or a viewpoint, but provides a linear strip of heterogeneous perspectives. The height difference in this case offers the possibility to look at the city and its dense tissue of buildings and streets from a new perspective. As the photograph shows, the Elevado becomes a structural catwalk and the city becomes the scenery. This can moreover be experienced when walking along the three kilometres of the highway, when extraordinary pieces of street art, new greened façades, and window theatres appear. Hence, this linear belvedere is rooted in a situation of ephemeral and dynamic perception.

Thus, in summary the present article discusses the old question of public space in the urban periphery and especially the role of architecture and infrastructure within the periphery. Therefore, it questions the use and the meaning of the term "periphery" especially for urban contexts which are dissolved and cannot be described by the traditional duality of centre and periphery. Instead the example of the Minhocão shows a new perspective on the urban realm, where periphery and centre, seen as an urban condition much more than a geographical position, can be at the same time in one place. Thus the thesis argues that places of inner-city periphery, as the infrastructural axes in São Paulo, deserve a closer look, as they are important fields of potentials which have the capacity to give form to a new collective sphere. As such, they are an important challenge for the contemporary profession of architecture.

Bibliography

Aquino E., Shanski K. (2014) *Beachscape*. Available online: http://www.coolgardens.ca/BEACHSCAPE, accessed 9.6.2017.

Avermaete T. et al., ed. (2007) "Urban Formation and Collective Spaces". In: *Oase 71: Urban Formation and Collective Spaces*, Rotterdam, Nai Publishers, pp. 2–4.

Barbosa E. (2012) "Minhocão Multiples Interpretations". In: *Arquitextos*, São Paulo, Year 13, n. 147.03, Vitruvius, retrieved from http:// www.vitruvius.com.br/revistas/read/arquitextos/13.147/4455/en>.

Childs M. (2008) "Storytelling and Urban Design". In: *Journal of Urbanism: International Research on Placemaking and Urban Sustainability*, 1:2, pp. 173–186.

De Mello Franco F. (2011) "Contrary and Complementary". In: Leite Rosa ed. (2011) *Microplanning*, Urban Creative Practices São Paulo, pp. 134–147.

Leite Rosa M. (2015) *From Modern Infrastructures to Operational Networks; The Qualification of Local Space at Existing Large-Scale Utility Infrastructure: A Method For Reading Community-Driven Initiatives; The Case Of São Paulo*. PhD Thesis, Munich, Technische Universität München, Lehrstuhl für Städtebau und Regionalplanung.

LSE Cities (2014) *Annual Report of the LSE Cities 2014–2016*. London School of Economics and Political Science, available online: LSECiti.es/Report2016, accessed 24.7.2016.

Sloterdijk P. (2002) *Die letzte Kugel*. Frankfurt am Main, Suhrkamp.

Building Beyond the Periphery

Philip Norman Peterson

Figure 1. Paläon. HolzerKobler Architects. Photo: Jan Bitter

To begin with, I'd like to attempt to define the term periphery. Near to the sites of the projects I will present today is a particular European phenomenon, the Hollowcore as defined by Rem Koolhaas. Amsterdam, Brussels, Dortmund, and Cologne define, more or less, the outer boundaries of a networked periphery. The Hollowcore defined by Rem Koolhaas in the exhibition catalogue *Content* from 2004 is in fact a periphery that includes non-peripheral cities and lies between the larger cities of London, Paris, and Berlin. Beyond this periphery are places such as Nebra, Schoeningen, St. Peter-Ording, Cuxhaven, Schleswig, and Warnemuende. In particular I'd like to evaluate the qualities of these extra-peripheral places. Places beyond the periphery are located more than 200 kilometres from a major city in relation to the task of making an architecture.

The first project I'd like to present is an archaeological research and experience centre called paläon. Paläon is in its own right a small archaeological museum housing a permanent exhibition, a temporary exhibition space, pedagogic rooms, an archaeological laboratory, a shop, and a restaurant with spaces for meetings and events. The museum is located next to the archaeological site where seven wooden spears were discovered in 1994. Those are over 300,000 years old and therefore turned the current research upside down as they are the oldest hunting weapons known to humankind.

Figure 2. Paläon. HolzerKobler Architects. Photo: Jan Bitter

Figure 3. Paläon. HolzerKobler Architects. Photo: Jan Bitter

The "Schöninger Speere" were found on the edge of a coal mine and are on the property of the coal mine. From the discovery to the realisation of thc museum was a long way and obviously such a project involves many people. I'd like to single out four men who played a significant role in deciding where the building should be located and how it should be financed.

The archaeologist Hartmut Thieme is outstanding for his persistence in the face of doubt and pressure from the mining company. After many years of mining, the site Mr. Thieme had located was to be mined in the mid 1990s. In a last minute act the director of the mine, Klaus Friedrich, finally gave in and rerouted the mining in order to preserve the site. This costly act saved the site from being destroyed. Shortly after this decision, Mr. Thieme made the sensational find.

What was so sensational about it? The dating of the spears puts it in the time of the Homo heidelbergensis. The fact that many horse skeletons were found in combination with the spears implies a complex group hunt. Until this sensational find, archaeologists believed that the Homo heidelbergensis were not capable of complex communications. This awareness refuted the theory, and the history books were corrected in accordance with these newly found facts.

What was to be done with the found artefacts? It took about ten years after the find until Dr. Wolf-Michael Schmid, the president of the Chamber of Industry and Commerce of Lower Saxony invited Prime Minister, Christian Wulff, to visit the site. This region of Lower Saxony was and is a coal-mining region. The coal-mining was diminishing, which led to a reevaluation of the economic future of the area. The economic future of Lower Saxony should be partially oriented towards culture and tourism. Wolf-Michael Schmid was not only able to convince Christian Wulff of the value of locating the museum at the site of this find; he was also able to secure the necessary funding for the entire project.

For the town of Schoeningen, paläon was to be a significant cornerstone in the new economic development of not only Schoeningen but the entire region.

It is relevant to understand the weight and importance of the building characteristic of all extra-peripheral locations. Typically, as in Schoeningen, the place has had a long period of lack of development. The new culturally significant theme is to be housed in an architecture that not only fulfills the functional requirements but also, and more importantly, symbolizes a new beginning for an economically weakened area. Schoeningen, as said, was and is a coal-mining area. In addition to that it was a border town between the former East and West Germany during the time of the Iron Curtain. It thus became a dead-end which led to a decline in population and economic strength. The discovery of the spears and the decision to erect a museum on the site paved the way for the beginning of a new era.

Our approach to design is rooted in communicating the content and reacting to the context. The design for the new museum is from one point of view an attempt to address the issue.

Figure 4. Watt Besucherzentrum. HolzerKobler Architects. Photo: Jan Bitter

Figure 5. Watt Besucherzentrum. HolzerKobler Architects. Photo: Jan Bitter

We began by analysing the spears and their particular qualities. Their technical and aerodynamic nature is very sophisticated. The flight-path is very precise, and so the vector is an appropriate symbol of this. By orienting the vectors towards points of interest on and around the site as in the archaeological site, we positioned the vectors in the direction of the coal mine, the mountain of Brocken, and the city centre of Schöningen. These lines formed the outer shell building.

Then we organised the spatial programme around the path through the building. The sequence of approach, entry hall, access using the main stair directly to the second floor, and the temporary exhibit, through the permanent exhibit, down to the first floor and the visitors laboratory, the archives, and returning to the entry hall, shop, and cafe determined the organisation of the interior spaces and remoulded the exterior.

The mirrored façade was an attempt to make the building both ephemeral and through the form of the building simultaneously distinctive. To make a building that is present and absent at the same time, depending on the light and the reflection of the weather on its surface. The large cut-like windows on the façade mark the points where the view-lines exit and enter the building.

The exhibition architecture is based on the cellular structure of the bone of a horse. The ins and outs of the space-making form give the exhibition its rhythm while providing the necessary exhibition cabinets and spaces for the scientific narrative of the exhibition. Surrounding and within this element are the thematic narratives created by artists such as Misha Shenbrot, Alexej Tchernyi, and Stephan Hüsch. The combination of low-threshold (artistic) and scientific information ensures the communication at varying levels. There is something for all visitors, that is to say, something for the "skimmer, swimmer, and deep diver".

The final station in the permanent exhibition is the 270° cinema which provides the opportunity to tell the story in yet another medium and from another perspective. One exits the permanent exhibition into the three-story atrium space. This is the core space, a space for reorientation. It provides a view onto the coal mine, as well as a display of the diverse laquerwork specimens or "lift-offs" hung as paintings on the multi-storied wall, a positive model of the mine which shows what might have been there before, and a video installation dealing with the story of strata or archaeological layers in a playful manner.

Arriving at the first level, the path leads to the visitors' laboratory, and the display windows offer a view into the real research centre where one can experience the entire archaeological process from the found artefacts to cleaning, analysis, and documentation.

The building becomes in its architectural expression a symbol for the museum, easily recognizable. It offers itself as a symbol of a new start used in advertising, on stamps and clothing. The fact that the architecture is unique to its purpose allows it to effectively market itself and thus fulfill its roll as a cornerstone to the future of tourism in this extra-peripheral region.

Figure 6. Watt Besucherzentrum. HolzerKobler Architects. Photo: Jan Bitter

Figure 7. Watt Besucherzentrum. HolzerKobler Architects. Photo: Jan Bitter

The second project I'd like to present is a visitors' centre for the Unesco World Heritage site of the Wadden Sea in Cuxhaven. Inspired by the stilt houses on the North-Sea Coast of Germany the Wadden Sea Unesco World Heritage Visitor Centre symbolises the rebirth of Cuxhaven in the beginning of the twenty-first century. It was the first project in Cuxhaven since the Doeser Strandhaus from 1953 that attempted to start a cultural revitalisation.

Like the Doeser Strandhaus, the Wadden Sea World Heritage Visitor Centre began with an architectural competition. We started with the idea of a stilt house inspired by the wooden stilt structures on the North-Sea Coast of Germany—but it soon became clear that the task was to design a simple readable house which focused on marking and informing about the Wadden Sea in Cuxhaven. The inspiration of the stilt house combined with a desire to build using sustainable materials led to the decision to use wood for the entire structure.

The protruding glassed-in staircase not only marks and protects the entrance to the building but intuitively wakens the curiosity of the visitor and the desire to enter. Upon reaching the top of the main stair, the visitor is not only introduced to the theme of Unesco World Heritage sites around the world but is also confronted with the place by the framed view through the first of two large windows. The window frames the heathland outside of the building. It also works as a frame from the outside of the building, framing the large-scale back-lit aerial photograph of the Wadden Sea landscape. Our focus throughout the design and building was on the views from inside showing the magnificent landscape of the Wadden Sea. One day, while leaving the site, I pointed out the building and this particular aspect to a taxi driver, Mr. Graf. Upon seeing the aerial photograph framed, from the outside, by the heathland window, he was overwhelmed and spontaneously suggested that the project is a sort of "forced sensual seduction" (zwang-sinnliche Verführung).

Continuing through the exhibition, the visitor is informed about the specific attributes of the Wadden Sea in Cuxhaven. By means of the flooding model, media stations showing weather conditions, a physical book of tides, video interviews, collages, and a diorama, the visitor is guided to the larger of the two main windows. The Wadden Sea window fills the entire wall, thus practically bringing the entire Wadden Sea into the exhibition space. In this area the plant and animal life of the Wadden Sea are explained and displayed.

The programme of the house is rounded off at the uppermost floor with seminar rooms, laboratories, offices, and a library. The aspect of sustainability culminates with the solar collectors on the roof. The levels of energy gained are displayed in the exhibition.

Clearly the main attraction of significant places within the extra-periphery is the main attraction. Good architecture succeeds in calling attention to and informing about the uniqueness of the place. Distinctive architecture alone is not enough to attract a visitor to an extra-peripheral location—but it helps.

A Creative Alliance for Urban Rivers

Paola Sabbion

Watercourses are elements of the urban landscape around which deep environmental transformations have occurred. However, from peripheral areas along streams and rivers it is still possible to trigger the next rocess of change. Urban rivers have been heavily transformed worldwide since the industrial revolution. Anthropic activities, such as factories and infrastructure, flood control features, and engineered works have altered river environments, removing riparian habitats, hindering watershed processes and ecological integrity. Impervious surfaces have increased within river basins, and this physical transformation of the environment has often produced a condition of economic and social deprivation, which has led the poorer and marginalized populations to occupy the most degraded urban areas. This has occurred in many cities, especially where metropolitan areas experienced explosive development in the twentieth century.

Although watercourse control has been based on hydraulic engineering for centuries, this approach is gradually changing. Cities are increasingly required to implement targeted solutions not only for defense against possible flooding, but also for the improvement of the living environment's quality. To achieve these aims, considering hydraulic and engineering aspects is not enough: in addition it is necessary to pursue the preservation of the ecosystems and the restoration of river habitats through new approaches inspired by natural processes (Furlong et al. 2016). As a result, in recent decades interest in river restoration has considerably increased, along with a new attention to the functions of rivers and the ecosystem services they can provide. Remarkably, the most ambitious projects recently achieved have involved the central areas of cities, while peripheral areas were often ignored. Nevertheless, some neglected neighbourhoods have precisely been the main scene of important struggles carried out by local community organisations worldwide, including riverfront development, brownfield regeneration, creation of open spaces, and environmental health improvement.

In many major cities in the United States, Australia, and North Europe, the integration of river infrastructure into the urban fabric has developed with the aim of improving water availability, preventing floods, and providing health and quality advantages to life. There is therefore a broad consensus that urban areas should adapt to climate change by being intergrated into natural cycles and creating more water-sensitive cities (Ward et al. 2012). Hence, rivers are becoming one of the centres of interest around which communities have aggregated to trigger the revitalisation of the most degraded peripheral urban areas. Bottom-up initiatives and the sharing of intentions between local organisations and public entities have recently triggered successfully river recovery processes.

Figure 1. Abandoned fruit market used as the venue of a temporary event. Photo: Paola Sabbion

Different cases in Europe and USA demonstrate how bottom-up and top-down logics can be useful to solve peripheral issues. However, in both cases the whole urban, geographic, and social framework needs to be carefully analysed in its complexity in terms of political adjustment, administrative reform, and social justice.

New technologies can be useful tools both for searching for information and for the involvement of populations. An increasing complexity can be steered by the construction of shared intentions and the involvement of dynamic creative energies.

In the United States, voluntary actions started by citizens and volunteer associations have notably and frequently led to an improvement of environmental and social conditions. For example, American cases of the ongoing rehabilitation of the Brox River (New York) and Los Angeles River (Los Angeles) demonstrate the effectiveness of bottom-up initiatives and collaborations between local governments and volunteer associations in areas characterised by environmental, economical, and social issues. By contrast, in Europe, community involvement is characterised by a more institutional approach, although it is noticed that planning practices are gradually moving towards a larger inclusion of local communities. European cases demonstrate the effectiveness of top-down policies, where attention has been focused on environmental needs, citizenship involvement, quality of public space, and also on economic and touristic benefits (see, for example, the case of Paillon in Nice and of Madrid Rio in Madrid; Perini, Sabbion 2016).

In fact, if local participation in the United States is based on a deep-rooted tradition, Europe is traditionally top-down oriented. However, recent planning practices in EU are gradually including community needs. In particular, activists, volunteers, and civil society organisations have enthusiastically embraced initiatives supporting city greening projects and actions, demonstrating that green infrastructure can be "the ecological framework for environmental, social, and economic health, in short, our natural life-support system" (Benedict, McMahon 2012, p. 1). In this scenario, community engagement must necessarily find a new ground of shared initiatives oriented toward the integration of subjects at different levels (national, regional, administrative, and community). Even more so in peripheral areas, designing "resilient cities" should mean designing natural and social spaces able to "accommodate complex patterns of diversity" (Montgomery 1998, p. 106).

Ultimately, it is possible to look at cities, in particular where public engagement is not yet deeply rooted, through the lenses of the revised concept of the "Creative City", which defines a paradigm for making cities more vital and liveable through people's creative capital. This definition implies being aware of a growing demand by people for desirable places to live by re-creating values of belonging, continuity, safety, and the opportunities for interactions. This is all the more true in peripheral areas, where the main concern of inhabitants is to re-create a sense of identity and a sense of place, as well as to renovate access to natural values. If, according to Charles Landry, creativity can come from any source, including anyone who addresses issues in an inventive way (and not only from artists or creative economic actors), this scenario should include architects, public administrators, businessmen, social workers, and scientists who together address innovations and urban quality. Therefore, communities can nowadays find new allies in their struggle for a better living environment. The "Creative City" paradigm entails a more productive and innovative making of attractive places. In addition, it should "encourage social inclusion, cultural participation, poverty alleviation" (Mould 2015, p. 2). But this is not an easy recipe. In fact, Florida's initial definition of Creative City "drew a considerable amount of criticism for its hyperbolic advocacy as well as for its elitism and its tendency to obscure the potential implication of the 'creative class' in exclusionary forms of urbanism" (Guano 2017, p. 6). In the past years, policies derived from the Creative City paradigm have actually become rhetorical, having led to negative effects on the social fabric and

Figure 2. Creative designers and people from the neighbourhood participating in a Festival. Photo: Paola Sabbion

In the contemporary city, periphery is defined by a series of marginal areas. These places are often the most fragile, but also the richest in opportunities. Some fringe areas, such as the transition between “city and country”, or coastal sea and inland waterways' urbanised territories, have a greater complexity due to the opportunity to interface human with natural systems. In particular, river corridors are particularly weak but interesting ecotonal regions: transition areas between different biomes and social dynamics. In fact, in these areas social conflicts and bottom-up forces sometimes tend to concentrate and arise, actively playing a leading part in political processes and urban transformations.

cultural diversity. Such policies, criticised for being just a globally replicable "trend", have produced "homogenous urban spaces internationally", becoming "a justification for an already ongoing process of economic urbanisation characterised by privately led investments" (Mould 2015, p. 3). To avoid these risks, being a creative city today means pursuing new ways of transformation that are not incorporable by a capitalist system that is simply addressed to making profit. This implies "creating a more culturally vibrant and diverse place free from hegemonic political rhetoric" and "enacting more social justice without conquering space", finding "alternative ways of experiencing the city" (Mould 2015, p. 112). This new approach requires a shift from focusing on growth and production to a more imaginative city, producing the favourable framework conditions for citizens to become active agents of change. For this aim, a "creative milieu" is necessary. It is defined as "a place within which a critical mass of local councillors, entrepreneurs, intellectuals, social analysts, artists, promoters or students might operate, possessing the requisites for global interaction and where spatial intercourse creates new ideas, products, services and institutions, contributing to the city's regeneration and improved status" (Carta 2007, p. 15). It could be a street, a square, a park, or even an urban river. In this creative milieu significant interactions and connections networks should stimulate new ideas collected by institutions. These networks may include informal associations, business clubs, or marketing consortia, and public–private partnerships though which activists working on the ground can find powerful allies and decision-makers can meet innovative ideas (Landry 2008, p. 169). This means also avoiding being "victims of capitalistic systems that tend to consume bottom-up energies by satisfying them in a way that neutralizes their subversive potential" (Mould 2015, p. 167), a strategy able to assure that "the city of the future will be a city of culture, a city generating new culture" (Carta 2007, p. 5).

From this point of view the case of the city of Genoa (Italy) is paradigmatic, because it shows peculiar organisational and performative practices of social movements which constitute "social dramas as collective enactments of crisis and resolution as well as geographic debates on the resistive spatialities" (Guano 2017, p. 17). The creative class in Genoa is a product of the precarity that began in the early 1970s and, ultimately, is a reaction to deep social inequities. Nevertheless it reflects "the skills, experiences, and sensibilities of individuals who are themselves adept consumers of urban cultures, and who, in producing and selling symbolic goods and experiences, are exercising their agency in shaping the urban experience of their publics" (Guano 2017, p. 17). In particular, in 2013, activists founded an organisation (Amici di Ponte Carrega) in a heavily urbanised area on the banks of the river Bisagno, which was badly affected by a flood in the 1970s and then by the 2011 and 2014 river overflows. During these past flooding events, most residents were forced to leave their homes, but a spirit of cooperation and solidarity arose. It was shared by a community that was, despite everything, alive and pulsating, proud and full of ideas. The common objective of creating a more liveable neighbourhood in complex and heavily urbanised surroundings developed after the first flood clean-up efforts. Significantly, this local community has sought, from the beginning, the support of some national heritage and environmental protection entities as well as of scientific institutions such as universities, to find allies against ongoing real estate plans, which included the construction of new shopping centres in the river basin, in a high hydrological risk

Figure 3. Tour in the riverbed of Bisagno attending a botanical walking lecture. Photo: Paola Sabbion

Each city is the home to a complex plot of narrations. These stories have, in some sense, their own life and they can change every time they are narrated. In this perspective, stories represent an extraordinarily effective tool both to create a shared vision among citizens and to reorient the perception of the city from the outside. Thus, stories are powerful resources and devices. They can be effective in foretelling the future of a city, or, on the contrary, causing an inertia in addressing the necessary changes of urban spaces.

condition. They involved other environmental associations, volunteers, and the “creative class” of the city, to create awareness of landscape values in the valley and a new sense of place. The last activities concern political activism and also walking lectures to local historical and cultural places, as well as volunteer recovery of ancient architectural artefacts in the valley, guerrilla gardening, and temporary events. In 2016, temporary stalls assembled in an abandoned fruit market created a festival of cultural events for a short period of time, inviting the participation of small firms, music bands, freelancers, and artists. This was made possible thanks to continuous dialogue and cooperation that sought out the legitimation of both local administrators and higher entities. The walking lectures in the riverbed, which are organised as tours in the urban nature to discover a number of forgotten botanical species, have met with great success and are repeated every year. This is an interesting example of story-telling by which the lecturer illustrated the history of the relationship between people and different plants of the river habitat that were used for food, or for pharmaceutical or medical purposes.

The central role of the river in triggering this change demonstrates that green infrastructure initiatives can be an effective tool for building social capital by bringing together people with different perspectives, helping to “forge bonds where they did not previously exist” (Benedict, McMahon 2012, p. 231). The river, integrated in a green infrastructure network, has the potential to gradually contribute to reinforcing trust and collaboration; “by highlighting the involvement and contributions of once opposing players, a project can find common ground and build the foundation for future dialogue” (Benedict, McMahon 2012, p. 231). In conclusion, this series of experiences show that in the Italian context the cooperation between different levels and institutions is characterised by an increasing complexity, and that the involvement of dynamic creative energies is crucial for the rehabilitation of suburbs and the weakest peripheral areas.

Bibliography

Benedict M. A., McMahon E. T., The Conservation Fund (2012) *Green Infrastructure: Linking Landscapes and Communities*. Island Press.

Carta M. (2007) *Creative City: Dynamics, Innovations, Actions*. Actar Birkhauser Distribution.

Florida R. (2005) *Cities and the Creative Class*. New York, Routledge.

Furlong C., De Silva S., Guthrie L., Considine R. (2016) “Developing a Water Infrastructure Planning Framework for the Complex Modern Planning Environment”. In: *Utilities Policy*, 38, pp. 1–10.

Guano E. (2017) *Creative Urbanity: An Italian Middle Class in the Shade of Revitalization*. University of Pennsylvania Press.

Landry C. (2008) *The Creative City: A Toolkit for Urban Innovators*. London, Sterling, Earthscan.

Montgomery J. (1998). “Making a City: Urbanity, Vitality and Urban Design”. In: *Journal of Urban Design*, 3:1, pp. 93–116.

Mould O. (2015) *Urban Subversion and the Creative City*. Oxon, New York, Routledge.

Perini K., Sabbion P. (2017) *Urban Sustainability and River Restoration: Green and Blue Infrastructure*. London-New York, Wiley Blackwell.

Ward S., Lundy L., Shaffer P., Wong T., Ashley R., Arthur S., Armitage N. P., Walker L., Brown R., Deletic A., Butler D. (2012) “Water Sensitive Urban Design in the City of the Future”. In: *WSUD 2012 Water Sensitive Urban Design. Building the Water Sensitive Community, 7th International Conference on Water Sensitive Urban Design*. Barton, A.C.T. Engineers Australia.

Social Innovation: From Practices to New Territorial Development Models

Martina Massari

The Nature of the Challenge

There is growing evidence that increasing complexity, environmental challenges, and fragmentation issues in contemporary territories call for deep changes in urban and territorial development paradigms. The consequence of a series of long-term trends that undermine urban and welfare systems, the processes of social inclusion, and economic development are now clear, with the progressive weakening of social ties connecting individuals (Moulaert et al. 2009). The contraction of welfare policies and the introduction of new enabling technologies have opened up the way for new and old actors (city and urban "makers", social enterprises, active communities, etc.), and for the promotion of innovation practices addressing the diffuse need to build a new generation of more user-centred and collaborative services, as a possible approach to urban and territorial development.

In this context, we are witnessing a multitude of intellective interactions generating several initiatives of "disintermediation" in the production of public services, assimilated under the "buzzword" social innovation, defining an ecosystem of practices of civic origin, exploring and experimenting "new ideas and solutions to meet social needs and at the same time create new relationships of collaboration." (Murray et al. 2010). These are described as new manifestations of participatory practices, which overcome the rhetoric of participation, and are able to achieve the power of a "de facto" public policy (Fareri et al. 2009), where tangible bottom-up action replaces complex planning strategies and the role of public institutions is transformed into mutual learning and knowledge exchange (Foster et al. 2016). Social innovation is not a new concept: people have always been looking for new solutions to pressing social needs. Nevertheless, the growing number of civic initiatives along with the diffusion of new enabling technologies, is recently taking on such dimensions as to lead to the assumption that these changes are not only intervening in the resolution of people's needs, but are laying the foundations for a new development paradigm. After several years of experiences and literature, it is time to promote the "up-scaling" of the many urban innovation experiments and then reformulate patterns of action according to urban planning tools.

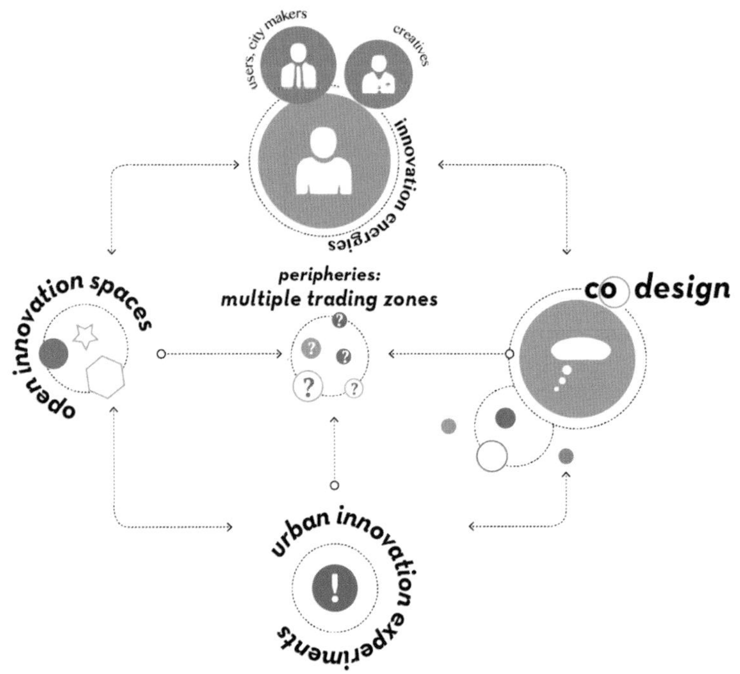

Figure 1. Peripheries, as trading zones, trigger urban innovation experiments. Graphic: author

New ways of Making the City are emerging: not only designed, but also experimented by its citizens. The size of civic actions that are already underway and the heterogeneity of the actors promoting them imply the emergence of a phenomenon that deserves to be critically investigated in order to understand its innovative organisational systems, design capabilities, and ambition of growth. There is a clear evidence of the mobilising power and creative potential of peripheral contexts as trading zones, and of the existence of important innovation energies in conflict areas that are able to trigger long-term dynamics of urban transformation.[1] The time has come to consolidate the many on-going urban innovation experiments, promote their "up-scaling" (Brandsen et al. 2016), and then reformulate patterns of action according to urban planning tools. Reading the phenomena from the twofold perspective of social innovation practices and regeneration policies, and understanding the historical transformation power of their intertwining work, allow us to extract the design principles, tools, and transformation dynamics and finally implement them in an Urban Circular Model. Through the tools of open innovation spaces and environments where knowledge becomes a device for innovation, new opportunities for reading peripheries open up, considering not only the subsidiarity perspective, but also a co-creation perspective that recombines the territorial capital to provide a competitive advantage for overcoming inequalities.[2]

Research Leads

These premises impose an approach to the contemporary city capable of generating new forms of urbanity, starting from the territorial capital, by reactivating existing local resources through the (re) combination of the assets embedded in the territory (Moulaert et al. 2009). Such a paradigmatic change, must be able to remodel the different forms of personal engagement and empowerment and their empirical interconnections and to consider individuals as agents (Sen 2007) instead of passive recipients of external interventions.

When related to urban systems and their disputed areas, discussion about innovation often takes the form of technological solutions applied as a superimposed layer, intended as a moment that breaks with the past and the traditions of places. At the same time, however, several scholars state that the political, urban, social context usually triggers the conditions for the growth of social innovations, "the space given to them, the opportunities for sustainability and the scope for policy learning" (Brandsen et al. 2016, p. 8). According to Deleuze's definition, social innovation takes place in opportunity spaces (Hillier 2005) at the micro-level, enabling creative strategies at the macro-level.

With these premises, those initiatives are considered socially innovative that, thanks to context-related conditions, use a collaborative methodology, reverberate with social and spatial change in complex systems, invest a significant portion of the territorial capital, and generate considerable impact on the territory. The research process described in this chapter will investigate how social innovation practices could be engaged and assimilated in a Circular Urban Model, which allows them to be "up-scaled" (Murray et al. 2010) and to become part of the ecosystem of regeneration policies. The research will begin with a better comprehension of the concepts of space-related social innovations in service co-production, exploring their design tools and protocols and depicting the space conditions that influence civic actions and the evolution of emergent spatial and policy configurations. Lastly, the goal is to identify which policy arrangements and practices are needed to exploit the possible benefits and to try to develop mutual learning by imagining a model for urban and territorial development.

Approach and Strategy

Narrowing the extensive field of inquiry, the interest of this research concerns the practices that are intertwined with urban regeneration and able to produce changes at the spatial, social, and ultimately institutional level. In some cases these experiences pursue collective utility through the form of the enterprise, and according to a temporary and light action, they ultimately generate added value in service creation through the mobilisation of common resources (Calvaresi et al. 2016). It seems finally necessary to understand how their innovative action would constitute long-term leverage and influence the public and formal praxis of urban and territorial planning, and how the public can enhance and permit these phenomena to be scaled.

Figure 2. Kilowatt in Bologna, a hybrid community hub for social innovation. Photo: Lorenzo Burlando

A crucial need to rethink territorial models has been encouraged by the boost of new practice-based innovation environments, often located in marginal places and able to provide a context for new modes of social activism. An aging policy model corresponds to the current complexity of these territories; bringin new efficiency, quality, and identity to these territories has thus become essential for addressing emerging social issues in terms of services, inclusion, and cultural growth. Considering innovation as a highly path-dependent methodology (Moulaert and Vicari Haddock 2009), with a mutual exchange and learning relationship within this context, it is clear that the starting point for a new model must be the territorial capital and—even more—the one embedded in fragile and challenging places.[3] In this scenario, the collective figures of social innovators can explore the potential of places' transformation by testing the power of pooling resources, problems, and opportunities, and seeking new territorial patterns. This is a combinatorial, exploratory approach, working in the territories as if they were laboratories, handling multiple ingredients, working and repositioning scraps, inventing adaptive strategies, proceeding with incremental steps, and ultimately generating added value. The initiatives that are considered capable of producing added value in the territory allow territorial resources, products, and services to increase and evolve, and the possibility of territorial innovation to grow.

This work will develop reflections on the socio-spatial impacts of socially innovative actions, and how and on the means and the service design principles (Deserti, Rizzo 2014) iniatives born at the local level can be transformed into integrated urban policy mechanisms. Starting from a theoretical framework, the research suggests two reflections. The first highlights the risk that these initiatives, working on public spaces and generating social value, run towards the production of "individualisms" affecting the success of long-term sustainability, often as a result of poor interactions with institutions.

This insight requires a review of the traditional cognitive patterns of policy makers and urban planners (Carta 2013) that are able not only to define new knowledge for the plan, but also to identify new planning tools capable of achieving the synergy of practices with policies. In Italy some administrations have already undertaken pathways to change the instruments and regulations governing these relations. It would be useful to investigate the meaning of this change and whether it represents an evolution of policy integration or a drift towards the instrumental use of active citizenship, which reduces it merely to an addition to the strategies of de-financing public policies. The other hypothesis concerns the mutual relationship between social innovations and the space in which they arise and develop.

The objective is to explore in depth the role of the specific innovation-triggering spaces and their capacity to contaminate—starting from micro-scale initiatives—the territory. The possible relations between the two heterogeneous dimensions of institutional programmes and the spontaneous and unpredictable ecosystems of co-creation allow us to read the issue from the point of view of places of intermediation—or transaction (Crosta 1998)—that facilitate the encounter and exchange between actors, stakeholders, and institutions. These hybrid spaces can be useful bridges between urban governance mechanisms and micro-scale environments, aspiring to become drivers of social and spatial innovation. Urban and Territorial Living Labs, Community Hubs, Neighbourhood Centres, as open innovation spaces and context-driven environments, are some of the useful models for integrating different levels of government and practices. Intermediation spaces act as interfaces to allow energies, resources, and opportunities, emerging from the territory, to incisively contribute to the redefinition of the urban public sphere and thus identify concrete opportunities for verifying in the field the feasibility of forms of collaboration among social and institutional actors for the production of public goods.

Implementation and Assessment

Given the complexity of the issue, the theoretical framework will be addressed on a specific case. Using the Metropolitan City of Bologna as a point of observation, the project will outline a map of the city's urban transformations that have been fundamentally guided by the combined action of practices and policies. This mapping experiment will allow us to define what is called the "Bologna model", which organise the territorial capital and defines the transformative power of the mutual learning action among its various actors.

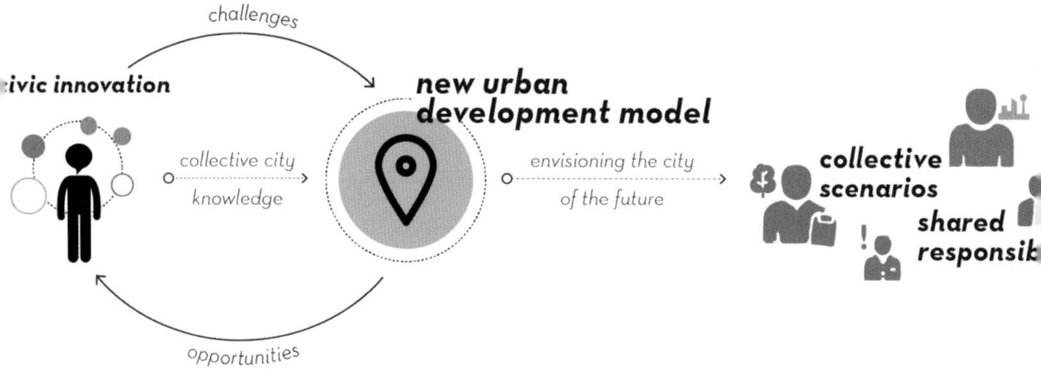

Figure 3. The representation of the city becomes a collective action transforming challenges into opportunities. Graphic: author

The radical transformations occurring in urban arenas are helping to rewrite their representations and maps. The meaning of space changes, because the way it is experienced by the community that inhabits it mutates. We are facing the manifestation of an experienced-city idea (Deserti and Rizzo, 2014): the city's potential for being read escalates when the point of view shifts towards generative practices of new places of sociability.

In this vision, citizens are empowered to narrate the city through their innovative actions. The active role of inhabitants contributes to the overcoming of implicit labelling; based on the postulate of peripheries=degradation, it allows us to shift to a vision where challenges are opportunities, giving the inhabitants the capacity to co-generate public arrangements. Within these processes, the agency of individuals creates value through micro-actions and fosters the possibility of its distribution. When dealing with urban systems, the importance of user-driven innovations is crucial because it transforms citizens from users into co-producers of collective knowledge and narratives.[4] The consequence of the enabling of those instances of change—which are already creating communities—contributes to the definition of a new urban development paradigm. The intertwining action between community, space, and public policies prefigures a new development model in which envisioning and describing the future is a collective process that concerns scenarios in which a variety of actors are committed and responsible.

The analysis will be useful for anchoring the theoretical framework and drawing out a cognitive pathway for comparison to international case studies. The work on Bologna will be completed with an application phase that would, on the one hand, contribute to the cognitive framework for the collective action of transformation of the urban system, and on the other, allow us to begin the prefiguration of the descriptive, analytical, prescriptive model expected as final output. The model will evolve by putting forward the hypothesis that only by using local knowledge and existing resources of territorial capital will it be possible to achieve concrete and tangible improvements in the quality of regenerated public space. The action-research will be implemented—within the European project ROCK—first in Via Zamboni, a controversial central area with a number of social pressures having a clear impact on public urban space.[5]

Notes/Bibliography

1 The paradigm of Open Innovation was theorised by Chesbrough. See Chesbrough H. W. (2003) *Open Innovation: The New Imperative for Creating and Profiting from Technology.* Boston: Harvard Business School Press.

2 For the concept of trading zones see Galison, P. (2010) "Trading with the Enemy". In: Gorman M.E. ed. (2010) *Trading Zones and Interactional Expertise: Creating New Kinds of Collaboration*. MIT Press, Cambridge, MA, pp. 25–52.

3 For the definition on territorial capital see Camagni R., Dotti N. F. (2010) "Il sistema urbano", In: Perulli P., Pichierri A. eds. (2010) *La crisi italiana nel mondo globale: economia e società del Nord.* Torino, Einaudi.

4 See Franke N. (2014). "User-Driven Innovation". In: *The Oxford Handbook of Innovation Management*, Oxford University Press.

5 *ROCK Regeneration and Optimisation of Cultural Heritage in Creative and Knowledge Cities* is a European project led by the University of Bologna, aiming at organizing the University area in the form of Cultural and Creative District. www.rockproject.eu ROCK's actions have the ambition to connect previously separated socio-spatial systems through technical and ecological processes and generate new, shared values. The project takes into account the innovation ecosystems present in the territory and inserts them into a newly conceived Urban Circular Model. The intersection point with the ROCK project is to experiment with new regeneration scenarios, which have the ambition to lead to the prefiguration of shared, collective models of local development.

Brandsen T., Cattacin S., Evers A., Zimmer A. eds. (2016) *Social Innovations in the Urban Context*. Cham, Springer International Publishing.

Calvaresi C., Pederiva I. (2016) "Community Hub: rigenerazione urbana e innovazione sociale". In: Bidussa D., Polizzi E. eds. (2016) *Agenda Milano. Ricerche e pratiche per una città inclusiva*. Milano, Fondazione Feltrinelli.

Carta M. (2013) *Reimagining Urbanism. Città creative, intelligenti ed ecologiche per i tempi che cambiano*. Trento-Barcellona, ListLab.

Crosta P.L. (1998) *Politiche. Quale conoscenza per l'azione territoriale*. Milano, Franco Angeli.

Deserti A., Rizzo F. (2014) "Design and Organisational Change". In: *Design Management Journal*, 9(1), pp. 85–97.

Foster S., Iaione C. (2010) "The City as Commons". *31 Yale Law & Policy Review*, pp. 286

Fareri P., Giraudi M. (2009) Rallentare. Il disegno delle politiche urbane. Milano, FrancoAngeli.

Hillier J. (2005) "Straddling the Post-Structuralist Abyss: Between Transcendence and Immanence". In: *Planning Theory*, 4/2005.

Moulaert F., Vicari Haddock S. (2009) *Rigenerare la città. Pratiche di innovazione sociale nelle città europee*. Bologna, Il Mulino.

Murray R., Caulier-Grice J., Mulgan G. (2010) *The Open Book of Social Innovation*. London, Nesta and Young Foundation.

Territorial Creativity in Peripheral Contexts: Urban and Regional Effects of the Recycling of the Añana Saltworks

Federica Scaffidi

Figure 1. Socially innovative recycling process. Graphic: Federica Scaffidi

This study analyses the theory and the practice a recycling paradigm in peripheral areas in which brownfield sites are situated. This recycling paradigm is studied for its ability to give an innovative role to peripheries and to dynamise and renovate territorial metabolism. This paper presents the methodology and the results of the research conducted in Salinas de Añana. This is an interesting example of activation of new urban and regional metabolism by the recycling of a brownfield located in the rural area of Vitoria-Gasteiz. These interventions promote territorial creativity with innovative actions by the local community; therefore, this example is not only limited to the "musealisation" of this resource. The reactivation of the Añana saltworks' life cycle started in 2000 when the "Plan Director para la recuperación integral del Valle Salado de Salinas de Añana" was fulfilled in response to citizens' needs to recover the site. The main objective of the plan was to create new life cycles for the area, focusing activity on the recovery of this cultural resource and on the development of the natural and urban landscape. The integral recovery of the site aimed at regenerating the brownfield and achieving socio-cultural and economic regional development, as claimed during an interview by the former Master Plan director Juan Ignacio Lasagabaster. The Valle Salado Foundation was founded to reach this objective. It generates positive externalities for the town and for the whole Province of Álava.

Figure 2. Local development: new services and business for Salinas de Añana. Graphic: Federica Scaffidi

The spatial-social interaction generates a territorial dynamisation that contributes to the development and transformation of contemporary regions. The interrelation between recycling and social innovative practices creates a regenerative process able to achieve this objective. Indeed, recycling strategy activates disregarded spaces and re-configures urban and regional areas by improving the original life cycle and creating new ones (Bocchi, Marini 2014), whereas processes of social innovation create a change over a longer period and economic equilibrium is achieved. Furthermore, contemporary literature affirms that social innovation is characterised by better satisfaction of a collective need, innovation in relations, better use of resources, structural impact, and economic strength (Caroli 2015).

Therefore, a socially innovative recycling process needs to connect the transformation strategy itself to local actors creating new values for the site in a structural way. The socially innovative rrecycling has to answer to three main questions: What? Who? How?

The first question introduces the typology of the process; it must be open and innovative and has to reactivate the weakened sites of contemporary regions. Who should generate this process? Social activators and local stakeholders have to be identified. The third question focuses on the modalities for recycling a place in a social innovative way by creating new economies and a structural impact—a spatial-social process thus contributes to the regional development.

Methods

The research was divided into three phases of work and a qualitative methodology was adopted. The first phase of research addressed the study of plans and initiatives developed by the community of Salinas de Añana; it was developed in bibliographical studies that consulted books, newspapers, and scientific journal articles.
The second phase of research was based on the local analysis of Salinas de Añana and analysed urban plans, projects, and programmes developed by regional institutions, local associations and foundations. The third phase of research was developed by defining the categories of local actors to be interviewed, proceeding with dialogic surveys and qualitative semistructured and/or unstructured interviews with Añana's inhabitants and re-cycling promoters. The analysis was developed by dialogic surveys which, unlike the exploratory surveys, are not only intended to observe and describe a place but to interpret it through interaction with social actors. The social actors identified to be examined in depth for the case study were divided into five categories:

I. The Basque Government of Álava;
II. The Municipality of Salinas de Añana;
III. The Valle Salado Foundation;
IV. The Gaztgak Society;
V. The citizens of Salinas de Añana.[1]

This step has been necessary to verify the information acquired from theoretical studies, to evaluate whether the Añana saltworks can be truly identified as a case of recycling and whether it has contributed to local development of this peripheral area, and to understand the role played by the Foundation.

The Role of the Foundation as Activator of Territorial Creativity

In 2009, the Valle Salado de Añana Foundation was established as a non-profit entity created with the aim of recovering and enhancing the saltworks. The foundation has the task of managing the saltworks and is engaged for the objectives of the "Plan Director", focusing its mission on the economic and social recovery of the valley and on ensuring the integrity of the activities in the territorial context. This foundation has given rise to a dynamic economic engine that has generated a change in the urban ecosystem. Indeed, the foundation produces the Añana salt whose sale is contributing to the self-financing of the project. The regenerated production activity has enabled the economic reactivation of this abandoned brownfield. The initiatives started by the foundation are revitalizing this province through innovative initiatives in three different scenarios: education, tourism, and production. The foundation, furthermore, represents a connection between institutions and the territory, a bond between the different stakeholders. The Añana saltworks offers new opportunities for the Basque region and defines new management models that can be adapted to other territorial contexts by defining new economic, social, and cultural strategies.

Figure 3. Interrelations between settlements and landscapes. Graphic: Federica Scaffidi

Territorial capitals located in peripheral areas have an essential role in the reactivation of these places. Why? Because their position at the boundaries of the polarities could generate innovative interrelations between urban settlements and landscapes. Therefore, they have to be recognised and developed. This would create new possibilities to enhance the region and generate new flows, new physical and intangible connections between polar sites and peripheries. This represents a resource of development thanks to the reactivation of neglected and weakened areas located in marginal places by changing the point of views. As Maurizio Carta affirms (2016, p. 95): "Discontinued or shrinking settlement systems, health or sports services that have fallen into disuse, and infrastructural networks undergoing transformation must be addressed through actions of functional change, clustering, or reinvention, thanks to which unused components are re-created without destroying them, by changing their functions, pursuing a generative perspective, and increasing their creative resilience." Through these actions, the underused or neglected spaces can breathe new life into socially innovative recycling processes.

This intervention aims to reactivate the entire region, creating new local economies and sociocultural offering for local communities and contributing to local development.

Salinas de Añana: Strategies Developed to Activate New Life Cycles

The "Plan of touristic dynamism of the gastronomic product" was drafted to define some guidelines for pursuing and developing tourism in the Salt Valley. Five strategic lines and sixty actions concerning tourism activities have been defined, such as infrastructure improvements and signage, and the recovery, promotion, and marketing of the product (Valle Salado 2014). The plan aimed to strengthen salt-marketing policies, enhancing the salt's positioning in the market. The plan foresees a development of the touristic offering from the enhancement of the existing resources and is divided into culture, nature, wellness, and gastronomy. Through tourism, a process of continuous self-reinforcement is activated, thanks to the increased visits, the economic dynamism of the province, the recovery of its heritage, the growing commercial demand for Añana salt, and the positioning of the brand.

These interventions have benefited the municipality of Salinas de Añana and the surrounding area, encouraging a "rejuvenation" of the town. The main streets that connect to the saltworks have been improved and signage and public parking have been introduced to facilitate the accessibility of tourists. In 2013 a plan to beautify the city, the so-called "Plan de embellecimiento", was created; Juan Carlos Medina, the mayor of Salinas de Añana, affirmed that the aim of this intervention is the reconnection between the old town and the saltworks, which are now physically separated by the street, but are gradually being connected through the cultural initiatives promoted by the Valle Salado Foundation, the Álava Government, and the Añana City Council. Nowadays, the Álava Government is developing a Management Plan, called "Plan General de Ordenación Urbana", which disciplines local urbanisation and land-use and promotes the development of the Salinas de Añana. During an interview, Macarena Ruiz Redondo, the Head of the Urbanism Office, stated that the "General Management Plan" envisages the territory as a system. The recycling of Añana saltworks has brought benefits to the territory, strengthening connections with the village of Salinas de Añana, which is also a cultural site to be enhanced.

The Local Effects of the Recycling of the Añana Saltworks

From the analyses it has been shown that the Añana saltworks (157 inh.) are experiencing cultural, touristic, and economic growth due to the recycling action. This intervention, in fact, led to the presence of new flows of visitors (Valle Salado Foundation showed an increase of visitors from 5,692 in 2005 to 74,112 in 2015). The economic growth was fostered by the sale of Añana salt and tourist services managed by the Valle Salado Foundation. The commercialization and sale of the Añana salt in 2015 exceeded the previous year with an increase of 73,232 Euro, of overall 474,562 Euro (Valle Salado 2015). Through its activities, the "Valle Salado" of Añana contributes to the achievement of a partial economic sufficiency of the project thanks to the production, marketing, and sale of salt. This is exemplified by the exponential growth obtained in the last years. The marketing and sale of Añana salt generates an economic activity that contributes to the self- sustaining and financing of the Salt Valley reactivation project.

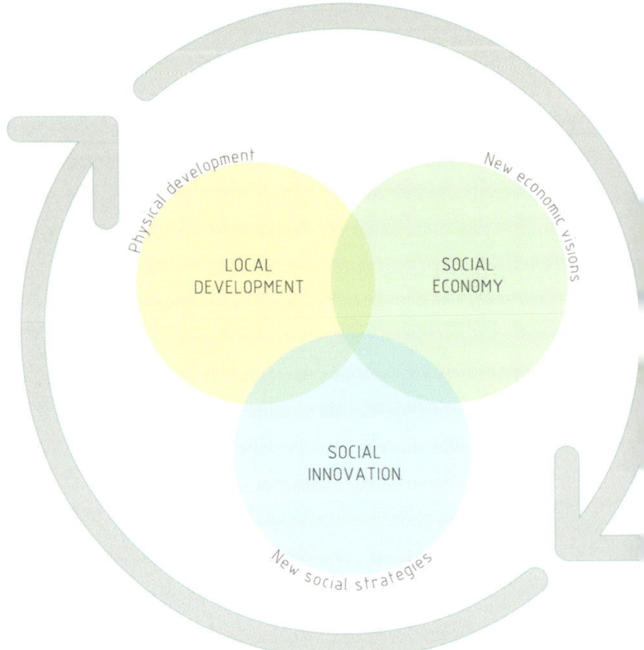

Figure 4. Innovative social-spatial scenario. Graphic: Federica Scaffidi

Rebuilding people's perceptions of peripheries is an arduous process. To reach this goal it is important to activate some strategies for social innovation that aim to develop places by improving relations among stakeholders. According to Ani Matei and Adela Dorobandtu (2015, p. 490): “The social economy contributes to developing a social cohesion-generating economy forming new mentalities for the local ‘social-economical environment’”. Accordingly, people have to be involved in a process that generates new mentalities and contributes to local development. The regenerated vision of peripheries creates new dynamisms that improve the quality of the space and defines new habitats. The regenerated image of a peripheral context creates new investments from people of other sites, defining innovative and creative flows. For this reason, the human aspect has a relevant role in the reactivation process of peripheries. The human factor influences the space. The interactions between the two aspects generates more impulses for the local development; for this reason social economy and social innovation strategies play an important role in regional enhancement. They contribute to building the connections between people and place, generating a sense of belonging to the place and new profitable dynamics for the whole territory.

The recycling process adopted in the saltworks allowed the recovery of these weakened resources, which had been neglected, but it also contributes to the economic, touristic, social, and cultural development achieved by the local community and the whole context in terms of accommodation, leisure, and socio-cultural services. In recent years, the salt mine landscape has attracted many visitors, making the "Comarca de Añana" into a tourist destination: businesses and citizens can consequently benefit from the success. The visit and entry balance of 2015 corresponds to a record of 70,114 people and a revenue of 707,643 Euro for visits and sales, 121,554 Euro more than the previous year (Valle Salado 2015). From 2005 to 2015, the number of visitors to the Salinas of Añana grew continuously. The interviews revealed that some renovation work and the opening of new business activities were carried out by citizens from Vitoria-Gasteiz and other towns. Thus, a flow of people has occurred between the surrounding cities and Salinas de Añana. Furthermore, new services were created such as a social centre, info point, parking, and a conference room, and people from other towns invested in the recovery of some buildings to create new businesses. The recycling process is not limited to the saltworks but it is extending to the whole town. The reuse of these places led to a new economy and new services for the inhabitants, users, and tourists.

From the analyses carried out we can see that the process has given rise to an economic and cultural dynamisation that has generated a change in the urban ecosystem. This contributes to the creation of a development model that is not limited to the reuse of the resource but generates new autonomous realities able to define new flows. This is a long-term process made possible by the quality of the site, the quality of the salt product, and the ability of the local activators. This innovative process has made it possible to reactivate the brownfield, creating a cultural place that can survive over time. The foundation, as non-profit entity, aims to create an economic model oriented toward the constant regeneration of the place thanks to its ability to autonomously support the process and to create an integrated development of the site creating new dynamics for this peripheral context and new creative possibilities for a weakened and abandoned place.

Note/Bibliography

1 The Gaztgak Society is composed of the owners and salt workers of Salinas de Añana.

Bocchi R., Marini S. (2015) "Re-cycle Italy. Alla ricerca di nuovi cicli di vita per i territori dello scarto e dell'abbandono". In: *Techne* 10/2015. Firenze University Press, pp. 16–18.
Caroli M. (2015) *Modelli ed esperienze di innovazione sociale in Italia. Secondo rapporto sull'innovazione sociale.* Milano, Franco Angeli.
Carta M. (2016) "Innovation, Circularity and Local Development". In: Carta M., Lino B., Ronsivalle D. ed. (2016) *Re_cyclical Urbanism: Visions, Paradigm and Projects for the Circular Metamorphosis*. Rovereto, List Lab, pp. 92–103.
Dorobantu A. D., Matei A. (2015) "Social Economy: Added Value for Local Development and Social Cohesion". In: Procedia Economics and Finance, 26/2015. Elsevier, pp. 490–494.
Fundación Valle Salado de Añana (2015) *Memoria de Actividades 2015*.
Fundación Valle Salado de Añana (2011–2014) *Plan de dinamización turística del producto gastronómico 2011–2014*.
Plata Montero A., Landa Esparza Mikel (2011) "Pasado, presente y futuro del Valle Salado de Añana (Álava, País Vasco)". In: *Rev. Int. Estud. Vascos*, 2/2011, pp. 719–739.
Plata Montero A. (2009) "Arqueología de las salinas. El método de estudio de un paisaje cultural construido". In: *Kobie*, 28/2009, pp. 255–266.

The Perception of Space and Time in the New Rural-Peripheries

Giorgia Tucci

Figure 1. Aerial view of the Vega of Granada, rural periphery of Granada. Photo: PactoVisual

Over the last decade the interest in the identification of development scenarios for local contexts has renewed within the model of macro-regions, which encompass areas related conceptually to each other beyond their geographical localization. One of these is the Mediterranean area, intended as a theoretical concept that interprets the idea of "Mediterranean character". The Mediterranean multi-city is the place of relationships and exchanges among different landscapes and cultures, "contaminated" by the wide networks of relationships that touch the shores of this sea with ideas, styles, techniques, and knowledge, which spread their effects along the whole costal area. Thanks to the biodiversity along the Mediterranean coasts, there are very heterogeneous urban centres that keep changing and evolving with a continuous territorial consumption, which today has outlined "the global shape of the Mediterranean city" as defined by Cardarelli (1987, p. 84). The interest to focus on rural and coastal Mediterranean cities is not, however, a novelty; already more than a decade ago in the objectives of European projects (e.g., Europe 2000+), the Latin Arc was identified as one of the eight "interested regions" for the development programmes of "transnational perspectives of the European territory". Among other issues, it notes: "in the 80s, the demographic change has stabilized or even reversed for natural demographics reasons or for immigration of "new rural dwellers" coming from the urban space. Rural areas have been able to attract inhabitants, but also economic activities, because of their proximity to highly urbanised areas

Figure 2. The pattern of night lights shows populations concentrated mainly along the coastlines.
Source: M. J. Wilkinson, NASA-JSC, 21 October 2014

Today we are faced with a situation in which the cities of the coast have been consolidated in some aspects thanks to decades of urban sprawl; in other aspects, however, the opposite has occurred, especially in contexts where urban growth has spontaneously occupied peripheral areas. The so-called sprawl towns, which superimpose themselves over the surrounding rural territory, have given way to formless and chaotic expansion of the urban core over the years. Since the seventies, research about processes of growth and decline of the cities has not been limited to a merely urban perspective but has investigated all phenomena of economic globalisation that incorporate and act upon urban spaces, identifying these "not only as object of study, but also as a strategic reference for the theory of a wide range of social, economic, and political processes in the current era" (Sassen, 1997). These complex dynamics and the current revolutionary phenomena are shaping new perspectives in the evolution of rural suburbs that are emerging nowadays thanks to the progress of technology in contemporary society and the close connection to the development of primary activities. Faced with this varied context, what is the present-day architect's position towards the planning of this "new" Mediterranean countryside farmland in terms of production and environmental development?

and their touristic character" (Report Europe 2000+, p. 112). As part of these ongoing evolutionary processes, Mediterranean coastal cities are on the one hand being consolidated through decades of immigration and urban sprawl. But on the other hand, they are also undergoing a process of complete change, in which they are experiencing difficulties in recovering their own identity, especially where they have expanded to chaotically occupy peripheral areas through the construction of infrastructure and large commercial-industrial districts. Along their borders, they have thus become truly extended cities, in which rural land has given way to a formless appropriation of the urban fabric.

We should not forget that the agricultural and rural dimensions of the Mediterranean have been, and still continue to be, central and essential elements for its economy and society. The wealth of natural resources and the diversity of landscapes make the Mediterranean a unique echo-region. However, many factors continue to undermine this fragile ecoystem: industrial development, incessant construction (in Italy, for example, about five million hectares of agricultural land were urbanised between 1971 and 2010, according to data from Mipaaf, ENEA, and Ispra), unfair social habits, the constant increase of pollutants, and the progressive reduction of primary resources such as water resources.

Despite international efforts over the last thirty years or so to protect and preserve this unique landscape, it continues to deteriorate as a result of increased pressure on the environment. The impact of climate change, the threats to the biodiversity of the area, the soil erosion and the emissions caused by energy consumption are strong evidence of the increasing vulnerability of this space. To it is added the serious phenomena of drought and the desertification processes with dramatic consequences for the rural territories. Aggravating the conditions and disparities between the shores of this sea, there are also social dynamics such as the scourge of poverty in the southern Mediterranean farmlands; the deficient collective infrastructure (access to water, services, and education); the lack of efficient management policies (for example, in the legal organisation of producers); the weakness of civil society; and logistical gaps.

There is thus a need to "identify the common basic elements to frame cities, regions, and Mediterranean networks into a unified perspective" in order to "define these models in comparison to theoretical 'global' models and processes and so [create] an urban theory that can combine the achievements of modern planning with the concepts and experiences related to Mediterranean specificities" (Pace 1998, p. 3). This intention is as ambitious as it is complex. Both the risk of "forgery" and of implementing approximate general theories about urban planning represent possible, dangerous elements, and it's necessary to be careful. Even within the community strategies that incorporate macro-areas and "multi-cities", the principle that each area is a "locus solus" (Rossi 1972, p. 4) should be maintained, with an inherent cultural, physical, and local biodiversity, and it is therefore difficult to frame any one area within common replicable models. It is therefore clear that the outcome of framing the features of this complex landscape is a complicated effort, namely "in comparison to theoretical 'global' models and processes [and therefore according to] an urban

Figure 3. Ortophotos Andalucia Coast, Adra; from 1956 to 2016, the spread of greenhouses along the coastline. Graphic: author, based on Google Earth

The advent of mass technological systems, new processes of governance in urban planning, the awareness of strategies for recycling degraded urban spaces, and the integration of these spaces into the community have outlined an epochal paradigm shift; the antithesis of urban-rural or metropolitan-periphery is therefore largely outdated. Today's small and medium rural Mediterranean cities are the result of the evolution of these phenomena and the various strategic planning processes of the twentieth century (Rome Treaty 1957), which have radically changed the balances and models of life in rural areas. Many of these areas, however, were able to reinvent and adapt themselves to the new requirements in terms of:

- socio-cultural aspects, promoting inclusion and social hybridization;
- environmental issues, focusing new attention on issues relating to the consumption of resources and preservation of the landscape;
- economic activities that aim to improve the seaside activities;
- agricultural programmes adapting to the to the rural development programmes.

To approach the study of this Mediterranean landscape in a consistent and non-reductive way, it is necessary to understand that there cannot be only one "method" of planning that could can correlate every single aspect that makes up the city without generating superficial planning and the danger of homogenising the territories.

theory that can combine the achievements of modern planning with the concepts and experiences related to Mediterranean specificities" (Pace 1998, p. 3). Nevertheless, if this global framework incorporates realities as socially, culturally, and economically different as those of northern and southern Mediterranean countries, the results can only belong to a purely theoretical sphere. In order to "restrict" the context within which this article aims to provide new ideas and discussions, we will focus on the countries of the Northern Mediterranean, that is, the Latin Arc (Spain, France, Italy). This coastal area is particularly interesting because it has been, and still continues to be, subject to significant changes, mostly due to the incessant urbanisation caused by the Industrial Revolution, but also because of the difficult socio-cultural integration (mostly caused by heavy immigration), recent critical economic conditions, and the effects that globalisation and enormous technological advances have had on the development prospects of these realities. Many of these areas, however, have been able to reinvent and adapt themselves to these new requirements, specifically in terms of:

- Socio-cultural aspects: promoting inclusion and social hybridization, such as the case of Jardin de Perpignan. Starting in 1997, forty-five companies in Perpignan—a major agricultural town on the southern French coast, in an area with more than 120,000 inhabitants—have implemented an agricultural development programme favouring short chains and, in 2006, were able to create a recognisable brand.

- Environmental issues: focusing new attention on issues relating to the consumption of resources and preservation of the landscape, as in the case of the Vega of Granada, which was, for a long time, the centre of protection plans and programming strategies. In 2001 the drafting of the Plan General de Ordenación Urbana de Granada, or PGOU, tried to solve the problems of the agricultural areas of the Vega by proposing regeneration policies. In 2006 and in the following years a proposal was begun for the creation of the Parque del Milenio in order to safeguard the agricultural areas as a heritage of the city.

- Economic activities: aiming to improve the seaside activities, such as the Côte d'Azur in the southern France, which is one of the leading examples of enhancement of the Mediterranean coastal-tourist industry. Famous all over the world, this area has been able to promote itself, maintaining a specialization in the agricultural sector, especially in the floral and horticultural business (about one-third of national production comes from this area) and winery activities, with over nineteen productions labelled DOC.

- Agricultural programmes: adapting to rural development programmes such as the Huerta of Valencia. The Plan de acción territorial de la Huerta de Valencia is linked to the European territorial strategy and is based on: polycentric development; structuring of dynamic, attractive, and competitive urban regions; and a conservation of the natural and cultural heritage. In the Dobris report, the Huerta was defined as one of the last six remaining experiences of existing Mediterranean gardens on the edge of urban centres in Europe.

Figure 4. Thermal image of the CIMMYT-Obregón station acquired from the thermal camera at two-meter resolution. Source: CIMMYT and Instituto de Agricultura Sostenible (IAS), 14 February 2013, www.cimmyt.org

Within a framework that considers contemporary phenomena, the renewed interest in the reoccupation of the farmland—or “rurbanisation”, to quote Sorokin, Zimmerman, and Galpin—has generated a concept that significantly changed the relationship in the urban-rural dichotomy, approaching the concept of rural-urban continuum. This process will have to be rethought so that it can adapt to future changes in which the perception of space, context, and environment will be radically changed. “The city, in fact, seems less and less topical and territorial and more and more teletopical and deeply extraterritorial, in which central and suburban geometric notions are losing their meanings” (Virilio 1996, pp. 6–9).

The technological revolution that affects rural peripheries and the agricultural sector is indeed the result of the now inseparable existence of technological devices that have entered permanently into the everyday life of each of us to become an extension of the same person. Should these be considered a key element in dealing with governance issues related to rural development?

The strong rural character of these areas has, therefore, enabled many cities along several coastal sections to consolidate their economy on agricultural production—beginning in the mid-twentieth century—and to compete nationally and internationally in the global market with quality materials (for example, the Andalusian coast has a considerable export of fruits, vegetables, and olive oil; or the Ligurian Coast, with its export of flowers and potted herbs). The progressive *rapprochement* of agricultural and rural dynamics is a phenomenon that has especially affected the younger generation in recent years. In fact, the number of under-30s who, despite their high levels of educational attainment, choose agricultural activity, is constantly increasing; this entails consciously leaving the prospects of precarious jobs to move in rural suburbs and reinvent themselves in the role of entrepreneur-farmers, probably also prompted by the economic crisis of this decade, too.

Just think that only in Italy in 2013 were founded more than twelve thousand agro-start-up and designed a huge amount of agricultural Apps, trading platforms and new technological devices and services developed for agricultural purposes.[1] The amazing potential of today's technology offerings has recently found fertile development in agribusiness (from digital agronomists to Big Data for farming), becoming an indispensable element for optimising production, reducing costs, and better protecting the environment thanks to monitoring and automation devices and the awareness of this recent class of young farmer-entrepreneurs (commonly nicknamed farmers 2.0), who have a strong propensity towards progress and innovation. Will it be possible, by promoting the innovation of tools and space in these new agricultural suburbs, to align the objectives that Mediterranean agriculture must impose on itself to become globally competitive, aiming to promote environmental sustainability, energy efficiency, and the enhancement of the production of eco-friendly processes, keeping the identity character of this coastal landscape but approaching new prospects for sustainable development?[2]

Notes/Bibliography

1 Sources: www.farmingwithapps.com; www.novagricoltura.com.
2 Objectives discussed at the conference VI ICAS 2012 International Conference on Agricultural Statistics in Rio de Janeiro.

Cardarelli U. (1987) *La Città Mediterranea. Primo rapporto di ricerca.* Napoli, Istituto per la Pianificazione e la Gestione del Territorio.
Castells M. (1972) *La question urbaine.* Paris, François Maspero.
European Commission (1994) *Europe 2000+. Cooperation for European Territorial Development*. Bruxelles-Luxembourg, Office for Official Publications of the European Communities.
Sassen S. (1994) *Cities in a World Economy*. Thousand Oaks, Pine Forge Press, trad.it (1997), *Le città nell'economia Globale*, Bologna, Il Mulino.
Bertrand H, Lacirignola C. (2007) "Dieci pilastri per l'agricoltura del Mediterraneo". In: *Centre international de hautes études agronomiques méditerranéennes*, *Agriregionieuropa* 10/2007.
Pace G. (1998) *Modi di pensare e vedere la città mediterranea*. Napoli, Istituto di Ricerche sull'Economia Mediterranea.
Rossi A. (1973) *L'architettura della Città*. Venezia, Marsilio Editori.
Sorokin P., Zimmerman C.G. (1929) *Principles of Rural-Urban Sociology*. New York, Henry Holt and Company.
Virilio P. (1996) "La freccia del tempo". In: *Domus Dossier* 4/2016.

Repositioning of Peripheral Villages: Case Studies in Indonesia

Listen Prima

This research examines the repositioning of perspectives for peripheral villages in South Sumatera, Indonesia, in regards to local development in sustainability frameworks. Many peripheral villages have lost their original characteristics due to the excessive growth of industrial and urban needs of expanding urban agglomerations, which influences people to move to the cities and which also causes changes in the buildings, settlements, and landscapes of the villages. Furthermore, local capacities and potential offer an advanced perspective of local development (Mascio 2015, p. 201) in economic, social, and cultural aspects. However, the existing condition of peripheral villages has not yet been addressed for development.

By analysing buildings types and construction, settlement and landscape structures, and culture and tradition in the research framework, threads and challenges are defined for possible approaches and criteria to maximise local potential. In the approach and as criteria, creative interventions are used as the main consideration in order to define their influence on local development in the context of sustainability.

Local Potential

South Sumatera Province shows significant sites of local potential, such as Lubuk Sepang and Bangke, which have been chosen as the case study areas. The settlement forms of Lubuk Sepang and Bangke are a group of houses dominated by heritage buildings. The transport system in these villages uses the main road without any alternative access to the village. Thus, the possibility of improving the infrastructure will support the proliferation of local development. In addition, the system of the landscape to use the local potential, such as the regional watershed. This water resource also bears the chance for energy self-sufficiency, which has not developed yet. The isolated location triggers the local people to meet their own needs, especially in terms of food production.

In terms of demography, the age composition of the local population is unbalanced due to significant number of movements towards the large urban areas. Based on the recent years (BPS-Statistics of Sumatera Selatan Province 2017, pp. 45–46), the total population in the capital city of South Sumatera Province, Palembang is 19.63% (4405.17 population density per square kilometre), whereas in the capital city of Lahat Regency, Lahat, it is 4.87% (92.49 population density per square kilometre). On the other hand, the number of the inhabitants is still increasing. The challenge of overpopulation is crucial for South Sumatera Province, as generally for Indonesia. By considering

Figure 1. Creative intervention process in the local development. Graphic: Listen Prima

Globalisation is provoking changes in many sectors of development. The changes are strongly related to environmental, social, economic, political, and developmental components. More-over, local development concepts in Indonesia are mostly dominated by the industrial sector. This has been centralised in the urban agglomerations, which creates a significance different level or gap of development between city and peripheral areas.

Hence, the urban agglomerations growing with urbanisation attract population from the peripheral areas, because of better jobs, entertainment, and education, especially for young people. Thus, the population remaining in the peripheral areas or villages consists mostly of elderly and children. Based on BPS-Statistics of Lahat Regency (2016), in the case study areas of Lubuk Sepang Village and Bangke Village, the percentage of the elderly is approximately 14% (over 60 years old) and of children is approximately 30% of the total population. This demographic condition influences the level of productivity and the limits of local development in the peripheral areas.

However, the chance to boost local development focuses on working with local potential to improve the quality of life for the local area (Jelic et al. 2015, p. 146). This local richness is expressed as forms of cultural and natural resources, skills, and knowledge in the peripheral villages, which also refer to the customs and traditions of local communities.

the population growth and its consequences in terms of pressure on space, it is important to find creativc ways for both maintaining and boosting the use of local cultural and natural resources. All these components bear potential to support the villages as a new place not only for sustaining local needs but also supporting the national development of Indonesia. All these components, highlighted in the case study areas, represent the capacities of an alternative paradigm of spatial and local development and also build on settlement and landscape characteristics of the territory.

Spatial and Local Development

Spatial development is a complex composition between the importance of territory and its relation to other aspect of development. The goal of spatial development is to set up an adequate advantage of a certain territory (UN-Habitat III 2016). As Alberto Magnaghi (2000, p. 8) writes, "a territory is the historical outcome of the process in the long-term joint evaluation of the human settlement and the environment". Moreover, spatial development goes beyond political-administrative, nation-state, or former geographic concepts of region that come from direct spatial, cultural, legal, economic, and social relations (Schröder 2017, p. 20). A consideration of the territory as component of spatial development aims to lead to the definition of productive spaces for the local people. Productive space can be described as the forming of the space as an innovative method by creating smarter and more responsive territories that enhance the social and cultural profitability, value creation, and production of jobs (Carta 2017, p. 38).

As K. Desmet and E. Rossi-Hansberg (2014, p. 1211) mention, the innovative method in spatial planning in certain territories is to be seen as more important than just adding aesthetic values to respond to global challenges, in terms of planning and development. In addition, an enhancement of the peripheral villages through developing their economic condition and their social and culture role points toward the importance of local development, especially in Indonesia. Moreover, the intervention of supporting factors is needed, such as the development of infrastructure facilities. Hence, the local potential of the spatial and structural elements of the peripheral villages, which include the landscape, will be optimally explored for the local development.

Possible Approaches and Criteria

The context of sustainable development is actually discussed as an important issue in Indonesia. The Indonesian government has set up a sustainable development agenda in the National Long-Term Development Plan 2005–2025 (Ministry of the National Development Planning Agency 2017) as the guideline for the implementation in the provincial and regional levels. However, building construction, which mostly facilitates the industrial sector in the larger urban agglomerations, dominates the development growth of Indonesia. This is shown by the significant gap of recent growth rate of gross invested capital in building construction and other sectors in Indonesia.

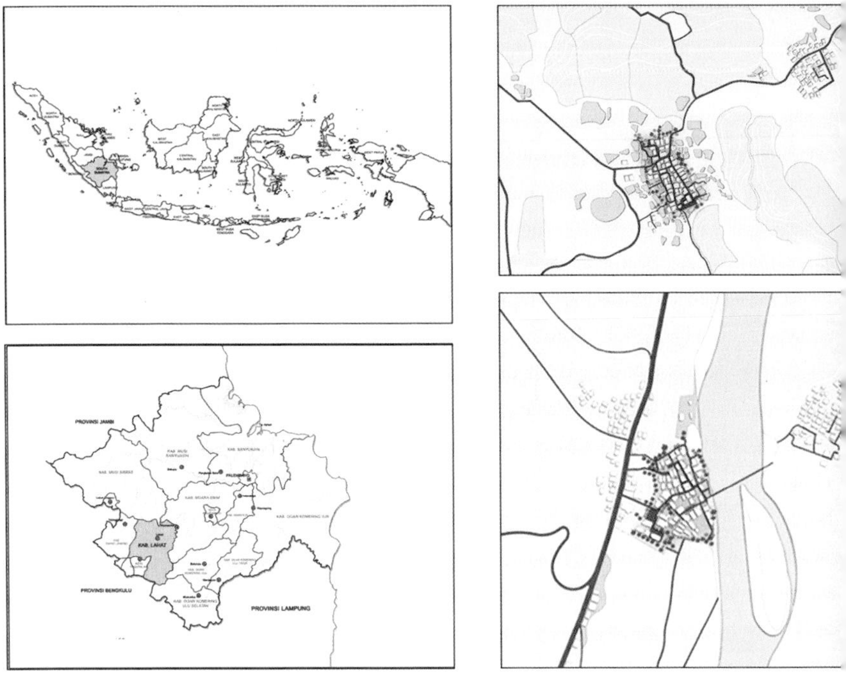

Figure 2. Indonesia, South Sumatera Province, and the Villages Lubuk Sepang and Bangke.
Graphic: Listen Prima, Ulfa Kun Aulia

Indonesia is a country formed by islands, with specific characteristics as local values of the area. The local values refer to its territories, people, and culture and provide the perspective for local development to promote peripheral villages. As stressed by the United Nations Sustainability Development Goals, all nations have declared to end poverty, protect the planet, and ensure prosperity for all as part of a sustainable development agenda. This research is an integrated approach for exploring the characteristics, roles, and potentials of villages in South Sumatera Province, Indonesia, as case study areas. In South Sumatera Province, as in many parts of Indonesia, structure and functions of the built environment in many villages have changed. Nevertheless, villages such as Lubuk Sepang and Bangke still maintain special characteristics, such as traditional buildings, historical settlements and pattern, specific sceneries and special geographic locations, such as near the river and in a hillside area. The aim of this research is to analyse further these components as significant potentials for local development.

The average percentage of invested capital building construction is 6.18%, while the average percentage of invested capital in another sector is 3.44% (BPS-Statistics Indonesia 2017, pp. 192–193). Hence, the problems provoked by urbanisation, such as the disproportionate age gap of populations in villages, are increasing in Indonesia, as shown for the case study areas of Lubuk Sepang Village and Bangke Village. To address this issue, the villages do need sustainable development perspectives oriented towards the long-term development. In order to set a possible framework and methods of creative intervention, this research aims to analyse some requirements in order to maximise its contribution to local development.

Analysing the local capabilities and potentials of the peripheral villages is seen as fundamental in the planning process. The next steps are to formulate the principles of good practices as the spirit of the development, and to measure targets for and to classify the significance of the local areas. Creative interventions can trigger the evolution and contemporary metamorphosis of local potentials and their contexts, within the complex changes of physical, global, and societal aging of cities and the environment (Walczak 2015, pp. 49–52). The local potentials and their contexts, such as in peripheral villages, could be improved by optimising the local resources including the characteristics of buildings, settlements, and landscapes, using the area in new and more productive ways, proposing incentives for private ownership, improving the communication with the local people as the main power of the local development, and proposing funding avenues and cost estimations for the success of the creative project.

Figure 3. People and cultural expression in the case study areas. Photos: Listen Prima

As one of the most populated countries in the world, Indonesia has many large urban agglomerations that are more intensively developed in the industrial sectors and as urban settlements. The development gap between cities and rural areas makes the former more attractive for local communities.

By analysing the local capacities and potential, the demand of local communities can be better addressed, in order to draw a scenario based on local values through adapted analytical and conceptual methods. Moreover, the community involvement in the development process is a main factor for controlling and balancing spatial transformation.

Furthermore, improved development of peripheral villages generally may influence the expansion and change of urban areas, by reducing extensive stresses in terms of the number of inhabitants, problems of poverty, environmental degradation, and other challenges. Thus, local development of the peripheral villages may improve the quality of life not only for local communities but also in a wider sense, by offering alternative perspectives and experiences beyond the cities.

Bibliography

BPS-Statistics Indonesia (2017) *Gross Regional Domestic Product of Provinces in Indonesia by Expenditure 2012–2016*, Jakarta, BPS-Statistics Indonesia, pp. 192–193, available online at: https://www.bps.go.id/index.php/publikasi/index?Publikasi%5BtahunJudul%5D=&Publikasi%5BkataKunci%5D=PDRB&yt0=Tampilkan, accessed on 10.11.2017.

BPS-Statistics of Lahat Regency (2016) *Unified Database for Social Coverage Program, Document Project of the National Team for the Acceleration of Poverty Reduction (TNP2K) of Lahat Regency*, available online at: http://bdt.tnp2k.go.id/index.php/data/sebaran-kab-kota, accessed on 10.11.2017.

BPS-Statistics of Sumatera Selatan Province (2017), *Sumatera Selatan Province in Figure 2017, Palembang, BPS-Statistics of Sumatera Selatan Province*, pp. 45–46, available online at: https://sumsel.bps.go.id/index.php/publikasi/index?Publikasi%5BtahunJudul%5D=&Publikasi%5BkataKunci%5D=sumatera+selatan+dalam+angka&yt0=Tampilkan, accessed on 10.11.2017.

Carta M. (2015) "Planning for the Rur-Urban Anthropocene". In: Schröder J., Carta M., Ferretti M., Lino B. eds. (2011) *Territories: Rural-Urban Strategies*, Berlin, Jovis, pp. 36–53.

Desmet K., Rossi-Hansberg E. (2014) "Spatial Development", In: *American Economic Review*, Vol. 104, No. 4, pp. 1211–1243.

European Commission (2015) Cultural Heritage Counts for Europe Report, CHCfE Consortium, p. 9, Krakow

Jelic S., Jandric M., Zivkovic M., Milovancevic Z. (2015) "Determinant of Household and Regional Rural Areas", In: *Agriculture & Forestry*, Vol. 61, pp. 143–148.

Magnaghi A. (2000) *The Urban Village: A Charter for Democracy and Local Self-Sustainable Development*. 2ed Books, London-New York, pp. 41–44.

Mascio D. (2015) "Analytical Drawings of Architectural Built Heritage". In: Walczak, A. ed. (2015) *Envisioning Architecture: Image, Perception and Communication of Heritage*, Lakowa, Lodz University of Technology, p. 201.

Ministry of the National Development Planning Agency, Indonesia (2017) *Document of National Long-Term Development Plan 2005–2025*, Jakarta, Ministry of the National Development Planning Agency, available online at: https://www.bappenas.go.id/id/data-dan-informasi-utama/dokumen-perencanaan-dan-pelaksanaan/dokumen-rencana-pembangunan-nasional/rpjp-2005-2025/rpjpn-2005-2025/, accessed on 8.11.2017.

Schröder J. (2017) "Towards an Architecture of Territories". In: Schröder J., Carta M., Ferretti M., Lino B. eds. (2017) *Territories: Rural-Urban Strategies*, Berlin, Jovis, pp. 14–35.

UN-Habitat III (2016) *The United Nations Conference on Housing and Sustainable Urban Development*, United Nation Habitat, available online at: http://habitat3.org, accessed on 9.11.2017.

United Nations Sustainability Development (2015) *Sustainability Development Goals, 17 Goals to Transform Our World*, Department of Public Information, United Nations, available online at: http://www.un.org/sustainabledevelopment/sustainable-development-goals, accessed on 9.11.2017.

Walczak A. ed. (2015) *Envisioning Architecture: Image, Perception and Communication of Heritage*, Lakowa, Lodz University of Technology, pp. 49–52.

Infrastructural Urbanism in the Construction of the Triple Frontier: Simultaneous Territories in the Global Flow

Jesús Pereira Cubilla

Figure 1. *Point de vue du Gras* or *View from the Window at Le Gras*.
Photo: Nicéphore Niépce in 1826. Public domain

> Man knows that the world is not made on a human scale,
> and he wishes that it were.
> *André Malraux, 1945*

"Point de vue du Gras" or "View from the Window at Le Gras" is the title of the first photograph known to the world taken by the French inventor Nicéphore Niépce in 1826 showing the rural countryside of his town, Le Gras. After years of tests, Niépce invented the heliographic process when he managed to write with the sunlight inside of a camera obscura after eight hours of exposure. Nicéphore called his work "Point de vue" [point of view], not knowing that his invention would forever change the way we see the world. The magazine *Life* listed "View from the Window at Le Gras" among the one hundred photographs that changed the world. So the question to answer is now: how much urban exposure must the rural have in order to remain rural? Or, how much rural exposure must the urban need in order to remain urban? Or, is the answer already given by Lefebvre's urban revolution: "society has been completely urbanised" (Lefebvre 1970)? On the basis of the hypothesis that all cities in the world share a common bond, it might be said that they are, above all, a part of nature modified by the will of humankind. "Cities are an act of will" (Bacon 1967), and understanding how this "will" takes shape in the physical world requires a new look at the conceptualisation of urban areas, because their illumination often rests paradoxically in their

Figure 2. The Cantino Planisphere. Source: Anonymous, 1502. Public domain

“What you see depends on where—and when—you are looking from” (Brotton 2012): We can set our point of view at the beginning of the sixteenth century at one of the renowned documents in which European and American history collide, also known as “The Cantino Planisphere”, “America’s birth certificate” as the author describes it (Brotton 2012). We can identify a lot of information in it but we will refer to the vertical line that represented the limits between the Empire of Portugal and the Kingdom of Spain, established in the Tordesillas Treaty at the end of the fifteenth century. The map has always been open to different interpretations and now what we must be focused on is not to drawn map itself but the undrawn one. The main concept that will serve as a starting point is very simple: the drawn map portrays the known world of that time and the undrawn map, which is of course absent, represents the unknown world. The Cantino Planisphere ended up not only being a revolutionary map but a reification of the world at the tipping point of America’s discovery: the drawing of limits; and it is in this process that we can find the conception of the territory as infrastructure.

relationship to the darkest rural areas. However, it seems that everything is heading for a new "semantic nightmare" (Koolhaas 1992), and in order to avoid this, the main focus will be on infrastructure due to its ability to rescale and reshape entire territories throughout the history of urbanisation. Patterns derived from this "infrastructural urbanism" have proved this idea. Stan Allen defines it as: "Going beyond stylistic or formal issues, infrastructural urbanism offers a new model for practice and a renewed sense of architecture's potential to structure the future of the city. Infrastructural urbanism understands architecture as a material practice as an activity that works in and among the world of things, and not exclusively with meaning and image" (Allen 1999). In order to approach this potential energy that infrastructure has in turning the territory into an artifice, Claude Raffestin makes a revealing affirmation by saying that "the territory is not space"; according to him, territory and space, are two completely different things, but they do complement each other. "Space is always a precondition of the territory. Space is data, the territory a construction" (Raffestin 2005). If space is data and the territory is a construction, then we can read the construction of the territory through data.

The case study of this thesis focuses on an area known as the "Triple Frontier" in the middle section of the Paraná River (the second largest river in South America) where Paraguay, Brazil, and Argentina currently share common borders. This area has been profoundly transformed by large infrastructural projects during the second half of the twentieth century. Imagining the main rivers of South America in relation to the current political limits, fusing them like a palimpsest, the limits do not correspond to the biophysical environment that isolates countries like Bolivia and Paraguay as landlocked countries. Today people see water as a limit, but our ancestors saw it as a bond, as a liquid territory. "Some say that the Paraná River separates the coasts of the three countries. But, in reality, it is a liquid thread that sews them, turning them into a fourth country of legend" (Varela 1943). In that context, no one remains isolated. Evidence for this can be found in all the cities founded during the colonisation process, because these cities were strictly related to the natural environment and its mission to keep exploring, controlling, exploiting, and using the territory as an infrastructure, which can be defined today as a "set of systems, works and networks that sustain modern societies and economies" (Bélanger 2009).

Through the data we can visualize how infrastructure was deployed throughout the territory; roads, bridges, hydroelectric installations, and dams are new axes of centrality, a transition into a new condition of human artifice, which changes not only virgin nature but also the daily life of people, altering the relationship between people and even their perception of time and space in the new conception of infrastructure as the territory. When the landscape itself is the sum of nature and the artificial, it can be seen as an integrated infrastructure system (Perrotti 2012). To fully understand the case study, the construction of the Triple Frontier territory, we must explain crucial aspects of Latin American history that played a key role in the configuration of the Triple Frontier, particularly the history of Paraguay and Brazil. The numerous territorial dismemberments of Paraguay gave birth to the common borders under study. Paraguay had the longest and uninterrupted dictatorship in modern history from the 1950s to the 1990s: all the infrastructure in the region was built

Figure 3. Earth at night. Source: Composite image by NASA

The main discussion centuries ago was entirely another one while Columbus and Vasco Da Gama started the first world known space race. Moving forward in time almost five hundred years we can see now the same place but an entirely new world. Compiled from over four hundred satellite pictures ending in a composite image by NASA shows us the earth at night as sharp as a portrait photo. The same as in the Cantino Planesphere, it's quite impressive how the lighted areas form constellations of human settlements across the continents.

But what about the dark ones? What is urban and what is rural? How much "urban exposure" must the rural have, in order to be considered rural? How much "rural exposure" must the urban have, in order to be considered urban?

during the dictatorship period. The Brazilian geopolitical initiatives of the 1930s were known as "The March to the West", as the country tried to occupy its hinterland towards the west of its territory. The Paraguayan geopolitical reaction was known as "The March to the East", as a response to these Brazilian interests but in the opposite direction towards Paraguay's own hinterland (Mora 2008). The urban disciplines of the 1950s were submerged, or perhaps sinking, in a technocracy that reached a tipping point with the construction of Brasilia. The three main infrastructural elements in the construction of the Triple Frontier emerged from the articulation of geopolitical initiatives as generators of new productive and economic rural and urban patterns. Each piece of the infrastructures almost meant the foundation of a new city. In the Parguayan context, for example, we have in chronological order: in 1960, the first national road from the capital city of Asuncion to the Triple Frontier; in 1965, the Fraternity Bridge; and finally, in 1984, the Itaipu Dam.

Perspective needs distance, in time and in space, to conceive these crucial moments of infrastructural urbanism. In 1960, the capital of Paraguay is separated from the Triple Frontier—spatially, by 300 kilometres; and temporally, the difference between the dates of their founding differ by 420 years. With the arrival of the road, the city began to grow a little until it stopped because it lacked a connection to Brazil. In 1965, the Fraternity Bridge became the first international bridge between Paraguay and Brazil; it was the first such articulation on a continental scale. The etymological meaning of the Guaraní word "Paraguay", is "water that flows towards the sea", which is the same meaning that the Paraguayans gave to the bridge because it opened, through Brazil, "a way to the sea" and therefore to international commerce. "Building skyscrapers is the nearest peace-time equivalent of war" (Starrett 1928). Imagine building the world's largest dam (at that time) in an enclave like the Triple Frontier which turns rapidly into an infrastructural implosion and later on into an infrastructural explosion; the country had never seen anything like it—except for the war. The Itaipu dam provides the 80% of the energy consumed in Paraguay and the 30% of the total amount needed in Brazil and is still the world's most productive hydroelectric system. Thanks to the degree of territorial articulation achieved by the infrastructure, the Triple Frontier ended up joining the built environment with the natural environment, establishing one of the world's most active free trade zones after Miami and Hong Kong. Therefore, it gave birth to a continental node formed by three cities acting as one, and related to global trade flows and to the metropolises of São Paulo and Buenos Aires. "Freedom is given to us by technology" (Mendes da Rocha 2007), but it must be ethical. The aim of this work is to shed a light on the understanding that the region's metabolism is based on the relationship between simultaneous territories—meaning territories of commerce, energy, and agricultural production—in a new urban and rural context, since "... the rise of cities as strategic economic spaces is the consequence of a much deeper structural transformation evident in all developed economies" (Sassen 2011) in a global trade flow. Hence, the capacity of infrastructural urbanism to reshape entire territories means that they must go beyond fulfilling their primary function and seek resilience in systemic interaction ensuring the sustainable regional infrastructural integration of South America.
"Eppur si muove" (Baretti 2010).

Figure 4. Photomontage. Graphic: Jesus Pereira

These two images can help tracing a common link and establish a parallelism between the two worlds that produced them. In both worlds, the available technological instruments helped to trace each world. Technology as *techne*, *techne* as knowledge, knowledge as light. Therefore, if we take a closer conceptual look at the Cantino Planisphere, the visible part of the drawing represents the recently discovered land. It would be accurate to say, then, that those territories are "enlightened" areas. And the absent drawing representing the yet undiscovered territories would be the obscure areas. As in the NASA photograph, we still consider those areas to be enlightened where the "urban" is currently settled, and "areas with no light" the darker areas to be where the "rural" is. The discussion still needs a new look at the "urban" because its "enlightened" areas often paradoxically rely on the darker areas, which are misunderstood as "rural". Thus—as in the time of the Cantino Planisphere—the urban discipline is prevented from seeing the rural differently, as the rural is not even in the visible field as the urban is, and consequently it proves impossible to rethink the rural.

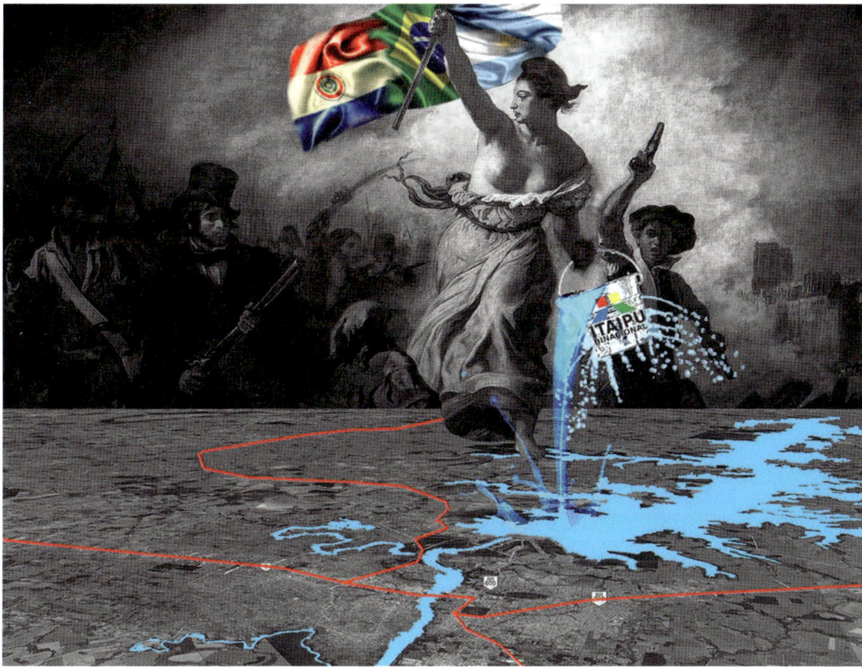

Figure 5. Photomontage. Graphic: Jesus Pereira

Bibliography

Allen S. (1999) *Points + Lines: Diagrams and Projects for the City*. Princeton, Architectural Press.
Bacon E. (1976) *Design of Cities*. London, Penguin.
Baretti G. (2010) *The Italian Library: The Lives and Works Of The Most Valuable Authors Of Italy (1757).* Montana, Kessinger.
Bélanger P. (2010) "Redefining Infrastructure". In: Mostafavi M. and Doherty G. (2010) *Ecological Urbanism*. Baden, Lars Müller.
Brotton J. (2012) *The History of the World in Twelve Maps*. London, Penguin.
Cristaldo J. (2013) *Continental Hub: Infrastructure, Energy and Territorial Transformations*. Boston, Harvard University Press.
Fernández H., et. al. (2016) *About the Recent Landscape: From the Image to the Territory*. Madrid, ICO Foundation.
Koolhaas R. (1992) "OMA/Rem Koolhaas: 1987–1992". *Madrid, El Croquis* N°53, p. 15.
Lefebvre H. (2003) *La révolution urbaine. Translated by Robert Bononno*. Minneapolis, University of Minnesota Press.
Malraux A. (1948) *Les Noyers de l'Altenburg*. Paris, Gallimard.
Mitchell J. (1999) E-topia. Cambridge, MIT Press.
Mora E. (2008) *Field 9: A Development Pole on the March to the East*. Asunción, El Lector.
Perroti D. (2011) "Landscape as Energy Infrastructure". In: Czechowski D., Hauck T., Hausladen G. (2015) *Revising Green Infrastructure*. Florida, CRC Press, pp. 71–90.
Pisani D. (2007) *Paulo Mendes da Rocha: Complete Works*. Barcelona, Gustavo Gili.
Raffestin C. (2005) *From the Nostalgia of the Territory to the Desire for Landscape*. Florence, Alinea.
Sassen S. (2011) *Cities in a World Economy*. California, Sage Publications.
Starrett W. (1928) *Skyscrapers and the Men who Build Them*. New York, Scribner.
Varela A. (1984) *The Dark River*. Buenos Aires, Editorial Directa.

List of Authors

Alessandro Betta. Architect, master's degree from the Polytechnic University of Milan. He has been lecturer at Polytechnic University of Milan and at the University of Trento. His thesis project has been published in the *Theory of Weakness* collection and has been awarded with the third prize of the YAA Award of the Alpine Convention. Curator of the project *Atmospheres* at the Milan Design Week and the Biennale of Venice. Currently PhD candidate at the University of Trento.

Nicola Valentino Canessa. Architect, PhD in architecture. Lecturer in design culture at the University of Genoa. Coordinator, since 2009, of GIC-LAB (Genova Intelligent Context). Professional experience in the office of Stefano Boeri, and as founder of Goagroup; since 2015, he directs Go-Up office of architecture, with P. Raffetto. Founder, in 2004, and president of *PdA_Pensieri di Architettura*. PdA deals with the promotion of young architecture. Since 2008, president of the Young Architects of Genoa.

Marta Carrasco Bonet. Architect and urban planner, master's degree from Polytechnic University of Catalonia UPC, currently PhD candidate. Since 2016, lecturer at the Department of Urban Planning, University of Girona. 2011–2015, researcher at the Department of Urbanism and Territorial Planning of UPC, coordinating national and international research projects. Since 2010, co-director of *Mixité—Territory, Art, and Community*, developing transversal projects of participation-action research.

Daniele Caruso. Master's degree from the University of Naples Federico II in urban, environmental, and landscape planning with a thesis focused on infrastructure recycling as multi-scale armature of landscape. PhD candidate with a thesis on the role of blue infrastructure for sustainable urban development.

Maurizio Carta. Architect and urban planner, PhD. Full professor of urban and regional planning at the Department of Architecture of the University of Palermo; current President of the Polytechnic School of the University of Palermo. Senior expert in strategic planning, urban design, and local development. Author of several urban, landscape, and strategic plans in Italy. He is directing the *Smart Planning Lab* with the aim to improve the smartness of cities and communities. He has been member of the steering committees of the Italian Society of Urban Planners (SIU), the Accademia Urbana (AU), and the National Institute of Urbanism (INU). From 2009–2011 he has been Councillor for Urban Regeneration and Strategic Planning of the City of Palermo. He has been visiting professor at several international universities and institutions. Author of several publications, e.g: *Next City: Culture City* (Meltemi, 2004), *Creative City* (List, 2007), *Governare l'evoluzione* (Franco Angeli, 2009) *Re-think, Re-load, Reimagining Urbanism* (ListLab, 2014), *Urban Hyper-Metabolism* (with B. Lino, 2015), *The Fluid City Paradigm* (with D. Ronsivalle, Springer, 2016), *Re-cyclical Urbanism* (with B. Lino and D. Ronsivalle, List, 2017), *Augmented City* (List, 2017).

Annalisa Contato. Architect and architectural engineer, second level master's degree in valorisation and management of minor historical centres, PhD in urban and regional planning with a thesis focused on polycentrism, city networks, and gateway cities. Since 2014, research fellow in urban studies at the Department of Architecture of the University of Palermo. Research focus on the Inner Area of Sicani in Sicily, for integrated urban and territorial planning and the smart land paradigm.

Alissa Diesch. Architect, lives and works in Bogotá, Colombia, where she holds a DAAD scholarship for her doctoral research. Lecturer and researcher at the University La Gran Colombia of Bogotá. diploma from Technische Universität München TUM in 2012, with a thesis on the transformation of a former sugar cane factory into a cultural centre in Mauritius. Since 2016, PhD candidate at TUM, with Prof. Sophie Wolfrum as thesis supervisor.

Raffaella Fagnoni. Architect, Associate professor in design and chair of the master's programme in product and event design of the Department of Architecture and Design DAD of the University of Genoa. She is also deputy coordinator of PhD course in architecture and design, and coordinator of the PhD curriculum in design. She is member of the governing council of the Italian Design Society SID, since 2014. Her research interests focus on social design, working on different topics, from cultural heritage to health and environment, urban life, reuse and re-cycle. She obtained her diploma from the University of Florence. Selected publications: Fagnoni R. (2009) "Design and New Behaviors: Project Responsibility, Social and Cultural Connectibility", in: *Strategic Design Research Journal*, vol. 2, 2/2009; Fagnoni R. (2011) "Lo spazio pubblico urbano. Connettibilità sociale, colore, comunicazione", in: Spadolini M.B. ed. (2011) *I colori di Cornigliano*; Fagnoni R. (2016) "Core Values For Re-Cycle Social Innovators", in: Ricci M., Schröder J. eds. (2016) *Towards a Pro-Active Manifesto.*

Nadia Fava. Architect, PhD in architecture from Polytechnic University of Catalonia UPC. Lecturer in urban planning at the University of Girona and responsible for the research group Architecture and Territory. Her work focuses on urban history and planning, mainly on urban evolution, city food retailing, and rural development. Publications in international academic books and in peer-reviewed journals, including *Journal of Urban History* (2016) and *Town Planning Review* (2015).

Maddalena Ferretti. Architect, PhD. Associate professor in architectural and urban design at the Department of Civil and Building Engineering and Architecture of the Università Politecnica delle Marche. 2012–17 university researcher and lecturer at the Institute of Urban Design and Planning of Leibniz Universität Hannover, director of the research group for building and settlement development in the BMBF research project Regiobranding. Professional architect in the field of architecture, landscape, and urban design. She obtained her diploma in architecture and urban planning studies from Roma Tre University; PhD in the international research doctorate programme in architecture "Villard d'Honnecourt" at IUAV University of Venice. Books: *Land Stocks. New operational landscapes of city and territory* (LISt Lab, 2016) and *La Fabbrica del Gas all'Ostiense. Luogo e forma di un'area industriale* (with M. Furnari, S. Bernardi, C. Pagani, Gangemi, 2006).

Giulia Garbarini. Architect, master's degree from the University of Genoa in 2013. Since 2014, PhD candidate in environmental engineering at the University of Trento, with a doctoral scholarship in the 30th cycle. Her thesis is entitled *Smart Landscapes: The Architecture of the "Micro Smart Grid" as a Resilience Strategy for Landscape*. Since 2014, teaching assistant for the course landscape architecture, University of Trento. In 2017, visiting scientist at Leibniz Universität Hannover.

Manuel Gausa Navarro. Architect, PhD. Full Professor of landscape architecture and urbanism at the Department of Architecture and Design DDA of the University of Genoa. Director of GIC-Lab (Genoa Intelligent Contexts Laboratory), a research laboratory of urban and regional design at DAD, that carries out national and international research projects. The Lab aims to explore and integrate the complex, articulate and celebrate diversity, and promote and give impetus to a multilevel interaction to design new spaces and transversal scenarios (territorial, urban, landscape architectural, and social) with a new relational logic (open) and informational (advanced). His projects have included: MED.NET.COAST: Network identity of Mediterranean cities; RE-CYCLE: Reactivation Strategies and Urban Landscape; UNIVER(C)TY: The Urban Role of the University System; LANDSCAPES INFRASTRUCTURE: Infrastructure Osmotic Over Sector Policies. In 2012-2015 he has been Academic and Scientific Director (Dean) of IAAC Insitute of Advanced Architecture of Catalonia. Since 2015 he is lead professor in theory and advanced knowledge studies, IAAC-TAK, and member of the scientific committee as IAAC-Founder.

Sarah Hartmann. Architect, university researcher and lecturer at the Institute of Urban Design and Planning of Leibniz Universität Hannover, since 2012. Architectural studies at Universität Stuttgart and Technische Universität München TUM, diploma from TUM 2012. For her thesis she has been awarded with the ALR Bayern award. 2010–12 researcher for the European project AlpHouse, 2012–15 researcher for the European project AlpBC Alpine Building Culture. In 2012 collaboration with RicciSpaini office for architecture and urbanism in Rome. Co-director of the workshop *Urban Elements* (2014) in the sessions programme of the Biennale of Venice. PhD candidate at the Faculty of Architecture and Landscape Sciences of LUH, with a thesis entitled *Monuments of Everyday Life: Interplays of City, Infrastructure, and Architecture in São Paulo.*

Antonio Ippolito. Architect and engineer, PhD candidate in cities and landscapes at the University of Basilicata in Matera. He is also co-founder of Are_lab integrated architecture. His work is concentred on the identification of new strategies for urban regeneration through the paradigm of Nature_City for sustainable urban development.

Barbara Lino. Architect, PhD, university researcher in urban planning at the Department of Architecture of the University of Palermo. She writes about cities, suburban regeneration, and local development strategies. She is member of the SicaniLab, the local development laboratory of the Sicani Interior Area in Sicily, and has been involved in research projects as PRIN "Re-cycle Italy". She also collaborated in applied research, most recently for the Palermo strategic plan, the Palermo Port master plan, the management plan for the Arab-Norman Palermo, Monreale and

Cefalù World Heritage Site. Contributions to conferences, workshops, and journals at national and international level. Recent publications: *Periferie in trasform-azione. Riflessioni dai „margini" delle città* (Alinea, 2013), *Urban Hyper-Metabolism* (with M. Carta, Aracne, 2015).

Luciana Macaluso. Architect, PhD in architectural design. She works at the Department of Architecture of the University of Palermo and has been lecturer at the University of Palermo and at the University of Parma. She has participated in the PRIN research project "From the Urbanized Countryside to the Extending Town", from 2011–13. She has been awarded with a DAAD Grant for Young Researchers in 2014–15 as visiting researcher at Leibniz Universität Hannover. Her publications include: *The Main Church of Gibellina* (Roma, 2013) and *Rural-Urban Intersections* (Parma, 2016).

Martina Massari. Architect, master's degree from the University of Ferrara, with a thesis on the urban and territorial regeneration of the island of Lampedusa; second level professional master's degree in management of small historic centres from La Sapienza University of Rome. She is a PhD candidate in architecture and design cultures at the University of Bologna, with a doctoral scholarship in the 32nd cycle. Her work is focused on social innovation practices and their relationship with urban policies.

Jessica Smeralda Oliva. Architect, PhD candidate in urban, regional and landscape planning at the Department of Architecture of the University of Palermo. Visiting PhD student at IHS Rotterdam in 2016. She contributed to conferences and workshops at national and international level. Her research interests are focused on urban resilience and regeneration, landscape, and ecological urbanism.

Jesús Pereira Cubilla. Architect, PhD candidate at the Department of Urbanism and Territorial Planning of UPC Polytechnic University of Catalonia. Assistant professor at the Faculty of Architecture, Design, and Art of the National University of Asunción, since 2012. Member of the Paraguayan UN-Habitat III Committee, in 2015–16. Partner in the Panoplia Urban and Architecture Design Research Studio in Asunción, since 2012.

Philip Norman Peterson. Architect, Born in Fergus Falls, USA, Philip Norman Peterson completed his architecture studies at the University of Illinois in Chicago in 1989. After working for John Melvin and Partners in London and Marina Stankovic in Berlin, he joined the office of Max Dudler Zürich/Berlin in 1992. In 2006 he started working at Studio Daniel Libeskind as Deputy Project Supervisor and was responsible for Westside Leisure- and Shopping Centre at Bern Brünnen. Since 2009 he has been working for Holzer Kobler Architekturen as project supervisor for projects such as the *paläon* research and experience centre in Schöningen. As managing director of Holzer Kobler Architekturen Berlin GmbH since 2011, he has been responsible for projects such as the UNESCO World Natural Heritage Wadden Sea Visitor Centre in Cuxhaven, the modular housing project EBA51 in Berlin and for the conversion, extension, and scenography at the Castle Gottorf.

Listen Prima. Junior lecturer and researcher at the Department of Architecture, Universitas Sriwijaya, Indonesia; master's degree in planning from the University of Adelaide, Australia. Her research focus is on heritage architecture and regional planning in Indonesia. PhD candidate at the Faculty of Architecture and Landscape Sciences of Leibniz Universität Hannover; funded by BUDI-LN Scholarship of Kemristikdikti-LPDP (Indonesian Endowment Fund for Education).

Mosè Ricci. Emeritus of the Italian Republic for Art and Culture, architect and urbanist. His research examines the relations between landscape, contemporary urbanism, and architecure and concerns ecological performing projects, *Recycle*, resilience, sensitive landscape design, and ecological urbanism. He is full professor of architectural design and urbanism and chair of the architectureal design studio at the University of Trento. He graduated in architecture in 1982 at La Sapienza University of Rome. In 1996–97, he was Fulbright recipient and visiting scholar at GSD, Harvard University; from 2008–09, visiting professor at Technische Universität München TUM; in 2015, visiting professor of advanced urbanism at IAAC Barcelona. Since 1999 he has been member of the scientific board of the Villard International Seminar and since 2004 of the Villard International Doctorate. He has been member of the steering committee of the Italian Society of Urban Planners (2003–05, 2007–11). Selected publications: *New Paradigms* (List, 2012), *UniverCity* (List 2010), *iSpace* (Meltemi, 2008), *RISCHIOPAESAGGIO* (Meltemi, 2003). Recipient of several prizes in international competitions, exhibited in the Biennale of Venice in 1996 and in 2012.

Chiara Rizzi. Architect, international PhD, university researcher in architectural and urban design at the University of Basilicata in Matera. The main theme of her research is involving ecological issues and collaborative approaches in design strategies. She is author of several chapters in edited books and of articles in international peer-reviewed journals. Her books include: *Fourth Landscape* (2014), *Joao Nunes: Progettare paesaggi* (2016), and *La città dell'Altro Adige* (2016).

Paola Sabbion. Architect, PhD. Lecturer at the Department of Architecture and Design DAD of the University of Genoa. Her work includes urban studies, landscape architecture, planning policies, and planning practices. She is author of the books *Paesaggio come esperienza: Evoluzione di un'idea tra storia, natura ed ecologia* (Franco Angeli, 2016) and (with K. Perini) *Urban Sustainability and River Restoration: Green and Blue Infrastructure* (Wiley Blackwell, 2017).

Federica Scaffidi. Architect, PhD candidate in urban, regional, and landscape planning at the University of Palermo. Her research interests concern local development and *Recycle* strategies, with a focus on brownfield reactivation and social innovation. She was a visiting research fellow at Leibniz Universität Hannover and at the Polytechnic University of Madrid.

Gaia Sgaramella. PhD candidate in landscape planning at the University of Trento, where she received her master's degree in architectural engineering. Her major research interests include the ecological relationship between landscape and motorway elements, as service areas and noise barriers. She is holding a doctoral scholarship in the 30th cycle.

Jörg Schröder. Architect and urban planner, Full professor and Chair for Regional Building and Urban Planning at the Faculty of Architecture and Landscape Sciences of Leibniz Universität Hannover; currently Dean of Research of the Faculty. Research focus on *Architecture of Territories*, urbanism and territorial design, metropolitan and urban-rural visioning, strategic planning, territorial innovation and resilience, design research. Diploma in architecture from Technische Universität München TUM in 1998; university researcher and lecturer with TUM from 2002–10, director of the research group *AlpHouse* 2010–12. Recent R&D projects: Rurbance—Rural-Urban Inclusive Governance Strategies and Tools for Sustainable Development, funded by ERDF; AlpBC—Capitalising Knowledge on Alpine Building Culture, funded by ERDF; Regiobranding, funded by BMBF German Federal Ministry of Education and Research. Recent publications: *Territories—Rural-Urban Strategies* (with M. Carta, M. Ferretti, B. Lino, Jovis, 2017); "Foodscapes: Architectures of Food for the Metropolis Hamburg" (with S. Hartmann; in: *Food Revolution 5.0*, 2017); *Scenarios and Patterns for Regiobranding* (with M. Ferretti, Jovis, 2018), *Creative Heritage Agenda* (2017).

Emanuele Sommariva. Architect, PhD in urban design from the University of Genoa. University researcher and lecturer at the Institute of Urban Design and Planning of Leibniz Universität Hannover, since 2012. Involved in the PRIN research project Recycle 2012–16. His research interests include landscape evolution, sustainable planning, and the relationship between agriculture and the city. He has been visiting PhD scholar at Technische Universität München TUM in 2011. Since 2009, at the Department of Architecture and Design of the University of Genoa, he has contributed to teaching and collaborated for research projects (COST Urban Allotment EU 2012–16; EU MED 2011–13; Interreg-Maritime INNOLABS 2011). Recent publications: *Creating City. Urban Agriculture. Strategies for City Resilience* (LISt Lab, 2015) and "Cultivar Ciudades", in: *Ecologías Emergentes* (Santiago de Chile 2016).

Luca Torrisi. Master's degree from the University of Palermo, PhD candidate in urban, regional, and landscape planning at the Department of Architecture of the University of Palermo. Expert in integrated planning for sustainable development. Winner of the UrbanPromo Giovani2 contest.

Giorgia Tucci. Architect, PhD candidate in architecture and design at the University of Genoa. Her research focus is on the identity of rural cities and the relationship between rural landscapes and the city itself, through territorial strategies (economic, energetic, environmental, and social), combined with new technological systems and innovative planning approaches.

DYNAMICS OF PERIPHERY

Atlas for Emerging Creative and Resilient Habitats

DAAD Hochschuldialog mit Südeuropa 2017-18
gefördert durch den Deutschen Akademischen Austauschdienst
finanziert aus Mitteln des Auswärtigen Amtes (AA)

The atlas DYNAMICS OF PERIPHERY is published in the programme HOCHSCHULDIALOG MIT SÜDEUROPA, co-funded by DAAD German Academic Exchange Service, financed by the German Federal Office of Foreign Affairs, in collaboration between the Chair for Regional Architecture and Urban Planning of Leibniz Universität Hannover and the Department of Architecture of the University of Palermo.

Leibniz Universität Hannover
Abteilung Regionales Bauen und Siedlungsplanung
Prof. Dipl.-Ing. Jörg Schröder
www.staedtebau.uni-hannover.de

Università degli Studi di Palermo
Dipartimento di Architettura
Prof. Arch. Maurizio Carta
www.unipa.it/maurizio.carta

Cover: Jörg Schröder, Photography: Sarah Hartmann

Editors: Jörg Schröder, Maurizio Carta, Maddalena Ferretti, Barbara Lino

Copy-editing: Michael Thomas Taylor
Design, setting, and lithography: Jörg Schröder, Maddalena Ferretti, Barbara Lino, Anna Pape
Printed in the European Union

Bibliographic information published by the Deutsche Nationalbibliothek.
The Deutsche Nationalbibliothek lists this publication in the Deutsche Nationalbibliografie; detailed bibliographic data are available on the Internet at http://dnb.d-nb.de.

jovis Verlag GmbH
Kurfürstenstraße 15/16
10785 Berlin

www.jovis.de

jovis books are available worldwide in selected bookstores. Please contact your nearest bookseller or visit www.jovis.de for information concerning your local distribution.

ISBN 978-3-86859-511-6